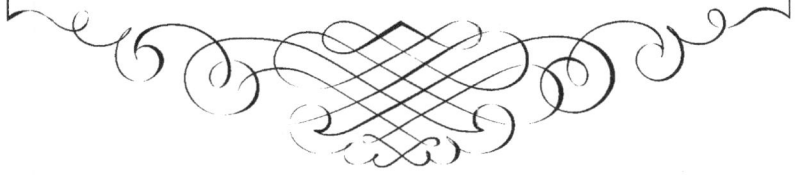

ISBN 978-1-332-19489-6
PIBN 10296594

1 MONTH OF
FREE
READING

at

www.ForgottenBooks.com

By purchasing this book you are eligible for one month membership to ForgottenBooks.com, giving you unlimited access to our entire collection of over 1,000,000 titles via our web site and mobile apps.

To claim your free month visit:

www.forgottenbooks.com/free296594

SEVEN CENTURIES IN THE

KNEELAND FAMILY

by

STILLMAN FOSTER KNEELAND

NEW YORK

1897

"KNEELAND OF YAT ILK"

THE ORIGINAL KNEELAND COAT OF ARMS.
GRANTED TO JAMES KNELAND[2] BY ROBERT
THE BRUCE, AFTER THE BATTLE OF BANNOCK-
BURN IT IS SHOWN AT PAGE 118 OF "HERALDIC
MANUSCRIPTS EMBLAZONED BY SIR DAVID LYND
JAY," IN 1542 PUBLISHED IN 1878 BY DAVID
LAING. IT IS NOW USED BY THE KNEELANDS
OF GREAT BRITAIN AND THEIR DESCENDANTS,
THE CLELANDS

"*IN THE NAME OF KNEELAND*"

COAT OF ARMS GRANTED BY MARY STUART TO
MAJ WM. KNELAND (10), AND BROUGHT TO
THIS COUNTRY BY HIS GRANDSON, JOHN
KNEELAND (12), IN 1630. THE ORIGINAL IS
STILL IN THE POSSESSION OF THE FAMILY

PREFACE.

Some ten years ago the "Encyclopedia of Contemporary Biography" of New York, published a biographical sketch of the writer, which contained an alleged genealogical summary of the Kneeland family in this country. A little study satisfied me that the editor was several miles out of the correct path in his data. Spurred on by the discovery of this fact, I commenced a systematic inquiry into the heretofore of the family, running back several centuries, and in the completion thereof have examined critically some thousands of volumes and tens of thousands of names, inscribed on musty records in the cobwebbed archives of the past.

Although the history, prior to 1800, has been mostly made up from bible entries, public records, historical and genealogical works, the continuation could never have been perfected but for the assistance of numerous members of the family, to whom general credit is herewith given and specific mention is hereinafter inserted.

The fact that not a single criminal act has appeared to mar a history covering nearly seven centuries, has, after all, made the work a labor of love. That fact is a wonderful stimulus to each living and future member of the family, and a warning against being the first to break the record of such a law-abiding, honorable race.

I will not insult the intelligence of my readers by claiming for this work absolute accuracy. The sources of information have not always been of the highest character; but I have given the matter the benefit of such judicial discrimination as an experience of over a quarter of a century at the bar ought to have endowed me with, and have stated the result as the best possible solution that can be reached by me, at this late day, of the problems involved in the somewhat tangled skein of evidences gathered together during the past ten years. With the aid of individual criticisms, and the tardy suggestions and statements that always, in a work of this kind, lag along a few days too late, some worthier successor will, I hope, build upon this feeble foundation, a monument worthy of the race.

STILLMAN FOSTER KNEELAND.

NEW YORK, 1897.

TO MY WIFE,
MARY STUART WILSON KNEELAND,
A ROYAL DESCENDANT OF A ROYAL FAMILY,
THIS VOLUME IS DEDICATED
AS A PEACE OFFERING
FOR THE MANY HOURS DEVOTED TO HER SOMETIME RIVAL,
THE KNEELAND GENEALOGY.

TABLE OF CONTENTS.

PART VI.

THE TIMOTHY KNEELAND FAMILY.

(Nos. 761 to 1,427.)

PART VII.

JONATHAN KNEELAND'S FAMILY.

(Nos. 1,428 to 1,782.)

PART VIII.

DR. HEZEKIAH KNEELAND'S FAMILY.

(Nos. 1,783 to 1,853.)

PART IX.

THE DAVID KNEELAND FAMILY.

(Nos. 1,854 to 2,086.)

PART X.

LOCAL BRANCHES OF THAT ILK.

(Nos. 2,087 to 3,254.)

PART I.

PRELIMINARY OBSERVATIONS.

---

a.—SYSTEM OF GENEALOGY.

b.—CHARACTERISTICS.

c.—GENESIS.

a.—SYSTEM OF GENEALOGY.

From the perusal of several thousand genealogical works, I have been struck with the variety of systems adopted or adapted by the writers to designate the different families and the several members of the same family. The New England Genealogical Society finally formulated a plan which is known by its name and is in most common use. To the ordinary intellect that system is quite confusing. It has two separate sets of numbers, between which one stumbles most blindly. I have found the same difficulty in comprehending the arrangement of the matter in many of these works, and particularly in the indexing. The Long Island Historical Society, where much of my delving after material has been made, has about three thousand genealogical works. It is necessary to examine each of these books to ascertain whether the family one is searching for is connected with any of the families there represented. There is a special index in many of the books that enables you to ascertain the fact at a glance. In others you plod all through the work—usually commencing in the middle and working both ways—to arrive at any conclusion in the matter. There is such a proclivity to profanity, such a corruption of morals, such a destruction to the nervous system, such an exasperation in this work, that it ought to be made a penal offense to publish a book without a proper handle to it.

Whether the system originated for this book will prove as puzzling to some authors as their works have to me, is a matter of indifference, provided the persons for whom it is intended—the members of our clan—can find a name immediately, and having found it can run it back to all of its predecessors. All works have three sets of numerals: First, the individual number, which designates the person and locates him in the book, thus: "**286** *Thomas Jones*," which means, or is supposed to mean, that in chronological order this particular Jones is numbered 286. Second, the family number, which distinguishes him from the other children in the same family, thus: "**286** xi *Thomas Jones*," the xi meaning that he is the eleventh child of his father. Third, the genealogical number, which shows the number of generations he is removed from the first, thus: "**286** xi *Thomas Jones*[7]," means that he is the seventh in descent from Patrick Jones, who had the honor of originating the particular line of Jones in question.

So far, all is serene. It is in the individual numbers that confusion gets confounded. We will suppose that this *Thomas Jones* was a man of mark or became the head of a numerous family. It is clear that in such a case he cannot be allowed to rest with the simple notice that he is the eleventh child of John Jones. When his name appears again, how shall he be tagged? Many books simply give him his original number over again. It then pops up, we will say, after No. 420, thus:

"**420,** v *Jonathan Jones*[9], born Jan. 10, 1843."
"**286,** THOMAS JONES," etc.

You will notice that he is considerably out of joint. One has to hunt all the way down from 287 to 420 to locate him, in fact to find out whether he turns up again at all. My system differs from all others in that I give him a new number, "421," in addition to the old, which is preserved in parenthesis to show his original position in line. Where the name first appears I point out where it comes up again, thus:

"**286** xi *Thomas Jones*[7], born June 6, 1810 (of whom hereafter, 421)."

"He who runs may read" the fact that his name will come up in chronological order next after No. 420. Turning directly to No. 420, we will find the next item as follows:

"**421** (286) THOMAS JONES[7]," etc.

By this method there is but one set of figures to designate the location of individuals, and there you are. You cannot get mixed up.

It is customary to give the entire ancestry wherever the head of a family is entered, thus:

"**421** (286) THOMAS JONES[7] (James[6], John[5], John[4], James[3] Michael[2], Patrick[1])."

When we consider that our record runs 675 years and covers 22 generations, it will be perceived at once that this would be most unwieldly. I therefore give the entire record at the head of each chapter, and at the head of families give the American branch and then skip to the first name, "Alexander[1]." The abbreviations will be readily understood—*b* stands for born, *m* for married and *d* for died. I have endeavored to make the captions and indexing complete, even at the expense of undue space. The book is divided into parts, chapters and numbers. The title of the part is the first heading on the left hand and of the chapter on the right hand pages. The second heading gives the name of the individual who is under consideration. The index will explain itself.

With apologies for 'this extended explanation of a system that I claim to be so simple, I raise the curtain for the main performance.

b.—CHARACTERISTICS.

Strong of constitution, religious, combative, self-opinionated, honest, temperate, too much given to hospitality and humanity to be over-frugal or over-rich, yet withal independent, mirthful, happy, intensely desirous of the goodwill of others, always holding to a goodwill of themselves (or, as the Scotch put it, having a great "conceit of themselves"), hopeful, good-natured, cheerful, always inspiring hope and cheer in others—these are the tendencies of the race, however much they may differ in the individual.

Perhaps a leading characteristic is best shown by the first will recorded in America by one of the clan, which bequeaths a rapier, a cutlass and two guns, and the inventory revealed a family Bible. This denotes the gentleman, the fighter and the Christian. The same qualities are designated by the family crest: " He bearest Sable; a Lyon rampant, *Or*, holding in his Dexter paw an Escutcheon, *Argent*, charged with a cross," etc. Here we have the same trinity—Nobility, designated by the fact of a coat of arms; Strength and Courage, shown by the lion rampant, and Christianity, by the cross.

One of the natural results of a hardy constitution and temperate habits is longevity. This is well proven in the history of this family. Although it has been established by actuaries that the average life of human beings is under twenty years, a glance at the record hereinafter set forth shows that the average in this family is over fifty years, and in several branches, over seventy-five years. In the writer's family there were ten sons and one daughter. All are living, and the average age is over forty-five. Probably the oldest living twins in this country are the Kneeland sisters, formerly of Hartford, Vt., born in 1809. One of them had thirteen children, of whom one died in the army during the late war, *and all the others are living*. She has forty-eight grandchildren and a small army of great-grandchildren.

Another peculiarity of the race is that its line of life has never been coiled into a noose. This makes the writing easier *and the gaps fewer.*

According to well established tradition, the Kneelands were among the ancient Vikings that overran Northern Europe prior to the Tenth Century, and finally settled in Scotland and elsewhere, becoming lairds of the captured lands.' We have no trace of our family prior to the Thirteenth Century, the record commencing with *Alexander Kneland*, who was born about 1225.

Burke, in his "Landed Gentry," p. 227, title "Cleland," says: " The family of Cleland (formerly spelled Kneland) is of great antiquity in Scotland. Their Coats of Arms, tradition states, were acquired through being hereditary foresters to the ancient Earls of Douglas. The first of the family of whom there is any record was Alexander Kneland. He was living in the reign of Alexander III and married Margaret, daughter of Adam Wallace, of Riccartoun, Scotland. She was the sister of Sir Malcolm Wallace, who was the father of Sir William Wallace."

Anderson, in his " Scottish Nation," Vol. II, p. 617, under the title of " Kneland," says: " *Kneland*, a surname derived from the lands of Kneland, in Lanarkshire. The first of the family on record, Alexander Kneland, of that ilk (*i. e.*, Alexander Kneland, of Kneland), living in the time of Alexander III, married Margaret, daughter of Adam Wallace, of Riccartoun, grandfather of Sir William Wallace, the hero of Scotland," etc.

Both Burke and Anderson make the mistake of locating Alexander Kneland in Lanarkshire. The error probably arose from the fact that the Kneland estate was located in that county. As a matter of fact, Alexander Kneland resided in Gowrie, where he was in the enjoyment of a lucrative living. The Lanarkshire lands were granted by Bruce to Alexander's son, James Kneland, for gallant services in the battle of Bannockburn, and remained in the family for four centuries, as we shall see hereafter.

At the end of his chapter on " Cleland " (Scottish Nation,

Vol. I, pp. 643-4), Anderson says: "The name was formerly Kneilland, with the 'K' pronounced. In 1603, Andrew Kneilland was Justice depute, and there are several instances of Cleland of Cleland being called Kneland of Kneland; thus, of the persons who were 'delated' for being art and part in the death of King Henry Darley, were William Kneland, of that ilk and Arthur Kneland, of Knowhobbilhill—afterwards softened into Connoblehill—in the parish of Shotts."

This William Kneland is the one referred to as William Cleland[10] in Burke's "Landed Gentry," as follows: "William Cleland, the 10th of that ilk, eminent for his loyalty to Queen Mary," etc. Both he and his son, Capt. John Kneeland, were eminent in their devotion to this luckless Queen, but all the records give the name as "Kneland," instead of "Cleland."

As we have noted, upon the primal stem of the Kneeland family were grafted many branches different in spelling but retaining all the attributes of the good old stock.

THE CLELANDS. This was the first and most important offshoot. It came about in the beginning of the Seventeenth Century. Even the name of the estate was changed, and "Kneland, of Kneland," became "Cleland, of Cleland." How this came about and to what extent it prevailed, is fully set forth in Part II herein.

The old homestead of "Kneland" is thus spoken of in the "Statistical account of Scotland": "At 'Cleland,' in Lanarkshire, coal is found 9 feet thick." (Vol. I, p. 775).

"'Cleland,' now the property of North Dalrymple, Esq., on the South Calder, is a large and elegant seat. The grounds around it are elegant and picturesque, deriving great beauty from the bold and richly wooded banks of the stream on which it is situated." (*id.*, Vol. VI, p. 784).

"The United Presbytery of Hamilton and Lanark held their first meeting at Cleland. The following is an extract from their first record: 'At Cleland, Sept. 6, 1687, Session I. * * * A little above the house, in a rock on the bank of the Calder, is a cave which is said to have been the hiding-place of the persecuted in the troublous times.'" (*id.*, Vol. VI, p. 968).

All this really relates to "Kneland," and refers to the

c.—GENESIS.

lands granted by Bruce to James Kneland in the beginning of the Fourteenth Century.

The change from Kneland to Cleland was a slight one at that time. The name was originally pronounced K-neland. The "K" being sounded, it was pronounced as if spelled Cneland. The change to Cleland was, therefore, only the substitution of a single letter.

The Clelands now use the original Kneeland Coat of Arms—a hare with a hunting-horn suspended from its neck; and as a crest, a falcon upon a mailed hand, with two grey-hounds for supporters. This has probably been in the family since the days of Bruce. But the Kneelands of America use the Coat of Arms granted by Queen Mary to Major William Kneland, the grandfather of the brothers who came here in 1630, which is hereinafter described. As a matter of fact, we are entitled to the use of either or both of these emblems.

THE KNELLS. This modification came about a little later. They adopted the Coat of Arms granted by Queen Mary to Major William Kneland, and used in the American family: A lion rampant holding a cross, with a demi lion rampant in the crest—except that they changed the cross to the crest.

THE NEWLANDS. In due course of time the English method of pronunciation made the "K" a silent letter, as at present. After this the new names always commenced with an "N," and we have Neelands, Neylands and Newlands. The latter family, which is a very honorable one, have a Coat of Arms (representing the Newlands of Totness and Devon) precisely similar to the Knell's, except that there are three lions rampant in the Coat of Arms, the Crest remaining the same— a demi lion rampant charged with a cross.

The Newlands of Scotland have, like the Kneelands, a lion rampant in both the Coat of Arms and the Crest, but they have no cross. From the fact that the estate of "New-land," in Scotland, is situated on the river Calder, in close proximity to the Kneland estate, it is probable that they both formed a part of the original lands granted to James Kneland by Bruce, and the absence of the cross shows that they adopted the Coat of Arms granted to Major William Kneland by Queen Mary, except the emblem of Popery—the cross.

2

The Newlands of Southampton received their Coat of Arms in 1620. The origin thereof is thus stated in Burke: "Descended from Roger Newland, of Newlands, County of Southampton, who, having failed in the attempt to effect the escape of Charles I from Caresbroke Castle, suffered death on the Scaffold, exclaiming, 'Deprived of my life and my property, I leave to my posterity, *Le nom les armes la loyaute*,' which has since been retained as the motto of this branch of the family."

The similarity of the original Newland Coat of Arms with that of the Knells and Kneelands, together with the similarity of names, is so marked (when we consider the fact that there is no other recorded instances of a cross held in the dexter paw of a lion rampant) as to clearly demonstrate a common family. As the Kneelands are first in point of time, it also follows that they were the original family, and we having retained both the original spelling and the Coat of Arms, are certainly entitled to the order of precedence.

NEELAND. But to follow still further the history of the race and their constant tendency to depart from the original spelling, we have only to look to the recorded events in this country. Of the two brothers that came from Scotland in 1630, the younger (Edward) settled in Ipswich, and for over a century names of this branch were spelled phonetically "Neland," "Nealand," "Neeland," etc. One of this branch settled in the Southern States and is now known by the name of "Neyland."

Attributes. However the clan changed its name, it never lost its attributes, its love of liberty, together with the desire and ability to fight its battles. In times of peace they have been men of peace; in times of war, warriors—emblematic of the Scotch thistle, that pricks only when pressed from the outside.

Our Honored Ancestors. From a pedigree in the possession of the present Rose-Cleland, I extract the following as the persons from whom the Kneeland family are descended, through intermarriages of ancestors: Sir John Mowatt; Sir John Herring; Sir John Hamilton, ancestor of the Lords of

Burgany; Earl of Bothwell, third husband of Queen Mary Stuart; Lord Darnley, second husband of Queen Mary Stuart; Alexander Stewart, High Steward of Scotland; James the Fifth of Scotland; James Douglass, ancestor of the Earls of Morton; William de Hay, ancestor of Lord Hay; Sir Alexander Livingston, ancestor of the Earls of Lilienthow; Sir James Douglass, Earl of Dalkeith; Gilbert Graham, Earl of Strathern; William Ross, Earl of Ross; Adam Gordon, Lord Gordon; Robert the Bruce, King of Scotland; Adam Wallace, grandfather of Sir William Wallace; Cedric, King of the West Saxons; Charlemagne; Alfred the Great; Capet, King of France; Rollo, Duke of Normandy; Baldwin the Third, Earl of Flanders; Siward, Earl of Northumberland; William the Conqueror; Malcolm Canmore, King of Scotland; Hugh Keviloch, Earl of Chester; Wallern, Earl of Mallert; Roger de Bellamont, Lord of Port Andeman; Rudolph de Gauder, Earl of the East Angles; Hugh de Grantmesnil, Great Steward of England; Norman de Leslie, ancestor of the Earls of Rothes; and the families of Burgundy, Valois and Vermandois.

All this and more is set forth in Burke's "Landed Gentry," title "Cleland." Personally, I do not stand sponsor for the truth of all this ancestry, though history proves much of it. I simply give it from Burke, who is trusted by all aspirants and adored by all hero worshippers.

> " Howe'er it be, it seems to me
> 'Tis only noble to be good ;
> Kind hearts are more than Coronets,
> And simple faith, than Norman blood."

PART II.

SCOTTISH CHIEFTAINS OF THE CLAN-KNELAND.
(NOS. 1 TO 30.)

DEDICATED TO THE MEMORY OF

JAMES KNELAND, ESQ.,[2]

THE SQUIRE AND "NE'R CUSYNG" OF

SIR WILLIAM WALLACE,

THE DEFENDER AND FRIEND OF

KING ROBERT THE BRUCE,

AND THE ANCESTOR OF A LONG LINE OF KNEELANDS

EQUALLY HANDY WITH THE SWORD, THE

PEN AND THE PLOW.

CHAPTER I.

THE "PARSON O'GOWRIE" AND KNELANDS OF THAT ILK.

(Nos. 1 TO 10.)

1. ALEXANDER KNELAND[1]. Born about 1225. He was named after the reigning King of Scotland, Alexander III; was a wealthy prelate residing at Kilspendie, in Gowrie, Scotland, and married Margaret Wallace, of Riccartoun, who was the daughter of Adam Wallace, of that place, and the aunt of Sir William Wallace. He was therefore the uncle, by marriage, of Sir William, who resided with and received his early education and love of liberty from him. This venerable old man is thus referred to by Henry, the Minstrel—Blind Harry—in his "Wallace and Bruce," (Book I, lines 151 to 155), speaking of Sir William Wallace in his boyhood:

> "The Knight his fadyr, thedyr he thaim sent
> Till his Wncle that with full gud content,
> In Gowry duelt, and had gud lewyng ther;
> Ane agyt man, the yuhilk resawt thaim far."

Kerr, in his "History of Scotland," (Vol. I, p. 119) says of this Parson O'Gowrie: "It is said in the Schotichronicon that an uncle, who was a priest, strongly inculcated on William Wallace the following sentence in monkish latin, desiring him to preserve it in his memory as the invariable guide of his life: 'Dico tibi verum, libertas est optima rerum; nunquam servili sub nexu vivite fili' (Ford XII, iii.)" "Verily I say unto you, liberty is the best of things; never live under a servile yoke."

In Kinlock's "History of Scotland," p. 133, we find the following reference to Parson Alexander Kneland: "He (Wallace) had grown up with an instinctive hatred for the

English which was fostered by his uncle, a priest, who was perpetually bewailing the banished freedom of his unhappy land."

Many writers on Scottish history have confounded this uncle with the Parson of Dunipace, who befriended Wallace in after years. These are clearly separate individuals living in separate localities and with manifestly divergent opinions. The latter uncle, or "eyme," as he is invariably called by Blind Harry, advised Sir William, in the midst of his difficulties, to give up the contest and accept a gift of lands and peerage under the English King. The Parson O'Gowrie could never have brought himself to that way of thinking. The former is always spoken of by Harry as the "wncle," and the latter as the "eyme" of Wallace. Although these words have been considered as equivalent, yet the distinction was notably observed by the bard.

It is clear that the Parson of Dunipace was a Wallace. The name of the other uncle does not appear in Harry's poem. Kerr, after speaking of the Dunipace uncle, says: "Another uncle is mentioned as aged and having a good living at Kilspendie, in Gowrie, but whether paternally or maternally related does not appear." (Vol. I, Kerr's "History of Scotland," p. 120).

I do not find, from the Canonical Records of Scotland, that any uncle of Wallace was a *Catholic* prelate. He probably was at the head of a dissenting church. I find, from a thorough examination of records, that the Gowrie uncle was neither a brother of Sir Malcolm Wallace (who was the father of Sir William) nor a Crawford (the maiden name of his mother), all the Wallaces and Crawfords being otherwise accounted for. As Malcolm Wallace only had one sister, Margaret, who married Alexander Kneland, it follows that Alexander Kneland *must* have been the uncle to whom Wallace was indebted for his early education and love of liberty, and Scotland indebted for the inspiration of that love. We have no record of his family except his eldest son and heir.

2. JAMES KNELAND[3] (*Alexander*[1]). "The second of that ilk." It would have been impossible to have been the son

of the prelate that instilled into the mind of Wallace such an enthusiastic love of liberty without being filled with the same zeal. James Kneland was more than a lover of liberty. He was pre-eminently a fighter for it. He was one of those sterling, zealous, unwavering, brave Scottish chiefs that gave Scott and Burns a basis for their inspiration, and the world its admiration for the "Heroes of Scotland." James Kneland had the rare privilege of being individualized in poetry. The earliest of the Scotch poets—Henry the Minstrel—writing two hundred years after his death, but basing his poem on the History of Wallace (now extant) written by John Blair, who was Sir William's chaplain, speaking of the assembling of the chiefs before the battle of Stirling, says (Book III, line 35, etc.):

> " Kneland was yar, ner cusyng to Wallace,
>   Syne baid with hym in mony peralouss place."

Again, speaking of the sea fight of the " Red Rover," the same bard says:

> " And thar war part in his falowship,
>   'Twa Wallace, was his kynsman full ner
>   Crawfurd, Kneland, was haldyn till him der."

Later on, in the same fight, he puts it in the mouth of Wallace to say (Book IX, line 133, etc.):

> " Kneland, cusyng, cum take the ster on hand
>   Her on the waill, ner by the I sall stand."

It will be noted from a full reading of Blind Harry's historical verses, that Wallace, who had learned that the Scottish nobility were not to be depended upon, relied for advice and assistance upon a band of relatives constituting the lesser barons of Scotland. They included the three sons of his uncle, Sir Richard Crawford, the Sheriff of Riccartoun, Adam, Richard and Simon Crawford; his cousin, James Kneland, and his nephew, Edward Littell, "and Edward Littil his sister's son so der." United with these were a few other boon companions, most conspicuous of whom were Squire Robert Boyd and John Blair, his chaplain.

James Kneland [2].

How he listened to this band of followers appears from the following (Book III, line 325, etc.):

> " Than Wallace said till gud men him about;
> ' I will no pess for all this felloune dout,
> Bot gif it pless bettir to yow than me.'
> The Squire Boids him ansuerd sobyrle,
> ' I gif conseill or this gud Knycht be slayne
> Tak pess a quhill, supposs it do us payne.'
> So said Adam the Ayr of Rycardtoune :
> And Kneland als grantyt to thair opynoun.
> With thair consent Wallace this pess has tayne
> As his eyme wrocht, till ten month was gayne,
> Boyd and Kneland past to thar placis hayme,
> Adam Wallace to Riccartoun by name."

In this same book we have an account of one of the minor fights with the English :

> " Wallace in deide he wrocht so worthely,
> The Squire Boyd and all thair chewalry,
> Litil, Kneland, gert off thair enemys de,
> The Inglissmen tuk playnly part to fle.
> A hundreth dede in feild was lewyt thar,
> And thre yemen that wace menyde for mar."

Again, in Book V, line 250, etc.:

> " Gud Robert Boid on till a tavern yeid.
> With twenty men that douchty was indeid.
> Kerle turnyt with his master agayne,
> Kneland and Byrd, that mekill war off mayne."

In Book IV, lines 135, etc., we find Wallace in trouble :

> " And mony othir was full woo that day.
> Robert the Boide stall of the toune his way,
> And Kneland als, befor with him had beyne.
> Thai had leuir haif seyne him with thair eyne,
> Boide wept sor, said " our leider is goyne
> Amang our fays he is set him allayne."
> Than Kneland said, " Fals fortoun changis fast
> Gret God sen we had euir with him past."

James Kneland joined his cousin, Sir William Wallace, in 1296, in his attempt to restore the liberties of the country. He was present at most of the exploits of Wallace, particularly at Loudoun Hill, July, 1296; the battle of Stirling,

John Kneland [4].

September 13, 1297, and the disastrous battle of Falkirk, July 22, 1298. He sailed with his illustrious cousin to France and assisted in the sea battle with " Thomas of Longueville," commonly called the " Red Rover." After the death of Sir William, he firmly supported the cause of King Robert the Bruce and was present with his eldest son, John Kneland, at the battle of Bannockburn, where he was severely wounded. For his loyalty and good service that King gave to him several lands in the Barony of Calder, West Lothian, in Linlithgow-shire (now Lanarkshire), which remained in the family for several hundred years (see Burke's "Landed Gentry," title "Cleland," and Anderson's " History of Scotland "). He was succeeded by his eldest son and heir :

3. JOHN KNELAND[3] (*James*[2], *Alexander*[1]). This is the first on record of a long race of John Kneelands and John Clelands. While yet a boy he fought with his father in the battle of Bannockburn, under Robert the Bruce, and there-after took a hand in every opportunity to strike a blow against the foes of Scotland, ending his active career by being captured with the reigning monarch, David the Second, at the battle of Durham or "Neville's Cross," October 17, 1346. He was a staunch adherent and follower of Alexander Murray, of Both-well, and of " Robert the Steward," afterwards King Robert II. His eldest son and heir was :

4. JOHN KNELAND[4] (*John*[3], *James*[2], *Alexander*[1]). A John Kinieland—the first record we have of that spelling—was severely wounded while leading a band of Scotchmen at the unfortunate battle at Poitiers, in 1357, which led to the treaty of Berwick, October 3, 1357. As John Kneland, Sr., fought in the battle of Bannockburn, in 1314, and at Dunham, in 1346, it cannot be presumed that he could have survived to fight for his sovereign in 1357. As the warriors seem to have been confined to the heirs " of that ilk," I am safe in putting this John down as John, Jr., who spelled his name as then pronounced, and as some of his successors still spell it. This is all the information I can gather of John[4], and is more than Burke or Cleland-Ross discovered, for, with them, there was a

break in the chain from John[3] to William[7]. I have, after much scurrying around, succeeded in finding Knelands during this interim which supply the missing links.

5. JOHN KNELAND[5] (*John[4], John[3], James[2], Alexander[1]*). What right a Kneland of Calder had to interfere in the quarrels of Donald, lord of the isles, after the old house of Douglass had been made satisfied with the condition of affairs at the beginning of the Sixteenth Century, is more than I can understand, except it may be a touch of the Irishman's desire to hit a head wherever he could see it. Certain it is, however, that we find the name of John Kneland in the conflict at Harlow, May 17, 1412, the "Otterburn" of the "Northern Ballads." As this fills a gap between John[4] and William[6], I shall claim it as our own and brand him John Kneland[5]. That is all I know about him or the aforesaid gap, and this is from historical ballads rather than from history. There is, however, this to be added—the name stated is John Kneland *of that ilk*, meaning John Kneland who resided at *Kneland*. As no one could occupy this property except the heir, and as the date is too late for John Kneeland[4], and as the sixth heir was William, it necessarily follows that it must have been the eldest son of John Kneland[4], viz., John Kneland[5].

6. WILLIAM KNELAND[6] (*John[5], John[4], John[3], James[2], Alexander[1]*). Little is known of him except that he was a man of education and much given to hunting. Burke, in his "Landed Gentry," confounds him with his son William[7], who succeeded him. He (William[6]) was one of the witnesses, in 1445, to the charter of the lands of Watston, granted by James, Lord Hamilton, to Sir William Baillie, of Hoprigg. How this act could be ascribed to William[7] when the latter was not old enough to be married until 1462, is more than I can comprehend, any more than I can understand the statement that he was William "Cleland," in the face of the fact that it is written "Kneland" in the deed.

7. WILLIAM KNELAND[7] (*William[6], John[5], John[4], John[3], James[2], Alexander[1]*). "The seventh of that ilk." In other words, the seventh Kneland, of Kneland, or residing at Kneland,

Alexander Kneland[8].

was married in 1462—soon after James the Third had ascended to the throne of Scotland—to Jean Somerville, daughter of William de Somerville, second Lord Somerville by his wife, Janet Mowat, daughter of Sir John Mowat. From this marriage descended the several branches of the Kneland family, to wit—Kneland of Faskine, Kneland of Monkland and Kneland of Cartness, making, with Kneland of Kneland, four sons who became heads of distinct families.

A short reference to these families may now be in order. The Cartness family terminated in an heiress previous to the middle of the Eighteenth Century, who married Sir William Vere, of Blackwood, in the same county. William Kneland, of Faskine, was killed, together with his cousin, Alexander Kneland[8], of Kneland, at the battle of Flodden, in 1513. About the beginning of the Seventeenth Century, Sir James Kneland purchased the barony of Monkland from Sir Thomas Hamilton, of Binning, first Earl of Haddington, but his son, Ludovick, sold it to James, Marquis of Hamilton. On the sixth of September, 1615, this Sir James Kneland, of Monkland, was, with two others, indicted for "treasonable resetting Jesuites, hearing of mass," etc., offences very seriously punished in those days, but the diet was deserted against them. Sir James was sometimes called "Cleland," and is one of the first of the Knelands to spell his name in that way. The Monkland family, which is still extant, spell their names at present with a "K," but give it in the form of the old pronunciation— "Kineiland." (See "Kineiland, of Monkland," in the works on Heraldry by Berry and Burke). This is the only one of the several branches that preserves intact the original Kneland Coat of Arms, as shown in the work of Sir Thomas Lyndsay, issued in 1542, though the Clelands have the same, with slight modifications.

8. ALEXANDER KNELAND[8] (*William*[7], *Wiliam*[6], *John*[5], *John*[4], *John*[3], *James*[2], *Alexander*[1]). "The eighth of that ilk." He was very much of a fighter, a strong partisan and friend of King James IV, of Scotland, and was killed at the fatal battle of Flodden, on the ninth day of September, 1513. To a charter of the date of 1498, there was appended a

James Kneland [9].

seal of this Alexander Kneland, upon which was a hare salient with a hunting horn about his neck. It is just possible that this Coat of Arms was given to him by King James IV to commemorate their hunting exploits. The Crest is equally significant of its origin: A falcon standing on a sinister hand glove ppr.; supporters, two greyhounds ppr. Motto, over the Crest, "Non sibi"; under the arms, "Je pense a qui pense plus."

Tradition states that this Coat of Arms was acquired at a very early date and related to their position as hereditary foresters of the Earls of Douglass. It cannot be objected that a hare would not have a horn around his neck at a period prior to the adoption of powder for hunting purposes. It is a fact that gunpowder was not extensively manufactured or used for sporting in England until the days of Elizabeth, nearly a century after this period. But "hunting horns" had been in use from time immemorial. Some were made to call the hounds and falcon, and others for drinking purposes. That the Kneelands were expert huntsmen at the time of King James IV and of his successor, James V, is evident from the fact of their attendance on those monarchs in that capacity. It is probable that their Coat of Arms had been in the family from the earliest period of Heraldry. If not, then they must have been given by Bruce to James Kneland with the lands conferred upon him, or by King James III or IV, in commemoration of their hunting exploits.

9.   JAMES KNELAND[9] (*Alexander*[8], *William*[7], *John*[6], *John*[5], *John*[4], *John*[2], *John*[1]). "The ninth of that ilk." An eminent man in the time of King James V, whom he frequently attended at hunting. He married a daughter of Hepburn, of Bonnytown, who was the son of Patrick, Lord Halles, Earl of Bothnell. King James was probably one of the best examples of the Stuart family, save and except the founder thereof, Robert III. He was a vigorous administrator and protected the poor from oppression by the nobles. From his intimate relation to the common people, he was often termed the "King of the Commons," and his incognito was "the gude man of Ballinbreich." To this popular monarch James Kneland was a favorite courtier, and fought bravely for him in the disas-

trous field at Solway Moss, November 25, 1542, where he was severely wounded. James V had several "natural" sons, and one of his granddaughters of that ilk married a grandson of James Kneland, but his only legitimate heir was the unfortunate Mary Stuart, Queen of Scots, who was devotedly loved and defended by the son and heir of James Kneland, of Kneland.

10. MAJ. WILLIAM KNELAND[10] (*James*[9], *Alexander*[8], *William*[7], *William*[6], *John*[5], *John*[4], *John*[3], *James*[2], *Alexander*[1]). "The tenth Kneland of that ilk," who was, as above suggested, eminent for his loyalty to Queen Mary of the Scots. The Queen's favor and his known attachment to her and desire to further her supposed wishes, led him into difficulties, for he was suspected of being privy to the sudden taking off of Her Majesty's discarded husband and cousin, Lord Darnley. William Kneland, of Kneland, and Arthur Kneland, of Knowhobbihill, in the parish of Shotts, were "delated"—that is, accused in court in connection with this affair.

It will be remembered that Lord Darnley was blown up by gunpowder while confined by sickness in the house known as "Kirk of Field," on the tenth day of February, 1567. The parties to this crime were, undoubtedly, the Earl of Bothnell, who planned, and his servants who executed it. Their confessions prove this much. But who the accomplices were has from that day to this been debated without conclusive answer. That they were persons high in favor with Mary is evident, as her own skirts were not free from stain. The charge against the two Knelands, although unproven, had a decided influence upon the future of the family, and may have been instrumental in splitting it into fragmentary branches, each following its own ideas of spelling the family name.

The Queen, having been educated in France, was an ardent Catholic, at a period when the Reformation was in the full vigor of early manhood in her Scottish Kingdom. Naturally, her most intimate supporters were of the old faith, notwithstanding the breach thus made with others of the same family who were the followers of John Knox. It is probably for this reason that the Coat of Arms given by the Queen to

Major William Kneland [10].

William or his son, Captain John Kneland, which contained, in addition to the lion of Scotland, the cross of Rome, was not accepted by those of the same name not closely connected with the crown. Capt. John Kneland, who was a younger son of Major William Kneland, and who, having a touch of the old Viking forefathers, adopted the sea for a profession, retained the original parchment creating the Coat of Arms, and the precious document is still in the possession of his descendants in America, and was reproduced in part by other branches of the family, as we have shown elsewhere.

The eldest son and heir of this William Kneland [10], who succeeded to the estate of Kneland, changed the spelling of the name to "Cleland," and we find that to be the name of the Knelands of that ilk and of the estate thereafter. Whether this was done consciously to draw a line of demarkation between the Papist forefathers and the Protestant descendants, and to eliminate a name then under suspicion of a crime, or whether it occurred through accident, will probably never be determined. Certain it is, that from that time forward the Knelands, of Kneland, became the "Clelands, of Cleland." As, however, they were of the same old stock and just as much Kneelands as if they had never changed their name, I will consider them in the next chapter, and then proceed with the American history, which commences with the sons of Capt. John Kneland [11], and which never departed from the old name, although it did break from the old faith.

CHAPTER II.

THE CLELAND FAMILY.

The career of the Kneeland family after they adopted the new mode of spelling is so illustrious as to make it a source of regret that the departure ever took place. They continued the use of the original Coat of Arms, typical of their life as foresters, and also continued their record as warriors and added to it a new feature in the domain of literature. We take pleasure, therefore, in completing the history of this branch of the family to the present time.

11. *William Cleland*[11], of that ilk, was the eldest son and heir of Major William Kneland[10], the loyal friend of Mary Stuart, Queen of the Scots. He married a sister of Walter Stewart, first Lord Blantyre, daughter of Sir John Stewart by his wife, Margaret, daughter of James Stewart and granddaughter of King James V.

12. *Alexander Cleland*[12], of that ilk, married Mary, sister of John Hamilton, first Lord Bargany, and the youngest daughter of Sir John Hamilton, of Bargany, and his spouse, Margaret Campbell, daughter of Rev. Alexander Campbell, Bishop of Brechen, who was descended from the Duke of Argyle. By her he had several sons, the eldest of whom sold the lands of Kneland (then designated as Cleland) to a cousin of his own name. From this point the heirship is broken. Burke's account, taking up the third son, John Cleland, who was the ancestor of the Rose-Clelands, who were subscribers to Burke.

13. *John Cleland*[13], of Laird Braes, in the parish of Zeswalt, was the third son of Alexander Cleland[12], and was born about 1623. In consequence of some disagreement with

3

Richard Rose-Cleland, Esq.[19]

his elder brother, he retired in disgust to a small property called Laird Braes, in the parish of Zeswalt, and about the year 1651, M. Katharine Ross, descended from the Rosses, in Henning. He died in 1683, leaving his son and successor:

14. *James Cleland*[14], of Laird Braes, born in 1652. He was married, 1690, to Agnes Inness, a descendant of the Innesses, of Bennell. She died in 1711 and he died in 1717, leaving issue: (i.) John, b. in 1692 (of whom hereafter); (ii.) Mary, b. in 1694, m. her third cousin, James McEwan.

15. *John Cleland*[15], of Whithorn, in Wigtonshire, Scotland, was the only son and heir of James Cleland[14]. He was factor to James, fifth Earl of Galloway, and in 1731 m. Margaret Murdock, only child of Murdock, provost of Whithorn. They had issue:

16. (i.) *James*[16], b. May 4, 1736 (of whom hereafter[18]).

17. (ii.) *Agnes*[16], b. Sept. 14, 1740; m. Lieut. Richard Rose, of the East India Co. Regiment, by whom she had an only child, James Dowsett Rose, who inherited the Cleland estate and assumed the additional surname of Cleland (of whom hereafter).

18. (16) *James Cleland, Esq.*[16], of Newton Ards, County Down, Ireland, was the only son and heir of John Cleland[15], m. in 1770 to Sarah, only child of Capt. Patrick Baird, the uncle of Gen. Sir David Baird. He died May 14, 1777. He had no issue and was succeeded by his nephew.

19. *James Dowsett Rose-Cleland, Esq.*[17], hereinbefore mentioned, was born March 24, 1767. He inherited an Irish estate situated in the County of Down and located there, where his descendants still reside. He was living at the time Burke's "Landed Gentry" was published, and was the representative of the family and subscriber to Burke at that time. He had several children, the eldest being:

20. *James Dowsett Rose-Cleland, Esq*[18], who inherited the Irish and Scotch estates and resided at Rath Gael House, in Bangor. He had several children, the oldest of which, bearing the same name, died without issue in 1856, the estates descending to:

21. *Richard Rose-Cleland, Esq.*[19], the second son, who retained the family residence, Rath Gael House, in Bangor, County.

of Down. He was born in 1836 and married in 1861 to Elizabeth Wilhelmina, eldest daughter of Robert Kennedy, Esq., of Lisburn, County of Antrim. Their eldest son and heir was:

22. *James Dowsett Rose-Cleland*[20], who was born in 1852.

We have now completed the history of the Kneeland family in great Britain in a direct line, running twenty generations and covering nearly seven centuries. Before taking up the American Branch, I propose to give a sketch of other members of the family abroad who indulged in the fancy of spelling their name " Cleland."

23. *Samuel Cleland*[18], son of James Dowsett Rose Cleland[17]. He resided at Stormont Castle, in the County of Down, and had as his eldest son and heir :

24. *John C. Cleland, Esq.*[19] He resided at Stormont Castle, Dundodald, County Down, was educated at Eton, is a Justice of the Peace, and was formerly High Sheriff for the County of Down ; is also Lord of the Manor of Stormont and Patron of the living of Dundonald. He married Theresa Maria, daughter of Capt. Thomas Leyland, of Haggerstown Castle, Northumberland. Their eldest son and heir was :

25. *Arthur Charles Stewart Rose Cleland*[20], born in 1862, and resides at Stormont Castle.

26. *James Cleland, Esq.*[20], son of Hugh Cleland, Esq., and probably grandson of Samuel Rose Cleland,[18] was born in 1857, and resides at Ruband House, Kirkcubbin, County of Down, Ireland. He is a magistrate of the County and the owner of several estates therein.

27. *Maj.-Gen. William Douglas Cleland, E. J. C. S.* This representative has more rank, but probably less honor, than the Col. William Cleland (of whom hereafter). I know nothing of this august descendant of the Kneelands except the statement in Burke's Heraldry of the name and title as above, with the addition of the fact that he was the son of the late Lieut. Robert Cleiland, R. N., and grandson of Col. Robert Cleland, who was the grandson of Major William Kneland[10], the tenth Kneland of that ilk, making use of the word " Cleland," instead of " Kneland," which we have shown to be erroneous, as applied to the gallant Major.

28.   *Lieut.-Col. William Cleland and his Literary Descendants.*   We now come to the consideration of one of the most
celebrated of all the descendants of Alexander Kneland[1], the
Parson O'Gowrie, Lieut. Col. William Cleland, equally eminent
as poet, scholar and soldier.   He was the son of Thomas
Cleland, hereditary game-keeper to the Marquis of Douglass
and the fourth in descent from Major William Kneland[10] (see
Woodrow's " History of the Sufferings of the Church of Scotland," Vol. I, p. 524).

In a proclamation issued after the battle of Drumclog,
June 1, 1679, he and his brother are described as " James and
William Cleland, brothers-in-law to John Haddoway, merchant
in Douglass,"   Possibly the most accurate sketch of his life is
contained in the " Dictionary of National Biography," title
" Cleland," where all previous records are carefully analyzed.
In relation to his place of birth it is there stated :   " From
references in his poems to the county town of Dumfries, and
to the rivers Nith and Onnan, it has been supposed that he
was a native of Dumfrieshire, but further investigation shows
that he was born and brought up near Douglass Castle, in
Lanarkshire, where the Marquis of Douglass chiefly resided."
That is the location of the lands of " Kneland," and it is clear
from this and other facts relating thereto that he was the great-
grandson of William Cleland[11], and a cousin (four times
removed) of John Kneland[13], who founded the Society of
Scots in Boston.

Chambers' Biographical Encyclopedia fixes the date of
his birth at 1671, but this is clearly erroneous, as the college
records show that he was educated at the University of St.
Andrews, where he entered St. Salvator's college in 1676, and
matriculated in 1677.   It also appears that he successfully
planned the victory at Drumclog, which took place June 1,
1679.   It cannot be conceived that these achievements could
have been consummated, even by a Kneeland, before arriving
at the age of ten years.   The date of birth given in "The
National Biography" is undoubtedly correct.   Even this
placed him in an important command at the age of 18.   It is
significant that he belonged to a family of wealth and influence to have enabled him to secure, in those days, the educa-

tional privileges and position in the army of the Lowlands. It must be remembered that in addition to the fact that the Knelands had then been for centuries attached to the house of Douglass as hereditary foresters, they were, themselves, one of the oldest families among the landed squires of Scotland. It was probably due to the influence of the Marquis of Douglass that he secured his appointment to the head of the Cameronian Regiment, as hereinafter stated.

When only 18 he held command as a captain in the covenanting army of Drumclog and Bothwell Bridge. He seems to have stepped directly from the university into the field of arms; for it is known that he was at college just before completing his eighteenth year, at which age he enjoyed the rank above mentioned in the Whig army. Although he probably left the country after the affair at Bothwell, he is found spending the summer of 1685, in hiding, among the wilds of Clydesdale and Ayrshire, having, perhaps, returned in the unfortunate expedition of the Earl of Argyle. Whether he again retired to the continent is not known, but after the revolution he re-appears on the stage of public life, in the character of lieutenant-colonel of the Earl of Angus' regiment, called the Cameronian Regiment, in consequence of its having been raised out of that body of men for the purpose of protecting the convention parliament. That Cleland had now seen a little of the world appears from a poem entitled, some lines made by him upon the observation of the vanity of worldly honors, after he had been at several princes' courts.*

Cleland, before he left college,' had writen some highly fanciful verses, of which we have preserved a copy below : †

> " In conceit like Phæton,
>   I'll mount Phœbus' chair,
>   Having ne'er a hat on,
>   All my hair a-burning,
>   In my journeying,
>   Hurrying through the air.

---

*We also observe, in Watts' Bibliotheca Britanica, that he published "Disputatio Juridica de Probationibus," at Utrecht, in 1684, which would imply that he studied civil law at that celebrated seminary.

† These form part of a poem entitled, " Hollo, my Fancy," which was printed in Watson's Collection of Scottish Poems, at the beginning of the last century.

Lieut.-Col. William Cleland.

Fain would I hear his fiery horses neighing!
And see how they on foamy bits are playing!
All the stars and planets I will be surveying,
   Hollo, my fancy, whither wilt thou go?

   O, from what ground of nature
     Doth the pelican,
   That self-devouring creature,
   Prove so froward
   And untoward
     Her vitals for to strain!
And why the subtle fox, while in death's wounds lying,
Doth not lament his wounds by howling and by crying!
And why the milk-white swan doth sing when she's a-dying!
   Hollo, my fancy, whither wilt thou go?" etc., etc.

It is a strong mark of the early popularity of Hudibras that, embodying though it did the sarcasms of a cavalier against the friends of civil and religious liberty, it nevertheless traveled into Scotland and inspired a poet of the entirely opposite party.

He composed a poem in the Hudibrastic style, upon the celebrated expedition of the Highland host, which took place in 1678. His object was to satirize both the men who composed this expedition and those who directed it to take place. It chiefly consists in a ludicrous account of the outlandish appearance, senseless manners, and oppressive conduct of the northern army. So far as satire could repay the rank cruelly of that mode of constraining men's consciences, it was repaid—for the poem is full of poignant sarcasm, expressed in language far above the poetical diction of that day. It was not published, however, till 1697, nearly twenty years after the incident which called it forth, when at length it appeared in a small volume, along with several other poems by the same author. We present the following specimen of the composition, being a description of the Highlanders:

   " Some might have judged they were the *creatures*
   Call'd *selfies*, whose customes and features
   Paracelsus doth descry,
   In his occult philosophy,
   Or *faunes*, or *brownies*, if ye will,
   Or *satyres*, come from *Atlas* hill:

Or that the three-tongu'd tyke was sleeping,
Who hath the *Stygian* door a-keeping.
Their head, their neck, their leggs and thighs
Are influenced by the skies;
Without a clout to interrupt them,
They need not strip them when they whip them,
Nor loose their doublet when they're hanged.

      *   *   *   *

" But those who were their chief commanders,
As such who bore the pirnie standarts;
Who led the van and drove the rear,
Were right well mounted of their gear;
With brogues, and trues, and pirnie plaides,
And good blue bonnets on their heads,
Which on the one side had a flipe,
Adorn'd with a tobacco-pipe.
With dirk, and snap-work, and snuff-mill,
A bagg which they with onions fill,
And, as their strict observers say,
A tasse horn filled with usquebay.
A slasht-out coat beneath her plaides,
A targe of timber, nails, and hides;
With a long, two-handed sword,
As good's the country can afford—
Had they not need of bulk and bones,
Who fight with all these arms at once?
It's marvellous how in such weather
O'er hill and moss they came together;
How in such storms they came so far;
The reason is, they're smeared with tar,
Which doth defend them heel and neck,
Just as it doth their sheep protect—

      *   *   *   *

" Nought like religion they retain,
Of moral honestie they're clean.
In nothing theyre accounted sharp,
Except in bagpipe and in harp.
For a misobliging word,
She'll durk her neighbour o'er the boord,
And then she'll flee like fire from flint,
She'll scarcely ward the second dint.
If any ask her of her thrift,
Forsooth, her *nainsell* lives by theft."

Lieut.-Col. William Cleland.

Colonel Cleland was not destined long to enjoy his command in the Cameronian Regiment, or the better times which the revolution had at length introduced. In August, 1689, the month after the battle of Killiecrankie, he was sent with his men to take post at Dunkeld, in order to prepare the way for a second invasion of the Highlands. The remains of that army which Dundee had led to victory, but without gaining its fruits, gathered suddenly into the neighborhood, and, on the twenty-first of August, made a most determined attack upon the town. Cleland, though he had only eight hundred men to oppose to four thousand, resolved to fight it out to the last, telling his men that, if they chose to desert him, he would stand out by himself for the honor of the regiment and the good cause in which he was engaged. The soldiers were animated so much by his eloquence and example, that they withstood the immense odds brought against them and finally caused the Highlanders to retire discomfited, leaving about three hundred men behind them. Perhaps there was not a single skirmish or battle during the whole of the war of liberty —from 1639 to 1689—which conferred more honor on either party than this affair at Dunkeld. Cleland, to whom so much of the glory was due, unfortunately fell in the action, at the early age of twenty-eight. He was employed in encouraging his soldiers in front of the Dunkeld house, when two bullets pierced his head and one his liver, simultaneously. He turned about and endeavored to get back into the house, in order that his death might not discourage his men, but he fell before reaching the threshold.

From Burton's " History of Scotland " (p. 140, etc.), we have a vivid account of this battle : " While they proceeded, a new and powerful element was brought into the strife. The regiment of the armed Cameronians was sent northward by the council to aid in the subjugation of the Highlands. They were led by a remarkable commander—their Lieutenant-Colonel, William Cleland, not yet in his thirtieth year. His comparative youth might have rendered him unacceptable to the stern fathers of the Societies, and it is still more wonderful that they should have accepted one endowed with worldly accomplishments and heathen learning, and even given to the

DEATH OF COL. WILLIAM CLELAND

No. 28

vain art of poetry. * * * But his true command over them was in a powerful response to the higher tones of their own enthusiasm. Like Cromwell and Dundee, he could feel all they felt, yet point the strength of his zeal to a definite object by the unerring guidance of a clear judgment, and he crowned his short life with an achievement fit to have been given another laurel to those more renowned heroes. * * * On the morning of Wednesday (Aug. 21, 1689), the whole Highland army of 5,000 men covered the hills. Cleland, with great skill, drew in his outposts, signaling them how to retreat and fire from cover to cover, until they came within the general barriers. The wild host, like hungry hyenas, disappointed for a moment of their doomed prey, came close around to make their general rush. They expected to get over the dykes and commence the slaughter, but they were driven back by pikes and halberds, and retreated nearly as quick as they came. The attempt was repeated over and over with the same success.

"To protect themselves from this fierce open fighting, the Highlanders occupied the houses of the village and fought from under cover. The Cameronians, assailed thus, finally took to the offensive in a manner as daring and original as it was effective. A party of men were sent with blazing fagots on the end of long pikes, who set fire to the dry thatch of the houses, and the village was speedily in flames. This ferocious warfare lasted till eleven o'clock at night. When wearied out with the pertinacity of the defenders, the Highlanders took no order of retreat but scampered off at once to the hills, and the besieged, after many demonstrations of exultation, contempt and defiance, betook themselves to thanksgiving for a deliverance which, they believed, and as it turned out, was complete. Thus an army exceeding four thousand men was beaten back by Cleland's regiment of 800."

29. *Col. William Cleland.* It is stated by the editor of the Border Minstrelsy, that this brave officer was the father of a second Colonel Cleland, who flourished in the *beau monde* at London, in the reign of Queen Anne and George I, and who, besides enjoying the honor of having his character embalmed in the Spectator, under the delightful fiction of Will Honeycomb, was the author of a letter to Pope, prefixed to the Dunciad.

John Cleland.

30. *John Cleland,* the son of this latter gentleman, was also a literary character. He was born in 1709, and received a good education at Westminster school, where he was the contemporary of Lord Mansfield. He went on some mercantile pursuit to Smyrna and remained there several years. After his return from the Mediterranean he went to the East Indies, but, quarreling with some of the members of the Presidency of Bombay, he returned home. After living for some time in London, in a state little short of destitution, he was tempted by a bookseller, for the sum of twenty guineas, to write a novel, which was published in 1749, in two volumes, and had so successful a run that the profits are said to have exceeded £10,000. This book was severely criticised. It is related that, having been called before the privy council for this offense, he pleaded his destitute circumstances as his only excuse, which induced the president, Lord Granville, to buy the pen of the unfortunate author over to the side of virtue, by granting him a pension of £100 a year. He lived many years upon this income, which he aided by writing occasional pieces in the newspapers and also by the publication of various works.

He published a novel called the "Man of Honor" as an *amende honorable* for his flagitious work, and also a work entitled, "The Memoirs of a Coxcomb." His political essays, which appeared in the public prints under the signatures, "Modestus," "A Briton," etc., are said to have been somewhat heavy and dull. He wrote some philological tracts, chiefly relating to the Celtic language, but it was in songs and novels that he chiefly shone. In the latter part of his life he lived in a retired manner in Petty France, Westminster, where he had a good library, in which hung a portrait of his father, indicating all the manners and *d'abord* of the fashionable townsman at the beginning of the eighteenth century. Though obliged to live frugally, in order that he might not exceed his narrow income, Mr. Cleland occasionally received visits from his friends, to whom his conversation, enriched by many observations of foreign travel and all the literary anecdote of the past century, strongly recommended him. He spoke with fluency the languages of Italy and France, through which countries, as well as Spain and Portugal, he had traveled on his return from the East Indies. He died in his house in Little France, January 23, 1786, at the age of eighty.

In regard to the questionable volume written by Cleland —" Fanny Hill, or the Memoirs of a Woman of Pleasure," it is only fair to his memory to state the fact that, as originally written, it was very favorably noticed in the *Monthly Review* (Vol. XI, pp. 451-2), and that thereafter a bookseller (Dry-butter) is said to have altered the language for the worse and then printed the edition that received public condemnation. The fact that the privy council on a full hearing of the matter, not only acquitted Cleland, but condemned Drybutter to the pillory, is evidence that much, if not all, the obloquy that the author was under should have been transferred to this publisher. The other books written by him were : " Memoirs of a Coxcomb " (12mo., 1751); a series of dramatic works, including " Titus Vespasian " (8 vols., 1755); "The Ladies' Subscription " (8 vols., 1755); " Timbo Chiqui, or the American Savage " (8 vols., 1758) ; a course of educational works relating to the connection of the Celtic with the English language, including " The Way to Things by Words, and to Words by Things," and several minor essays of a like nature. To this he added several volumes of a lighter character, including the " Man of Honor " (London, 1763, 12mo., 3 vols.), and " Surprises of Love " (London, 1765, 12mo). In my opinion, this author was the victim of another's cupidity and rascality. At any rate, it is clear that he was one of the most distinguished litera-teurs of his day and should not be unduly weighted down by another's crime.

Thus endeth, for the present, the ante-American history of the Kneeland family. I have re-written portions of it about a dozen times as new facts have turned up, and intend, in the indefinite future, when, if ever, my " ship comes in," to visit Scotland and re-write it from original records instead of from historical data. If this book had been published when originally announced, or within six months thereafter, these two chapters would not have appeared, as it was not until the autumn of 1896 that I discovered the first trace of the Scotch annals.

Dr. Thomas Cleland, a representative of the American descendants of the
Clelands and Knelands of Scotland.

PART III.

THE ORIGINAL BOSTONIANS.

(NOS. 31 TO 349.)

DEDICATED TO THE MEMORY OF

JOHN KNEELAND[13],

FOUNDER OF THE SCOTS' CHARITABLE SOCIETY,

AT BOSTON, IN 1657;

THE OLDEST SOCIAL ORGANIZATION IN AMERICA.

John Kneeland¹².

Children of John and Mary (Dunbar) Kneeland.

32.   (i.)   JOHN¹², b. about 1575 (of whom hereafter, 36).
33.   (ii.) EDWARD¹², b. about 1580 (of whom hereafter, 645).
34.   (iii.) WILLIAM¹², b. about 1583 ; came to America about
            1635, with his brother, Philip.

      Little is known of him except through tradition. He
was probably named after his uncle, William Cleland.

35.   (iv.) PHILIP¹², b. about 1590.

      It is recorded that he came to America with his
brother, William, some years after the two elder brothers
arrived—probably about 1635. Two years later (1637) he
was living at Lynn, Mass. (see "Genealogical History of
N. E.," by Savage, p. 171). Nothing is known of his
descendants, but it is probable that he and his brother
were the ancestors of the Newlands of this country.
William Newland was living in Lynn, some years later,
and he may have been William Kneeland, brother or son
of Philip.

36.   (32.) JOHN KNEELAND¹² (*John¹¹—Alexander¹*).

      Eldest son of Capt. John Kneeland¹¹ and grandson of
Major William Kneland¹⁰, of Lanarkshire, Scotland. According to tradition, he was born at Glasgow, which is quite probable, as his father was a mariner and abandoned the old
inland homestead. He and his brother, Edward Neland,
arrived in Massachusetts Bay about 1630, on board one of his
father's vessels freighted with provisions for the Pilgrims. He
brought his wife and aged mother. She sickened during the
voyage and died soon after reaching America. Tradition says
that before she embarked she exacted a promise that she
should not be buried at sea. She went into a trance and was
supposed to be dead, but, true to their promise, the sons
brought the body with them. After reaching land she revived
and lived for several years after. The brothers disposed of
their cargo at good advantage, and John settled near the
future town of Boston, and Edward at Ipswich, Mass. For
convenience, I will designate their descendants respectively as

John Kneeland¹³.

the "Boston family" and the "Ipswich family," and pursue the history of the former to the end before taking up the latter.

John Kneeland¹² married Mary Stewart, daughter of Walter Stewart, first Lord of Blantyre and a descendant of James V. Her aunt, of the same name, married his uncle, William Cleland¹¹ (see No. 11).

Children of John and Mary (Stewart) Kneeland.

37. (i.) JOHN¹³, b. Aug. 2, 1632; d. Aug. 11, 1691, æ. 59 (of whom hereafter, 39).

38. (ii.) BARTHOLOMEW¹³, b. Oct. 10, 1633; was living when John's will was made. No further record.

39. (37.) JOHN KNEELAND¹³ (*John¹², John¹¹—Alexander¹*).

Little is known of his life excepting what is gleaned from his unsigned will, which was dated in 1684 and recorded in the Boston record of wills. He there makes an abortive attempt to leave to his brother, Bartholomew, his house and grounds near Sudbury, and then: "I give my biggest gun and my cutlass to my eldest son, my best gun and my rapier to my youngest son." Inasmuch as he left a widow and six children, it is evident that it is just as well that Bartholomew's history is unknown. I very much fear this autograph will was the result of undue influence on his part. Fortunately, it was unsigned and the house and grounds went, with the family Bible and muniments of war, where they would do the most good. It is evident that he was a man of importance in Boston, as his name is often mentioned in connection with public matters. He was one of the founders of the Scots' Charitable Society, in 1657 (p. 34, Gen'l Hist. of N. E).

In the old burial ground at Roxbury appears the last record of John Kneeland¹³, in the following quaint style: "Here lyes ye Body of John Kneeland aged 59 years & 9 days died ye 11th of Aug. 1691."

John Kneeland¹³ married Mary Hawkins, daughter of Col. James and Mary (Mills) Hawkins, who was a prominent builder of Boston and the son of Richard Hawkins, "mariner,

John Kneeland[18].

of that towne." Mary Mills was the daughter of John Mills, Esq., who came over in the fleet with Gov. Winthrop, and was No. 33 of the First Church, his wife, Susannah, being No. 34. He was the first town clerk of Braintree, Mass., and the descendant of a long line of "predecessors in the ministry." Jane Hawkins, wife of Richard and grandmother of Mary (Hawkins) Kneland, was for many years under banishment to Portsmouth, R. I., for supposed tendency to Quakerism.

It appears from Boston records that on March 12, 1638, Jane Hawkins was given liberty till the beginning of May, " and in the meantime she is not to meddle in surgery or physic, drinks, plasters or oils, nor to question matters of religion except with the elders for satisfaction." On June 2, 1641, she was "ordered to depart from Massachusetts to-morrow morning and not to return again thither, upon pain of severe whipping, and her sons were bound in £20 to carry her away according to order." She was taken to Portsmouth and, notwithstanding the frequent petitions to the court by her children, was never allowed to return. The husband and wife both died the same year—1656—and I have yet to learn that they have since been separated on account of religious scruples. It is difficult to understand that her Puritan perse-cutors came to this country for religious liberty (?). A memo-randum of these records will be found at p. 94, "Genealogical Dictionary of Rhode Island."

Children of John and Mary (Hawkins) Kneeland.

40. (i.) MARY[14], b. Oct. 6, 1659; d. Oct. 19, 1660, æ. 1 yr.
41. (ii.) HANNAH[14], b. July 10, 1663; d. Jan. 18, 1749, æ. 86.
42. (iii.) MARY[14], b. April 15, 1666; d. May 17, 1756, æ. 90.
43. (iv.) JOHN[14], b. Nov. 29, 1668; d. Aug. 5, 1740, æ. 72
    (of whom hereafter, 47).
44. (v.) SOLOMON[14], b. Feb. 17, 1671; d. Dec. 5, 1743, æ.
    72 (of whom hereafter, 112).
45. (vi.) RUTH[14], b. July 30, 1673; d. Jan. 10, 1705, æ. 32.
46. (vii.) RACHAEL[14], b. Jan. 20, 1675; unmarried; d. Sept.
    14; 1753, æ. 78.

John Kneeland [14].

47. (43.) JOHN KNEELAND [14], (*John* [13], *John* [12], *John* [11] —*Alexander* [1]).

Eldest son of John Kneeland [13], " builder," of Boston ; born November 29, 1668. In some deeds he was described as " bricklayer," in some, under the more pretentious title of " builder." He evidently learned the trade from his uncle, James Hawkins. He married Mary Green, daughter of Samuel Green, Jr., and granddaughter of Samuel Green, the old Cambridge printer, who published, in England, the famous Cambridge Bible. Her brother, Timothy Green, was the partner of her son, Samuel Kneeland, in the publishing business. He was the husband of Mary Flint, a daughter of Col. John Flint, of Salem. This is the fourth generation that married a Mary. They had eight children. These names and dates are mostly from Bible records, but are confirmed in full from the official records of the " Towne of Boston."

Children of John and Mary (Green) Kneeland.

48. (i.) MARY [15], b. Sept. 12, 1692; m. (1) Dec. 12, 1718, Andrew Brown, and (2) John Turner; had nine children; d. June 7, 1780, æ. 88.

49. (ii.) JOHN [15], " builder "; b. Nov. 14, 1694; married four times and had thirteen children; d. Feb. 16, 1774, æ. 80 (of whom hereafter, 56).

50. (iii.) SAMUEL [15], " printer "; b. Jan. 31, 1697; m. Feb. 8, 1722, Mary Alden, great-granddaughter of John Alden and Priscilla; had eleven children; d. Dec. 14, 1869, æ. 72 (of whom hereafter, Chap. VII).

51. (iv.) JOSEPH [15], " housewright "; b. July 20, 1698; m. Nov. 8, 1722, Elizabeth Chamberlain; had five children; d. Oct. 12, 1760, æ. 62 (of whom hereafter, 96).

52. (v.) SARAH [15], b. Jan. 4, 1700; m. June 2, 1726, Michael Horner; had four children; d. Nov. 10, 1782, æ. 82 (of whom hereafter, 104).

53. (vi.) JAMES [15], b. Sept. 9, 1701; d. Aug. 25, 1702; buried in King's Chapel Burying Ground.

John Kneeland[15].

54. (vii.) HANNAH[15], b. May 10, 1703; m. April 16, 1734.
    Jeremiah Townsend, of New Haven; had seven
    children; d. Jan. 10, 1786, æ. 83 (of whom here-
    after, Chap. V).

55. (viii.) RACHEL[15], b. Aug. 11, 1705; m. (1) April 5,
    1722, Samuel Foster, (2) Timothy Parmerly, of
    Bradford; had eight children; d. July 10, 1776,
    æ. 71.

This is a remarkable record. Excluding James, who died
in infancy, the ages are as follows: Mary, 88; John, 80;
Samuel, 72; Joseph, 62; Sarah, 82; Hannah, 83; Rachel, 71;
making an aggregate of 538 years, or an average of 77 years.
Including James, 1 year, we have have 539 years, or an average of 67 years. Again, the seven children had fifty-seven
children, or an average of eight each, and the father lived to
know his sixty-four children and grandchildren, with treble
that number of great-grandchildren.

56. (49.) JOHN KNEELAND[15], (*John*[14], *John*[13], *John*[13],
    John[11]—*Alexander*[1]).

This is in some respects the most remarkable character in
the whole line of Kneelands. He married the first of four
wives in 1719, and the last in 1743. His first child was born
in 1720 and the last in 1754, thirty-four years afterwards, and
when he was sixty years old. He was one of the best known
and most respected citizens of Boston. He was a large owner
of real estate, Kneeland's Wharf and Kneeland Street being
named after him, on account of his large holdings in that
locality. He built the original "Old South Church," the successor of the "Old South Meeting House," which was built
by his father, John Kneeland[14]. He owned pew No. 17 in
the Old South Meeting House, and No. 15 in the new one.
Four generations of Kneelands owned pews and were members of this church. He also built the original John Hancock
house, the old Court House and Jail, in Boston. About 1750,
he retired from the building trade and is thereafter designated
in deeds as "merchant" or "shopkeeper."

His will, drawn in 1769 and filed in 1774, devises a "Mansion house on Union St., near Sudbury," four houses and lots

John Kneeland[15].

on Hawkins Street, and bequeaths a stock of goods in store and other property, including a "quarto Bible." This Bible has been in the family over 300 years. It was printed in London, in the year 1576, by Christopher Barker, "dweeling in Powell's Churchyard at the sign of the Tiger's Head." It was originally the property of Capt. John Kneeland, and passed by will or inheritance through the entire succession of John Kneelands, and thence to Richard Kneeland, Esq., of Westford, Mass., and has since passed down the line of Richard Kneelands to the present possessor, Lucius Richard Kneeland, of Middlesex, Vermont. One of the most cherished reminiscences connected with this heirloom is the fact that when during the Revolution, families gave up their jewelry to help the patriot cause, the gold clasps on this book were taken off and used for that purpose.

Down to the time of John Kneeland[15], the two heirlooms —the Coat of Arms and the Bible—went together to the eldest son John. But the latter had two sons of that name. To the first he gave the Coat of Arms, through whom it descended to his great-granddaughter, Alice Julia Gould, of Boston, who now holds it; and the Bible went to his second son John, who, dying intestate, passed it over to his eldest living brother, Richard.

Prince's Chronology, published in 1851, includes John Kneeland[15] and his brother Samuel, the printer, in a pretentious list of Boston's "Four Hundred," headed with the following descriptive title: "The individuals whose names are given in the following list may be justly regarded as the principal Literati of New England, who flourished about the beginning of the last century. The great majority of them were born before 1700, some as early as 1670." This was the beginning of the long line of "blue books" that have since been thrown upon a suffering humanity.

A bit of early history is gleaned from the statement of the executors of John Kneeland, who credit themselves, in 1786, with the value of pew No. 15, in the Old South Meeting House, destroyed by the enemy in 1774.

John Kneeland[15].

Children of John[15], by Elizabeth Green, m. Jan. 29, 1719.

57. (i.) SAMUEL[16], b. Feb. 2, 1720.
58. (ii.) JOHN[16], "merchant"; b. Aug. 6, 1722; m. Jan. 14, 1748, Sarah Mulberry; had three children; d. Dec. 10, 1751 (of whom hereafter, 70).
59. (iii.) WILLIAM[16], "gentleman"; b. Jan. 1, 1724; unmarried; graduated Harvard College in 1744; d. May 10, 1748, æ. 24.
60. (iv.) BARTHOLOMEW[16], "merchant"; b. Nov. 11, 1725 (of whom hereafter, 85).
61. (v.) DORCAS[16], b. Oct. 21, 1727; m. Jan. 10, 1755, Wm. Clough; d. Dec. 30, 1758.

By Prudence Clark, daughter of Timothy Clark, Esq., m. March 18, 1731.

62. (vi.) PRUDENCE[16], b. Jan. 2, 1733; m. Nov. 9, 1749, Deacon Samuel Penhallow, of Portsmouth, N. H. (of whom hereafter, 88).

By Mehitable King, m. Dec. 9, 1735.

63. (vii.) BENJAMIN[16], "scrivenor"; b. Jan. 20, 1737. He purchased from his brother, Bartholomew, December 14, 1772, the property known as "Fanueil House, Cornhill. This could not have been the progenitor of Fanueil Hall, as that was a market place. It may have been the homestead of Mr. Fanueil.
64. (viii.) MEHITABLE[16], b. March 23, 1738; m. (1) Oct. 3, 1763, Samuel Torrey; (2) John Simpkins, upholsterer. She was a widow at the time of the Boston Massacre, March 5, 1770, and her brother Bartholomew lodged with her (see Bartholomew, No. 85).
65. (ix.) MARY[16], b. October 19, 1740; m. Sept. 22, 1763, Philip Freeman, Jr. She died prior to 1769.

John Kneeland[16].

By Abigail Martin, m. Dec. 23, 1743.

66. (x.) EDWARD[16], "pewterer"; b. Oct. 20, 1747. He was captain of a Boston company of guards under Gen. Gates in the Revolution of 1779. Was in Boston at the time of the census, in 1790.

67. (xi.) ABIGAIL[16], b. April 28, 1750; m. John Hinckley, auctioneer (of whom hereafter, 89).

68. (xii.) RICHARD[16], "gentleman"; b. Nov. 30, 1752 (of whom hereafter, Chap. VI).

69. (xiii.) JOHN[16], "auctioneer"; b. Oct. 8, 1754; m. Nov. 1, 1778, Grace Perkins. Lived in his own "Mansion House" on Orange Street; d. Aug. 1, 1790, æ. 36. His widow Grace was living in 1798 (see Boston census).

70. (58.) JOHN KNEELAND[16] (*John*[15], *John*[14], *John*[13], *John*[12], *John*[11]—*Alexander*[1]).

Second son of John Kneeland[15], builder, of Boston. Little is known of him. From descriptions in the earlier deeds, of "Brazier," he was probably at first in the hardware business but afterwards became a general merchant. He was the only one of a long succession of Johns that died early. He married Sarah Mulberry and had three children. His will is filed in Boston. He died January 10, 1754. His widow subsequently married Hon. Samuel Abbot, the guardian of her minor children. They had no children. He was a merchant in Boston, established in 1753. They succeeded in amassing a large property and retired to Andover. He died there April 1, 1812, leaving a fortune of nearly half a million, $100,000 of which was left to charity. She died February 12, 1816 (see Abbot family, p. 26).

The following is from Appleton's Encyclopedia: "Samuel Abbot, a wealthy Boston merchant, one of the founders of the Andover Theological Seminary, was born at Andover and died April, 1812, aged 80. In 1807 he made a donation of $20,000 towards establishing the seminary, and at his death left it $100,000 in addition. He also gave away large sums for various charitable objects. He was a conscientious and upright man of rigidly methodical habits. He lived with his wife, Sarah (Mulberry) Kneeland, about fifty years, and received a great deal of aid from her in conducting his business."

Children of John and Sarah (Mulberry) Kneeland.

71. (i.) JOHN[17], b. Oct. 14, 1748; married three times; had one son and three daughters; d. Aug. 4, 1831, æ. 83 (of whom hereafter, 74).

72. (ii.) SARAH[17], b. March 18, 1750; d. Jan. 15, 1782, æ. 32.

73. (iii.) ELIZABETH[17], b. Nov. 19, 1751; d. June 20, 1781, æ. 30.

74. (71.) JOHN KNEELAND[17], merchant of Andover (*John*[16], *John*[15], *John*[14], *John*[13], *John* [12], *John*[11] —*Alexander*[1]).

We come now to the consideration of the seventh and last of the direct succession in the male line of John Kneelands. Perhaps I cannot better sum up his life than by quoting a private letter to me from his granddaughter, Alice Julia Gould, as follows: " He was a man of large and sympathetic heart, and ever most happy when relieving the wants of those in trouble and distress. Great confidence was placed in his business qualities, being most strictly honest and just. He held many offices of trust and represented Andover twenty-one years in the Legislature, to general acceptance. A strong advocate of temperance, who knew not the filthy weed in any form. He died at the age of eighty-three, greatly respected and universally lamented. To me his memory will ever be very dear."

An incident in his career may as well be recited here, from p. 136, Vol. I, Old R. Hist. Ass'n, as follows: "Gen. Lafayette left Boston, June 20, 1825, for Concord. At Andover line he was met by a company of cavalry and escorted to the vicinity of the Institution, when he was met by citizens of the town and addressed in their behalf by Mr. Kneeland, an aged man (he was then seventy-seven years). To the address, Lafayette made an appropriate response." His granddaughter, Alice Julia Gould, distinctly remembers this incident. She was in Andover at the time.

John Kneeland[17].

He married Ann Hobart, daughter of Col. Samuel Hobart, of Hollis, N. H. Col. Hobart was a distinguished soldier and citizen of New Hampshire. He first enlisted as lieutenant in Capt. Marston's company of Col. John Effies' regiment, raised in 1762 "for securing His Majesty's conquest." He served at Crown Point and other places (see Rev. Rec. of N. H., p. 24). On April 21, 1775, the Provincial Congress appointed Col. Nathaniel Folsom to take command of the N. H. troops, "to assist our suffering brethren in the Province of Massachusetts Bay." Among these troops was Col. John Stark's regiment, in which was Maj. Samuel Hobart, and he served at the battle of Bunker Hill where a number of the Hollis men were killed. He was afterwards promoted Paymaster of all the New Hampshire troops, with rank of Colonel, and served in that capacity until the close of the war. His youngest daughter, Ann, married John Kneeland, of Andover.

Children of John and Ann (Hobart) Kneeland.

The descendants of John Kneeland[17] I give in his own language, copied from the Bible bequeathed by him to his granddaughter, Alice Julia Gould, in whose handwriting are the items after his death:

"My father, John Kneeland, Jr., married Sarah Mulberry, January 14, 1748.

"I was born October 14, 1748. Married to Ann Hobart, of Hollis, N. H., by Rev. Daniel Emerson, Feb. 14, 1774.

75. "January 18th, 1777 a son born at Billerica, Mass.; baptized by the name Samuel Abbot[18]. (He was named after his stepfather, Hon. Samuel Abbot, of Boston, who was the guardian for John and his sisters under their father's will). He —Samuel Abbot Kneeland[18]—was a young man of great promise. He graduated at Harvard in 1797 and died in 1817, æ. 40, without issue. He was the last male descendant in the line of John Kneelands.

76. "Dec. 20th, 1778, a daughter born; baptized by Rev. Dr. Cooper, by the name of Nancy. (She was the only one of the family that had issue).

John Kneeland[11].

77. "Feb. 14, 1780, a daughter born; lived about one hour and a half.

"Feb. 16, 1780. Between the hours of 3 & 4 o'clock my dear wife died, aged 25 years, 4 months and 17 days.

"Feb. 20th, 1780. The remains of my dear wife, with her babe in her arms, was buried in the King's Chapel, 'Family Tomb,' on Tremont Street, belonging to my grandfather, John Kneeland. (This was John Kneeland[15], the builder).

"My sister, Elizabeth, died at Andover, July 21st, 1781, aged 30 years.

"My sister, Sarah, died at Portsmouth, N. H., Jan. 15, 1782, aged 32 years.

"Rebecca Austin married John Kneeland, by Rev. Mr. Clarke, May 20, 1783. (He thus announces in the third person his second marriage).

78. "Jan. 26th, 1785, a daughter born; baptized by the name of Sarah Abbot[18], by the Rev. Mr. Thatcher.

"This dear child died (1786) aged 16 months and 3 days buried in the 'Kneeland Family Tomb.'"

This was his last child, all dead but Samuel Abbot and Nancy. He now turns to his daughter's family:

"Aug. 16th, 1804, daughter Nancy married Mr. Joseph Hall, of Montreal, Canada, by Rev. Mr. French.

79. "A daughter born to them July 14, 1805; babtized by the name of Alice Julia[19]."

I take this from her copy of the Bible record made in a clear, smooth hand, written at the age of 87 with all the freedom and dash of a schoolgirl. She was 92 in July of this year (1897). Joseph Hall, her father, was a successful merchant of Montreal.

80. "A second daughter born March 31, 1809; baptized by the name of Rebecca Kneeland[19].

"March 8, 1810. The younger of these dear children died, aged 11 months and 9 days; buried at Andover.

"Sept. 5, 1817. My only son, Samuel Abbot Kneeland, died after 5 days' illness, aged 40 years, 7 months and 18 days."

A. Julia Gould

No. 79

John Kneeland[17].

(Who can picture the old man's agony as he wrote these words. The last hope of male issue in the long line of John Kneelands vanished).

"Aug. 17, 1818. My dear wife died after a lingering illness; buried in Andover.

" June 6th, 1820, Priscilla Abbot married John Kneeland."

(He thus announces his third marriage. Priscilla Abbot was born June 1st, 1770, and died Feb. 10th, 1830. She was the daughter of Phœbe Chandler and Hon. Isaac Abbot, of Andover, Mass. The latter was a lieutenant in and wounded at, the battle of Bunker Hill. He was born Feb. 13, 1745; died June, 1836, and was the first postmaster of Andover (see Chandler family, p. 374).

"Nov. 17, 1825. My grandmother Alice Julia Hall, was married to Dr. Daniel Gould, of Reading, Mass." (This was about the time that, when heading a delegation of citizens from Andover, he made the welcoming speech to Lafayette, hereinbefore referred to).

81. " 1826. A daughter born to them, Rebecca Austin Gould[20].

" 1828. The dear child died, aged 22 months.

82. "A second daughter born, Aug. 31, 1829, named Rebecca Austin[20].

83. "Dec. 25, 1831. A daughter born, named Alice Julia Hall Gould[20].

84. "A son born Oct. 24, 1834, named John Kneeland Gould[20]. (Thus the name was continued in the tenth generation).

"My wife, Priscilla, died Feb. 17th, 1830, aged 59 years, 8 months and 17 days."

(This is the last record in the handwriting of the last of the continued race of John Kneelands).

The next year his granddaughter, to whom the Bible was bequeathed, continued it as follows:

"Aug. 4th, 1831. My dear grandfather died, aged 83 years.

" July 24th, 1854. My dear mother died, aged 76 years. (Nancy Kneeland[18]).

John Kneeland[17].

"My good husband died March 22d, 1856. A kind, devoted husband and father, a skillful and sympathizing physician and a warm-hearted and true friend.

"Oct. 22d, 1863. My daughter, Alice Julia Hall, married to Frank T. Dwinell, of Boston. (They had one daughter, Alice Frances Dwinell, born Aug. 17, 1869: died Ang. 18, 1869).

"My daughter, Rebecca Austin, married Sept. 2, 1876, to George E. Cofran, of Boston."

This ends the Bible record, and Mrs. Gould adds, in her communication to me:

"John Kneeland Gould, unmarried. This ends all I can tell you of our branch of the Kneeland family. Only four of us left to tell the tale *and if the days of marvels are past, all there ever will be.*"

CHAPTER IV.

COLONIAL DESCENDANTS.

Having traced for ten generations the genealogy of the John Kneelands of America, we proceed to take up the other members of the several families with which they were connected and which, with them, make up the "Boston family." The period of their history covers the entire Eighteenth Century, ending with the Revolution and the birth of a new nation. It will be noted that while the Ipswich family contributed more soldiers, the Boston family, being located in the thick of the fight, rendered equal or greater service to the good cause. They were officials of the Boston government and contributed largely of time and money to the final success of the patriot army.

85. (60.) BARTHOLOMEW KNEELAND[16] (*John*[15], *John*[14], *John*[13], *John*[12], *John*[11]—*Alexander*[1]).

Third son of John Kneeland[15] and Elizabeth Green, born Nov. 11, 1725. Bartholomew was a merchant and one of the solid men of Boston in the days of the Revolution and prominently connected with the dark tragedy that baptized the newborn Republic, "The Boston Massacre." It will be remembered that a British fleet anchored in Boston Harbor in 1768 and two regiments that came with them were quartered on Boston Common. There were continual clashings between the soldiers and citizens, but no bloodshed until the evening of March 5, 1770, when, under the pretext of protecting a sentry stationed by the Brick Church at Washington and King streets, the soldiers fired upon the people assembled in King street, killing several and wounding others. This was the beginning of the end of English rule.

Bartholomew Kneeland[16].

Webster, speaking of it, said: "From that moment we may date the severance of the British Empire." John Adams says: "On that night the formation of American independence was laid. Not the battle of Lexington or Bunker Hill, not the surrender of Burgoyne or Cornwallis, were more important events in American history than the battle of King street, on the fifth of March, 1770."

One of the first men assaulted on that eventful occasion was Bartholomew Kneeland. In a deposition taken two or three days later, he relates his experience as follows: "I, Bartholomew Kneeland, of Boston, merchant, being of legal age, testify and say that on Monday, the 5th inst. (being at my lodgings at the house of my sister, Mrs. Mehitable Torrey, widow of the late Samuel Torrey, (deceased), about 15 minutes after 9 P. M., hearing a bell ring which I supposed was for fire, went immediately to the front door, followed by Mr. Matthias King, Mrs. Torrey and two others of the family. Standing at the door for the space of four or five minutes, I saw a number of soldiers with drawn broadswords and bayonets in the main street, near the town pump, making a great noise. One of the soldiers, when nearly opposite me, said, 'Damn you, what do you do there? Get in.' To which I made no answer. The same soldier immediately crossed the gutter and came to me, pointing his naked bayonet within six inches of my breast. I told him to go along and then I retired into the house. In about half an hour after, I heard a volley of small arms fired off in King street, and upon inquiry was told that three men were killed and others wounded." (See "History of Boston Massacre," by Kidder).

Bartholomew died intestate in April, 1792. His widow, Susannah (Sewell) Kneeland, a relative of Chief Justice Sewell, took out letters of administration May 7, 1792. The inventory, among other things, specified: "One pew, No. 6, Old South Meeting House; Mansion House, 73 Cornhill; Land at Bath, Lincoln County, Me.; Stock of dry goods," etc.

The character and size of this mansion appear in the census for direct taxation made at Boston, where it is put down to Mrs. Susannah Kneeland. The lot contained 22,550 square feet, and the house 2,120 square feet; "3 story, brick, with 24 windows. Value, $5,000."

The census of householders of Boston in 1790 gives:

Name.	Heads of Family.	Girls under 16.	Males, including head of family.
Bartholomew Kneeland,	2	..	4
John Kneeland, - -	2	3	5
John Kneeland, -	1	1	2
Capt. Edward Kneeland,	1	2	1

The Boston directory of "Merchants, Mechanics and Traders," for 1789, gives: "John Kneeland, store, 15 Butler's Row. Bartholomew Kneeland, Shopk'r, 73 Cornhill."

The census for occupants of houses in 1798 includes, among the others, Grace Kneeland. This was probably Grace Perkins, widow of John Kneeland, auctioneer, who died in 1790.

I give these items of a general nature to show record verifications of certain of the family about the time of Bartholomew's death, during the nineties of 1700. Of course, these do not include all the people of the name of Kneeland in Boston at that time.

Children of Bartholomew and Susannah (Sewell) Kneeland.

86.　(i.) WILLIAM[16], b. at Boston, Aug. 11, 1778; d. at Boston, Nov. 24, 1809.

87.　(ii.) ELIZABETH[16], b. at Boston, March 19, 1780; m. Sept. 18, 1782, Rev. Asa McFarland, D. D. She was his third wife.

The following, copied from Bouton's "History of Concord," (p. 440) gives a full sketch of her life, character and work: "Died in this town, Nov. 9, 1838, Mrs. Elizabeth McFarland, aged 58 years, widow of the late Rev. Asa McFarland, D. D., the only daughter of Bartholomew Kneeland, a respected merchant of that place, and Susannah (Sewell) Kneeland. Her grandfather, Samuel Sewell, of York, Me., was a kinsman of the distinguished Chief Justice Sewell, of Massachusetts. Possessed naturally of superior endowments of

Abigail Kneeland[16].

mind and heart, with good education, refined manners and of
singular conscientiousness, humility and devotion of spirit,
Mrs. McFarland rendered herself eminently useful in the
station which she occupied. In her domestic relations she
was a pattern of industry, order, frugality and diligence. By
her charity, her self-denial, simplicity in dress and manners,
her eminent social qualities and, above all, by that " ornament
of a meek and quiet spirit," which she always wore, she greatly
endeared herself to all who knew her without exciting the
envy of any. She was one of those who not only 'devised'
but 'executed' liberal things. She first suggested the plan of
the New Hampshire Cent Institution, in 1804, and of the
Concord Female Charitable Society, in 1812. She originated
the first female prayer meeting held in town, which is sustained
until this time. Of the many excellent women that have
adorned society in Concord and whose memory is precious, it
may be said with respect to her, 'Many daughters have done
virtuously, but thou excellest them all.'"

88. (62.) PRUDENCE KNEELAND[15], sixth child of John
        Kneeland, the builder.
    "Samuel Penhallow married Prudence Kneeland about
1715, no issue. Dea. Penhallow and wife, walked with Christian uprightness, and abundant in good works. The Deacon
was also a Magistrate, and administered justice in his sphere
without fear or favor. To quote from a late historian, 'Justice
Penhallow was a strict constructionist, believing with C. J. Jay
that Justice should be administered faithfully, impartially and
without delay.' He recognized only two distinctions of character of those living under and being entitled to the protection
of the law, viz.: Obedience to, and disobedience of those laws.
Neither the possession of wealth nor any adventitious condition
of life of the accused could influence the old Deacon."
(Brewster).

89. (67.) ABIGAIL KNEELAND[16] (*John[15], John[14], John[13]
        John[12], John[11]—Alexander[1].*)
    Eleventh child of John[15], the builder. Married John
Hinckley, auctioneer, of Boston, the grandson of one of the
most distinguished of the Plymouth Governors, Gov. Hinckley.

Joseph Kneeland[15].

He was a member of the "Ancient and Honorable Artillery," and was a much respected citizen of Boston. They had six children, as follows:

Children of Abigail[16] and John Hinckley.

90. (i.) ABIGAIL[17], married her cousin, Joseph Kneeland; no children.
91. (ii.) MARY[17], married Edward Clinch, merchant, of Boston. They had four children, who died young. She died at Dorchester, in 1858, aged 88.
92. (iii.) JOHN[17], was a bachelor. Died at Andover at an advanced age.
93. (iv.) SOPHIA[17], died young.
94. (v.) HARRIET[17], died young.
95. (vi.) ELIPHALET[17], died young.

96. (51.) JOSEPH KNEELAND[15], housewright (*John[14], John[13], John[12], John[11]—Alexander[1]*).

Third son of John[14], the builder. The term "housewright" expressed in deeds by him, probably refers to a house furnisher, a business intimately connected with that of his father and of his brother John, who were builders. In 1731 he is described as "goldsmith." But little is known of him. He married Elizabeth Chamberlain, by whom he had two sons and three daughters. He died intestate. His widow and son Nathaniel, merchant tailor, and his cousin, William Clough, husband of Dorcas Kneeland, were on the administration bonds. He left a store and other personal property, also a "Mansion House and land in Sudbury street, Boston, where he resided." His tombstone can now be seen in King's Chapel Burying Ground. "Here lies y[e] body of Mr. Joseph Kneeland, died Oct. 12, 1760, aged 62 years." The following statement of the descendants of Joseph Kneeland[15] is taken from the Boston Records:

Children of Joseph and Elizabeth (Chamberlain) Kneeland.

97. (i.) JOSEPH[16], b. Aug. 22, 1723.
98. (ii.) ELIZABETH[16], b. Feb. 17, 1725; m. April 27, 1749.
99. (iii.) MARY[16], b. Feb. 7. 1726.

Sarah Kneeland[15].

100. (iv.) NATHANIEL[16], merchant tailor; b. May 3, 1729;
m. Sarah Hastings; had three daughters, viz:
101. (i.) *Sarah*[17]. She was born Jan. 8, 1760, and was a
"spinster" in 1786.
102. (ii.) *Elizabeth*[17], b. Jan. 10, 1765; m. Zebediah
Johnson, and was a widow in 1786.
103. (iii.) *Abigail*[17]. b. Aug. 10, 1778.
He (Nathaniel[16]) died intestate Feb. 26, 1786, æ. 60.
Estate was administered March 17, 1786. He was a
soldier in the Revolution for three years. He resided on
Hawkins Street, where he had a "Mansion house and
lands."
103A. (v.) PRUDENCE[16], b. Feb. 23, 1731.

104. (52.) SARAH KNEELAND[15] (*John*[14], *John*[13], *John*[12],
John[11]—*Alexander*[1]. Second daughter of John
Kneeland[14]. Married Michael Homer, Jan. 21,
1726. She had four sons and three daughters.
(This record is taken from the "Genealogy of the
Homer Family.")

Children of Sarah Kneeland and Michael Homer.

105. (i.) WILLIAM HOMER[16], b. 1727; he married and had
one son:
106. *Joseph Warren Homer*[17]. He married and had
one son:
107. Peter Thatcher Homer[18], of No. 27 Mount
Vernon street, Boston.
108. (ii.) MICHAEL HOMER[16]; married; one of his sons was:
109. *Rev. Dr. Jonathan Homer*[17], of Newton, Mass.,
A. M., S. T. D., S. H. S., who died without
issue in 1843.
110. (iii.) JACOB HOMER[16].
111. (iv.) JOHN HOMER[16].
Besides these there were three daughters, one of whom
married Hon. John Jay, a relative of Governor Jay.

112. (44.) SOLOMON KNEELAND[14], leather dresser, (*John*[13], *John*[12], *John*[11]—*Alexander*[1]). Second son of John Kneeland[13]; b. at Boston, Feb. 17, 1671.
A prominent and successful business man of the "towne of Boston," often referred to in the old records. He amassed a large property and was generally respected as one of the staunch patriotic citizens in the stormy days of the Revolution.

Children of Solomon and Mary (Hawkins) Kneeland.

113. (i.) SAMUEL[15], b. April 26, 1697; m. Elizabeth Smith, Dec. 14, 1718; had three sons and two daughters; d. Jan., 1770, æ. 73 (of whom hereafter, 120).

114. (ii.) SOLOMON[15], falconer; b. Sept. 23, 1698; m. Aug. 2, 1727, Lydia Lowder; had two sons and two daughters; d. July 20, 1784, æ. 86 (of whom hereafter, 126).

115. (iii.) JOSEPH[15] b. Dec. 14, 1700; m. Feb. 12, 1728, Mary Warton; had two sons and three daughters; d. (of whom hereafter, 141).

116. (iv.) MARY[15], b. Oct. 15, 1702.

117. (v.) BENJAMIN[15], b. July 22, 1707.

118. (vi.) HANNAH[15], b. April 10, 1709 (of whom hereafter, 148).

119. (vii.) MARTHA[15], b. July 1, 1711; m. Dec. 19, 1728, John Symmes (of whom hereafter, 167); d.
(The foregoing is from the Boston Records).

120. (113.) SAMUEL KNEELAND[15] (*Solomon*[14], *John*[13], *John*[12], *John*[11]—*Alexander*[1]).
Eldest son of Solomon[14]. Born at Boston, April 26, 1697. Not much is known of his life. He married Elizabeth Smith, and lived in Boston. In 1783 he was a hotel-keeper and for many years was an assessor of the "Towne" of Boston. He amassed quite a fortune for the Colonial times and died intestate at the ripe old age of 73. He received, in 1735, a grant of land in Narragansett Township, as an heir-at-law of his grandfather, Capt. Samuel Pollard, for services rendered in the expedition of 1675 (King Philip's War).

Solomon Kneeland[15].

Children of Samuel and Elizabeth (Smith) Kneeland.

121. (i.) ELIZABETH[16], b. Feb. 17, 1720.
122. (ii.) WILLIAM[16], b. Oct). 31, 1721 ; d. Oct. 25, 1722.
123. (iii.) MARY[16], b. Oct. 2, 1722.
124. (iv.) WILLIAM[16], Esq., "gentleman"; b. July 21, 1724; lived in Boston and Cambridge ; never married; d. Jan. 14, 1753.
125. (v.) ROBERT[16], b. April 10, 1726; no trace of his history.

126. (114.) SOLOMON KNEELAND[15] (*Solomon[14], John[13], John[12], John[11]—Alexander[1]*). Second son of Solomon[14] and Mary Pollard; born at Boston, Sept. 23, 1698.

He was an extensive real estate owner in Boston. Lived on Orange street and purchased "eight acres of pasture land in Roxbury." He educated his children thoroughly, sending his eldest son to Harvard and bequeathing him a substantial sum to assist him in his fight against that institution (of which hereafter). He was a wealthy and respected merchant and one of the Four Hundred of "Y^e towne of Boston." Although "aged," he was in the Lexington "Alarm-list" of John Haskins' company, in 1773-5, and took part in the preliminary skirmish for liberty and the battle of Bunker Hill. He died in 1784, aged 86. His family were members of the "Old South Church," owning pew No. 6. I find the following in the diary of J. J. Barnsted, the sexton, under date of September 23, 1723: "Solomon Kneeland took his turn to look after ye boys 3 Sabbaths and a fast day." He married Lydia Richardson.

Children of Solomon and Lydia (Richardson) Kneeland.

127. (i.) LYDIA[16], b. March 16, 1728; m. her cousin, James Richardson, distiller, of Boston ; they had no children; she died Dec. 17, 1796, æ. 69.
128. (ii.) WILLIAM[16], Esq., "gentleman"; b. May 28, 1732; grad. Harvard, 1751 ; m. Elizabeth Holyoke, daughter of Dr. Edward Holyoke, of Cambridge; d. Nov. 2, 1788, æ. 56 (of whom hereafter, 131).

Dr. William Kneeland[16].

129. (iii.) SOLOMON[16], "leather dresser"; b. July 8, 1736; unmarried; died intestate, June 10, 1784, æ. 48; Wm. Kneeland, Esq., Executor. Schedule of property covered house and lot, "leather dressing yard in the south part of Boston" (probably inherited from his grandfather, Solomon[14], leather dresser), also "sundries taken while the town was in possession of the British, in 1783, by Wm. Bate, who then had charge of his Tannery." Inventory signed by "Oliver Wendel," grandfather of Oliver Wendell Holmes.

130. (iv.) MARY[16], b. April 11, 1739; unmarried.

131. (128.) DR. WILLIAM KNEELAND[16] (*Solomon[15], Solomon[14], John[13], John[12], John[11]—Alexander[1]*). Second son of Solomon Kneeland[15]; b. at Boston, May 28, 1732.

This is one of the characteristic Kneelands. A scholar, ambitious, and a born fighter. He was, with one other exception, the only sympathizer with the Mother Country in the great struggle for liberty. In Paige's "History of Cambridge," we find the following (p. 417): "May 15, 1775. The Committee of Safety voted that 'the Quarter Master General remove as many of the three Companies to the mansion house of Dr. William Kneeland as the house can accommodate.' This was on the South East corner of Mt. Auburn St. and Winthrop Sq., and was demolished not long ago." This was published in 1877.

Another publication, "Loyalists of American Revolution," has the following: "Kneeland, William, of Cambridge, Mass., Physician. He graduated at Harvard Univ. in 1751, and was elected Steward of that institution by the Corporation in 1778; but as he had been deemed unfriendly to the cause of American independence, the overseers objected to the choice and refused to concur. The former body accordingly requested his predecessor to resume his duties until another Steward could be chosen. The discussions that arose in the case do not belong to this place, further than to say that the corporation objected, and have since exercised the right of electing

Joseph Kneeland[15].

that officer without action on the part of the overseers. Dr.
Kneeland was Overseer of the Poor, Registrar of Probate, and
for several years President of the Mass. Medical Society."

Dr. Kneeland's wife was of the celebrated family of Hol-
yokes. She was the granddaughter of President Edward Holyoke of Harvard University, and the second daughter of Dr.
Edward Augustus Holyoke, of Cambridge. He, Dr. Edward,
was the first person on whom the degree of Doctor of Medicine was conferred by Harvard College. He also received
the degree of L.L. D., and was the first President of the
Massachusetts Medical Society (Dr. Kneeland was the second
President). He was also President of the American Academy
of Arts and Sciences; President of the Salem Athenæum,
the Essex Historical Society and the Salem Dispensary.

Children of Dr. William and Elizabeth (Holyoke) Kneeland.

132.   (i.) LYDIA[17], unmarried; d. about July, 1837.
133.   (ii.) ELIZABETH HOLYOKE[17], unmarried; d. Dec., 1826.
134.   (iii.) MARY[17], m. Levi Hedges, L.L. D. He is a promin-
       ent member of the Boston Bar. They had the
       following children:
135.   (i.) *William Kneeland Hedges*[18].
136.   (ii.) *Frederick Henry Hedges*[18].
137.   (iii.) *Edward Holyoke Hedges*[18].
138.   (iv.) *Josiah Dunham Hedges*[18].
139.   (v.) *Harry L. Hedges*[18].
140.   (vi.) *Elizabeth Holyoke Hedges*[18].

Having followed to the end the descendants of Solomon
Kneeland[15], we take up the other children of Solomon Kneeland[14], leather dresser, to wit:

141.   (115.) JOSEPH KNEELAND[15], "goldsmith" (*Solo-
       mon*[14], *John*[13], *John*[12], *John*[11]—*Alexander*[1]). Third
       son of Solomon Kneeland[14]; b. at Boston, Dec. 14,
       1700; he married Mary Warton, and had six child-
       ren, as follows (taken from Boston Records):

Children of Joseph and Mary (Warton) Kneeland.

142. (i.) JOSEPH[16], "goldsmith "; b. Feb. 13, 1730; m. Mirriam Phillips; lived in Westford. Had one child (*Lydia*, b. April 4, 1747); d. Oct. 10, 1805, æ. 75.
143. (ii.) MARY[16], b. Jan. 3, 1731.
144. (iii.) SARAH[16], b March 5, 1733.
145. (iv.) JOHN[16], b. Oct. 11, 1736.
146. (v.) SARAH[16], b. April 18, 1740.
147. (vi.) JAMES[16], b. March 10, 1742.

148. (118.) HANNAH KNEELAND[15] (*Solomon*[14], *John*[13], *John*[12], *John*[11]—*Alexander*[1]). Daughter of Solomoh Kneeland, of Boston; b. at Boston, April 10, 1709; m. Ephraim Abbot, of Andover, Mass. They settled in Amherst, N. H. (see Abbot family[18], also History of Amherst, p. 478), and had eight children, as follows:

Children of Hannah Kneeland[15] and Ephraim Abbot.

149. (i.) EPHRAIM ABBOT[16], b. at Amherst, Dec. 16, 1742; m. Dorothy Styles; d. in Goffstown, in 1827.
150. (ii.) HANNAH ABBOT[16], b. March 12, 1745, at Amherst; m. Jas. Shattuck, of Hollis, N. H.
151 (iii.) KNEELAND ABBOT[16], b. at Amherst, May 17, 1748; m. ——— Stanley, of Vermont, and had six children:
152. (i.) *Moses*[17].
153. (ii.) *Abiel*[17].
154. (iii.) *Betsy*[17].
155. (iv.) *Sarah*[17].
156. (v.) *Mary*[17].
157. (vi.) *Jacob*[17].
158. (iv.) SARAH ABBOT[16], b. June 14, 1751; m. Wm. Codman, of Deering, N. H.
159. (v.) DORCAS ABBOT[16], b. Aug. 7, 1752; m. Geo. Wiley.
160. (vi.) ESTHER ABBOT[16], b. March 6, 1755; m. Benj. Pike, Jr., of Amherst; settled in Montpelier, Vt., and had four children:

Martha Kneeland[15].

161.   (i.) *Mary[17].*
162.   (ii.) *John[17].*
163.   (iii.) *Stephen[17].*
164.   (iv.) *Samuel[17].*
165.   (vii.) ABIGAIL ABBOT[16], b. July 30, 1756; m. Samuel
            Twiss, of New Boston, April 25, 1781.
166.   (viii.) DANIEL ABBOT[16], b. April 1, 1762; m. Sarah
            Stevens, July 28, 1786.

167.   (119.) MARTHA KNEELAND[15] (*Solomon[14], John[13],
            John[12], John[11]—Alexander[1]*). Youngest daughter
            of Solomon Kneeland[14]; b. at Boston, July 1, 1711.
    This is all that we can find as to the descendants of
Solomon Kneeland, the second son of John Kneeland[13],
except a reference in the " Symmes Memorial" to his youngest
daughter, Martha, who married Col. John Symmes, Dec. 19,
1728. John Symmes was the third son of Rev. Thomas
Symmes. His character is thus given in an obituary notice
published in the *Boston Gazette* of March 1, 1764: " Monday
evening last, died here after a few days' illness, John Symmes,
Esq., in the 58th year of his age, Lieut.-Colonel of the Militia
of this town. He was a gentleman of a very courteous and
affable disposition, industrious, honest in his dealings with
mankind, and pious towards God." They had one son:
168.   THOMAS[16], b. Sept. 8, 1729, who married Rebecca
            Marshall, March 22, 1753.
    He (Thomas) was a member of the Ancient and Honor-
able Artillery, of Boston, and the grandfather of the author of
" Symmes Hole."

CHAPTER V.

THE TOWNSEND FAMILY.

(NOS. 169 TO 213.)

Contrary to established usage, I give in the case of Hannah Kneeland[15] the descent in the female line beyond the third generation. This exception is not founded so much on the distinguished character of the Townsend Family, with whom she united, as on the unusual compliment shown by retaining the name Kneeland in the Townsend family for over a century and a half. Hon. William Kneeland Townsend, the present possessor of the name, is a distinguished author and jurist, and one of the professors of Yale University.

169. (54.) HANNAH KNEELAND[15] (*John*[14], *John*[13], *John*[12], *John*[11]—*Alexander*[1]). Third daughter of John Kneeland[14], the celebrated builder, of Boston, and Mary Green, the granddaughter of Samuel Green, the publisher of the Cambridge Bible.

She was the sister of Samuel Kneeland[15], printer to the Governor's Council and the House of Representatives. Hannah Kneeland was born May 10, 1703, and joined the Old South Church April 16, 1722. She married Jeremiah Townsend, of Boston, April 16, 1734, and died at New Haven, July 30, 1744. Her husband was a lineal descendant from Sir Roger Townsend, of Lynn, England,. He was baptized in the Old South Church, November 18, 1711, and died at New Haven, January 6, 1803. They resided in Boston until May 20, 1739, when they settled in New Haven, where the family has ever since resided.

Isaac Townsend[16].

Children of Hannah Kneeland[15] and Jeremiah Townsend.

170. (i.) JEREMIAH TOWNSEND[16], b. in Boston, January 20, 1735; m. Abigail Woodbridge; d. in New Haven, Sept. 24, 1794.

171. (ii.) ISAAC TOWNSEND[16], b. in Boston, July 18, 1735; d. Nov. 28, 1736.

172. (iii.) ISAAC TOWNSEND[16], b. in Boston, July 22, 1739 (of whom hereafter, 178).

174. (iv.) JOHN TOWNSEND[16], b. in Boston, July 22, 1739; d. in New Haven, Nov. 30, 1739.

175. (v.) SAMUEL TOWNSEND[16], b. in New Haven, Oct. 14, 1740; m. Sarah Treadway,; d. Aug. 29, 1795.

176. (vi.) HANNAH TOWNSEND[16], b. Nov. 29, 1742; d. May 31, 1773.

177. (vii.) MARY TOWNSEND[16], b. Jan. 10, 1744; d. Aug. 11, 1744.

178. (172.) ISAAC TOWNSEND[16], (*Hannah Kneeland*[15], *John*[14], *John*[13], *John*[12], *John*[11]—*Alexander*[1]). Second son of Jeremiah Townsend and Hannah Kneeland[15]; b. in Boston, July 22, 1739; m. Elizabeth, daughter of Jacob Hitchcock, of Springfield, Mass. She was a cousin of Maj.-Gen. David Wooster, killed near Ridgefield, Conn., May 2, 1777, in the battle with the British forces under Gov. Tryon. Her sister, Abigail, married Capt. Ezekiel Hayes, great-grandfather of ex-President R. B. Hayes. They resided first at New Haven, then for many years at Stratford, where most of their children were born. They then returned to New Haven and spent the remainder of their lives there. He died in June, 1818, and his wife, Nov. 9, 1792.

Children of Isaac Townsend and Elizabeth Hitchcock.

179. (i.) ELIZABETH TOWNSEND[17], b. Nov. 1, 1762; d. Jan. 15, 1852.

180. (ii.) ISAAC TOWNSEND[17], b. Feb. 4, 1765 (of whom hereafter, 188).

181. (iii.) KNEELAND TOWNSEND[17], b. March 20, 1757.

Isaac Townsend[17].

182. (iv.) JACOB TOWNSEND[17], b. April 10, 1769; m. (1) Eunice Clark; (2) Eunice Atwater; d. May 7, 1852.
183. (v.) ABIGAIL TOWNSEND[17], b. Sept. 4, 1771; d. May 30, 1814.
184. (vi.) MARY TOWNSEND[17], b. Jan. 29, 1774; d. Dec. 26, 1788.
185. (vii.) SARAH TOWNSEND[17], b. in 1776; m. Joel Atwater; d. May 1, 1844.
186. (viii.) ANNE TOWNSEND[17], b. May 20, 1779; d. Nov. 18, 1861.
187. (ix.) WILLIAM TOWNSEND[17], b. May 12, 1781; m. Maria Lampson; d. July 28, 1849.

188. (180.) ISAAC TOWNSEND[17] (*Isaac[16], Hannah Kneeland[15], John[14], John[13], John[12], John[11]—Alexander[1]*). Eldest son of Isaac Townsend[16] and Abigail Hitchcock; b. at New Haven, Feb. 4, 1765.

In 1781, when only 16 years of age, he enlisted under Col. Meigs, and served until the close of the Revolution. During the war of 1812 he and his son, Prof. Isaac H. Townsend, were captured by one of the English vessels cruising on Long Island Sound, and taken to Plum Island and there detained on board the Pomone until ransomed. He held the rank of Captain. With this exception, his life was spent in successful mercantile pursuits from which he retired on an ample fortune soon after the second war with England. He commenced business in New Haven about 1789, with a branch house in South Carolina and agencies in New York and London, in which latter place he was for many years represented by his brother, Kneeland Townsend. He was largely interested in landed estates in Virginia, Vermont, Connecticut and Ohio, establishing, with his brothers in the latter State, the town of Townsend, Huron County. He married Rhoda Atwater, of Hamden, Conn, April 11, 1795, and had eight children.

Children of Isaac Townsend[17] and Rhoda Atwater.

189. (i.) WILLIAM KNEELAND TOWNSEND[18], b. at New Haven, June 3, 1796 (of whom hereafter, 197).

Isaac Townsend[17].

190. (ii.) ELIZABETH MARY TOWNSEND[18], b. Feb. 18, 1798;
     m. Isaac Beers, Nov. 26, 1821.
191. (iii.) ISAAC ATWATER TOWNSEND[18], b. Dec. 2, 1799;
     d. June, 1803.
192. (iv.) CHARLES HENRY TOWNSEND[18], b. April 26, 1801;
     d. June 11, 1847.
193. (v.) ISAAC HENRY TOWNSEND[18], b. at New Haven,
     April 25, 1803; d. June 11, 1847.
     He was one of the first scholars of his day and a
thorough gentleman. He entered Yale College in the
class of 1818, and during the four years' course was not
once absent from recitation. Graduated with distinguished honors in 1822, having made the salutatory
oration of his class. Two years after, he graduated at the
law school with honors and was admitted to the bar in
1824. He was Justice of the Peace, a director of the
New Haven and Northampton R. R., and organized, with
others, the scheme for utilizing the abandoned bed of the
Farmington Canal, securing thereby a most valuable fran-
chise. He was a director of the New Haven Bank, a
member of the City Council, and representative from
New Haven to the Connecticut assembly. He was appointed the first Professor of Jurisprudence of the newly
created Law Department of Yale College in 1847, a position
he had previously held in the Law School. Afterwards, in
the same year, June 11, 1847, he died without issue.
194. (vi.) JANE MARIE TOWNSEND[18], b. May 1, 1805; d.
     Dec. 15, 1814.
195. (vii.) GEORGE ATWATER TOWNSEND[18], b. Oct. 28, 1807;
     m. (1) Julie Sanford; (2) Mildred Parker.
196. (viii.) EMILY AUGUSTA TOWNSEND[18], b. Sept. 28, 1810;
     m. David Sanford, of Newtown, Conn., Oct. 5,
     1831; d. Feb. 6, 1875.

197. (189.) WILLIAM KNEELAND TOWNSEND[18] (*Isaac*[17], *Isaac*[16], *Hannah Kneeland*[15], *John*[14], *John*[13], *John*[12], *John*[11]—*Alexander*[1]). Eldest son of Isaac Townsend[17] and great-grandson of Jeremiah Townsend and Hannah Kneeland; b. at New Haven, June 3, 1796; educated at Hopkins Grammar School, and succeeded to his father's mercantile business at New Haven and elsewhere.

He was a most successful business man, a director of the New Haven Bank, President of several corporations and associations, a lieutenant of the Second Company of the Governor's Horse Guards, a Justice of the Peace and Representative to the Connecticut Assembly from the town of East Haven. He married, December 3, 1820, Eliza Ann, eldest daughter of Hervey Mulford, Esq., and a descendant of Capt. Lyon Gardiner, the first patentee and Lord of the Manor of Gardiner's Island. About 1830 he retired from business and bought from his father and uncle the beautiful homestead at Raynham, now a part of the city of New Haven. They had nine children, as follows:

Children of William Kneeland Townsend[18] and Eliza A. Mulford.

198. (i.) WILLIAM ISAAC TOWNSEND[19], b. Nov. 28, 1822, at New Haven,; m. April 22, 1850, Elizabeth B., daughter of Col. Mason A. Durand. They had one daughter:

199. *Elizabeth Durand Townsend*[20], b. Feb. 11, 1851; d. May 27, 1857.

200. (ii.) JAMES MULFORD TOWNSEND[19], b. Jan 20, 1825, at New Haven; m. Sept. 1, 1847, Maria Theresa Clark, of Middletown, Conn. They had:

201. (i.) *William Kneeland Townsend*[20], b. at New Haven, June 12, 1848 (of whom hereafter, 210.)

202. (ii.) *James Mulford Townsend*[20], b. Aug. 26, 1852 (of whom hereafter, 213).

203. (iii.) GEORGE HENRY TOWNSEND[19], b. in New Haven, Dec. 28, 1826; m. Mary Gertrude Buckelen, of Jamesburg, N. J.

William Kneeland Townsend[20].

204. (iv.) FREDERICK ATWATER TOWNSEND[19], b. in New Haven, Mar. 23, 1829; m. Jane, daughter of Roger Sherman Prescott, Esq., of New Haven.

205. (v.) ROBERT KAIKE TOWNSEND[19], b. in East Haven, Dec. 22, 1831; m. Almira N. Tuttle, of Fair Haven, Conn., March 21, 1853; d. June 30, 1857.

206. (vi.) CHARLES HERVEY TOWNSEND[19], b. at East Haven, Nov. 16, 1833; m. April 26, 1871, Mary Ann Hotchkiss, of New Haven.

This is all the sketch the modest author gives of himself. Nevertheless, it is to his admirable work entitled, "The Townsend Family, of Lynn, in Old and New England," that the records of this family have been preserved. To him alone am I indebted for the information herein inserted as to the descendants of Hannah Kneeland, who passed away nearly a century and a half ago. Many of us only have the pleasure of knowing him through the fruits of his labors, but judging therefrom we unhesitatingly class him as one of the chiefs in a family of intellectual giants.

207. (vii.) TIMOTHY BEERS TOWNSEND[19], b. Nov. 21, 1835.

208. (viii.) EDWARD HOWARD TOWNSEND[19], b. April 8, 1840; m. Alice Eliza Maltby, April 28, 1869. They had one child:

208A. *Maud Townsend[20]*, b. June 21, 1871; d. July 25, 1871.

209. (ix.) ELIZA MULFORD TOWNSEND[19], b. Dec. 3, 1842; m. Oct. 13, 1863, Charles Augustus Lindsley, of New York.

210. (201.) WILLIAM KNEELAND TOWNSEND[20] (*James M.*[19], *Wm. Kneeland*[18], *Isaac*[17], *Isaac*[16], *Hannah Kneeland*[15], *John*[14], *John*[13], *John*[12] *John*[11] —*Alexander*[1]). Eldest son of Jas. M. Townsend, Esq., b. at New Haven, June 12, 1848; graduated from Yale College in 1871, with high honors.

After an extended European trip, he entered Yale Law School (1872), taking both the Jewell and Civil Law Composition prizes and graduating, in 1874, second in his class. On his return from a second European trip he was admitted and

William Kirkland Townsend

No. 210

began the practice of law in New Haven. He took the post-graduate course at the Law School, and received the degree of M. L. in 1878 and D. C. L. in 1880. He has held several important positions of trust in New Haven. In 1881, he published a law book entitled, "The New Connecticut Civil Officer," and was appointed Professor of Pleading in Yale College, and later was appointed Judge of the U. S. Court. He married, July 1, 1874, Mary Leavenworth Trowbridge, of New Haven. They had two children:

211.   (i.) WINSTON TROWBRIDGE TOWNSEND[21], b. June 10, 1878.

212.   (ii.) MARY LEAVENWORTH TOWNSEND[21], b. Dec. 6, 1879.

213.   (202.) JAMES MULFORD TOWNSEND[20] (*Jas M.[19], Wm. Kneeland[18], Isaac[17], Isaac[16], Hannah Kneeland[15], John[14], John[13], John[12], John[11]—Alexander[1]*). Second son of James Mulford Townsend, b. at New Haven, Aug. 26, 1852.

He graduated at the Hopkins Grammar School in 1869; entered Yale in 1870, and graduated in 1874 with an oration, and was chosen one of the Commencement speakers. He won both the junior and senior Townsend prizes; was one of the editors of the *College Courant*, and received the De Forest prize (the gold medal then considered the highest collegiate honor at Yale, "awarded to that scholar of the senior class who shall write and pronounce an English oration in the best manner"). After taking a second trip to Europe, he studied law in the well-known law office of Chittenden & Hubbard, and upon the retirement of Mr. Hubbard, became a member of the new firm of Chittenden, Townsend & Chittenden. Mr. Townsend, though still a young man, ranks well up among the leading lawyers of the metropolis.

CHAPTER VI.

THE DESCENDANTS OF RICHARD KNEE-LAND, ESQ.

(NOS. 214 TO 349.)

214. (68). RICHARD KNEELAND[16] (*John*[15], *John*[14], *John*[13], *John*[12], *John*[11], *William*[10], *James*[9], *Alexander*[8], *William*[7], *William*[6], *John*[5], *John*[4], *John*[3], *James*[2], *Alexander*[1]). Twelfth son of John[15], the builder; b. at Boston, Mass., Nov. 30, 1752.

Richard Kneeland went from Boston to Westford, Mass. He there married, January 4, 1775, Martha Hall, youngest daughter of Rev. Willard Hall, who graduated at Cambridge in 1792. They had ten children. He was drowned in March, 1800, during a freshet in which the Concord River carried away his house, several others of the family barely escaping with their lives. He held several important positions in his town and county, was for a number of years County Treasurer, and was one of the select committee appointed to receive George Washington at Cambridge, after the close of the Revolutionary War. The "History of Westford" says: "He held the office of Town Treasurer at the time of his death—a thoroughly honest man." His Bible, which bears the thumb-marks of much study, contains the following account of the birth of his several children, the same being a verbatim copy of the original record in the handwriting of Richard Kneeland[16]:

215. (i.) "MARTHA KNEELAND[17], daughter of Richard Kneeland and Martha, his wife, was born August 12, 1776—Monday. (She was married, and died April 20, 1848, æ. 72.)

216. (ii.) "RICHARD KNEELAND[17], son of Richard Kneeland and Martha, his wife, was born April 1, 1778 —Wednesday. (Of whom hereafter, 284.)

217. (iii.) "BENJAMIN KNEELAND[17], son of Richard Kneeland and Martha, his wife, was born February the 13th, 1780—Sunday. (Of whom hereafter, 225.)
218. (iv.) "WILLIAM KNEELAND[17], son of Richard Kneeland and Martha, his wife, was born March 7, 1782 —Thursday. (He died Nov. 11, 1809—see Boston Records.)
219. (v.) "JOHN WILLARD KNEELAND[17], son of Richard Kneeland and Martha his wife, was born September 3, 1784—Friday.
220. (vi.) "JAMES KNEELAND[17], son of Richard Kneeland and Martha, his wife, was born December 9, 1786 —Saturday. (Of whom hereafter, 247.)
221. (vii.) "MARY KNEELAND[17], daughter of Richard Kneeland and Martha, his wife, was born February 25, 1789—Wednesday. (She married Dr. Amos Bancroft, of Croton, Mass.)
222. (viii.) "EDWARD MARTYN KNEELAND[17], son of Richard Kneeland and Martha, his wife, was born July 9, 1791—Monday.
223. (ix.) "SAMUEL KNEELAND[17], son of Richard Kneeland and Martha, his wife, was born May 8, 1794— Thursday. (Of whom hereafter, 232.)
224. (x.) "BARTHOLOMEW KNEELAND[17], son of Richard Kneeland and Martha, his wife, was born July 21, 1797—Friday."

225. (217.) BENJAMIN KNEELAND[17](*Richard*[16], *John*[15] *John*[14], *John*[13], *John*[12], *John*[11]—*Alexander*[1]). Second son of Richard[16]; b. at Westford, Feb. 13, 1870. ↗ 7 ↗ ↘

He lived in Westford, and died intestate in 1830, leaving a widow, Eve (Cogswell) Kneeland, and the following living children:

Children of Benjamin and Eve (Cogswell) Kneeland.

226. (i.) AUGUSTA[18].
227. (ii.) MARIA[18].
228. (iii) EVE[18]. She died in 1838.

6

Dr. Samuel Kneeland[18].

229. (iv.) CAROLINE COGSWELL[18]. She married Francis
      Bartlett, "Gent."
230. (v.) SARAH[18].
231. (vi.) FLETCHER[18].

232. (223.) SAMUEL KNEELAND[17] (*Richard*[16], *John*[15],
      Jonn[14], *John*[13], *John*[12], *John*[11]—*Alexander*[1]), b.
      May 8, 1794. Was a successful merchant. He
      married, Oct. 5, 1820, Nancy Burt Johnson. They
      had three children.

Children of Samuel and Nancy (Johnson) Kneeland.

233. (i.) SAMUEL[18]. b. Aug. 1, 1821 (of whom hereafter, 238.)
234. (ii.) EDWARD[18], b. April 30, 1823; died young.
235. (iii.) NANCY B.[18], b. Oct. 10, 1827; m. Hon. William
      M. Wallace. He then married his late wife's sister,
      Juliana Johnson, by whom two children were born,
      as follows:

236. (iv.) HENRY[18], b. Aug. 22, 1830.
237. (v.) JULIANA[18], b. Jan. 16, 1832; m. Judge Jacob Story,
      and now lives in Winona, Minn.

238. (233.) DR. SAMUEL KNEELAND[18] (*Samuel*[17],
      Richard[16], *John*[15], *John*[14], *John*[13], *John*[12], *John*[11]
      —*Alexander*[1]).

This is one of the landmarks in the history of the race.
Perhaps the best summary of his life is contained in "Appleton's Encyclopedia," to which he was a contributor. It is as
follows:

"KNEELAND, SAMUEL, an American naturalist, born in
Boston, 1821. He graduated at Harvard College, in 1840, and
at the medical school of the same institution in 1843, and
studied in Paris till 1845. Subsequently he practiced medicine
in Boston, taught anatomy in the Harvard school, was connected for two years with the Boston Dispensary, was for five
years Secretary of the Boston Natural History Society, and
for two years of the American Academy of Arts and Sciences.
He also explored Brazil, the copper region of Lake Superior,

Samuel Kneeland

No. 238

Dr. Samuel Kneeland[18].

and the Hawaiian Islands. From 1862 to 1866, he was Surgeon in the army, first under Gen. Burnside, but for most of the time serving in New Orleans and Mobile, afterward Commander of the Loyal Legion. In August, 1866, he was appointed Secretary of the Massachusetts Institute of Technology, and Professor of Zoology and Physiology in that institution, which position he held twelve years. In the summer of 1874 he visited Iceland, at the time of its millenial celebration, for the purpose of studying the volcanic phenomena of that island. He edited the 'Annual of Scientific Discovery' from 1866 to 1869, wrote most of the zoological and many medical articles in the 'New American Encyclopedia' and the 'American Encyclopedia,' and contributed largely to scientific periodicals.

"Besides a translation of Andry's 'Diseases of the Heart' and an edition of Smith's 'History of the Human Species,' he has published the 'Wonders of the Yosemite Valley and of California' (Boston, 1871), 'An American in Iceland' (Boston, 1876), and 'The Land of Hemp and Sugar, or a Winter's Residence in the Philippine Islands,' the result of a trip around the world in 1881-2. He lectured on his travels before the Lowell Institute, Boston, the Cooper Union, and the Geographical Society, New York, and the Peabody Institute, Baltimore. His favorite studies were volcanic and earthquake phenomena, to obtain a knowledge of which he has visited most of the regions of the globe subject to such catastrophies, and the semi-civilized races of men in America, Asia and the Pacific Islands. Of these he had several hundred photographic illustrations taken from nature and from life, embracing California, Isthmus of Panama, Japan, China, Philippine and Sandwich Islands, Straits Settlements, Ceylon, Red Sea, Suez Canal, Iceland and Mediterranean volcanoes. 1884-5 he spent in Copenhagen, studying the antiquities and customs of the Scandinavian Vikings."

On August 1, 1849, he married Eliza Maria Curtis, of Cambridge, who was the granddaughter of Gen. Paul Curtis, of Revolutionary fame. They had:

Children of Samuel and Eliza (Curtis) Kneeland.

239. (i.) SAMUEL[19], b. at Boston, Dec. 10, 1850 (of whom hereafter, 245).

240. (ii.) ELIZA CURTIS[19], b. Oct. 21, 1852; m. Benj. L. M. Tower, a distinguished member of the Boston Bar. They have four children:

241.   (i.) *George Homer*[20], b. June 20, 1872.

242.   (ii.) *Eliza Kneeland*[20], b. Dec. 16, 1880.

243.   (iii.) *Benjamin Curtis*[20], b. June 20, 1884.

244.   (iv.) *Adeline Lane*[20], b. June 20, 1884.

245. (199.) SAMUEL KNEELAND[19](*Samuel*[18], *Samuel*[17], *Richard*[16], *John*[15], *John*[14], *John*[13], *John*[12], *John*[11] —*Alexander*[1]). Eldest son of Dr. Samuel Kneeland[18], now living at Hull, Mass.

Married at Boston, Oct. 18, 1880, to Hannah Lincoln Souther, the fifth descendant of Gen. Benjamin Lincoln, who commanded the American forces in Boston, after the evacuation by the British, and was afterwards with Washington.

Child of Samuel and Hannah (Souther) Kneeland.

246. SAMUEL KNEELAND[20] (*Samuel*[19], *Samuel*[18], *Samuel*[17], *Richard*[16], *John*[15], *John*[14], *John*[13], *John*[12], *John*[11]—*Alexander*[1]).

Thus, for the second time, we have struck the twentieth generation and the end, but, fortunately, the male issue in this instance is still extant.

247. (220.) JAMES KNEELAND[17], *Richard*[16], *John*[15], *John*[14], *John*[13], *John*[12], *John*[11]—*Alexander*[1]). Sixth child of Richard Kneeland Esq. and Martha, youngest daughter of Rev. Willard Hall, b. at Westford, Mass., Dec. 9, 1786, and died Sept. 11, 1862.

He married at Boston, Oct. 28, 1813, Margaret Beckford (see Boston Records). She was born November 7, 1889, at Salem, Mass., and died August 16, 1843. He resided in Boston, Mass., until about 1836, when he removed to Illinois, where the majority of his descendants still reside. They had eleven children, as follows:

Children of James and Martha (Beckford) Kneeland.

248. (i.) MARGARET[18], b. Feb. 14, 1814.
249. (ii.) CHARLES W.[18], b. April 27, 1815 (of whom hereafter, 262).
250. (iii.) JAMES A.[18], b. Aug. 2, 1817; d. Aug. 2, 1822 (Boston Records).
251. (iv.) LAURA ANN[18], b. Jan. 7, 1818; d. April 28, 1851.
252. (v.) BENJAMIN, B.[18], b. Dec. 20, 1820 (of whom hereafter, 271).
253. (vi.) JAMES W.[18], b. Feb. 22, 1822; d. May 10, 1851.
254. (vii.) ELIZA A.[18], b. Nov. 2, 1825.
255. (viii.) JOHN W.[18], b. Aug. 18, 1827; m. Maria Dix, Jan. 25, 1855, and d. April 1, 1895. He settled in Griggsville in 1836; was a soldier both in the Mexican and the Civil Wars. Children:
256.   (i.) *Willard E.*[19], b. Dec. 20, 1855; m. Nellie Penstour, June 21, 1894; living in Griggsville, Ill.
257.   (ii.) *Charles Henry*[19], b. July 31, 1857; living in Griggsville, Ill.
258.   (iii.) *Andrew Wilson*[19], b. July 20, 1863; d. Sept. 17, 1865.
259. (ix.) ELLEN A.[18], b. Oct. 2, 1829; m. ———— Hunt; d. Jan. 6, 1873.
260. (x.) CAROLINE E.[18], b. Sept. 4, 1832; d. Aug. 9, 1834.
261. (xi.) GEORGE S.[18], b. Nov. 24, 1833; m. Ella E. Wilson, Nov. 14, 1881. She was b. Dec. 22, 1854. They reside at Blocksburg, Cal. Children:
261A.   (i.) *George Wilson*[19], b. Jan. 22, 1883.
261B.   (ii.) *Lloyd B.*[19], b. Oct. 17, 1884.
261C.   (iii.) *May Belle*[19], b. Aug. 26, 1886.
261D.   (iv.) *Leota*[19], b. Oct. 7, 1888.

262. (249.) CHARLES W. KNEELAND[18] (*James*[17], *Richard*[16], *John*[15], *John*[14], *John*[13], *John*[12], *John*[11], —*Alexander*[1]). Eldest son of James Kneeland and Margaret Beckford; b. April 27, 1815; m. Elizabeth P. Jackson.

She was born May 2, 1820. They settled in Griggsville, Ill., in 1836, and for many years he was a merchant of that place. He still resides in Griggsville.

Children of Charles W. and Elizabeth P. (Jackson) Kneeland.

263.   (i.) HARRIET ANN[19], b. April 30, 1842; d. Dec. 5, 1877; m. James M. Higgins. They had one child:

264.   *C. M. Higgins[20].* They live at 843 N. Seventh St., Springfield, Ill.

265.   (ii.) CHARLES W.[19], b. Aug. 18, 1846; m. Mary L. Folger, April 29, 1868. They live at 45 Henry Street, Buffalo, N. Y. Children:

266.   (i.) *Anna Elizabeth[20]*, b. Jan. 30, 1869; d. July 25, 1869.

267.   (ii.) *Frederick Rowland[20]*, b. July 24, 1870; m. Jessie C. Cotton; now living in Cripple Creek, Col.

268.   (iii.) *George Jackson[20]*, b. Sept. 11, 1872; now living in Griggsville, Ill.

269.   (iv.) *Ralph Folger[20]*, b. Oct. 5, 1875; now living at 59 Congress Street, Milford, Mass.

270.   (v.) *Warren Francis[20]*, b. June 28, 1889.

271.   (252.) BENJAMIN B. KNEELAND[18] (*James[17], Richard[16], John[15], John[14], John[13], John[12], John[11] —Alexander[1]*). Fourth son of James and Margaret B. Kneeland; b. Dec. 22, 1820; m. (1) Mary Walker, Oct. 22, 1843; she d. Feb. 22, 1847; (2) Ellen Johnson, Nov., 1848; she d. Nov. 9, 1894. He settled in Griggsville, in 1834, and still resides there.

Children of Benjamin B. Kneeland, by his first wife, Mary Walker.

272.   (i.) CHARLES H.[19], b. Aug. 1, 1843; d. Oct. 1, 1845.
273.   (ii.) WILLARD H.[19], b. Oct. 24, 1846; d. Oct. 3, 1864.

Richard Kneeland[17].

By his second wife, Ellen Johnson.

274. (iii.) EDWARD[19], b. April 21, 1849; m. Lida Lampson, April, 28, 1881. They resided in Harvey, Ill., and have children, as follows:

275.   (i.) *Mystic E.*[20], b. June 23, 1882; d. Nov. 9, 1895.
276.   (ii.) *Sarah E.*[20], b. Dec. 3, 1883.
277.   (iii.) *Frank H.*[20], b. Sept. 21, 1885.
278.   (iv.) *Harold E.*[20], b. May 26, 1887.
279.   (v.) *Edward R.*[20], b. in 1889.
280. (iv.) GEORGE F.[19], b. Oct. 28, 1859; m. May A Dix, Nov. 23, 1882. She d. March 20, 1895, and he m. (2) Grace P. Sargant, April 26, 1896. He lives in Griggsville, Ill. Children by first wife:

281.   (i.) *Harry C.*[20], b. Sept. 1, 1883.
282.   (ii.) *Floyd*[20], b. August 15, 1884.

283. (216). RICHARD KNEELAND[17] (*Richard*[16], *John*[15], *John*[14], *John*[13], *John*[12], *John*[11]—*Alexander*[1]). Eldest son of Richard and Martha (Hall) Kneeland, of Westford, Mass.; b. April 1, 1778; m. Katharine Knight, of Claremont, N. H., about 1800, and settled in Waterbury in the spring of 1802, being one of the earliest settlers of that town.

He was, like his father, a Justice of the Peace for many years and was known as "Squire Kneeland," in the days when the title was a term of distinction. He died at Waterbury, Mass., February 17, 1868. at the age of 90. She died August 22, 1853. The following sketch of Squire Kneeland is taken from the Vermont *Historical Gazeteer:* "Richard Kneeland, Esq., who was favorably known to our residents in the second and third decades of the century, in early life lived in Boston, where he learned his trade of joiner by the long apprenticeship then necessary to entitle to a trade reputation, when a trade was something of a service. Mr. Kneeland raised a family of nine children. Two of the sons have represented other towns in the Legislature, one—the youngest—received a collegiate and medical education, but lived to practice his profession only a few years, dying young. The oldest daughter never married, but at least three we can recollect were well married and one is now living; also one son, Mr. Kneeland, lived to the age of 90, and died in Waterbury in 1867. He was always called Squire, was a man of extensive reading and had a peculiar cast of mind and was peculiar in his religious views."

Children of Richard and Katharine (Knight) Kneeland.

284. (i.) ORTENTIA[18], b. July 28, 1802; unmarried; d. Feb. 4, 1854.

285. (ii.) WILLARD HALL[18], b. April 27, 1805; m. Cleora Woods, Jan. 11, 1831. She was b. Nov. 16, 1810, and d. Sept. 12, 1891, æ. 81. He d. Jan. 13, 1875, æ. 70. They had four children:

286. (i.) *Samuel Pride*[19], b. Aug. 21, 1832, at Waterbury, Vt.; m. Feb. 18, 1856, at Lowell, Mass., Martha J. Spaulding. She was b. March 11, 1834, at Plainfield, N. H. They reside at Mooresville, N. C., and have no children.

287. (ii.) *Ianthe Cleora*[19], b. Jan. 19, 1836, at Waterbury, Vt.; m. Thaddeus Egrea Sanger, M. D., Oct. 29, 1856. He was. b. Mar. 12, 1832, in Troy, Vt. They reside at Littleton, N. H., and have three children:

288. (i.) Ellen Ingeberg Sanger[20], b. Dec. 22, 1866, at Littleton, N. H.

289. (ii.) Lillian Edith Sanger[20], b. April 20, 1873, at Littleton, N. H.; m. Dec. 26, 1895, to Frederick Elmer Green. He was b. April 10, 1873.

290. (iii.) Katharine Francis Sanger[20], b. April 7, 1879, at Littleton, N. H.

291. (iii). *Ellen Ophelia*[19], b. at Waterbury, Vt., July 4, 1840; m. Mark J. Russell, Dec. 13, 1865. He was b. Nov. 8, 1846. They reside at St. Johnsbury, Vt. Children:

292. (i.) Lucius Kneeland Russell[20], b. Dec. 12, 1867; d. July 19, 1870.

293. (ii.) Thaddeus Sanger Russell[20], b. Feb. 2, 1870; d. Aug. 30, 1872.

294. (iii). Fannie Ellen Russell[20], b. Jan. 16, 1874.

Richard Kneeland[17].

295.   (iv.) Grace Isabel Russell[20], b. Nov. 11, 1875.
296.   (v.) Henry Marcus Russell[20], b. Dec. 2, 1877.
297.   (vi.) Florence Mabel Russell[20], b. Apr. 11, 1879.
298.   (vii.) Perley Ray Russell[20], b. Nov. 23, 1880.
299.   (iv.) *Irenus Newcomb*[19], b. Dec. 12, 1846. m. Ellen
          Blake, July, 19, 1876. Resides in Milford,
          Kansas. They had children:
300.   (i.) Evangeline Cleora[20], b. May 30, 1877.
301.   (ii.) Ina Bertha[20], b. Oct. 15, 1879.
302.   (iii.) Katie Louisa[20], b. July 28, 1884.
303.   (iv.) Bessie May[20], b. May 19, 1887; d. May
          25, 1887.
304.   (v.) Richard Arthur[20], b. May 31, 1888.
305.   (vi.) Nellie Irene[20], b, Nov. 24, 1890.
306.   (iii.) MARTHA[18], b. Oct. 15, 1808; m. Ralph Parker in
          Jan., 1831. They had five children:
307.   (i.) *John Parker*[19].
308.   (ii.) *Edwin Parker*[19].
309.   (iii.) *Charles Parker*[19].
310.   (iv.) *Antensia Parker*[19].
311.   (v.) *Martha Parker*[19].
312.   (iv.) WILLIAM[18], b. April 9, 1811; m. Dorothy Jackman,
          Dec. 30. 1840; d. Dec. 16, 1891, æ. 80. They had
          one child, *Lucius Richard Kneeland*[19], b. Sept. 5,
          1891, through whom I have received much informa-
          tion relative to the descendants of Richard Knee-
          land, of Westford and Waterbury. He inherited
          the old Kneeland Bible, which has been in the
          family more than three centuries and is referred to
          in many wills and inventories of the dead and gone
          Kneelands. He lives at Middlesex, Vt. Married,
          March 17, 1890, Emma A. Wood. They have no
          children.
313.   (v.) MARY ANN[18], b. June 27, 1814; m. Baxter Whit-
          ney. They are both dead. They had four children:
314.   (i.) *Catharine Whitney*[19].
315.   (ii.) *Wallace Whitney*[19].
316.   (iii.) *Arthur Whitney*[19].
317.   (iv.) *Emma Whitney*[19].

318.   (vi.) HENRY[18], b. Sept. 25, 1819 (of whom hereafter, 326).
319.   (vii.) DR. LUCIUS[18], b. March 20, 1822; unmarried; d.
        at Orange Grove, Fla., Aug. 11, 1852, æ. 30. He
        was a young man of great promise. Received a
        collegiate education and then a medical course.
        Practiced medicine with great success for three
        years, and then death, that he had often defeated
        for others, claimed him for its own.
320.   (viii.) ADALINE[18], b. Sept. 17, 1825; m. William M.
        Wade. They reside with their son, Dr. Henry
        Wade, in Starksboro, Vt. They had five children:
321.   (i.) *William Wade*[19].
322.   (ii.) *Henry Wade*[19].
323.   (iii.) *Charles Wade*[19].
324.   (iv.) *Frank Wade*[19].
325.   (v.) *George Wade*[19].

326.   (318.) HENRY KNEELAND[18] (*Richard*[17], *Richard*[16],
        John[15], *John*[14], *John*[13], *John*[12], *John*[11]—*Alex-
        ander*[1]). Son of Richard and Catharine (Knight)
        Kneeland, b. at Waterbury, Vt., Sept. 25, 1819;
        m. March 27, 1849, Marie Sherman.
They reside at Westfield, Vt., and are highly respected
and influential citizens of that beautiful valley among the
green mountains of Vermont.

Children of Henry and Marie (Sherman) Kneeland.

327.   (i.) HOWLAND P.[19], b. at Waterbury, Vt., March 2,
        1843; m. Elinoir Warner, who was b. in Warren,
        Pa., Sept. 25, 1858. They settled at Nevada, Iowa,
        but soon after moved to Boone, Iowa, where they
        now reside. Children:
328.   (i.) *Zoe M.*[20], b. in Nevada, Iowa, May 11, 1876.
329.   (ii.) *Percy H. R.*[20], b. in Boone, Iowa, April 10, 1878.
330.   (iii.) *Clytie Z.*[20], b. in Boone, Iowa, July 11, 1882.
331.   (ii.) SEYMOUR L.[19], b. at Waterbury, Vt., Sept. 17,
        1845; m. Diantha E. Smyth. They reside in
        Lowell, Mass. Children:

Henry Kneeland[18].

332.   (i.) *Clarence Henry*[20].
333.   (ii.) *Winifred E.*[20], m. Arthur Bartlett and had one child :
334.   Harold Kneeland Bartlett[21].
335.   (iii.) KATHARINE L.[19], b. at Waterbury, Aug. 14, 1847; m. Dr. E. G. Hooker. Children:
336.   (i.) *Harold O. Hooker*[20], d. at the age of four.
337.   (ii.) *Jessie Maria Hooker*[20], m. Burt Atherton. They had a child :
340.   Beatrice Atherton[21], who resides in Waterbury, Vt.
341.   (iv.) ISABEL A. KNEELAND[19], b. at Waterbury, Vt., Dec. 20, 1850; m. C. M. Richardson. Their children are :
342.   (i.) *Ira Richardson*[20], m. Catharine L. Tobey. No issue.
343.   (ii.) *Henry Kneeland Richardson*[20], m. Florence Druckhammer. They had two children :
344.   (i.) Clarence D. Richardson[21].
345.   (ii.) Katharine I. Richardson[21].
346.   (iii.) *Gertrude Bernice Richardson*[20].
347.   (iv.) *Elizabeth Fanny Richardson*[20].
348.   (v.) *Flora Belle Richardson*[20].
349.   (vi.) *Orville C. Richardson*[20].

PART IV.

DESCENDANTS OF SAMUEL AND MARY (ALDEN) KNEELAND.

DEDICATED TO THE MEMORY OF

SAMUEL KNEELAND,

PUBLISHER AND STATE PRINTER, OF BOSTON,

WHOSE MARRIAGE TO

MARY ALDEN

MADE MANY MAYFLOWER DESCENDANTS

PROUD AND HAPPY.

CHAPTER VII.

SAMUEL KNEELAND AND MARY ALDEN.

(NOS. 350 TO 393.)

350. (50.) SAMUEL KNEELAND[15] (*John*[14], *John*[13], *John*[12], *John*[11], *William*[10], *James*[9], *Alexander*[8], *William*[7], *William*[6], *John*[5], *John*[4], *John*[3], *James*[2], *Alexander*[1]).

We come now to the consideration of one of the most charming characters of the race—Samuel Kneeland, Esq., publisher, of Boston. The history of printing in this country could never be written with Samuel Kneeland omitted. Neither could the history of Boston in the eighteenth century be properly compiled without including his family. He was named for his grandfather, Samuel Green, a printer, of Boston, and his great-grandfather, Samuel Green, of Cambridge, England, the publisher of the Cambridge Bible. The Greens were a family of printers, and the heritage was accepted by Samuel Kneeland and passed on to his sons, Daniel and John. It is safe to assert that at least three out of every four books published in Boston between 1705 and 1785 bear the imprint of Samuel Kneeland, Kneeland & Green, or D. & J. Kneeland, the latter being the sons of Samuel who succeeded him in business. In the Massachusetts *Gazette* of December 18, 1889, appears the following obituary notice: "Last Thursday noon, December 14, departed this life, 73 years of age, Samuel Kneeland, formerly an eminent printer of this town. He sustained the character of an upright man, a good Christian, and as such was universally esteemed. His funeral was very largely attended on Saturday evening."

From Appleton's "Cyclopedia of American Biography," I quote the following: "Kneeland, Samuel, printer, born in

Samuel Kneeland[1 5].

Boston, 1696, died there, Dec. 14, 1769. He was apprenticed to Benjamin Green, and was for many years printer to the Governor and Council, printing, also, the laws and journals of the House of Representatives. Besides many religious books and pamphlets, he published *The Gazette* from 1727 to 1741, and the *New England Weekly Journal* from 1741 to 1752."

Benjamin Green was his uncle and the father of Timothy Green, who was his partner, for many years. He was a close friend and associate of Benjamin Franklin, and for a short period was in partnership with his elder brother, James Franklin. *The Gazette*, referred to in the foregoing quotation, was the first paper printed in Boston, and the first but one printed in this country.

The most important work of Samuel Kneeland as a publisher has not, however, been generally recognized, inasmuch as under the peculiar laws of the mother country it could not, prior to the Revolution, be acknowledged. I refer to the printing of the first Bible published in America. I received hints of this work from various sources, but the first public statement to that effect is herewith clipped from a late Chicago paper.* This work was commenced by Kneeland &

---

*Is a Rare Treasure—First Bible Printed in America—New York man discovers an authentic copy of the celebrated book published in Boston in 1761, over a forged imprint.

John Anderson, Jr., of New York, has discovered an authentic copy of the celebrated Bible printed in Boston in 1761, by Samuel Kneeland and sent out with a forged imprint of the London printer, Mark Baskett. High authorities have crossed lances concerning even the perpetration of the forgery, ignoring altogether the possible existence of a copy, says the Boston *Globe.* Mr. Anderson has struck up the lances with the production of the indisputable copy. This announcement will create much interest among collectors and book fanciers everywhere, who have long followed with interest the pros and cons of the authorities concerning it. This book has, besides its peculiar value as a literary forgery, an aditional value in that it is now the first English Bible printed in America, and as "firsts," both in editions and in sequence, are of special value, this volume will bring a very large price when offered for sale.

It was long supposed that the Aitken Bible, published in 1781-2, was the first English Bible published in America, and the authorities, after long continued discussion on the existence of the forgery, agreed that the Aitken Bible must hold the distinction.

One man however—Isaiah Thomas, who wrote a valuable and authoritative history of printing—made the claim that there was such a forgery perpetrated, and stated certain facts about its issuance from the press with every appearance of sincerity and truth.

HISTORY OF THE PUBLICATION.

Thomas says in his book, published in 1810: "Kneeland & Green, of Boston, printed, principally for Daniel Henchman, an edition of the Bible in small quarto.

Samuel Kneeland[15].

Green, continued by Samuel Kneeland and completed by D. & J. Kneeland. I have had the pleasure of examining the volume referred to in this communication and have received confirmation of the story and assert my absolute belief as to its correctness.

Perhaps one of the best proofs of the versatility of Samuel Kneeland's mind, and of his perseverance and ability to succeed where others failed, is found in his connection with the claims of the descendants of the soldiers of King Phillip's War. Before starting out in the campaign against the Narragansetts, known as King Phillip's War of 1675, a proclamation was made in the name of the Colonial government that the soldiers, their heirs and representatives, in addition to regular pay, should have a special grant of the Narragansett lands, "provided they played the man (King Phillip), captured the fort where the great body of the enemy was entrenched and drove him out of the country." This feat having been per-

This was the first Bible printed in America in the English language. It was carried through the press as privately as possible and has the London imprint of the copy from which it was reprinted, viz: 'London; Printed by Mark Baskett, Printer to the King's Most Excellent Majesty,' in order to prevent a prosecution from those in England and Scotland who published the Bible by a patent from the crown or cum privilegio, as did the English universities of Oxford and Cambridge. When I was an apprentice I often heard those who had assisted at the case and press in printing this Bible make mention of the fact. The late Governor Hancock was related to Henchman and knew the particulars of the transaction. He possessed a copy of this impression. As it has a London imprint, at this day it can be distinguished from an English edition of the same date only by those who are acquainted with the niceties of typography. This Bible issued from the press about the time that the partnership of Kneeland & Green expired. The edition was not large. I have been informed that it did not exceed 700 or 800 copies."

Isaiah Thomas has always been noted for the accuracy of his statements, and this confirmation of his assertions regarding the printing of this Bible will be hailed with extreme satisfaction by those who have always regarded him as the fountain head of truth in such matters, and who do not care to see his statements disputed.

REASONS FOR THE FORGERY.

The reason for the forgery lay in the fact that there was at that time a law or regulation existing in England that no one could print a Bible without special letters patent from the crown. Dr. Green, of Boston, the well-known antiquarian, says that he never has heard of the law. He does not deny the existence of it, but merely says that he never has heard or it. On the other hand, eminent authorities, Thomas among them, insist that there was such a law.

The book is undoubtedly of American origin, as will be explained in detail further down this column. Granting this, the argument is all with the claimants for the existence of such a law. Kneeland & Green were well-known and prolific printers, and had an excellent reputation. If they had understood their rights, would they not have put

Samuel Kneeland[15].

formed, from time to time thereafter attempts were made to secure a fulfillment of the promise. Nothing was accomplished, however, during the first half century; in fact, none of the soldiers, in their own person, ever reaped the benefit of the proclamation. It was not until about 1733 that any proper steps were taken in their behalf. Samuel Kneeland, as one of the heirs of John Hawkins, who was wounded in King Phillip's War, and also representing, as "asine" (which, I suppose, meant "assignee"), one of the other heirs, went to work in a methodical manner to compel a realization of these antebellum promises. With great difficulty he succeeded in getting the interests of the heirs united. A committee of five was appointed with full power to act for all the others. Samuel was appointed a member of this committee, clerk, and also its manager. Through his labors the Narragansett townships Nos. 1 and 2 were set apart and divided up in severalty among the heirs. This work accomplished, he immediately set about to colonize the lands, and with great

their own names on the title page? The Bible remained unprinted in America until the close of the Revolution, barring the Baskett piracy. It would be seen that if the Bible could have been printed, it would have been by some of the numerous and enterprising printers of the colony.

DIFFICULTIES OF PRINTERS.

Mr. Anderson himself says on this point: "Early after the importation of the art of printing into England, the crown claimed a prerogative right in the statute book and in the English Bible, and this right seems to have been immediately recognized and supported. The first printer to style himself king's printer was Richard Pynson, in 1503. He was succeeded in time by Richard Grafton, who got himself in trouble in 1537 by printing an English edition of the Bible in Paris, for which he was imprisoned until he gave a bond of £100 not to print more English Bibles till the king and clergy had settled a translation. In 1540-1 he was restored to favor and entrusted with printing the folio English Bible under letters patent. From that day to this the right has been vested in certain printers, whose names are well known, in conjunction with the universities of Oxford and Cambridge.

"It will be readily seen that there was absolutely no occasion for any colonial prohibitory law. Why should there be? The king's prerogative right extended to all British territories, and this included the American colonies. I believe it is well known that we had regular censors of the press in America from the date of our first printing in 1640. Such being the fact, would they have allowed a Bible to be published openly, contrary to law, bearing an American imprint? In Barnes' history of the United States, the statement is made 'that to have printed the English Bible in America prior to the revolution would have been considered an act of piracy.'"

KEPT THE SECRET FOR YEARS.

Mr. Anderson has known of the existence of the work for some years, but until the present time did not care to impart his knowledge to the world. He has spent some difficulty succeeded in building up flourishing towns in the former abode of the Narragansetts. This work, manifestly for the benefit of the Commonwealth, received public recognition, a full statement of which I quote from the "History of Westminster, Mass" (p. 431).

"Early in the year 1735, Samuel Kneeland, clerk of the whole body of Narragansett grantees, a Boston printer, petitioned the General Court of the Province of Massachusetts Bay for a grant of land in recognition and part payment of services rendered in helping forward the settlement of certain new townships then recently established. The petition was favorably received and referred to a committee, who soon reported a bill in accordance therewith, accompanied by a plan of a tract of 500 acres lying southeast of Narragansett No. 2, and bounded partly on that township, partly on Wachusett pond and otherwise on common land. The report was adopted, and the lands were conveyed and confirmed to Mr.

time in searching to bring the book to light, and is entitled to much credit for his service to bibliography. The Bible is in a remarkable state of preservation, the binding being altogether sound and the leaves crisp. A careful collation shows that it lacks but five leaves, and two of these are in the Apocrypha. The New Testament is complete and perfect. It bears the autograph of Philip Livingstone, one of the signers of the Declaration of Independence, and contains also some interesting annotations, evidently in the same handwriting. There is contained in the volume an interesting family record, presumably of the Livingstone family, which begins with the year 1767, but six years subsequent to the publication of the work. All the entries are distinctively American. The Bible measures 7⅜ inches by 9 5-16 inches. It begins with the "Psalter, or Psalms of David, pointed as they are to be sung or said in churches." Following this are the usual forms of prayer, articles of religion, etc., the whole occupying twenty-eight leaves. Then comes the general title.

NO DOUBT OF ITS NATIVITY.

At the conclusion of the Old Testament proper is the inscription, "The End of the Prophets." The Apocrypha follows, and then comes the title page of the New Testament, similar to the general title, save that the name of Thomas Baskett is submitted for that of Mark. An index to the Bible and some tables occupy nineteen pages at the end.

It takes but a glance at the volume by one versed in the typographical art and possessing bibliographical knowledge, to locate its origin. It is distinctively and delightfully American. The binding alone would indicate its nativity. The "homemade" blind tooling on the sides and back, the stamped designs on the back, the quality of the paper on which it is printed, and the old red leather label "Bible,' to say nothing of its primitive leather board binding, denote beyond peradventure its early American origin.

There are a number of specimens extant of the typographical work of Mark Baskett, who was a master of his art, and it is only necessary to compare the real with the forgery to be convinced of the absurdity of any possible claim that this volume was

Samuel Kneeland[15].

Kneeland by the approving signature of Gov. Belcher, Dec.
29, 1735. He remained in possession several years, building
a house on the estate and making other improvements, though
probably never occupying it as a permanent resident. It was
known as the " Kneeland Farm," a designation it bore for a long
time thereafter. He afterwards sold it to Samuel Hews, of
Boston, and it passed through several hands to John Bowen,
of Lancaster, a wealthy man who occupied and greatly improved it. The latter being a loyalist, the property was con-
fiscated by the Provincial government and then passed into
the hands of Joshua Everett, in whose family it has since
remained. Many of the improvements of Samuel Kneeland
and John Bowen are still to be seen on this beautiful homestead."

On the eighth day of February, 1721, Samuel Kneeland
married Mary Alden, of Boston, a granddaughter of Captain
John Alden, of that town, and great-granddaughter of " John

printed in London by the real Mark Baskett. It is interesting to note, in the face of
this indisputable evidence of the authenticity of this volume, some of the comments of
well-known bibliographers.

In Bancroft's "History of the United States," Vol. V., p. 266, he says: "He
(Mr. Thomas) repeats only what he heard. Himself a collector, he does not profess
ever to have seen a copy of the alleged American edition of the English Bible. Search
has repeatedly been made for a copy and always without success. Six hundred or 800
Bibles in quarto could hardly have been printed, bound and sold in Boston, then a small
town, undiscovered. Nor would they all have disappeared. The most complete cata-
logues of English Bibles enumerate no one with the imprint which was said to have
been copied. Till a copy of the pretended American edition is produced, no credit can
be given to the second-hand story."

QUESTIONED ITS ORIGIN.

On page 60 of "Early Bibles of America," by Rev. Dr. John Wright, he says:
"Was Mr. Aitken's Bible the very first printed in America in the English language?
This question was vigorously discussed for many years, but with the light we now have
it should be considered settled." (In the negative.)

Mr. Anderson has discovered another point concerning the work, that will be of
interest to collectors. Whenever this work has been discussed it has been attributed to
Kneeland & Green, because the date assigned for its issuance was before the dissolution
of their partnership. He has fixed the publication date as 1761. History states that the
partnership was dissolved in 1752. Green went to New London, Conn., and Kneeland
remained at Boston till 1769. The date of the Bible has therefore settled that point and
proved that it was printed by Samuel Kneeland, and not by Kneeland & Green. Considering the fact that one of two known copies of the Cromwell Soldier's Bible sold
recently for $1,000, and that one of thirty-three copies of Aitken's Bible, mentioned
above, sold for $650, the inquiry naturally suggests itself, what would this Bible bring at
public sale?

Samuel Kneeland[15].

Alden and Priscilla," of the Mayflower (see Boston Records and the Alden Memorial, p. 24).

It is safe to assert that nothing that he ever did in his full life endeared him so much to his descendants as this same marriage. Of course, this young couple never dreamed of Longfellow or the immortality which, 250 years thereafter, he was to confer on his parentage. Verily, he "entertained an angel unawares."

John Alden was the last survivor of the Mayflower. He was born in 1599, and died at Duxbury, Mass., September 12, 1687, as the tombstone quaintly states, "in a good old age and full of years, and was gathered to his people, and his sons buried him." In 1621 he married Priscilla Mallens, who came over in the Mayflower with her father. They had at least eleven children—the exact number is not definitely determined—the oldest being Capt. John Alden, "mariner," who settled at Boston. He had fourteen children, including Nathaniel (No. 14, Alden Memorial), who was born at Boston, February 6, 1673. His eldest daughter, Mary, born February 6, 1673, married Samuel Kneeland, as hereinbefore stated. The fact of this relation is fully proven by the proceedings in court whereby the proceeds of lands granted by the government to Capt. John Alden, for services rendered and hardships suffered in the Canadian campaign, was distributed to his heirs, including "Samuel Kneeland and Mary (Alden) Kneeland, Timothy Green and Elizabeth (Alden) Green, grandchildren to the said John Alden, deceased, all of Boston in the County of Suffolk and Province of Massachusetts."

It will thus be seen that the partners, Samuel Kneeland and Timothy Green, were brothers-in-law as well as cousins. It may also be noted that the Kneeland and Alden families had previously been united by the marriage of Capt. Edward Kneeland[4], "mariner," of Ipswich, with another Mary Alden, as will be seen hereafter, (Chap. XVIII.)

Children of Samuel and Mary (Alden) Kneeland.

351. (i.) MARY[16], b. at Boston, Nov. 19, 1722; d. Feb. 24, 1724.
352. (ii.) SAMUEL[16], b. March 15, 1724; m. Mary Waters, Oct. 5, 1743; graduated at Harvard same year; d. in 1748. Children:

Samuel Kneeland[15].

353.   (i.) *Ebenezer[17]*, b. Jan. 1, 1745; m. Sarah Morris, Sept. 25, 1764. Child:

354.   Betsy[18], m. Zebediah Johnson.

355.   (ii.) *Alexander[17]*, b. Oct. 10, 1746; m. Mary ———— about 1771. Children:

356.   (i.) Debby[18], b, Jan. 6, 1773; m. Samuel Dwinnell, June 26, 1791. Their descendants still reside in Massachusetts.

357.   (ii.) Grace[18], b. April 7, 1775; m. Geo. Smith, Aug. 6, 1794. He was a mariner, residing in North Street at the time of the Boston directory of 1795.

358.   (iii.) Nancy[18], b. July 10, 1777; m. Nathan Simpson, Jan. 31, 1796, blacksmith.

359.   (iii.) *Samuel[17]*, b. May 10, 1748 (of whom hereafter, 587).

360. (iii.) DANIEL[16], b. at Boston, Nov. 11, 1725; unmarried; d. May 1, 1789. He was a printer and, in partner ship with his brother, John, succeeded their father in business. Many books printed 1745 bear the impress of "D. & J. Kneeland, Queen St., Boston." Samuel Kneeland, Kneeland & Green, Kneeland & Franklin, and D. & J. Kneeland continued the business on Queen Street over seventy years. He was for several years assessor of Boston and was personally associated with Samuel Adams, John Hancock and many of the leaders in the time of the Revolution.

361. (iv.) MARY[16], b. August 21, 1727; m. Thos. Walley, of Boston, June 12, 1749 (of whom hereafter, 393).

363. (v). JOHN[16], b. at Boston, Sept. 4, 1729; m. Abigail Phillips, Nov. 9, 1756. She was a cousin of Hon. John Phillips, who was the first Mayor of Boston and father of Judge Phillips. He was a printer and with his brother, Daniel, succeeded, under the name of D. & J. Kneeland, to his father's publishing business. He was a man of influence and held several public positions, including that of assessor of "the towne of Boston." He completed the

Samuel Kneeland[15].

publication of the first American Bible, commenced by Kneeland & Green. He died in 1776 and his brother Daniel succeeded him in business. Children:

364. (i.) *John[17]*, b. at Boston, June 10, 1757 (of whom hereafter, 558).

365. (ii.) *Mary[17]*, b. in Boston, Dec. 8, 1760.

366. (iii.) *Samuel[17]*, b. in Boston, Aug. 11, 1762.

367. (iv.) *James[17]*, b. in Boston, Jan. 10, 1765.

368. (v.) *Christopher[17]*, b. in Boston, April 16, 1768; m. Ruth Hopkins; d. in 1814. Letters of administration granted to his widow, Ruth, in that year.

369. (vi.) *James[17]*, b. in Boston, April 16, 1768.

√ 370. (vii.) *Edward[17]*, b. in Boston, Feb. 2, 1775 (of whom hereafter, 450).

371. (vi.) JONAS[16], b. at Boston, Oct. 10, 1731; unmarried. He was of a delicate constitution and always resided at his father's home in Boston. He died in 1775.

372. (vii.) TIMOTHY[16], b. at Boston, Jan. 1, 1734; m. (1) Lucretia Winslow, Nov. 1, 1752; and (2) Arista Dean, March 5, 1772 (Boston Records). He died in 1793, leaving as heir and next of kin, Henry Kneeland, Jr. As his brothers and sisters were not mentioned in the probate proceedings, it is clear that the latter must have been a descendant, as the term "Jr." is used. Timothy must, therefore, have had a son Henry, and the Henry in question must have been a grandson. The Boston Records do not show the birth of this son, but between 1750 and 1850 these records were by no means complete, and the absence of names neither proves nor disproves anything. It is known that Timothy had a country seat at Bedford, Mass., and it is known that Henry Kneeland, who fought in the revolution, enlisted from that place. The date of his birth, 1853, according to the enlistment papers, corresponds exactly with the time when Timothy would be expected to have an heir, he having married the year previous.

Ann Kneeland[16].

Timothy Kneeland was a man of substance and highly connected in Boston. He was for several years on the bond of Samuel Adams, who, prior to being Governor, was Collector of Boston. He, Timothy, also held several positions of trust during the revolutionary period in Boston, including that of chairman of the Board of Assessors. We have the record of only one of his children:

372A.   *Henry Kneeland*[17], b. Oct. 1, 1853. Resided at Bedford, near Boston, in the County of Middlesex, Mass. He enlisted in 1777 for three years, receiving by way of bounty, "20 head of cattle, 10 sheep and *one negro named Negus.*" He re-enlisted March 3, 1780, and was then "27 years old, 5 feet 9½ inches high, light complexion, dark hair and blue eyes." He married Mary Adams, March 15, 1766 (see Boston Records), and had one son:

373.   Henry Kneeland[18], b. about 1778.

374.   (viii.) ANN[16], b. at Boston, July 20, 1735; m. Joseph Gill (of whom hereafter, 378).

375.   (ix.) LYDIA[16], b. at Boston, Aug. 10, 1738; m. Nathaniel Phillips, Jan 15, 1762.

376.   (x.) ELIZABETH[16], b. at Boston, Dec. 4, 1739. No further record.

377.   (xi.) RACHEL[16]. No further record.

The above data are from the Boston Records.

378.   (374.) ANN KNEELAND[16] (*Samuel*[15], *John*[14], *John*[13], *John*[12], *John*[11]—*Alexander*[1]). Eighth child of Samuel Kneeland and Mary Alden; b. at Boston, July 20, 1735; m. John Gill, Esq., of Boston, who for many years had a large printing establishment on Nassau Street, in that city.

His brother, Hon. Moses Gill, of Boston, was elected Lieutenant-Governor of Massachusetts, in 1794, and held the position until his death. He was acting Governor after the death of Governor Sumner, June 1, 1799. We are indebted

Ann Kneeland[16].

to the "History of the Abbot Family" for the descendants of this couple, John Gill being the son of Elizabeth Abbot and John Gill, Sr.

Children of Ann Kneeland[16] and John Gill.

379. (i.) JOHN GILL[17], not married.
380. (ii.) NANCY[17], m. her cousin, Michael Gill and had several children.
381. (iii.) BETSY[17], m. Edward E. Powers.
382. (iv.) MOSES[17], adopted by his uncle, Hon. Moses Gill; graduated at Princeton, in 1784. and m. Susan Buttrick, of Princeton.
383. (v.) SARAH[17], b. July 18, 1770; m. Sept. 4, 1795, Mather Withington. He was b. July 28, 1759, and d. Jan. 13, 1831. Children:
384.   (i.) *Sarah Prince Withington*[18], b. June 20, 1796; m. Wm. Vose, March 24, 1814; d. Jan. 5, 1823. Children:
385.   (i.) Mather W. Vose[19], b. at Dorchester, 1816.
386.   (ii.) Wm. H. Vose[19], b. Aug. 2, 1818; unmarried; d. at Boston, June, 1846.
387.   (iii.) Sarah W. Vose[19], b. Nov. 8, 1822; d. Sept., 1823.
388.   (ii.) *Mary Preston Withington*[18], b. Sept. 19, 1800; m. Dec. 20, 1821, Jason Wadsworth, of Milton; d. May 3, 1825. Children:
389.   (i.) Mather W. Wadsworth[19], b. Oct. 27, 1822.
390.   (ii.) Henry A. Wadsworth[19], d. Sept. 30, 1824, æ. 9 months.
391.   (iii.) Augustus Wadsworth[19], d. Sept. 15, 1825, æ. 5 months.
392.   (iii.) *Ann Withington*[18], b. Jan. 10, 1805 ; unmarried; d. Oct. 7, 1831.
393. (vi.) POLLY GILL[17], m. Levi Pease Boston.

CHAPTER VIII.

THE LANGDON FAMILY.

(NOS. 394 TO 449.)

A separate chapter is given to this family and their descendants, the Barretts, Greenwoods, Haywards, etc., on account of their distinguished ancestry, reaching back to the choicest flowers of the Mayflower—John Alden and Priscilla —and of the equally distinguished descendants.

394. (361.) MARY KNEELAND[16] (*Samuel*[15], *John*[14], *John*[13], *John*[12], *John*[11], *William*[10], *James*[9], *Alexander*[8], *William*[7], *William*[6], *John*[5], *John*[4], *John*[3], *James*[2], *Alexander*[1]), b. at Boston, Aug. 21, 1727; m. Thos. Walley, Esq., June 12, 1749.

Thomas Walley was one of the wealthiest and most respected of Boston's merchants during the ante-revolutionary period. He was the father-in-law of Boston's first Mayor, Hon. John Phillips, and the grandfather of Wendell Phillips. His first wife was Mary, daughter of Samuel and Mary (Alden) Kneeland. She died soon after the birth of their first child:

395. MARY WALLEY[17], b. at Boston, June 12, 1749. She m. Capt. John Langdon, of Boston (of whom hereafter, 396).

There were two Langdon families in Boston from the earliest period of its existence. I have been unable to trace relationship between them, but from a careful study of the Boston Records, I am able to give the following as the correct ancestry of Capt. John Langdon. The genealogy of the Langdon family, contained in the N. E. Gen'l Register, gives John (b. 1650) and Nathaniel (b. 1695) as his grand-

Mary (Walley) Langdon[17].

father and father. I am satisfied that this is incorrect, as the John Langdon that was a son of Nathaniel was born in 1747, while we know from his age at the time of his death, as given in Vol. XV, N. E. Register, p. 185, that Capt. John Langdon must have been born in 1745.

BENJAMIN LANGDON[1]. The date of his birth is unknown, but he was living in the "towne" of Boston as early as 1640. He was a soldier in King Phillip's War, being a member of Maj. Samuel Appleton's regiment, and was wounded Dec. 19, 1675, at the attack on the Indian fort at Narragansett (see Bridges' "History of King Phillip's War," p. 109, and Mass. Archives, Vol. LXVIII, p. 104). He married Phoebe ———— and had one child:

> JOHN LANGDON[2], b. May 20, 1678, who married Eliza-
> beth ———— and had three children, including:
>> *John Langdon*[3], b. Oct. 17, 1698. He m. Mary
>> ———— and had several children, including:
>>> Capt. John Langdon[4], b. Nov. 19, 1745, who
>>> m. Mary Walley, as hereinbefore stated.

With this preamble we proceed to the genealogy proper.

396. (395.) MARY (WALLEY) LANGDON[17] (*Mary [Kneeland] Walley*[16], *Samuel Kneeland*[15], *John*[14], *John*[13], *John*[12], *John*[11]—*Alexander*[1]). Only child of Thomas and Mary (Kneeland) Walley, and granddaughter of Samuel and Mary (Alden) Kneeland; b. at Boston, June 12, 1749; m. Capt. John Langdon, of Boston.

He served an apprenticeship with Wharton & Ives, booksellers, his fellow-apprentice being Henry Knox, afterwards Major-General in the patriot army. In 1770 he commenced business for himself on Cornhill, but relinquished it at the outbreak of the Revolution. He raised a company of volunteers which did active service under his command during the campaign in Rhode Island. After the war Capt. Langdon was appointed to a position in the Custom House in Boston, which he held until his death in 1793. They had nine children, as follows:

Mary (Walley) Langdon[17].

Children of Capt. John and Mary (Walley) Langdon.

397. (i.) JOHN WALLEY LANGDON[18], bapt. March 8, 1772; m. Rebecca Cordis, of Charlestown, Aug. 26, 1794. He was a successful merchant in the tea trade with the principal house in Boston and branch houses at Smyrna and New York. He personally carried on the Smyrna house and his brother, Thomas W., the New York house for many years. They had the following children (see Hunnewell's "History of Charlestown, Mass).

398.   (i.) *Rebecca Cordis Langdon[19]*, bapt. at Charlestown, Mass., April 25, 1795.

399.   (ii.) *Mary Frances Langdon[19]*, bapt. at Charlestown, Dec. 3, 1797.

400.   (iii.) *Joseph Langdon[19]*, bapt. at Charlestown, Sept. 15, 1799. He was a merchant and succeeded his father at Smyrna, Turkey, where he resided at the time of his father's death, in 1860. He had for many years had charge of the Smyrna branch of the tea house of Langdon Bros.

401.   (iv.) *May Haswell Langdon[19]*, bapt. at Charlestown, April 12, 1807.

402.   (v.) *Charlotte Elizabeth Langdon[19]*, bapt. at Charlestown, Aug. 28, 1808.

403.   (vi.) *Octavus Augustus Langdon[19]*, bapt. at Charlestown, Nov. 14, 1813.

404. (ii.) MARY LANGDON[18], bapt. July 18, 1873; m. Dr. William P. Greenwood (of whom hereafter, 412).

405. (iii.) ELIZABETH LANGDON[18], bapt. July 3, 1774; m. William Lovett, Esq., Nov. 22, 1795.

406. (iv.) ABIGAIL HARRIS LANGDON[18], b. in 1776; m. in 1799 to Giles Lodge, Esq., and was the mother of Giles Henry Lodge, who graduated at Harvard in 1825, translator of Wickelmann's "History of Ancient Art among the Greeks," and of an art novel from the German of Von Sternberg, entitled "The Bringhel Brothers."

407. (v.) SARAH LANGDON[18], bapt. April 12, 1778; m. Henry Atchison, Esq.

Mary (Langdon) Greenwood[18].

408. (vi.) ANNA HURD LANGDON[18], bapt. Sept. 2, 1781; m. August, 1817, to John Bellows, Esq., president of the Manufacturers' and Mechanics' Bank and the father, by a former wife, of Henry W. Bellows, D. D., of New York.

409. (vii.) THOMAS WALLEY LANGDON[18], bapt. Oct. 5, 1783; m. Aug. 31, 1833, Mrs. Jane Weaver Ross, only daughter of Dr. John Greenwood, of New York. He resided in Boston and had charge of the business of Langdon Bros., at that place, until the main office was removed to New York. He then located in New York and resided there until his death. He died without issue, Dec. 17, 1860. The probate of the will gives as next of kin the following descendants of Capt. John Langdon: Francis W. G. Bellows, New York; Mrs. Harriet Allen, New York; Charlotte, wife of Dr. Chapman, Roxbury, Mass.; Mary S., wife of Rev. Samuel Barrett, Roxbury, Mass.; Amelia, wife of Geo. Bartlett, Roxbury, Mass.; Emeline, wife of Chas. Hayward, Roxbury, Mass.; Charlotte A. L. Cook, wife of Samuel W. Cook, Cambridge, Mass.; Rev. Alfred Greenwood, Natlick, Mass.; Joseph Langdon, Smyrna, Turkey; Amelia, wife of Mr. Prince, Smyrna, Turkey.

410. (viii.) CATHARINE AMELIA LANGDON[18], bapt. Dec. 25, 1785.

411. (ix.) CHARLOTTE AUGUSTA LANGDON[18], bapt. Dec. 31, 1801; m. Samuel W. Cook, Esq., and resided in Cambridge.

412. (404.) MARY (LANGDON) GREENWOOD[18], (*Mary [Walley] Langdon*[17], *Mary [Kneeland] Walley*[16], *Samuel*[15], *John*[14], *John*[13], *John*[12], *John*[11]—*Alexander*[1]).

The above line of Mary's could be carried back on the mother's side still farther, as Mary Kneeland's mother was Mary Alden, and her grandmother Mary Alden.

Mary Langdon[18] was the eldest daughter of Capt. John

Mary (Langdon) Greenwood[18].

Langdon and Mary Walley, and was born in Boston, July 10, 1873. She was married at Boston, July 23, 1796, to Dr. William Pitt Greenwood. This couple being the head of a numerous and distinguished line of descendants, I give, from the "Genealogy of the Barrett Family," compiled by William Barrett, Esq., a brief sketch of their lives.

Dr. William Pitt Greenwood was born in Boston, May 10, 1766. He was the youngest of five sons of Isaac and Mary (Tans) Greenwood, and a grandson of Prof. Isaac Greenwood, of Harvard College. He received the degree of D. D. S. from the Baltimore College. "He was an intelligent, cultivated gentleman, genial and courteous in his manners, pleasant, entertaining and instructive in conversation, and his honesty and truthfulness were of the very highest standard." He died at Boston, May 10, 1851, on his eighty-fifth birthday. His wife, Mary (Langdon) Greenwood, survived him but a few years. She died June 5, 1855, aged eighty years. She "was in form and features a very handsome woman. She possessed remarkably sound judgment, as well as poetic imagination and ability, and was for years a valued contributor to many literary periodicals. She was a devoted member of the church (King's Chapel, Boston) over which for so many years her eldest son was the beloved pastor. She delighted in relieving the wants of the needy and distressed, and her piety and faith were only equalled by her generosity and benevolence. Her conversational powers were remarkable and her wit and humor unsurpassed by any woman of her time. During her long and happy married life she held weekly receptions at which were present many of the most literary, cultured and distinguished men and women of Boston." They had ten children, of whom nine arrived at the age of maturity, as follows;

Children of Dr. Wm. Pitt Greenwood and Mary Langdon.

413. (i.) MARY SUSAN GREENWOOD[19], b. at Boston, April 19, 1805 (of whom hereafter, 435).

414. (ii.) FRANCIS WM. PITT GREENWOOD, D. D.[19], b. at Boston, Feb. 5, 1797. He graduated from Harvard in the class of 1814; studied theology under the direction of Rev. Dr. Henry Ware, and was settled

Mary (Langdon) Greenwood[18].

as pastor over the New South Church and Society, in Boston. In 1824, he became the colleague of Rev. Dr. Freeman, pastor of King's Chapel, Boston. This relation continued until 1827, when Dr. Freeman retired and Dr. Greenwood succeeded to the full charge of that church and society and remained as pastor until his death in 1843. " Dr. Greenwood was a man of very scholarly tastes and high scientific and literary attainments, and was greatly beloved, not only by his church and society, but by a host of other friends. Of the many able and beloved pastors of King's Chapel, no one was the superior of Dr. Greenwood." His children living in 1865 were as follows:

416.   (i.) *Mary Greenwood*[20], m. James Lodge, Esq., of Boston.

417.   (ii.) *Alice S. Greenwood*[20], m. George Howe, of Boston.

418.   (iii.) *Augustus G. Greenwood*[20], of Boston.

419. (iii.) EDWIN LANGDON GREENWOOD[19]. He resided at Roxbury, Mass., and died there, unmarried and intestate, March 4, 1862.

420. (iv.) ALFRED GREENWOOD[19]. He resided at Natick, Mass. No record of his descendants.

421. (v.) CATHARINE AMELIA GREENWOOD[19]. She m. Dr. George Bartlett. He died prior to 1864, leaving issue:

422.   (i.) *William Pitt Greenwood Bartlett*[20], who resided at Cambridge, Mass.

423.   (ii.) *Alice A. Bartlett*[20], who resided in Boston, Mass.

424. (vi.) EMELINE GREENWOOD[19], m. Charles L. Hayward, of Roxbury. He died Aug. 28, 1890, leaving the following issue:

425.   (i.) *Gertrude Langdon Hayward*[20], of Boston.

426.   (ii.) *Charles Langdon Hayward*[20], of Boston.

427.   (iii.) *William Pitt Greenwood Hayward*[20], Denver, Colorado.

428.   (iv.) *George Hayward*[20], of Boston.

429.   (v.) *Langdon Hayward*[20], of Boston.

Mary Susan Greenwood[19].

430. (vii.) ANGELINA GREENWOOD[19], m. Henry Warren, of New York. Their issue living in 1865 was as follows:

431. (i.) *Mary Winslow Warren[20]*, of New York.

432. (ii.) *Emma Greenwood Warren[20]*, of New York.

433. (iii.) *Angelina Langdon Warren[20]*, of New York.

434. (iv.) *Henry Warren[20]*, of New Mexico.

435. (413.) MARY SUSAN GREENWOOD[19] (*Mary Langdon[18], Mary Walley[17], Mary Kneeland[16], Samuel[15], John[14], John[13], John[12], John[11]—Alexander[1]*).
Counting the two successive Mary Aldens, this is the sixth in succession of Marys, her daughter, Mary Greenwood Barrett, being the seventh and her granddaughter, Mary Langdon Coffin, being the eighth, a concious tribute to Mary Langdon and an unconscious one to Mary Alden, the direct descendant of John Alden and Priscilla Mullens. She was the daughter of Dr. William Pitt Greenwood and Mary Langdon, born at Boston, April 19, 1805. She married Rev. Dr. Samuel Barrett, Sept. 11, 1832, the ceremony taking place at King's Chapel and administered by her brother, Rev. Dr. Francis William Pitt Greenwood, the pastor. Her husband, Rev. Samuel Barrett, D. D., was born in Royalston, Mass., August 11, 1795, being the eldest son of Major Benjamin Fiske Barrett. He graduated at Harvard in the class of 1818, and from the Divinity School of Harvard in the class of 1822. After a number of minor appointments he was ordained as the first minister of the Twelfth Congregational Society in the city of Boston, a part of which he held until 1858. He died at Roxbury, June 24, 1866.

Strong, brilliant and noble was the character and life-work of Dr. Barrett, but his consort, Mary Susan Greenwood, was in every way a fit companion in all his labors. Her daughter, Mrs. Chandler, in a letter to the compiler of the Barrett Genealogy, thus describes her: " It seems almost an impossibility for me to write anything that would do justice to my mother's life, her character being the most perfect one I have ever known. She was truly a noble woman—such a one as is seldom seen, but when once seen and known as we know her, can never be forgotten. Her intellectual qualities were very superior and had been carefully nurtured and trained; her tastes were refined and delicate; her range of reading was broad, elevating and pure; her love for and knowledge of music was very remarkable, and no one who has ever listened to the sweetness and pathos of her voice in singing will ever forget it. She was for two years the soprano singer in a voluntary choir in King's Chapel during the time her brother, Dr. Greenwood, was pastor. * * * To me she was and ever will be the one lovely and perfect woman, my beloved mother." She died at Roxbury, March 10, 1874, aged 68 years.

Children of Dr. Samuel Barrett and Mary Susan Greenwood.

436. (i.) MARY GREENWOOD BARRETT[20], b. June 15, 1833; m. at Roxbury, Oct. 13, 1864, to Henry Peleg Coffin, son of George Washington and Mary Winthrop (Spooner) Coffin, of Boston. They reside in Boston, where he is in the insurance business. They had one child:

437. *Mary Langdon Coffin*[21], b. in Boston, July 4, 1867.

438. (ii.) FRANCES LANGDON BARRETT[20], b. Dec. 27, 1834; m. in Boston, Oct. 19, 1858, to Henry Richmond Chandler, son of Samuel Ward and Elizabeth (Richmond) Chandler. He is a banker and broker in Boston. They had two children:

439. (i.) *Barrett Langdon Chandler*[21], b. at Nashville, Tenn., July 16, 1861; graduated at the Institute of Technology, Boston, in 1883, and is an expert chemist for Valentine & Co., manufacturers of varnishes, in New York City. He is unmarried.

440. (ii.) *Grace Greenwood Chandler*[21], b. at Roxbury, Mass., Oct. 10, 1864. She resides with her parents in Roxbury, Mass.

441. (iii.) GEORGE SAMUEL BARRETT[20], b. Sept. 5, 1836. He resides in Boston and is an accountant; unmarried.

Mary Susan Greenwood[19].

442. (iv.) CHARLES HENRY BARRETT[20], b. Sept. 9, 1838. He is a civil engineer and resides in San Francisco, Cal; unmarried.

443. (v.) ELLEN MARIA BARRETT[20], b. Jan. 10, 1841. She is unmarried and resides in Boston, Mass.

444. (vi.) GRACE CLEVELAND BARRETT[20], b. Dec. 15, 1844; m. Nov. 14, 1872, to Henry Chamberlain Valentine. He was born in Cambridge, Mass., April 21, 1830, and is president of Valentine & Co., manufacturers of varnishes in New York, and treasurer of the John Stephenson Co., Limited. They reside in New York City, and have two children:

445. (i.) *Langdon Barrett Valentine[21]*, b. at Spuyten Duyvil, N. Y., Oct. 12, 1873.

446. (ii.) *Susie Valentine[21]*, b. at Yonkers, N. Y., August 16, 1875.

447. (vii.) FRANCIS GREENWOOD BARRETT[20], b. July 7, 1848; m. Mary Louise Morris, and resides in Boston. She was born in New York. They have one child:

448. *Lewis Francis Barrett[21]*, b. Dec. 24, 1880.

449. (viii.) ARTHUR WILLIAM BARRETT[20], b. Nov. 24, 1857; d. at Thompsonville, Ga., Feb. 16, 1880, without issue.

CHAPTER IX.

EDWARD KNEELAND OF MAINE.

(NOS. 450 TO 557.)

450. (370.) EDWARD KNEELAND[17] (*John*[16], *Samuel*[15], *John*[14], *John*[13], *John*[12], *John*[11], *William*[10], *James*[9], *Alexander*[8], *William*[7], *William*[6], *John*[5], *John*[4], *John*[3], *James*[2], *Alexander*[1]). Youngest son of John and Abigail (Phillips) Kneeland and grandson of Samuel Kneeland and Mary Alden, was born at Boston, February 2, 1775.

He was left an orphan before he reached his first birthday. He became acquainted with Hon. Robert Hichborn, of Boston, when about ten years of age. This acquaintance probably came about through his grandfather, Samuel Kneeland, having some forty years before secured a settlement for the Hichborn family of their claims against the Government for the services of their ancestor in King Phillips' War. However that may be, it is true that young Kneeland was practically adopted by Mr. Hichborn and brought up at his home in what was then Prospect, Mass., (now Stockton Springs, Me.) where Mr. Hichborn had purchased an extensive property on Cape Jellison, near Fort Point, where is now located the summer hotel—" Woodcliffe "—and numerous cottages belonging to the summer residents. Left in straitened circumstances at his father's death and the attainment of his majority finding him in what was then a new and undeveloped section of the country, he became one of the pioneers of that region, settling upon a tract of public land a short distance from the residence of Mr. Hichborn. There are still standing on this property a house and stable built by Edward Kneeland during the early part of the present century. They were quite pretentious in their day but are now fast going to decay. They are located on the southern end of Cape Jellison, at the extreme northern end of Penobscot Bay and near the mouth of the Penobscot River (which takes its name from the Indian tribe of that name). It was here that Edward brought his wife, reared his family and died July 27, 1849. Edward Kneeland married Mary Staples of Prospect, Dec. 8, 1803. She was born Feb. 10, 1783 ; died April 20, 1874. They had eleven children.

Children of Edward and Mary (Staples) Kneeland.

451. (i.) EDWARD[18], b. Sept. 13, 1804 (of whom hereafter, 486).
452. (ii.) HENRY HICHBORN[18], b. July 7, 1806 (of whom hereafter, 508).
453. (iii.) ZINA[18], b. June 19, 1808 ; d. Sept. 23, 1830.
454. (iv.) CLARISSA[18], b. Oct. 21, 1810; m. Sept. 21, 1833, to Alfred Ridley, of Prospect ; d. Sept. 25, 1880.
455. (v.) JAMES S.[18], b. Jan. 20, 1813. He was a sea captain and was in command of a brigantine when he met his death by drowning in the Schuylkill River at Philadelphia, July 30, 1840. Married Caroline Clifford, of Prospect, by whom he had one child :
456.   *Mary S.[19]*, b. Oct. 25, 1840. She married June 26, 1863, Christopher Ridley, of Prospect, where she now resides. They have five children :
457.   (i.) Carrie E. Ridley[20], b. Aug. 4, 1866.
458.   (ii.) Nettie M.[20], b. Feb. 28, 1870.
459.   (iii.) Clara E.[20], b. Feb. 28, 1872.
460.   (iv.) Alfred C.[20], b. April 13, 1876.
461.   (v.) George C.[20], b. July 1, 1879.
462. (vi.) MARY[18], b. March 22, 1815; m. Nov. 9, 1835, to Dudley Gilman, of Prospect, where she still resides. They had three children :
463.   *Clarayette Gilman[19]*, b. Sept. 24, 1836; d. April 7, 1873.
464.   *Alvin Gilman[19]*, b. June 30, 1838 ; d. Oct. 20, 1879.
465.   *Dorinda A. Gilman[19]*, b. Dec. 24, 1840; m. William Richardson.

Edward Kneeland[11].

466. (vii.) ANDREW JACKSON[18], b. May 3, 1817; d. Oct. 30, 1825.

467. (viii.) WILLIAM[18], b. July 30, 1819 (of whom hereafter, 528).

468. (ix.) SARAH A.[18], b. March 31, 1822; m. Nov. 20, 1845, Miles Staples of Prospect; d. April 7, 1880. They had seven children:

469. (i.) *Madeline A. Staples*[19], b. Nov. 4, 1847; d. Sept. 6, 1849.

470. (ii.) *Ella I. Staples*[19], b. Nov. 3, 1850.

471. (iii.) *Agnes R. Staples*[19], b. July 12, 1854; d. May 30, 1883.

472. (iv.) *Ida M. Staples*[19], b. June 10, 1856.

473. (v.) *Oakes A. Staples*[19], b. May 25, 1860.

474. (vi.) *Electa S. Staples*[19], b. June 19, 1867.

475. (vii.) *Livia A. Staples*[19], b. March 12, 1868; d. June 5, 1880.

476. (x.) ELIZA[18], b. Jan. 17, 1825; m. Oct. 31, 1846, Capt. Jason W. Marden, of Prospect; d. in Astoria, Oregon, Jan. 29, 1884. They had eight children who live in Astoria, Oregon:

477. (i.) *Robert E. Marden*[19], b. Sept. 3, 1848; resides at Montesano, Washington.

478. (ii.) *Mary E. Marden*[19], b. Oct. 3, 1850; d. Nov. 29, 1886.

479. (iii.) *Albert S. Marden*[19], b. April 7, 1852; d. Sept., 1875.

480. (iv.) *Henry H. Marden*[19], b. July 29, 1854; resides at Victoria, British Columbia.

481. (v.) *George M. Marden*[19], b. March 17, 1864; d. July, 1886.

482. (vi.) *Fred Marden*[19], b. April 18, 1866; resides at Ilwaco, Washington.

483. (vii.) *Frank Marden*[19], (Twin of Fred) b. April 18, 1866; d. at Ilwaco, Washington, Feb. 27, 1892.

484. (viii.) *Horace S. Marden*[19], b. Dec. 15, 1869; d. Sept., 1877.

485. (xi.) NANCY[18], b. July 9, 1827; now living in Prospect, unmarried.

Edward Kneeland[18].

486. (451.) EDWARD KNEELAND[18] (*Edward*[17], *Samuel*[16], *John*[15], *John*[14], *John*[13], *John*[12], *John*[11],— *Alexander*[1]). Eldest son of Edward and Mary (Staples) Kneeland, born at Prospect, Mass., Feb. 10, 1783.

He spent the early part of his life on his father's farm on Cape Jellison. While a young man he, in company with his brother Henry, bought a tract of wild land in what is now Searsport, which they cleared and improved. After a few years he sold his interest to his brother and bought a tract of land of his father, in that part of what is now Stockton Springs, called Sandy Point, where he settled and spent the remainder of his life. Never of robust health, he outlived all his brothers, dying at his home June 15, 1880. He married (1) Abigail Cousens, May 1, 1828. She died Aug. 29. 1838; (2) Charlotte Black, Oct. 11, 1839. She died Aug. 5, 1865; (3) Mrs. Jane Carlisle, who survives him.

Children of Edward and Abigail (Cousens) Kneeland.

487. (i.) ANDREW J.[19], b. March 26, 1829; drowned Oct. 26, 1847.

488. (ii.) ELIZA A.[19], b. April 14, 1831; m. John M. Morin, Aug. 19, 1854. He died Feb. 22, 1887. They had five children:

489.   (i.) *Elden M. Morin*[20], b. June 14, 1855.

490.   (ii.) *E. Maria Morin*[20], b. Aug 13, 1857.

491.   (iii.) *Abigail C. Morin*[20], b. May 13, 1859.

492.   (iv.) *Califonia Morin*[20], b. July 8, 1868.

493.   (v.) *Herbert Henry Morin*[20], b. April 12, 1872.

495. (iii.) REBECCA A.[19], b. Oct. 4, 1833; m. March 15, 1856, Sewall W. Ginn. They had five children:

496.   (i.) *Edward S. Ginn*[20], b. Aug. 16, 1857; d. when three weeks old.

497.   (ii.) *Lottie Ginn*[20], b. Aug. 5, 1858; d. Oct. 19, 1869.

498.   (iii.) *Hattie J. Ginn*[20], b. Oct. 18, 1859.

499.   (iv.) *Sewall Ginn*[20], b. Nov. 18, 1860.

500.   (v.) *Susie W. Ginn*[20], b. April 5, 1862; d. July 3, 1884.

501. (iv.) MARY M.[19], b. Aug. 25, 1835; d. Oct. 2, 1839.

Children of Edward and Charlotte (Black) Kneeland.

502. (v.) JAMES O.[19], b. July 20, 1843; married (1) Orrissa
        Billado, March 2, 1870. She d. March 20, 1881;
        married (2) Caroline George. Had four children by
        first wife:

503. (i.) *Luther Adelbert*[20], b. Aug. 10, 1870.

504. (ii.) *Daughter*[20], b. in 1872; d. in infancy.

505. (iii.) *Hattie Lillian*[20], b. April 13, 1874; resides in
        Lewiston, Me.

506. (iv.) *Lottie May*[20], b. May 14, 1876; resides at
        Stockton Springs.

507. (vi.) JOHN C.[19], b. Aug., 1846; d. when three weeks old.

There were no children by the third marriage.

508. HENRY HICHBORN KNEELAND[18] (*Edward*[17]
        John[16], *Samuel*[15], *John*[14], *John*[13], *John*[12], *John*[11]
        —*Alexander*[1]). Second son of Edward and Mary
        (Staples) Kneeland, was born and reared on Cape
        Jellison.

A few years after he became of age, he and his brother,
Edward, purchased from the holders of the original patents,
Messrs. Montgomery & Sears, of Boston (it is from the last-
mentioned that the present town of Searsport takes its name),
a three hundred acre tract of land which was then covered
with the primeval forest, and set about to clear and improve
the same. Its location was then an unbroken wilderness,
several miles from even the semblance of a road, which made
it necessary for them to "swamp out" a rough wood road for
the bringing in of supplies, etc. During the first few years
their home was a log cabin, but with the advance of time they
caused the wilderness to disappear and the land to become
fruitful, so that after a while the log house was succeeded by
a comfortable farm house and, later on, one of still greater
pretentions took its place. After a time Henry bought his
brother's interest in their joint property and continued in the
occupation of a farmer and lumberman up to the time of his
death, on October 7, 1860. He and his brothers and sisters

were the great-grandchildren of Samuel Kneeland, Esq., the celebrated Boston publisher, by his wife, Mary Alden, and direct descendants of "John Alden and Priscilla."

Henry Hichborn Kneeland married Harriet Hichborn Rendell, of Prospect, October 20, 1828. She was born May 18, 1807. Her grandfather, John Rendell, came to America from a small town near London, England, about 1750, settling first in Salem, then in Bristol, Mass., and later, after losing most of his property through the medium of "accommodation" paper (all of which he redeemed, however), on what is known as Owl's Head, near Rockland, Me., where he purchased a 400 acre tract of land. During the Revolution he was taken from his bed at night by an English press-gang and taken on board a British man-of-war to act as pilot, he being well acquainted with the adjacent waters. He never returned. The British claimed that he was *lost* overboard off Monhegan and drowned. It was the general belief, however, that upon his refusing to take the vessel where the English commander wished most, to intimidate the inhabitants he was *thrown* overboard. His granddaughter, although a mere child at the time, well remembered the visit of the "redcoats" to Castine and Cape Jellison during the war of 1812-14, and took great delight in relating the circumstances to her grandchildren up to the time of her death, on April 10, 1896. They had ten children:

Children of Henry Hichborn and Harriet Hichborn (Rendell) Kneeland.

509. (i.) MARY R.[19], b. May 4, 1830; m. June 15, 1856, Wm. Kendall, of Fairfield, Me. He died at sea, of yellow fever, Sept. 2, 1862. Previous to her marriage Mrs. Kendall had been a school teacher, and upon her husband's death she took up her former occupation and has followed it continuously ever since, being at the present time one of the veteran school teachers of New England. Mr. and Mrs. Kendall had one child:

510.   *Fred L. Kendall*[20], b. Sept. 25, 1859. As a young
        man he followed the sea for several years,
        visiting all parts of the world. Beginning in
        the fo'c'sle, he advanced to an officer's position
        on different "deep water" craft, but when well
        on the way to the goal of every *American*
        sailor's ambition—a vessel of his own—he con-
        cluded that he had enough of the sea and would
        prefer spending his life on shore. He married
        Ida M. Chase, of Searsport, Me., January 12,
        1884. They reside at 12 Holden St., Dor-
        chester, Mass.

511.   (ii.) HARRIET H.[19], b. Jan. 7, 1832; lived in Massa-
        chusetts several years prior to her marriage. Mar-
        ried, July 15, 1868, at Holliston, Mass., to Isaac C.
        Closson. Mr. Closson was engaged in active busi-
        ness in Maine and Massachusetts for many years,
        but is now retired, residing with his wife at Sears-
        port, Me.

512.   (iii.) CLEMENTINE A.[19], b. July 3, 1833; m. Feb. 13,
        1871, Alfred Closson, of Searsport. He was cap-
        tain of various vessels engaged in the domestic
        trade, and was drowned in New York harbor, Dec.
        1, 1894. They had one daughter:

513.   *Carrie G. Closson*[20], b. April 7, 1873. She is a
        teacher in the public schools at North Sears-
        port, Me., where she and her mother reside.

514.   (iv.) NANCY J.[19], b. March 31, 1835; m. in Sept., 1862,
        Albert S. Nichols, of Searsport. She died April
        26, 1880. He died July 13, 1880. They had one
        daughter:

515.   *Sarah Annette Nichols*[20], b. July 15, 1863; m. June
        25, 1889, Otis Stewart Chessman, of Pittsburgh.
        The Chessmans were originally a New Hamp-
        shire family, Mr. Chessman's grandfather having
        emigrated to Western Pennsylvania during the
        early part of the present century. They have
        a family record which, it is claimed, can be
        traced back to the time of William the Con-

queror. They reside at Etna, Pa., and have one daughter:

516.   Ethel Nichols Chessman[21], b. Jan. 5, 1893.
517. (v.) CAROLINE[19], b. Dec. 3, 1839; married (1) Dexter Gray, of Paris, Me., Aug. 27, 1862; they had one child, who died in infancy. Mr. Gray died in June, 1868. Married (2) Daniel R. Stevenson, of Hampden, Me., Jan. 24, 1874. Mr. Stevenson died March 9, 1895. They had three children:
518.   (i.) *Daniel E. Stevenson*[20], b. June 11, 1879.
519.   (ii.) *William M. Stevenson*[20], b. April 6, 1882.
520.   (iii.) *Herbert L. Stevenson*[20], b. Jan. 24, 1886.
        Mrs. Stevenson lives in Orrington, Me.
521. (vi.) TWIN OF CAROLINE[19], b. Dec. 3, 1839; d. in infancy.
522. (vii.) JAMES HENRY[19], b. March 19, 1843 (of whom hereafter, 546).
523. (viii.) MILTON[19], b. Oct. 15, 1844 (of whom hereafter, 552).
524. (ix.) FRANK E.[19], b. Oct. 27, 1850; drowned in the Penobscot River, Bangor, Me., May 11, 1871.
525. (x.) ORRIE ELLEN[19], b. Sept. 21, 1852; m. Aug. 2, 1880, Capt. Wilton T. Randell, of Stockton, Me. He was lost overboard off Scotland Lightship, New York, Nov. 20, 1886, being in command of the barquentine "Henry L. Gregg" at the time. They had two children:
526.   (i.) *Clifford B. Randell*[20], b. Sept. 20, 1881.
527.   (ii.) *Alice Lillian Randell*[20], b. Jan. 9, 1886.

528. (467.) WILLIAM KNEELAND[18] (*Edward*[17], *Samuel*[16], *John*[15], *John*[14], *John*[13], *John*[12], *John*[11]— *Alexander*[1]). Eighth child of Edward and Abigail (Phillips) Kneeland, b. July 30, 1819.

He spent his boyhood on his father's farm, but began going to sea the year after he became of age. After following the sea for several years he bought a farm on Cape Jellison, spending his summers at home and going to sea winters, for ten or twelve years, most of his voyages being to the West

ETHEL NICHOLS CHESSMAN
No. 516

SARAH A. N. CHESSMAN   OTIS S. CHESSMAN
No. 515

NANCY J. (KNEELAND) NICHOLS

Indies and South America. At the end of this time he was shipwrecked on Nantucket Shoals and for a considerable length of time thereafter the sea had no charms for him. Later in life he owned and sailed the schooners "T. M. Richardson" and "The Eagle," chiefly in the domestic trade. He died at his home on Cape Jellison, Oct. 23, 1870. William Kneeland married Nancy H. Grant, of Prospect, Oct. 30, 1845. She was born March 19, 1826, and now resides in Stockton Springs, Me. They had nine children:

Children of William and Nancy N. (Grant) Kneeland.

529. (i.) WILSON G.[19], b. Dec. 1, 1848, "Master Mariner," at present captain of the schooner "John C. Smith," of Belfast. His home is in Medford, Mass., where his family resides. He married Nellie M. Macomber, Feb. 12, 1870. They had two children:

530. (i.) *Percy L.*[20], b. Aug. 28, 1871; d. Jan. 30, 1892.
531. (ii.) *Harold M.*[20], b. Sept. 7, 1876; resides at Medford, Mass.

532. (ii.) LINDLEY M.[19], b. Jan. 11, 1851; m. Dec. 11, 1875, Mary A. Eaton; resides in Searsport, Me. They had four children:

533. (i. and ii.) *Two Boys*[20], d. in infancy.
534. (iii.) *Hattie May*[20], b. July 15, 1881.
535. (iv.) *Eugenie L.*[20], b. Feb. 3, 1891.

536. (iii.) ALDANA[19], b. Nov. 25, 1852; m. Edwin C. Berry, of Stockton, Feb. 11, 1872, where they still reside.

537. (iv.) CLARA J.[19], b. July 19, 1854; m. Loren Ginn, July 18, 1886. They reside in Boston.

538. (v.) LIZZIE S.[19], b. Nov. 24, 1856; d. Oct. 23, 1870.

539. (vi.) ANNIE M.[19], b. Nov. 15, 1858; m. William C. Shute, of Stockton, Jan. 5, 1878. They reside at Port Madison, Washington.

540. (vii.) CHARLES[19], b. Sept. 5, 1862; m. Nellie H. Marden, of Stockton, April 14, 1888. They reside in Stockton Springs, and have two children:

541. (i.) *Marion W.*[20], b. Feb. 27, 1889.
542. (ii.) *Percy L.*[20], b. Oct. 13, 1894.

543. (viii.) HIRAM G.[19], b. April 28, 1864; d. Feb. 6, 1866.

James Henry Kneeland[19].

544. (ix.) EDWIN S.[19], b. March 6, 1869. Removed to Massachusetts in 1886 and has since followed a business life, with the exception of one year spent in attending the Bryant & Stratton Commercial School, at Boston. He is now head bookkeeper for the firm of A. W. Hurd & Co., at Lynn, Mass., and resides in Swampscott. He married Mamie E. Alburn, Aug. 12, 1891. They have one child:

545. *Blanche G.*[20], b. Oct. 18, 1892.

546. (522.) JAMES HENRY KNEELAND[19], *Henry*[18], *Edward*[17], *Samuel*[16], *John*[15], *John*[14], *John*[13], *John*[12], *John*[11]—*Alexander*[1]). Seventh child of Henry H. Kneeland, b. March 19, 1843.

He spent the early part of his life on his father's farm in Searsport (which was set off from the town of Prospect in 1845) and his father dying when he was but 17 years of age, he was left to care for the same with the aid of his younger brother. When 19 years of age he enlisted for service in the Civil War, being a member of Company K, Twenty-sixth Maine Volunteers. His term of service was spent in various parts of Virginia. Upon receiving his discharge from the army at the expiration of the time for which he enlisted, he returned to Searsport in extremely poor health, but home care and treatment having restored him somewhat and having conceived a desire to follow the sea (presumably a trait inherited from his ancestors) he celebrated his twenty-first birthday by shipping on board the barque "Evelyn," Capt. Henry A. Hichborn, for Cienfuegos, Cuba. One voyage, however, was enough to cure his longings in this direction (possibly aided by a fall from the royal-yard and a timely rescue in mid-air by a shipmate) and upon the vessel's return to Boston he returned home, caring for his mother's estate summers and teaching school winters until 1867, when he married and purchased a farm of his own. He continued in this occupation until 1875, when he went into the grocery and farm produce business, in which he has since continued, handling large quanities of eggs, poultry, wool, etc., for the Boston market. Has held various

JAMES H. KNEELAND
No. 546

HERBERT A. KNEELAND   FRANK E. KNEELAND
No. 549   No. 548

KATHARINE M. KNEELAND   I. RALPH KNEELAND
No. 550

HENRY W. KNEELAND
No. 551

town offices and was elected to the State Legislature in the avalanche of 1896, when " Maine went " as she did in the days of " Governor Kent," to the great satisfaction of a majority of our clan and of the country. James Henry Kneeland married Amanda H. Crockett, of Stockton, Me., March 23, 1867. She was born May 6, 1849. They reside in Searsport, and have four children :

Children of James Henry and Amanda H. (Crockett) Kneeland.

548. (i.) FRANK E.[20], b. July 27, 1870. It is to him that I am indebted for the genealogy of Edward Kneeland[16] and his descendants. He lived in Searsport until 1887. Since then he has been in mercantile business and resided in Boston, New York and the South. He now resides in Boston and has rendered most efficient work there for this book.

549. (ii.) HERBERT ALBION[20], b. May 26, 1873. He lived in Searsport until 1891 and has since resided in Portland and Boston, where he is now engaged in the insurance business with John C. Paige.

550. (iii.) KATHERINE M.[20], b. April 26, 1875. Fitted for teaching at the State Normal School, at Gorham, Me., where she graduated in 1893, and is now a teacher in the public schools at Searsport, Me.

551. (iv.) HENRY WILTON[20], b. Sept. 29, 1882. Now attending the Searsport High School.

552. (523.) MILTON KNEELAND[19] (*Henry H.*[18], *Edward*[17], *Samuel*[16], *John*[15], *John*[14], *John*[13], *John*[12], *John*[11]—*Alexander*[1]). Eighth child of Henry H. Kneeland, b. Oct. 15, 1844.

He spent his boyhood on his father's farm in Searsport, and in company with his elder brother, managed and carried on the same for several years after his father's death. He was a member of Company K., First Maine Volunteers, during the "late unpleasantness," after which he married and lived in Searsport until 1879, when he became attracted to the

Milton Kneeland[19].

"Garden of Maine," and moved to Presque Isle, in the northern part of the State. He resided there with his family until 1888 when, ill-health having incapacitated him for active work, he disposed of his property and returned to his native town, where he still resides, now greatly improved in health. Milton Kneeland married Sarah E. Hamilton, of Searsport, June 9, 1866. She was born July 28, 1848. They had five children:

553.   (i.) EUGENE M.[20], b. June 21, 1868. He lived in Searsport and Presque Isle, Me., until 1888, after which he spent several years in the watchmaking business in Waltham, Mass. He is now a jeweler and optician in Boston.

554.   (ii.) JOSIAH[20], b. Dec. 3, 1870; d. May 16, 1875.

555.   (iii.) EMILY F.[20], b. April 30, 1877. Now resides with her parents at Searsport.

556.   (iv.) CHARLES B.[20], b. June 29, 1882 d. Sept. 16, 1883.

557.   (v.) RAY E.[20], b. Oct. 21, 1886. Now attending school at Searsport.

CHAPTER X.

THE BOSTON FAMILIES.

(NOS. 558 TO 595.)

558. (364.) JOHN KNEELAND[17] (*John*[16], *Samuel*[15], *John*[14], *John*[13], *John*[12], *John*[11], *William*[10], *James*[9], *Alexander*[8], *William*[7], *William*[6], *John*[5], *John*[4], *John*[3], *James*[2], *Alexander*[1]). Eldest son of John and Abigail (Phillips) Kneeland, and grandson of Samuel and Mary (Alden) Kneeland, b. at Boston, June 10, 1757 (see Boston Records); m. Mary Adams.

The census of householders of Boston, taken 1790, gives his family as follows: "Heads of family, 2; girls under sixteen, 3; males, including head of family, 4." This corresponds with my record of children, received from a private source—Bible entries. He was described as "Brazier" in Boston deeds.

Children of John and Mary Kneeland.

559.   (i.) JOHN[18], b. May 1, 1777; m. Sarah Abbot. Children:
559A.   (i.) *John*[19], d. prior to 1857; unmarried.
560.   (ii.) *Henry*[19], d. in 1857; unmarried.
561.   (iii.) *Warren*[19], was adopted by Phillip Richardson and took his name. Children:
562.   (i.) Mary Olivia Richardson[20].
563.   (ii.) Susan White Richardson[20].
564.   (iii.) Phillip Henry Richardson[20].
565.   (iv.) Ebenezer Fox Richardson[20].
566.   (v.) John Warren Richardson[20].
                They were living in Marblehead, Mass., in 1857.
567.   (ii.) CHARLES[18], b. January, 1780.
568.   (iii.) KATHARINE[18], b. Dec. 6. 1783.

Martin Kneeland[18].

569. (iv.) MARY[18], b. March 17, 1786; d. Jan. 10, 1819, æ. 33; unmarried.

570. (v.) SARAH[18], b. Oct. 11, 1787.

571. (vi.) MARTIN[18], b. Sept. 6, 1789 (of whom hereafter, 572).

572. (571.) MARTIN KNEELAND[18] (*John[17]*, *John[16]*, *Samuel[15]*, *John[14]*, *John[13]*, *John[12]*, *John[11]—Alexander[1]*). Youngest son of John and Abigail (Phillips) Kneeland and great-grandson of Samuel and Mary (Alden) Kneeland, b. at Boston, Sept. 6, 1789; m. Mary Abbott, April 7, 1807.

He was a brass founder and coppersmith, succeeding, probably, to his father's business. Among other extensive contracts performed by him was the copper work on the Boston Lighthouse, which stands on "The Brewster's" Island, at the outer entrance to Boston Harbor.

Children of Martin and Mary (Abbott) Kneeland.

573. (i.) MARY[19], b. at Boston, Feb. 7, 1808; m. John B. Glover, "gentleman," of Boston. We have no further record except that he was, in 1847, appointed guardian to his brother's—Sylvanus'—children.

574. (ii.) SYLVANUS[19], b. at Boston, Dec. 15, 1809. He is described as "gentleman" in the records, from which I assume he had no particular occupation. He m. Elizabeth Church Reed, Nov. 15, 1835 (see Boston Records). She was the daughter of George Reed, familiar to the old Bostonians under the name of "Old George" Reed. He was for thirty-six years constable of Boston, and quite a noted character. Her mother was a Church, being a descendant of the Churchs of Colonial fame. She died prior to 1847. The Boston Probate Records of that year contain the appointment of John B. Glover, their "uncle by marriage," as guardian for the infant children of "Sylvanus Kneeland, of Boston, gentleman." The application was made by the following relatives: George Reed, Sarah Ann Fullick, Susan

Martin Kneeland[18].

(Reed) Kendall, Elizabeth Church Reed Gleason. John B. Glover certifies that there had come to his possession, $201, received of "Thomas Holden, executor of the will of George Reed, deceased, the grandfather of the minors within named." Sylvanus died in September, 1888. She died in 1852. They had three children:

575. (i.) *Sylvanus R.*[20], b. Aug. 30, 1834. He is in business in Boston under the style of The Kneeland Reflector Company, his business being the manufacture and sale of a patent device for intensifying the power of electric and other lights. Married Mary J. Sutton in 1858. They have three children:

576. (i.) Sylvanus Reed[21], b. July 5, 1859. He is engaged in the insurance business in Somerville, Mass. Was married, May 20, 1884, to Mary A. Berry, of Charlestown, Mass. They have two children:

577. (i.) *William I.*[22], b. March 17, 1885.
578. (ii.) *Sylvanus Roy*[22], b. Nov. 21, 1890.
579. (ii.) William B.[21], b. Aug. 21, 1861. His business is that of a traveling freight agent, with headquarters at 201 Washington St., Boston. He married Florence E. Briggs, of Adams, Mass., Nov. 24, 1884. They have no children.
580. (iii.) Elizabeth C.[21], b. March 4, 1863; d. Dec. 20, 1863.

581. (ii.) *Benjamin Church Reed*[20], b. Nov. 9, 1836. Learned and followed the trade of a machinist in early manhood. Was afterward in the steam and gas fitting business in Boston and Brockton for twenty years, and during the last twenty years has been in charge of the steam and gas fitting and gas heating department of the Walworth Manufacturing Co., of Boston. Married Melina I. Rendall, Nov., 1864. They had two children:

Samuel Kneeland[11].

582. (i.) Henry Church[21], b. Dec, 22, 1865.
583. (ii.) Daisy I.[21], b. March 17, 1870; m. Andrew Hull, in 1891.
584. (iii.) *William B.*[20], b. October 26, 1838. He is engaged in the plumbing business at North Cambridge, Mass. Was married, June 22, 1869, to Ellen M. Webber. They have no children.
585. (iii.) WILLIAM[19], died in boyhood.
586. (iv.) MARTIN[19], b. May 10, 1812; d. Jan. 12, 1852; married, and had two children, a son and a daughter, but have no further record.

587. (359.) SAMUEL KNEELAND[17](*Samuel*[16], *Samuel*[15], *John*[14], *John*[13], *John*[12], *John*[11]—*Alexander*[1]). Youngest son of Samuel and Mary (Waters) Kneeland and grandson of Samuel and Mary (Alden) Kneeland, was born in Boston, May 10, 1748.

He was a posthumous child, his father having died two months before his birth. His mother died soon after, leaving him an orphan. Not much is known of his history. Like his father, he died young, at the age of 51, and his wife died two years earlier. Her first name was Hannah; I have not been able to secure her surname. He enlisted at Boston in 1778, and served with distinction. After the close of the war he settled in Scituate, Mass., and remained there until his death, in 1796. He had three children, and possibly more. Those we have record of, are:

588. (i.) SAMUEL[18], b. at Scituate, Oct. 10, 1785. He was living at the time of his father's death in 1789. No record of him since.
589. (ii.) HANNAH[18], b. at Scituate, Nov. 10, 1789.
590. (iii.) JOSHUA[18], b. Jan. 14, 1792. He resided there until after his father's death in 1799, and then went to Braintree, Mass. From there he went to Quincy, where he was apprenticed to a tanner. After arriving at full age he went into business of tanning at Plymouth, Mass., where he resided for the remainder of his life. He married Harriet

Harlow, daughter of James and Hannah (Bagnall)
Harlow, Dec. 24, 1820. She was born March 4,
1794, and died Nov. 15, 1876. He died Nov. 15,·
1878. Her genealogy runs back on her father's
side to William Harlow, who came to Plymouth
in 1643: and on her mother's side to Richard
Warren, of the Mayflower. It will be noted, therefore, that the descendants of Joshua Kneeland are
lineally descended from John Alden and Priscilla,
of the Mayflower, on the male side, and from
Richard Warren, of the same ship, on the female
side. They had one child only:

591.   *John Kneeland*[19], b. in Plymouth, Mass., Nov. 25,
1821 (of whom hereafter, 592).

592. (591.) JOHN KNEELAND[19] (*Joshua*[18], *Samuel*[17],
Samuel[16], *Samuel*[15], *John*[14], *John*[13], *John*[12],
John[11]—*Alexander*[1]). Only son of Joshua and
Harriet (Harlow) Kneeland, b. in Plymouth, Mass.,
Nov. 25, 1821.

At the age of seventeen he commenced teaching school
at Plymouth, where he had previously acquired a common
and High School education, and from that time during his
entire life he was connected in some form with educational
matters. For thirty years—from 1841 to 1871—he taught
school in Plymouth, Hingham, Dorchester and Roxbury. He
then became Secretary of the Unitarian Sunday School Society for four years, but retained his connection with schools
through his membership of the Boston School Board. This
was followed with the position of the agent of the State
Board of Education which, in turn, was followed by his
appointment as Supervisor of the Public Schools in Boston,
which office he held for sixteen years, retiring in 1894, at the
age of 73. He resides at 31 Winthrop Street, Roxbury (Boston), Mass. He married (1), on June 4, 1848, Elizabeth Sampson, of Plymouth, daughter of Isaac and Elizabeth (Sherman) Sampson. She was born Jan. 15, 1824, and died Dec. 19,
1857. He married (2), Oct. 23, 1861, Mary Frances Fessenden,

widow of Charles F. Fessenden, and daughter of Albert Forbes Conant, of Boston. She was b. March 2, 1831, and died Sept. 1, 1876. He married (3), July 8, 1879, to Harriet Marie Miles, widow of Henry Townsend Miles, of Boston, and daughter of Timothy and Abby Phillips Daniell, of Needham. By his second wife he had one child, his only son:

593. HERBERT FORBES KNEELAND[20], b. at Boston, Nov. 20, 1862; m. Minnie Frances Jones, June 27, 1889. He is a member of the firm of Williams, Kneeland & Co., shoe manufacturers, of Braintree and Boston. They have two children, as follows:

594. (i.) *Marjorie Frances*[21], b. Nov. 27, 1891.

595. (ii.) *Elizabeth*[21], b. Feb. 11, 1893.

This is the Finis of the present record of the Boston family. It will be noted that the history of this branch ends where it commenced, in the goodly city of Boston.

PART V.

GENESIS OF THE IPSWICH FAMILY.

DEDICATED TO THE MEMORY OF
EDWARD KNEELAND[13],
WHO "FOUGHT THE GOOD FIGHT"
IN KING PHILLIPS' WAR.

CHAPTER XI.

THE COLONIAL PERIOD.

(NOS. 645 TO 760.)

645. (33.) EDWARD KNEELAND[12] (*John[11]*, *William[10]*, *James[9]*, *Alexander[8]*, *William[7]*, *William[6]*, *John[5]*, *John[4]*, *John[3]*, *James[2]*, *Alexander[1]*).

It will be remembered that the two brothers, John[12] and Edward[12], came to this country about 1630. John settled near Boston and Edward at Ipswich. For convenience of reference, the descendants of the former are termed "The Boston Family," and of the other "The Ipswich Family." The descendants of Edward Kneeland constitute nine-tenths of the Kneelands in this country.

Children of Edward Kneeland.

646. (i.) EDWARD[13], b. at Ipswich, in 1640; d. at the same place, in 1711, æ. 71 (of whom hereafter, 648).

647. (ii.) BENJAMIN[13]. All we know of him is the fact that there was a "Benjamin Neland, Jr.," at Ipswich, who was born prior to 1680. There are other Nelands shown by the Salem records who were extant about this time, but whence they came and whither they went I trow not. So far as I can discover, they were Melchisadeks, having neither ancestry nor posterity. They may have been children or descendants of children of Edward[12] who were not recorded in the town records of Ipswich, which were very meagre prior to the eighteenth century, or possibly children of Edward's brother, Phillip, who was living in Lynn, in 1637.

They did not receive such educational advan-

Edward Kneeland[13].

tages as the ·elder brother, John[12]. To this may, possibly, be attributed the fact that when they became separated by a wilderness of forest trees, Edward spelled his name phonetically, minus the silent " K." This may, however, have been the result of convenience, a sample of which we have in one who, in the present century, settled in Canada and dropped the " K" because it was too much trouble to explain its presence. Be the reason as it may, the fact is nevertheless true that down to about 1750, this branch of the family omitted the superfluous silent letter. We find, during this period, the name spelled in all manner of ways—" Neeland," " Neland," " Nealand," "Neiland," " Nelan," " Nealan " and " Neyland." It is usually put down, however, as it was inscribed in 1675, upon the roll of soldiers in King Philip's War, by the second member of this branch, " Edward Neland."

648. (646.) EDWARD KNEELAND[13] (*Edward[12], John[11] —Alexander[1]*). Eldest son of Edward[12]. He was born in 1740.

In a deposition of October 3, 1699, he is designated as " about 55," which makes his birthday about 1644, but several other depositions fix the date of his birth as 1740, and this appears from the record of his death in 1711, which gives his age as 71. Edward's wife was named Martha; the last name is not given, but inasmuch as we have no trace of a sister, and the records speak of his brother-in-law, Philip Fowler, of Wenham, it is probable that her name was Martha Fowler. His will was probated in Salem, and is dated Jan. 5, 1711. He makes specific mention therein of his sons, Edward and Philip; grandson, Edward Nealand; daughter, Martha Mackentine; son-in-law, John Graves, deceased, who left children; brother, Philip Fowler, of Wenham, and son, Benjamin Nealand, to whom he leaves his lot, No. 287, but " who has had his portions already." In a deed to his son, Edward, dated May 5, 1709, he mentions his son, John, and his brother-in-law,

John Kneeland[14].

Philip Fowler. The names of his children and the dates of their birth, hereinafter given, are taken from the records of births, in the town of Ipswich.

Edward Neland was granted "right of commonage" in Ipswich, in 1678. On April 28, 1664, he purchased from John Baker, a house and lands on Brook Street, Ipswich, and this is the first record we have of him there. If he had been born in 1644, he would not have been of age at that time. The early records of Essex and Salem contain many references to him, mostly from probate proceedings. That which most endears him to a long line of descendants is the fact that he was a soldier in King Philip's War, which gives them entrance to the "Society of Colonial Wars" and kindred organizations (see Bolge's History of King Philip's War," pp. 108 and 238).

Children of Edward and Martha (Fowler) Kneeland.

649. (i.) JOHN[14], b. at Ipswich, Sept. 30, 1670 (of whom hereafter, 655).

650. (ii.) MARTHA[14], b. at Ipswich, Jan. 10, 1675 ; m. ———— Mackentine. No further record.

651. (iii.) EDWARD[14], b. at Ipswich, Dec. 30, 1677 ; m. Mary Alden; d. in 1745, æ. 68 (of whom hereafter, 665),

652. (iv.) BENJAMIN[14], b. at Ipswich, July 7, 1679 (of whom hereafter, 671).

653. (v.) LYDIA[14], b. Oct. 10, 1683 ; m. John Graves; had among other children, a daughter, *Martha Graves*.

654. (vi.) PHILIP[14], b. at Ipswich, March 2, 1685 ; m. Martha Graves and settled in Topsfield, Mass. (Of whom hereafter, 726).

655. (649.) JOHN KNEELAND[14] (*Edward*[13], *Edward*[12], *John*[11]—*Alexander*[1]). Eldest son of Edward Neland[13]).

He resided at Ipswich, married Susanna ————, who survived him and was his widow in 1746. They had three children:

656. (i.) EDWARD[15], m. Ruth Hawkins. They resided at Ipswich and had the following children, as appears from Ipswich Records:

658. (i.) *Rebecca*[16], bapt. Jan. 2, 1713.

Capt. Edward Kneeland[14],

659.   (ii.) *David*[16], bapt. July 31, 1715; d. Mar. 9, 1736.
660.   (iii.) *Joanna*[16], bapt. June 2, 1718.
661.   (iv.) *Timothy*[16], bapt. Dec. 4, 1720.
662.   (v.) *Samuel*[16], bapt. May 19, 1723.
663.   (ii). JOHN[15]. No further record.
664.   (iii.) LYDIA[15]. No further record.

665.   (651.) CAPT. EDWARD KNEELAND[14] (*Edward*[13],
            Edward[12], *John*[11]—*Alexander*[1]). Second son of
            Edward[13], of Ipswich, b. Dec. 30, 1677.

He was a sea captain, located at Ipswich and trading on
the easterly coast of Massachusetts. He married Mary, second daughter of Capt. Timothy Alden, a fellow-mariner, and
son of " John Alden and Priscilla." Timothy is not recorded
in the "Alden Memorial," but the latter does not pretend to
give all the children of John Alden. Timothy's will mentions
his brother, Capt. John Alden, of Boston, who is known to
have been the son of the original John, of the Mayflower.

Possibly the Kneeland trait of assurance comes from their
many times great-grandmother, who is supposed to have shyly
said, "Why don't you speak for yourself, John?" Edward
Kneeland died "suddenly, July y[e] 7th, 1745," leaving a will
which confirms the record history of the family, as hereinafter
set forth. His widow, Mary (Alden) Kneeland, died May 12,
1753. They had the following children, all born at Ipswich,
as appears from the town records:

Children of Edward and Mary (Alden) Kneeland.

666.   (i.) JOHN[15], b. March 23, 1699; m. Susannah Chapman,
            Feb. 26, 1731. He must have died prior to 1750,
            as his widow, Susannah, that year married John
            Abbot, Esq., "gentleman," of Andover, Mass. He
            was living at the time of his father's death, in 1745.
            We have no record of any issue of this marriage.
667.   (ii.) MARY[15], b. Oct. 18, 1701; m. William Hambleton,
            Feb. 13, 1724. She was also living in 1745, when
            her father's will was probated. I have not investi-
            gated their descendants, but the strain of breeding
            was "sure enough Hambletonian," and therefore
            of the best.

Benjamin Kneeland[14].

668. (iii.) JOSEPH[15], b. April 17, 1704; m. Mirriam Allen. I am glad he married—though some of my friends may feel differently—as he was my ancestor. (We shall speak of him hereafter, 720.)

669. (iv.) EDWARD[15], b. Jan. 10, 1706. No further record.

670. (v.) REBECCA[15]. No record of birth, but she is named in her father's will. She was unmarried and living in Ipswich at the time of its probate, in 1745.

671. (652.) BENJAMIN KNEELAND[14] (*Edward[13], Edward[12], John[11], William[10], James[9], Alexander[8], William[7], William[6], John[5], John[4], John[3], James[2], Alexander[1]*). Third son of Edward Kneeland[13], of Ipswich; b. July 7, 1679; probably a farmer, but of a roving disposition.

He left Ipswich soon after his oldest son, Benjamin, Jr., was born—1705. From Ipswich he went to Framingham, Mass., where his daughters, Abigail (1707), Elizabeth (1708), and son, John (1710) were born (Temple's " History of Framingham "); thence to Oxford, Mass., where his sons, Joseph (1712) and Ebenezer (1714) were born (see History of Oxford); thence to Hebron, Conn., where his children Isaac (1716), Deborah (1719), Hezekiah (1722) and Edward (1724) were born (see Hebron Records); thence to Glastonbury, where he resided for a while. He returned, however, to Hebron, where he remained to the end of his days. He died Feb. 18, 1743, two years after his grandson, Benjamin[16], and three years before his son, Benjamin[15]. In 1736 he joined with his sons, Benjamin, John and Joseph, of Glastonbury, and Isaac, from Hebron, in the petition for a new town to be made up of parts of Glastonbury, Hebron and Colchester. The next year the same petitioners, except Benjamin, Sr., repeated the application. In 1747, three years after he had passed away, the last public work of Benjamin Kneeland received full fruition in the establishment of the present town of Marlborough. The records, however, were continued in the offices of the former towns until nearly the end of the century. To this is due the fact that many births in the Kneeland family that are popularly supposed to have taken place at Marlboro, are herein recorded in the adjoining towns.

Benjamin Kneeland was the ancestor of probably two-thirds of all the Kneelands to-day in this country. He married Abigail ———, who deserved and probably had another name, though it has not been discovered by me. The Hebron homestead consisted of 100 acres. It was purchased April 1, 1715, from Joseph Dewey, while Benjamin was yet living in Oxford, as appears from his description in the deed— "Benjamin Neeland, of Oxford;" in fact, the Oxford farm was not disposed of until January 29, 1717. The Hebron farm is described in the deed as being situated in "the great Plain, on the East side of the road to Windsor." This homestead was in the family over 150 years. Benjamin died at Hebron, February 18, 1744. His will was dated April 17, 1740, and was probated March 6, 1744. It mentions his wife, Abigail, his sons, Isaac, Benjamin, John, Joseph, Ebenezer, Hezekiah, Edward, and daughters, Abigail, Elizabeth and Deborah. He desires his children "may live in unity and be content with their father's will," which injunction, tradition says, was faithfully observed.

Children of Benjamin and Abigail Kneeland.

672.   (i.) BENJAMIN[15], b. at Ipswich, in 1705 (of whom hereafter, 689).

672A.   (ii.) ABIGAIL[15], b. March 12, 1707.

673.   (iii.) ELIZABETH[15], b. at Framingham, Mass., May 5, 1708; m. Benjamin Carrier, of Colchester, Conn, Feb. 6, 1734. They resided at Colchester, Conn. Children:

674.   (i.) *Benjamin Carrier*[16], b. Feb. 22, 1738.

675.   (ii.) *Josiah Carrier*[16], b. June 18, 1740.

676.   (iii.) *Elijah Carrier*[16], b. May 15, 1743; d. June 26, 1748.

677.   (iv.) *Philip Carrier*[16], b. June 20, 1745.

678.   (v.) *Rachel Carrier*[16], b. Sept. 6, 1747; d. in 1752.

679.   (vi.) *Mary Carrier*[16], b. July 15, 1749.

680.   (vii.) *Rachel Carrier*[16], b. Aug. 3, 1752.

681.   (viii.) *Elizabeth Carrier*[16], b. Nov. 25, 1753.

682. (iv.) JOHN[15], b. at Framingham, Mass., June 6, 1710 (of whom hereafter, 1426).
683. (v.) JOSEPH[15], b. May 16, 1714, in Oxford, Mass.; m. Lydia Adams, of Colchester.
684. (vi.) EBENEZER[15], b. at Oxford, Mass., Oct 7, 1714 (of whom hereafter, 703).
685. (vii.) ISAAC[15], b. at Hebron, Conn., May 15, 1716 (of whom hereafter, 739).
686. (viii.) DEBORAH[15], b. at Hebron, Conn., Dec. 9, 1719.
687. (ix.) HEZEKIAH[15], b. at Hebron, Conn., June 26, 1722 (of whom hereafter, 1783).
688. (x.) EDWARD,[15] b. at Hebron, Conn., Feb. 23, 1724 (of whom hereafter, 2142).

689. (672). BENJAMIN KNEELAND[15] (*Benjamin*[14], *Edward*[13], *Edward*[12], *John*[11]—*Alexander*[1]). Eldest son of Benjamin[14], b. at Ipswich, Mass., in 1705, and followed his father in his devious wanderings through Massachusetts and Connecticut.

He was a successful farmer and a man of liberal education, and had the honor of changing the spelling of the name from the phonetic method to the original and present style— "Kneeland." He was married twice ; first, to Mehitable Fuller, youngest daughter of John Fuller and sister of Deborah (Fuller) Kneeland, Dec. 5, 1725 ; second, to "ye widow Rachel Jones, August ye eighth day, 1738." Three generations of Benjamin Kneelands died within a period of five years— Benjamin Kneeland[16], Nov. 27, 1741 ; Benjamin Kneeland[14], Feb. 18, 1743 ; Benjamin Kneeland[15], June 20, 1746. The following children of Benjamin appear in the Hebron Records:

Children of Benjamin Kneeland—by Mehitable Fuller.

690. (i.) BENJAMIN[16], b. at Hebron, May 1, 1731; d. at Hebron, " Nov. ye 27th, 1741. This was the last of the direct line of Benjamin Kneelands.
691. (ii.) MEHITABLE[16], b. at Hebron, Dec. 10, 1732 ; d. Dec. 12, 1732.

Rev. Ebenezer Kneeland[16].

By Mrs. Rachel Jones. .

692. (iii.) PHOEBE[16], b. at Hebron, Jan. 15, 1730; m. Amos
        Carrier, of Colchester, Conn., June 6, 1745. Children:
693.   (i.) *Thankful Carrier*[17], b. March 28, 1746.
694.   (ii.) *Amos Carrier*[17], b. April 18, 1748.
695.   (iii.) *Rachel Carrier*[17], b. Nov. 4, 1750.
696.   (iv.) *Amaziah Carrier*[17], b. July 17, 1754.
697.   (v.) *Mehitable Carrier*[17], b. Feb. 9, 1756.
698. (iv.) MEHITABLE[16], b. at Hebron, June 15, 1734; d.
        March 27, 1740.
699. (v.) JABEZ[16], b. at Colchester, Conn., April 14, 1738;
        d. April 27, 1738.
700. (vi.) ELIZABETH[16], b. at Hebron, Oct. 8, 1739; d. Oct.
        10, 1739.
701. (vii.) EBENEZER[16], b. at Hebron, May 14, 1741 (of whom
        hereafter, 702).

702. (701.) REV. EBENEZER KNEELAND[16] (*Benjamin*[15],
        Benjamin[14], *Edward*[13], *Edward*[12], *John*[11]—*Alex-
        ander*[1]). Youngest son of Benjamin Kneeland[15],
        b. at Hebron, Conn., May 14, 1741.

The following, taken from "Loyalists of American Revolu-
tions," gives a correct sketch of his life and work: "KNEELAND,
REV. EBENEZER, Episcopal minister. He was graduated at
Yale College, in 1761, and four years afterwards went to England
for ordination. He served for a time as chaplain in the British
Army. In January, 1768, he was an assistant to the celebrated
Dr. Wm. Samuel Johnson (son of the more celebrated Dr. Sam.
Johnson, the contemporary of Shakespeare), who was the first
missionary of the English church to Connecticut, and located
at Stratford (named after Stratford-upon-Avon). Dr. Johnson had conceived the idea of making Stratford a resort for
young students of divinity, to prepare them for Holy Orders
and using Mr. Kneeland to assist him in his work. He speaks
of him in one of his letters as "very well qualified to continue
it when I am gone." On the death of Rev. Dr. Johnson, in
1772, Mr. Kneeland succeeded to the rectorship and probably
continued the missionary of the Society for the Propagation
of the Gospel, etc., until his death, April 17, 1777. His body

was buried in the church yard at Stratford. He married Charity, the eldest daughter of **Dr.** Johnson, but left no children.

The peculiar circumstances surrounding his death are told in the " History of the Church in Connecticut," by Beardsley. Speaking of the trials of this Church on account of its loyalty during the Revolution, he says (p. 317): " Several of the missionaries in Connecticut who continued to reside on their respective missions were forbidden to go beyond them, and others were placed for a time under heavy bonds and not allowed to visit even a parishioner without special leave from the selectmen of the town. This was the case with Mr. Andrews, of Wallingford, and also of Mr. Kneeland, of Stratford, the successor and grandson by marriage of Rev. Dr. Samuel Johnson, who thus died practically a prisoner in his own house, April 17, 1777."

703. (684.) EBENEZER KNEELAND[15] (*Benjamin*[14], *Edward*[13], *Edward*[12], *John*[11]—*Alexander*[1]). Third son of Benjamin Kneeland[14], b. at Oxford, Mass., Oct. 7, 1714; d. at Hebron, Conn., July 20, 1758. He m. Sarah Rowley, Jan. 9, 1746.

As she was a descendant of the Mayflower, I give herewith the lineage for the benefit of her descendants and those of her sister, Content Rowley, who married Isaac Kneeland[15]. Ebenezer died July 20, 1758. His will was made July 10, 1758, probated Dec. 11, 1758, and witnessed by Content and Hezekiah Neland. It mentions his wife, Sarah; sons, Ebenezer and Seth; daughters, Sarah and Deborah, and brother Isaac.

Biographical sketch of the Fuller family, ancestors of Sarah Rowley, wife of Ebenezer Kneeland, and Content Rowley, wife of Isaac Kneeland.

DR. SAMUEL FULLER and his brother, Edward Fuller, came over in the Mayflower. The former is stated to be one of the most important members of the Puritan family. He was the first resident physician in America and was of great assistance during the terrible struggles of that band for the first few years. Edward brought his wife, daughter and son,

Samuel, with him, leaving his son, Matthew, to complete his medical studies at home. The father, wife and daughter died the next year (1621) and the orphaned son Samuel, was adopted by his uncle, Dr. Samuel, who made him executor and co-heir. This nephew was one of the youngest members of the Mayflower and survived the rigor of these early years and was one of the last surviving members. He died October 31, 1683. His granddaughter, Deborah Fuller, married John Rowley, of East Haddam, Conn., and was the mother of Content Rowley, who married Isaac Kneeland, and of her sister Sarah, who was married to Ebenezer Kneeland.

The descent is given in the " Genealogical Notes to the Barnstable Families," as follows:

SAMUEL FULLER[1] came over on the Mayflower with his father, Edward, and his uncle, Dr. Samuel Fuller. He was married on April 8, 1635, to Jane, daughter of Rev. John Lothrop. The marriage service was performed by Capt. Miles Standish. A full history of the distinguished clergyman, Rev. John Lothrop, is given in Vol. II of the " Barnstable Families," at p. 170. He was graduated at Oxford, took holy orders, and after preaching for a few years at his native town, became the successor of Rev. Henry Jacob, the first pastor of the First Congregational Society, of London. He married, in 1620, and in 1632 was arrested with forty-two of his parisioners for promulgating a false doctrine, and confined in the New Prison until 1634, when he was released on condition that he should leave the country. Immediately after his release he went to New England and became, in 1635, the settled pastor of the church at Scituate. John Lothrop and his followers were held by the people to be martyrs in the cause of independence. No persecutions, no severity that their enemies could inflict, caused him or a solitary one of his followers to waver. They submitted without a murmur to loss of property, to imprisonment in loathsome jails, rather than to subscribe to the forms of worship that Charles I and his bigoted prelates endeavored to force on their consciences. Samuel and Jane (Lothrop) Fuller had several children, including :

JOHN FULLER[2], born about the year 1655. He married and had at least nine children, including

Ebenezer Kneeland[15].

DEBORAH FULLER[3], who married John Rowley, and became the ancestress of Sarah and Content Kneeland.

Edward Fuller's eldest son, Dr. Matthew Fuller, was educated in England. After receiving his diploma as a doctor he joined what was left of his family in America. Savage's "Genealogical Dictionary of N. E.," Vol. II, p. 215, and "Miscellaneous Records of Plymouth Colony," give much information as to Dr. Matthew Fuller and his descendants.

On this point I quote direct from Savage as follows, (p. 217): "MATTHEW FULLER, of Plymouth, son of Edward the first, b. in England, removed to Barnstable, 1652, a physician. Appointed surgeon of the force of the colony 1673, a captain 1675, as Thatcher says, and d. in 1678. By wife Frances he had (1) Mary, who married April 17, 1650, Ralph Jones; (2) Elizabeth, who m. 1652, Moses Rowley, etc." (Savage must have taken this from "Miscellaneous Records of Plymouth Colony," p. 47.)

Matthew's son, Lieut. Samuel Fuller, was killed in the first serious contest of King Philip's war. He was a Lieut. in Capt. Pierce's Plymouth Company which fell into a trap at Seekonk, where both of the officers and nearly all the men were killed by the Indians. A full account of this appears in Bodge Hist. of King Philip's War, pp. 330 to 332, and it is well-known history.

When the troops were raised for the final combat with the Narragansetts, Dr. Matthew Fuller (probably to avenge his son's death) gave up his staff position as Surgeon General (which he resumed again in December of that year, Bodge p. 136), and raised one of the Plymouth Companies at Barnstable and commanded it through the war with great bravery. (Bodge p. xii.)

"These three companies (Captains Prentice, Henchman and Mosely) marched out of Boston on the 26th and 27th and arrived at Swansey on the 28th (of June, 1675), having formed a junction with the Plymouth forces under Major (afterwards General) James Cudworth and Capt. Fuller." (p. 7.)

"During this time the Plymouth forces under Cudworth, Fuller and Church, were pursuing Philip into Pocasset, etc." (p. 7.)

10

Ebenezer Kneeland[15].

The following additional data relating to the Fullers is from the published Records of Plymouth Colony: "Lieut. Matthew Fuller was appointed by Gov. Prince, one of the Council of War for the Colony of Plymouth, Oct. 11, 1658 (Vol. 3, p. 153.) He held this position over twenty-five years, being associated with Capt. Myles Standish and Gov. Winslow and others."

It will be noted that he was then a Lieut. He had held that office only a fortnight for we have the fact that "Matthew Fuller appointed Lieut. of the Military Co. of Barnstable, October 15, 1652." (id. p. 17.) He evidently was not afraid to speak "right out in meeting," for we have the following:

"Lieut. Matthew Fuller being presented (that is indicted or charged) for speaking reproachfully of the Court (the Court was both a judicial and governmental body—it took the place of the present Court and the Legislature) and saying the law enacted about the minister's maintenance was a wicked and "Diuilish" (divilish) law, and that the diuell satt at the sterne when it was enacted," and having admitted the offense and appealed to the Court, was fined forty shillings." (id. p. 150.)

The expedition against the "Duch" in Long Island, June 20, 1654, was in command of Capt. Myles Standish and Lieut. Matthew Fuller. (Vol. 3, p. 55.) This expedition is stated to be "to afford assistance vnto thae design of reduceing the Duch to obedience vnto the State of England." It thus appears that one of our forefathers was bent on capturing New York. And he kept it up for about twenty years after, as we have the following: "Captaine Matthew Fuller was chosen the Surgeon-Generall for this expedition." This expedition was "The War agst the Duch of New York, organized Dec. 17, 1673." (Vol. 5, p. 136.)

This is the last memoranda during his life contained in the Plymouth records. Then came the real war against King Philip and the Narragansetts, in which the work of himself and his son, Lieut. Samuel Fuller, is set forth by Bodge and other writers of that eventful struggle.

The next record appears on p. 273 of Vol. 5, under date of 1678, and in substance is as follows: "Whereas, Capt.

Fuller at his death bequeathed a certain house to his grandson Samuel Fuller, son of Samuel Fuller, deceased, etc." This shows that the Lieut. Samuel Fuller killed at the beginning of the war was a son of Capt. Fuller and a brother of Elizabeth, who married Moses Rowley, Sr. The same proof exists on p. 62 of Vol. 5, where the Court selects for the assessment of damages done by the Indians, among others, Samuel Fuller, Capt. Fuller's son.

ELIZABETH FULLER[3], daughter of Dr. Matthew Fuller, married Moses Rowley, April 22, 1652. They had several children all named in Savage's "Genealogical Dictionary," (Vol. 2, p. 582), including the eldest son Moses (2) born November 10, 1654.

Both father and son removed to East Haddam, Conn., (a great rendezvous for the Plymouth people) in or about 1700.

The Cape Cod Annals give many references to Matthew and Samuel Fuller, and Moses Rowley, Sr. and Jr. They were there as late as 1698.

MOSES ROWLEY, the husband of Elizabeth Fuller, was the first of a long race of Moses Rowleys. He was probably the son of Henry Rowley, who was in Plymouth as early as 1630. (Savage.)

It appears from the Plymouth records (Vol. 1, p. 16) that Henry Rowley married Anna, the late wife of Thomas Blossome, October 17, 1633. As there was no record of any other Rowley at this time in Plymouth, it is evident that Moses, who was a child at the making of Palmer's will in 1637, must have been Henry's son and was born about 1634. Henry was admitted to the "Freedom of the Colonie," Jan. 1, 1634, (id. p. 32.)

I do not know when his father came to Plymouth, but I do know that Moses was very intimately associated with the earlier Puritans and very much loved by at least one of the original band. This appears from the will of William Palmer, of the Mayflower, dated Dec. 4, 1637. (See N. E. Genl. Reg. Vol. 4, p. 35.)

First: He appoints as executors, Bradford, Winslow and Prince (all of which were at times Governors of Plymouth). After giving one-third of his estate to his wife, he says: " I will

Ebenezer Kneeland[15].

to Rebecca, my grandchild, and Moses Rowley, *whom I love*, but not so as to put it in their father's or mother's hand, each five pounds, and also wish that young Rowley may be put with Mr. Partridge (who was their Minister of Duxbury), that he may be brought up in the fear of God, and to that end, if his father suffer, I give Mr. Partridge five pounds." To show that he loved them more than his own children, he coolly proceeds to give 46 s. to his son Henry and daughter Bridget. This is the first public mention we have of Moses Rowley, and it somehow escaped the attention of Savage, Farmer, Prince and all other historians and genealogists of the early days.

We have the following curious confirmation of the fact that Moses Rowley, Sr., of Barnstable, was the one mentioned in Palmer's will: "In respect of a will extant of William Palmer, deceased, the overseers of said will do allow unto Moses Rowley, of Barnstable, a cow, to bee valued for the price thereof as Mr. Thomas Spence and the said Moses Rowley shall agree, etc." (Vol. 5, Plymouth Records, p. 46, 1659.)

In the Annals of Cape Cod and in all records of Barnstable and Falmouth during the 17th century, Moses and his son born in 1654, are designated as Moses, Sr. and Jr.

Moses, Sr. moved to East Haddam about 1700 with his son and grandson Moses, and died there in 1705.

MOSES ROWLEY, JR.[4], born November 10, 1654, resided in Barnstable and Falmouth until about 1700, and then moved with their father, mother and family to East Haddam, Conn. He was several times elected as Constable of the county (then an office of considerable honor and responsibility) and he was Representative in 1692. (See Savage 582.) His mother, Elizabeth (Fuller) Rowley, on May 30, 1714, deeded to him and his sister Mehitabel's husband, John Fuller, her dower in the Falmouth property. She was then over 80 years old.

Moses, Jr. married Mary Fletcher, who was born in Barnstable in 1667 and died at East Haddam, June 9, 1764, aged 97. (See "East Haddam Records.") They moved to East Haddam shortly prior to 1700, bringing their children with them, together with his father and mother. The children of Moses, Jr., designated there as Moses, Sr., included Moses (3) (who married Martha Porter, September 7, 1707, and moved to Colchester, [E. Haddam Record]), and John, Ebenezer, Jonathan and Mehitabel, who with their father were baptized at East Haddam in December, 1704. (See E. H. Rec.) Moses Rowley, Jr., was a citizen in high repute in Barnstable Co. He died in East Haddam, July 16, 1635, aged 81 years.

JOHN ROWLEY[5], second son of Moses and Mary Rowley, born at Falmouth, Barnstable Co., married Sep. 11, 1716, Deborah Fuller, granddaughter of Samuel Fuller.

John moved to Colchester, Conn., about 1723, with their children, and that is how Isaac Kneeland and Ebenezer Kneeland became acquainted with Sarah and Content Rowley.

CONTENT ROWLEY[6], second child of John and Deborah (Fuller) Rowley, born at East Haddam, March 26, 1719, bapt. May 3, 1719, removed to Colchester in 1723, with her parents and married Isaac Kneeland, November 12, 1742, and was the mother of David Kneeland, Sr. Three of her sons served in the War of the Revolution.

SARAH ROWLEY[6], sixth child of John and Deborah (Fuller) Rowley was born at Colchester, Conn., Jan. 10, 1724, and married Ebenezer Kneeland, the father of Lieut. Seth Rowley Kneeland and the grandfather of Henry Kneeland, both of whom settled in New York City.

Children of Ebenezer and Sarah (Rowley) Kneeland.

704. (i.) SARAH[16], b. Oct. 3, 1746; d. Nov. 27, 1746.
705. (ii.) SARAH[16], b. at Hebron, Conn., Aug. 26, 1748.
706. (iii.) HANNAH[16], b. at Hebron, Conn., Oct. 29, 1749; m. Joseph Carrier, of Colchester, Sept., 1771. Their children, all born at Colchester, Conn., were:
708.   (i.) *Samuel Kneeland Carrier*[17], b. Jan. 10, 1773; d. Sept. 21, 1774.
709.   (ii.) *Ebenezer Carrier*[17], b. June 28, 1774.
710.   (iii.) *David Carrier*[17], b. May 12, 1776.
711.   (iv.) *Deborah Carrier*[17], b. Dec. 26, 1778.
712.   (v.) *Dolly Carrier*[17], b. May 27, 1781.
713.   (vi.) *Erastus Carrier*[17], b. April 14, 1784.
714.   (vii.) *Alfred Carrier*[17], b. April 3, 1789.
715.   (viii.) *Jerusha Carrier*[17], b. Sept. 21, 1791.
716.   (ix.) *Sarah Carrier*[17], b. April 3, 1796.

Ebenezer Kneeland[1 6].

716A. (iv.) DEBORAH[1 6], b. at Hebron,.May 6, 1750.
717.   (v.) EBENEZER[1 6], b. at Hebron, Sept. 8, 1753 (of whom
         hereafter, 718A).
718.   (vi.) SETH ROWLEY[1 6], b. April 29, 1757 (of whom here-
         after, 2087) .

718A. (717.) EBENEZER   KNEELAND[1 6]   (*Ebenezer[1 5],*
       Benjamin[1 4], Edward[1 3], Edward[1 2], Edward[1 1],
       John[1 0]—Alexander[1]). Eldest son of Ebenezer[1 5] and
       Sarah (Rowley) Kneeland, b. at Hebron, Sept. 8,
       1753.   He settled in Hartford, Conn., where he
       married about 1776, Mrs. Elizabeth (Sedgwick)
       Taylor, the widow of his deceased partner James
       Taylor, and daughter of William and Elizabeth
       (Brace) Sedgwick, of West Hartford.
     Ebenezer Kneeland and James Taylor were partners in
the business of dyeing and fulling, as appears by a deed from
his widow and her son by her first husband, taken from the
Hartford record :
     " June 1, 1795, Elizabeth Kneeland and William Taylor,
both of Hartford, for £220 quit claim to Reuben Wadsworth,
right in land on the south bank of Little River and west of
the 'Great Bridge,' extending from the west line of that part
of said bank leased by the town of Hartford to said Reuben
Wadsworth, unto the west line of a certain dye house now
standing on the bank of the river adjoining to the fulling mill
and which is called the lower mill-dam west of said bridge, *i. e.,*
one half of the above as it now lyeth in common and
undivided with James Taylor, together with half the shop, dye
house and fulling mill, and of all the tools and machinery,
thereto belonging." Ebenezer died Sept 20, 1786, and was
buried in the Centre Churchyard, Hartford. By his will,
Henry Kneeland, his eldest son, is given a double share, and
his children Sarah and Solomon each a single share of the
estate.   His inventory covered an interest in the dyeing establishment, a farm of 45 acres in Hebron and the usual personal
property and paraphernalia.
     Mrs. Elizabeth (Sedgwick) Kneeland, the wife of Ebenezer
and the mother of Henry Kneeland, of New York City, was

Ebenezer Kneeland[16].

a lineal descendant of Maj.-Gen. Robert Sedgwick, at one time Commander of all the Colonial troops. Savage, in his "Genealogical Dictionary of New England," gives the following sketch of his life (Vol. 4, p. 48):

"SEDGWICK, ROBERT[1], Charlestown, 1636, probably came in 1635, in the Truelove, aged 24; joined the church with his wife Joanna, Feb. 27, 1637, and was made Freeman 9th March following, when he was appointed Captain for the town and was chosen by the Court, next month, Representative and reappointed sixteen times. His neighbour Capt. Edward Johnson, in 'Wonder Works of Providence,' Chap. 26, of book 2 (the most valuable of that curious volume) assures us that he was 'wunst up in London artillery.' Garden and our records show that he was one of the founders of our artillery company, 1638; its Captain, 1640; Commander of Castle, 1641; head of the regiment of Middlesex, 1643; and last, Major-General of the colony. Soon afterwards he was called by Oliver Cromwell to military service with John Leverett (afterwards our Governor) and afterwards sent to Jamacia, recently conquered. There he died 24th May, 1656."

Savage then gives the descendants as hereinafter stated. They had five children, including:

WILLIAM SEDGWICK[2], settled in Hartford, Conn., and married Elizabeth Stone, the 7th child of Rev. Samuel Stone by his second wife Elizabeth Allen, of Boston (see Hist. of Hartford Co., Vol. 1, p. 262). Rev. Samuel Stone was b. in Hertford (then usually pronounced Hartford), Eng.; bapt. July 30, 1602. He was graduated at Cambridge in 1627; was curate at Sisted, County Essex, from June 13, 1627, to Sept. 13, 1630: came to New England with Hooker, Cotton and others of note, in the "Giffin," arriving at Boston, Sept. 4, 1633. He removed to Hartford in 1636, and was one of the original proprietors of that place. He served as Chaplain to the troops under Capt. Mason, in the Pequot War, 1637, and after the death of Hooker, was sole pastor of the First Church until his own death, July 20, 1663. William Sedgwick had but one child.

CAPT. SAMUEL SEDGWICK[3], b. in 1666; d. Mar. 24, 1735. He was a citizen of Hartford and married in 1689, Mary,

Joseph Kneeland[15].

daughter of Stephen Hopkins and granddaughter of John Hopkins, one of the original proprietors of Hartford. They had several children, including:

JONATHAN SEDGWICK[4], b. in 1793; m. Isabella Stebbins, March 7, 1716. They had several children, including:

WILLIAM SEDGWICK[5], b. Dec 21, 1717; m. May 8, 1740, Elizabeth, daughter of Henry Brace, of Hartford. Their eldest child was

ELIZABETH SEDGWICK[6], who was baptized July 5, 1741; m. (1) James Taylor, and (2) Ebenezer Kneeland. This descent from Gen. Sedgwick to Elizabeth (Sedgwick) Kneeland, is set forth in full in Godwin's "Genealogical Notes," p. 175, and is confirmed by the records of Hartford, Conn., and by many deeds, including the following: Deed from Jonathan Sedgwick, dated May 6, 1771 (Vol. 12, p. 242, Hartford deeds) to his grandchildren, the children of his son William; the first name of the grantee being Elizabeth, wife of James Taylor. Also deed of Dec. 18, 1793, from Elizabeth Kneeland to Dorus Barnard, of all her right in 12 acres in the town commons in common with the other heirs of William Sedgwick of Hartford.

Children of Ebenezer and Elizabeth Kneeland.

718B. (i.) Child buried May 17, 1778, æ. 5 months (Sexton's Record).

719. (ii.) HENRY[17], b. May 9, 1779; m. Anne Taylor and settled in New York (of whom hereafter, Chap. xli).

719A. (iii.) SARAH[17], m. Abel Thompson, of Hartford, May 29, 1796.

719B. (iv.) SOLOMON[17].

720. (668.) JOSEPH KNEELAND[15] (*Edward*[14], *Edward*[13], *Edward*[12], *John*[11]—*Alexander*[1]). Second son of Edward Kneeland[14] and Mary Alden, and great-grandson of John Alden and Priscilla; b. at Ipswich, April 17, 1704 (see Ipswich Records); m. Mirriam Alden.

They settled first at Topsfield, Mass., and several of his children were born there, as appears from Topsfield Records.

Philip Kneeland[14].

About 1745 he went to Westford, Mass., where Lydia was born in 1747 (see History of Westford, p. 459). From thence he went to Harvard, Mass., where his son, Joseph, was born, in 1752 (see History of Harvard and Harvard Town Records). Subsequently they moved to Gardner, Mass., where he remained until his death.

Children of Joseph and Mirriam (Alden) Kneeland.

720A. (i.) EDWARD[16], b. at Topsfield, July 25, 1735; d. Dec. 24, 1775, at Harvard, Mass. (see History of Harvard, p. 530).

721. (ii.) TIMOTHY[16], b. at Topsfield, Feb. 1, 1737 (of whom hereafter, 761).

722. (iii.) MIRRIAM[16], b. at Topsfield, March 13, 1739. She lived with her brother, Timothy; unmarried.

723. (iv.) DAVID[16], b. at Topsfield, Jan. 17, 1744; m. Sarah Smith, of Ipswich.

724. (v.) LYDIA[16], b. at Westford, in 1747.

725. (vi.) JOSEPH[16], b. at Harvard, Mass., Nov. 22, 1752 (of whom hereafter, 2693).

726. (654.) PHILIP KNEELAND[14] (*Edward*[13], *Edward*[12], *John*[11]—*Alexander*[1]). Youngest son of Edward Kneeland[13], of Ipswich, b. March 2, 1685; m. Martha Graves, Dec. 10, 1709; resided at Ipswich and became a prosperous merchant for those early days. He was probably named in memory of King Philip, whom his father had the pleasure of fighting ten years before his birth.

Children of Philip Kneeland and Martha Graves.

727. (i.) PHILIP[15], bapt. at Topsfield, April 13, 1715 (of whom hereafter, 731).

728. (ii.) SARAH[15], bapt. at Topsfield, June 17, 1716; m. Thos. Avery, Jan. 22, 1738.

729. (iii.) SAMUEL[15], bapt. at Topsfield, June 28, 1719.

730. (iv.) MARY[15], bapt. at Topsfield, May 21, 1721; m. Ephraim Abbot, of Andover, Mass., Feb. 1, 1745.

The above are from the Topsfield Records.

Philip Kneeland[15].

731. (727.) PHILIP KNEELAND[15] (*Philip[14]*, *Edward[13]*, *Edward[12]*, *John[11]—Alexander[1]*). Eldest son of Philip Kneeland[14], b. at Topsfield, Mass., April 15, 1715; m. Mary Potter, July 7, 1733.

He had two sons who fought in the Revolution and, although aged, was himself one of the "minute men." I have no record of his death, but have no doubt of the fact. His grandson, Nehemiah, was one of the founders of a new town in Maine which was named by him in honor of the home of his ancestors, "Topsfield."

Children of Philip and Mary (Potter) Kneeland.

732. (i.) PHILIP[16], b. at Topsfield, Mass., Jan. 10, 1735; m. Mehitable Emerson (of whom hereafter, 755).

733. (ii.) DAVID[16], b. Jan. 3, 1747. He was a farmer and served two years in the War of the Revolution; went from Topsfield to Bridgton, Me., in 1810, and finally settled at Otisfield, Me. He had two children:

734.   (i.) *Ephraim[17]*, and

735.   (ii.) *Asa[17]*.

They also settled at Otisfield, and still have descendants in that vicinity whose names shall be lost to the world unless they get into the legislature, the jail or in our second edition.

736. (iii.) AARON[16], b. Nov. 10, 1749; m. Hannah Ramsdell; had ten children; d. Oct. 4, 1833, æ. 84. She died June 10, 1844, æ. 88 (of whom hereafter, 2799).

737. (iv.) ABRAHAM[16]. He was a farmer and served three years in the Continental Army. His receipt for bounty is still preserved in the archives at Boston. He received his twenty head of cattle and his sheep, but evidently did not believe in slavery, as there is no record of any negro being thrown into the bargain, as in Henry Kneeland's case. So far as the world is concerned, his history ends with his enlistment.

739. (685.) ISAAC KNEELAND¹⁵ (*Benjamin¹⁴, Edward¹³, Edward¹², John¹¹—Alexander¹*). Born at Hebron, Conn., May 15, 1716. Son of Benjamin Kneeland and Abigail ——; farmer.

Settled at Hebron. Was one of the petitioners from that place for the new town of Marlboro. He married twice; first, to Sarah Beach, Nov. 8, 1739; she d. March 7, 1741. Second, to Content Rowley, Nov. 12, 1742; she was a sister of Sarah Rowley and a descendant of the Mayflower (see 703). He had three sons—Benjamin, Isaac and Jesse—in the War of the Revolution.

Children of Isaac Kneeland (see Hebron Records).
By Sarah Beach.

740. (i.) ISAAC¹⁶, b. at Hebron, Conn., Oct. 13, 1741 (of whom hereafter, 2503).

By Content Rowley.

741. (ii.) CONTENT¹⁶, b. at Hebron, Aug. 25, 1745; m. Elizur Tillitson, Jan. 17, 1764.
742. (iii.) SARAH¹⁶, b. at Hebron, Jan. 6, 1745.
743. (iv.) BENJAMIN¹⁶, b. at Hebron, Nov. 24, 1746.
744. (v.) JOSEPH¹⁶, b. at Hebron, Aug. 13, 1749 (of whom hereafter, 2248).
745. (vi.) DAVID¹⁶, b. at Hebron, April 23, 1752 (of whom hereafter, 1854).
746. (vii.) MINDWELL¹⁶, b. at Hebron, Conn., May 4, 1753.
747. (viii.) JESSE¹⁶, b. at Hebron, Conn., June 16, 1755 (of whom hereafter, 749).
748. (ix.) ELLIS¹⁶, b. at Hebron, March 19, 1762.

749. (747.) JESSE KNEELAND¹⁶ (*Isaac¹⁵, Benjamin¹⁴, Edward¹³, Edward¹², John¹¹—Alexander¹*). Son of Isaac¹⁵, b. at Hebron, Conn., June 16, 1755; m. Lucy Martin, and located in Chatham, Conn.

He served in the army during the war, was wounded and drew pension in New York State, under the act of 1818. This was the third son of Isaac Kneeland¹⁵ to serve in the Revolution. The records of the Congregational Church, at Chatham, show the admission to membership of Jesse Kneeland, Oct. 24, 1784. Sad to relate, on the same day, under the heading of "Satisfaction for offences," is the following: "Jesse Kneeland confessed himself guilty of a breach of Sabbath and profane swearing. Accepted." I am assured by the clerk of the church that this single breach of discipline showed him to be "a much better member than the average."

Children of Jesse and Lucy (Martin) Kneeland.

750. (i.) Infant child: unmarried; b. and d. May 31, 1780.
751. (ii.) JESSE[17], b. at Chatham, Conn., "Oct. ye 7, 1781 ;" bapt. Dec. 9, 1781.
752. (iii.) LUCY[17], b. at Chatham, "May ye 4, 1784;" bapt. July 25, 1784.
753. (iv.) REBECCA[17], b. at Chatham, "July ye 3, 1785 "; bapt. Aug. 28, 1785.
754. (v.) SALLY[17], b. at Chatham, June 6, 1787; bapt. July 13, 1788.

755. (732.) PHILIP KNEELAND[16] (*Philip*[15], *Philip*[14], *Edward*[13], *Edward*[12], *John*[11]—*Alexander*[1]). Eldest son of Philip Kneeland[15].

He was a farmer and speculator, accumulated considerable wealth and had several children by his wife, Mehitable Emerson.

Children of Philip and Mehitable (Emerson) Kneeland.

756. (i.) MEHITABLE[17], b. 1768; d. young.
757. (ii.) PHILIP[17], b. 1770; d. young. (This is the last of the direct line of Philip Kneelands).
758. (iii.) SARAH[17], b. April 15, 1773.
759. (iv.) EDWARD[17], b. March 10, 1776.
760. (v.) MARY[17]. Was living, unmarried, in 1798.

PART VI.

———

THE TIMOTHY KNEELAND FAMILY.

(NOS. 761 TO 1427.)

———

DEDICATED TO MY FATHER,

GARDNER KNEELAND,

THAN WHOM NO BETTER DISCIPLE OF MANLINESS,

OF GODLINESS AND OF TRUE GREATNESS EXISTS,

EITHER WITHIN OR WITHOUT

THIS GOODLY RACE OF KNEELANDS.

CHAPTER XII.

TIMOTHY AND MARIA (STONE) KNEELAND.

(NOS. 761 TO 777.)

761. (721.) TIMOTHY KNEELAND[16] (*Joseph*[15], *Edward*[14], *Edward*[13], *Edward*[12], *John*[11], *William*[10], *James*[9], *Alexander*[8], *William*[7], *William*[6], *John*[5], *John*[4], *John*[3], *James*[2], *Alexander*[1]), b. at Topsfield, Feb. 1, 1737. Son of Joseph[15] and Mirriam (Alden) Kneeland, grandson of Edward[14] and Mary (Alden) Kneeland.

He went with his father's family from Topsfield to Harvard, Mass., some time prior to 1762. I have not the exact date, but the records show that his pew in the town "meeting-house" was assigned by the "selectmen" of the town in 1766. "In March, 1766, it was voted to seat the meeting-house." Then follows a list of the seats. including, "Timothy Kneeland, ye third seat on ye right side" (History of Harvard, p. 200). We find from the same book (p. 489) this inscription on the tombstone of Timothy's mother: "Here lyes buried ye body of Mrs. Mirriam *Neeland*, wife of Joseph *Neland*, died March ye 15th, 1763, in ye 54th year of her age." Timothy married Moriah Stone, at Harvard, Feb. 11, 1761, and four of his children were born there. Afterwards, he moved to Gardner, Mass. From the "History of Gardner," we have a sketch of his life in that place and a statement of his eleven children and fifty-five grandchildren (see pp. 364-5). From this we extract the following:

"KNEELAND, TIMOTHY, from Harvard, was the third inhabitant of the town. He came here 1771 and located one and one-half miles west of the centre. He was a soldier in the Revolutionary War three years and three months. Although he had a large family of children, there are none of his de-

Timothy Kneeland[16].

scendants living in town at the present time. The exact spot
where he located was near the junction of the Wilder and
Kneeland brooks. At the time of his settlement it was an
unbroken wilderness for miles about him, with the exception
of the meadows which, it is supposed, were cleared by beavers
and was at that time producing large crops of grass. It is
probable that this was the principal inducement which led him
to settle in that place. He was a carpenter as well as a farmer
and was of great service to those who afterwars settled around
him. He had ten children, all of whom, with one exception,
lived to hold, and most of them had large families. Inasmuch as there are some things somewhat remarkable about
the family, it may be interesting to the reader to have a more
detailed account of it."

He enlisted three several times in the War of the Revolution, from Gardner, Mass., and served successively under
Lieut. Joseph Boynton, Col. Nathan Sparhawk and Capt.
Springfield, taking part, among other contests, in the Battle of
Benington, where "Molly Stark" did not become a widow.
He was acting as lieutenant in the latter battle, and I have
the sword and powder horn used by him at the time. The
sword was evidently made from a scythe and still bears the
dents and scars of battle. Returning home to Gardner after
the war was over, he hung up his sword and musket and,
taking down his scythe, commenced the battle of life. He
died April 4, 1818, at the age of 81.

Moriah Stone, wife of Timothy Kneeland, was a lineal
descendant on her mother's side of Degory Priest, of the Mayflower, and on her father's side of Capt. John Stone, the
celebrated Indian fighter of the early Colonial days. His wild,
ungovernable spirit brought him into constant clashings with
the strict disciplinarians of that Puritan age, as appears from
the "Log Book" of Gov. Bradford.

DEGORY (or Diggory) PRIEST, one of the Leyden exiles,
came over in the Mayflower with his brother-in-law, Mr. Allerton, and died a few days after his arrival. He married Sarah
(Allerton) Vincent, at Leyden. Cuthbert Cuthbertson brought
the wife and three children over in the Ann (see Dutch
Records and Savage's Gen'l Register). Priest, Allerton and

Timothy Kneeland[16].

Gov. Bradford were the only members of the Mayflower that had the distinguished honor of being admitted "citizens of Leyden." Cuthbertson afterwards married Mrs. Priest. He was her third husband. Degory and Sarah Priest had three children—one son, John, and two daughters, Moriah and Sarah.

John married Sarah Allerton and settled in Woburn. His oldest son, John Priest, Jr., was born at Woburn, about 1648. He married Rachel Garfield, March 10, 1678. On Dec. 1, 1675, he enlisted from Woburn in the Narragansett expedition (see History of Woburn). "The children of John Priest and Rachel Garfield were, John, b. 1681, and brought from Woburn," etc., mentioning others born at Bere Hill (History of Hartford, Mass., p. 559). From this it appears that John Priest, Jr., settled in Harvard and became John Priest, Sr.

The new John Priest, Jr. (b. in 1681) married Anna Houghton, and had several children, including Mariah (the name in the several generations is spelled Marah [first division of cattle in Plymouth], Moriah, Mariah, Maria, etc.), baptized in Lancaster, in 1721. The father, John Priest, finally located in Bolton, and died there Sept. 29, 1756, aged 75 (History of Harvard, p. 559). "Nov. 29, 1739, Oliver Stone married Maria Priest, of Bolton." Sergt. Oliver Stone was selectman in Harvard, Mass., in 1756 (History of Harvard, p. 421). He was in the company that marched to the relief of Fort William Henry, in August, 1757 (Id., p. 296). "Moriah, wife of Oliver Stone, d. June 13, 1754, aged 33 years. Ensign Oliver Stone d. Jan. 10, 1761, aged 41 " (Id., p. 524).

Children of Oliver and Moriah (Priest) Stone.

Note how these names are duplicated in the children of Timothy and Moriah (Stone) Kneeland.
- (i.)   Anna Stone, b. May 7, 1741.
- (ii.) Moriah Stone, b. July 12, 1743.
- (iii.) Sarah Stone, b. June 4, 1746.
- (iv.) Oliver Stone, b. July 25, 1748.
- (v.)   John Stone, b. July 6, 1751.
- (vi.) Anna Stone, b. April 28, 1754.

(History of Harvard, p. 565.)

11

Timothy Kneeland[16].

It will thus be seen that Moriah Stone, who married Timothy Kneeland, was on her mother's side fifth in descent from Degory Priest, of the Mayflower, the line being as follows: Mariah (Priest) Stone[5], John Priest[4], John Priest[3], John Priest[2], Degory Priest[1]. This branch of the Stone family came from Essex County, England. Their Coat of Arms, according to Burke, is: "Ar. three cinque foils sa on a chief az. a sun or. *Crest.*—Out of a ducal coronet, or, a griffin's head betw. two wings expanded, gu, bezantee."

Moriah Stone Kneeland was a woman of intellectual force and remarkable physical endurance. It is related that she could repeat entire books of the Bible, and that one night, between sunset and sunrise, she wove, on the old-fashioned hand loom, ten yards of cloth. Such were the parents of the celebrated Abner Kneeland and of a family of ten children, in which the earliest death was at the age of 63, and the latest of 98, the average of life being 77, notwithstanding the fact that two of the children were murdered.

Children of Timothy Kneeland and Moriah Stone.

762. (i.) MORIAH[17], b. at Harvard, Mass., Feb. 9, 1762; m. Josiah Nichols and settled in Verona, N. Y. They had six children. She d. at Verona at the age of 79. Children:

763.   (i.) *Audrien Nichels[18].*
764.   (ii.) *Sarah Nichols[18].*
765.   (iii.) *David Nichols[18].*
766.   (iv.) *Levi Nichols[18].*
767.   (v.) *Sabina Nichols[18].*
768.   (vi.) *Fanny Nichols[18].*

769. (ii.) OLIVER[17], b. at Harvard, Mass., April 21, 1764 (of whom hereafter, 778).

770. (iii.) JOHN[17], b. at Harvard, Aug. 12, 1766 (of whom hereafter, 842).

771. (iv.) MIRRIAM[17], b. at Gardner, Mass., May 1, 1769; murdered March 7, 1855.

From the History of Gardner (p. 324-5), we have a full account of the death of Mirriam and her widowed sister, Mrs. Phiney. They had been living alone in the

old homestead ever since the death of their father, in 1818. On the night of March 7, 1855, the murderer entered the house by breaking in a window. Both of his victims were killed in bed, beaten to death by a chair post. The bodies were not discovered until the evening of the next day. The selectmen offered a reward of $500, and Geo. Stacey was arrested and indicted for the crime. The evidence was very strong against him and there was no moral doubt of his guilt, but the jury acquitted him. He was afterwards tried and convicted in New York State for a burglary that he probably never committed. He died in the penitentiary at Sing Sing, and thus the original crime was avenged.

> " Though the wheels of God grind slowly.
> Yet they grind exceeding small;
> Though with patience he stands waiting,
> With exactness grinds he all."

From p. 325, History of Gardner, Mass., we have the termination of this sad affair, known throughout the country as the "Gardner Murder." "The funeral was attended at the meeting-house next Sabbath by a large congregation. Rev. A. Stowell preached a sermon on the text, ' They were lovely and pleasant in their lives, and in death they were not divided.' The congregation was so large that a part of the people repaired to the town hall where Rev. J. C. Paine preached from the text, ' Turn not to the right hand or to the left, remove thy foot from evil.' They were humble and exemplary Christians."

772. (v.) ASA[17], b. Sept. 20, 1771 ; m. Hannah Cheney ; had eleven children ; d. June 7, 1844, æ. 73 (of whom hereafter, Chap. XV).

773. (vi.) ABNER[17], b. April 17, 1774 ; m. four times ; had eleven children (of whom hereafter, 1239).

774. (vii.) LUCY[17], b. Nov. 8, 1776 ; m. Paul Stearns ; had eleven children (the magic number in this family); d. at Reading, Vt., Feb. 2, 1875, æ. 98 years, two months and twenty-six days (of whom hereafter, 1348).

Timothy Kneeland[16].

775.　(viii.) SARAH[17], b. March 19, 1779; m. James Phinney,
　　　　a sailor, who died without children.　She then lived
　　　　with her sister, Mirriam, at the old Gardner home-
　　　　stead until he was murdered at the age of 79 (see
　　　　Mirriam, No. 771).

776.　(ix.) EDWARD[17], b. Oct. 16, 1781 ; d. without issue.

777.　(x.) SILAS[17], b. Feb. 2, 1793; d. Aug. 27, 1862, æ. 69
　　　　(of whom hereafter, 1285).

CHAPTER XIII.

DESCENDANTS OF OLIVER KNEELAND.

(NOS. 778 TO 841.)

778. (769.) OLIVER KNEELAND[17] (*Timothy*[16], *Joseph*[15], *Edward*[14], *Edward*[13], *Edward*[12], *John*[11], *William*[10], *James*[9], *Alexander*[8], *William*[7], *William*[6], *John*[5], *John*[4], *John*[3], *James*[2], *Alexander*[1]).   Eldest son of Timothy Kneeland[16], b. at Harvard, Mass., April 21, 1764.

Moved with his father, in the year 1771, to Gardner, Mass.   He married Betsy Baldwin and settled at Poultney, Vt. From there, in about the year 1794, he moved to Chenango County, N. Y.   After three or four more shifts he finally, in 1805, settled down at Masonville, Delaware County, N. Y., where he cleared up, by the aid of a numerous family, a good farm, upon which he spent his remaining days, and his son Silas Kneeland[18] lived for eighty-four years.   Notwithstanding his roving propensities, Oliver was a prosperous farmer.   One of his sons, Rev. Levi Kneeland, was a Baptist minister of very marked talent and popularity, and each of his children received a liberal education for those early days.   He died April 15, 1832, aged 68 years.

Children of Oliver and Betsy (Baldwin) Kneeland.

779. (i.) ISRAEL[18], b. at Poultney, Vt., in 1795 (of whom hereafter, 792).

780. (ii.) LUCY[18], b. at Bainbridge, N. Y., in 1799; m. Daniel Welch.   Children:

781.   (i.) *Norton Welch*[19].

782.   (ii.) *Warren Welch*[19].

783.   (iii.) *Hannah Welch*[19].

784.   (iv.) *Mary Welch*[19].

Sally Kneeland[19].

785.   (v.) *Abner Welch[19]*.
786.   (vi.) *Olivia Welch[19]*.
        No further record.
787.   (iii.) SILAS[18], b. at Bainbridge, N. Y., Jan. 1, 1801 (of
        whom hereafter, 810.)
788.   (iv.) LEVI[18], b. in Masonville, N. Y., about 1803 (of
        whom hereafter, 841).
789.   (v.) ESTHER[18], b. in Masonville, N. Y., in 1805. She
        was unmarried and lived with her brother, Silas, at
        Masonville.
790.   (vi.) ABNER[18], b. at Masonville, in 1808; m. Deborah
        Weed, in 1836.
791.   (vii.) BETSY[18], b. at Masonville, in 1810; unmarried;
        lived with her brother, Silas.

792.   (779.) ISRAEL KNEELAND[18] (*Oliver[17]*, *Timothy[16]*,
        Joseph[15], *Edward[14]*, *Edward[13]*, *Edward[12]*, *John[11]*
        —*Alexander[1]*). Eldest son of Oliver Kneeland[17],
        b. Oct. 10, 1795; m. Susannah Welch, who was
        b. July 30, 1806, and d. July 29, 1872.
    She regained her maiden name by marrying, 2d, Marvin
Welch. He died March 25, 1852. I suppose she was Welch
when she died, as I have heard nothing to the contrary. Israel
died April 15, 1832, just two hundred years after his ancestor,
Edward Kneeland, came to this country.

Children of Israel and Susannah (Welch) Kneeland.

793.   (i.) SALLY[19], b. Jan. 6, 1824 (of whom hereafter, 797).
794.   (ii.) LUCY ANN[19], b. Dec. 29, 1825; m. Alfred C. Bailey,
        March 10, 1847; d. May 15, 1889.
795.   (iii.) HANNAH M.[19], b. March 12, 1829; d. April 5, 1834.
796.   (iv.) LOUISA M.[19], b. Oct. 28, 1830; m. Edward J.
        Davis, March 5, 1852.

797.   (793.) SALLY KNEELAND[19] (*Israel[18]*, *Oliver[17]*,
        Timothy[16], *Joseph[15]*, *Edward[14]*, *Edward[13]*, *Ed-
        ward[12]*, *John[11]—Alexander[1]*). Eldest daughter
        of Israel Kneeland and Susannah Welch; b. Jan.
        6, 1824; m. Sterling Brownson, Feb. 5, 1844.

Sally Kneeland[19].

Children of Sally Kneeland[19] and Sterling Brownson.

798.   (i.) JULIA C. BROWNSON[20], b. March 22, 1847; m. Dec. 25, 1867, to Gardner Bowman, a lumber dealer, at Sidney Centre, N. Y. They had the following children:

799.   (i.) *Edmond S. Bowman[21]*, b. Oct. 22, 1868; m. Nov. 9, 1891, to Anna Meings, of Holland, Mich. He is now in the manufacturing business in that place and has one child:

800.   Gardner Bowman[22], b. April 19, 1896.

801.   (ii.) *Frances M. Bowman[21]*, b. May 10, 1875.

802.   (iii.) *Berton B. Bowman[21]*, b. April 26, 1878.

803.   (iv.) *Fred N. Bowman[21]*, b. July 1, 1880.

804.   (v.) *Marion L. Bowman[21]*, b. Aug. 3, 1881.

805.   (vi.) *Lovernie J. Bowman[21]*, b. May 21, 1883.

806.   (vii.) *Truman Bowman[21]*, b. April 8, 1888; d. Jan. 25, 1896.

807.   (ii.) REV. TRUMAN G. BROWNSON, D.D.[20], b. April 2, 1851; m. to M. Franc Hayden, of Port Byron, N.Y., Oct. 13, 1880; graduated from Colgate University in 1877, and from the Union Theological Seminary, of Chicago, in 1883. He was ordained to the Baptist ministry in Three Rivers, Mich., and was pastor there; was also pastor at Albany, Oregon, 1884 to 1887, and was appointed President of McMinnville College, in Oregon, 1887, a position which he still holds.

808.   (iii.) REV. EDWIN J. BROWNSON[20], b. Nov. 17, 1852; m. Ella Gray, Nov. 7, 1879; graduated from Colgate University and Union Theological Seminary, of Chicago, now a part of the Chicago University; is a Baptist minister located (1897) at Warsaw, Ind.

Sally (Kneeland) Brownson married for a second time to Stillman Davis, and had one child:

809.   (iv.) ETTA A. DAVIS[20], b. Nov. 20, 1862; m. Harper W. Dewey, Dec. 28, 1880.

Stillman Davis died Dec. 29, 1879, and Sally married third, to Samuel W. Niles. He died Feb. 29, 1895. As her communication to me, under date of May 12, 1896, is signed "Sally W. Niles, of Sidney Centre," I assume that she has not remarried.

810. (787). SILAS KNEELAND[18] (*Oliver*[17], *Timothy*[16], *Joseph*[15], *Edward*[14], *Edward*[13], *Edward*[12], *John*[11], —*Alexander*[1]). Born in Chenango County, N. Y., Jan. 1, 1801; d. Dec. 25, 1886.

He could not have inherited his father's propensity for a change of base, for he remained at the homestead at Masonville, Delaware County, for over eighty years, and died there at the age of 86.   His cousin, John M. Stearns, writing in 1888, says of him: "I saw Silas about twenty years ago (1868). He was a widower, 72 years old, a Baptist deacon, one of the good old sort.   He never had been fifty miles from home and never rode on a railroad train.   He had two maiden sisters living with him, Esther and Betsy, and a married daughter, Samantha A. Scott, who kept house for him.   He used to write to me, but I have not heard from him in a dozen years, and presume he is dead."   He had been dead about two years at that time.   He married Ara Brown, daughter of Collins Brown, of Connecticut.   They had nine children.   Silas was a teacher as well as a farmer, and all his children who grew up were liberally educated and followed his example as school teachers in connection with their regular avocations.   His classical studies break out in the naming of the two sons who died in childhood, Quartus and Horace.

Children of Silas and Ara (Brown) Kneeland.

811. (i.) MARY ANN[19], b. at Masonville, N. Y., Jan. 6, 1826; d. Feb. 12, 1826.

812. (ii.) LEVI BROWN[19], b. at Masonville, N. Y., July 12, 1827 (of whom hereafter, 830).

813. (iii.) SAMUEL OTIS[19], b. at Masonville, N. Y., Jan 1, 1830; d. June 23, 1831.

814. (iv.) SARAH A.[19], b. at Masonville, N. Y., June 15, 1832; m. first, Warren Stilson, Sept. 21, 1856, by whom she had one child:

Silas Kneeland[18].

815.   *Florence E. Stilson*[20], b. Aug. 31, 1858; d. March
        30, 1875. Warren Stilson died June 10, 1875.
        Thus she lost husband and child the same spring-
        time. A few years later her sister, Martha, died,
        her last request being that Sarah should marry her
        husband and care for her children. This was done
        and so she married, second, **Geo. W. Boyd**, Feb. 7,
        1880. They now reside at Cannonsville, N. Y.

816.   (v.) QUARTUS[19], b. Dec. 13, 1834, at Masonville; d.
        May 19, 1890.
        Was not Silas a little "off" in his Latin or his
        mathematics? **Why** should the fifth child be
        Quartus? This record must be official as it comes
        with specific dates from **Mrs. Boyd. But Rev.**
        Lerwick L. Kneeland, his grandson, assigns Otis
        a place between Horace and Martha. This makes
        the name quite proper but I fear that it does so at
        the expense of the record. To leave him out dis-
        turbs the biennial characteristics of this family.

817.   (vi.) HORACE P.[19], b. at Cannonsville, Sept. 2, 1837; d.
        June 19, 1840.

818.   (vii.) MARTHA A.[19], b. April 7, 1840, d. April 14, 1879;
        m. Geo. W. Boyd, Nov. 27, 1862. Children:

819.   (i.) *Emma A. Boyd*[20], b. Oct. 14, 1863; m. Durward
            B. Seymour, Dec. 2, 1885. They reside at
            Cannonsville, N. Y. Children:

820.   (i.) Harold B. Seymour[21].

821.   (ii.) Frances A. Seymour[21].

822.   (ii.) *Virgil F. Boyd*[20], b. Sept. 29, 1865; m. Estelle
            Axtell, Sept. 26, 1889. They reside at Deposit,
            N. Y.

823.   (iii.) *Berkeley S. Boyd*[20], b. Aug. 30, 1868; m.
            Emma France, Dec. 19, 1894. Reside at Trout
            Creek, N. Y.

824.   (iv.) *Ernest L. Boyd*[20], b. Aug. 16, 1872; m. Kate
            M. Axtell, Oct. 4, 1893. One child:

825.   Pauline M. Boyd[21].
            They reside at Barboursville, N. Y.

826.   (v.) *Leslie L. Boyd*[20], b. Jan. 23, 1876; unmarried.

Levi B. Kneeland[19].

827. (viii.) HARRIET U.[19], b. at Masonville, Aug. 29, 1842;
      d. April 4, 1862.
828. (ix.) SAMANTHA A.[19], b. at Masonville, Jan. 17, 1846;
      m. Winfield Scott, Mar. 10, 1871. They had one
      child:
829.   *Andrew F. Scott[20]*, b. Jan 15, 1878, who died last
      year (1896).
      They reside at Masonville, N. Y., on the old Silas
      Kneeland homestead.

830. (812.) LEVI B. KNEELAND[19] (*Silas[18]*, *Oliver[17]*,
      Timothy[16], *Joseph[15]*, *Edward[14]*, *Edward[13]*, *Ed-
      ward[12]*, *John[11]—Alexander[1]*). Born at Mason-
      ville, N. Y., July 12, 1827; m. Harriet P. Neff; d.
      at Denver, Col., March 23, 1895 in his sixty-eighth
      year.
    He was for many years a consistent and efficient member
of the Baptist church at Masonville, N.Y., which, for a long time
he faithfully served as clerk. He removed to Colorado in 1887,
living first at Leadville, where his son, Lerwick L., was pastor
of the Baptist church, and afterward at Denver. Here he was
connected successively with the Judson Memorial, Galilee and
Bethel churches, being a deacon of the latter at the time of
his death. An exemplary Christian life, a sweet and gentle
spirit, a steadfast hope were his. There survive him, his wife,
daughter, Endora A., and four sons—L. S. Kneeland, of New
York, farmer; Rev. L. L. Kneeland and W. P. Kneeland, of
Denver, and F. L. Kneeland, of Portland, Oregon.

Children of Levi B. and Harriet P. (Neff) Kneeland.

831. (i.) LEANDER S.[20], b. in 1852, at Masonville, N. Y.;
      farmer; now living at Burlington Flats, N. Y. First
      wife, Roena S. Broad, by whom he had two daugh-
      ters, as follows:
832.   (i.) *Lena[21]*.
833.   (ii.) *Hattie[21]*.
      Second wife was Charlotte Barber, by whom he had:
834.   (iii.) *Howard[21]*.

Levi B. Kneeland[19].

835. (ii.) REV. LERWICK L.[20], b. at Masonville, Delaware County, N. Y., Oct. 11, 1854. Was early baptized into the Baptist church of that place. Graduated from Colgate Academy at the head of his class, in 1875, from Madison University—now Colgate University—in 1879, obtaining the degree of A. B., and from the Hamilton Theological Seminary, in 1882, obtaining the degree of A. M. During the third year of the college course he won three prizes for proficiency in scholarship, viz., the first prize in Greek, the first prize in Latin, and the second prize in essay writing. He was licensed to preach by the church at Masonville, N. Y., May 23, 1880; was ordained to the Baptist ministry by the church at Kankakee, Ill., Nov. 21, 1882. His chief pastorates have been at Kankakee, Ill.; Darlington, Wis.; Hudson, Wis.; Leadville, Col., and Denver, Col. He was married Nov. 23, 1889, to Miss Katie E. Bradley, born at Nunda, N. Y., July 12, 1864. Present address, Palmer Lake, Col., where he is engaged in home missionary work.

836. (iii.) ENDORA A.[20], b. at Masonville, N. Y., July 5, 1856; is unmarried and lives with her mother at Denver, Col. Address, Overland, Col.

837. (iv.) WILLIAM P.[20], b. at Masonville, N. Y., in 1858; graduated at Colgate University; took the prize in oratory; was Professor at Fort Edward Collegiate Institute; studied law, and is now at Denver, Col. Address, Overland, Col.

838. (v.) FREDERICK LINCOLN[20], b. at Masonville, N. Y., in 1860. Was an enthusiastic temperance worker in his early days. He enlisted in the regular army at New York City, and after serving about three years bought off his time and located at Portland, Ore., where he is interested in manufacturing. He is State Secretary of the Oregon Baptist Young People's Union.

839. (vi.) EDITH H.[20], b. and d. about 1862.

Levi B. Kneeland[19].

840. (vii). HOWARD GRANT KNEELAND[20], b. at Masonville,
N. Y., Feb. 19, 1866. Baptized into the Masonville
church, June 22, 1878. Entered Colgate Academy
in 1882; graduated from Coleman's Business College and taught in connection therewith at Newark,
N. J., 1885; seriously considered entering the
gospel ministry; removed with his parents to Leadville, Col. May 13, 1889, he was appointed government custodian of Pike's Peak by the Department
of the Interior; graduated from the Medical Department of Denver University, April 19, 1892; elected
resident physician of St. Luke's Hospital, at
Denver, Col., May, 10, 1892. Typhoid fever broke
out in the hospital through the use of impure
water, the fault of the management. Dr. Kneeland was one of the victims of the disease. After
three runs of the fever—a relapse, then a collapse
—a sickness of about ninety days, nature gave out
and he died Nov. 19, 1892, in his twenty-seventh
year, just as he was entering upon what promised to
be a very successful career. He was already gaining prominence among the medical fraternity by
his accurate diagnosis of disease, his faithful, skillful service and his winsome manner. He was soon
to have been married to Miss Alice W. Baker, of
Colorado Springs, whose untiring attention and
devoted service during the period of his sickness,
has forever endeared her to the family.

This is the history as given by his family.
Previous to receiving it, I had written the following:

While on a trip to California in 1889, my wife
and I stopped for a few days at Manitou Springs,
Col., and took advantage of the newly established stage line for a trip to the top of Pike's
Peak. Arriving at the apex, we were highly entertained by the U. S. Government Signal Service man
in charge of the station there, who took our photographs, and was especially kind to us on finding
that we were Kneelands. This was Howard Knee-

land, above named, and I here carve this epitaph to his general excellence and diplomatic suavity, showing him to be a true member of the clan.

841. (788.) REV. LEVI KNEELAND[18] (*Oliver*[17], *Timothy*[16], *Joseph*[15], *Edward*[14], *Edward*[13], *Edward*[12], *John*[11]—*Alexander*[1]).

Extract from the Baptist Encyclopedia: "Rev. Levi Kneeland was born in Masonville, N. Y., in 1803. At the age of fifteen he was converted and united with the Baptist church at Masonville; at twenty he was licensed to preach. A year later, in 1824, he entered Hamilton Literary and Theological Institution and remained four years. He was ordained at Packerville, Conn., Oct. 8, 1828, with a church just formed; established a branch church at Voluntown, and preached at Jewett City, Sterling and Plainfield, Conn, also assisted in protracted meetings at Norwich and elsewhere. Bold, aggressive, mighty in prayer, powerful in exhortation, full of illustrations, affable, sociable, intent on saving souls, and greatly beloved by his brethren. In the six years of his ministry he baptized more than three hundred. He died at Packerville, August 23, 1834, aged thirty-one."

No higher character could be given by ministerial associates than that thus voluntarily awarded to Levi Kneeland. He was a nephew of Rev. Abner Kneeland. The light of both of these celebrated preachers failed at the same time, one by death, the other by the extinction of faith in the God of the scriptures. If Abner Kneeland had passed away at the same time, great would have been his renown and greater his reward. He lived a blameless life according to his convictions. Who knows but what

" In the hereafter angels may
Roll the stone from his grave away."

In addition to the foregoing, we give the following sketch of Levi's life-work, from the " History of Windham County, Conn.," p. 505 : "Applying to the Baptist Home Missionary Society, Capt. Packard secured the services of a recent graduate of Hamilton College—Levi Kneeland, a nephew of the

Rev. Levi Kneeland[18].

able editor of the Boston *Investigator.* He was as earnest in promulgating the gospel as his kinsman in opposing it. In homes and school houses, in barns and groves, he proclaimed the message of salvation with great power and effect. A congregation quickly gathered around him and October 8, 1828, the Packerville Baptist Church was organized and Mr. Kneeland ordained to the ministry. Beginning with 21 members, its numbers were rapidly increased. Scarce a Sabbath passed without a baptismal service, and in eight months it numbered 101. A house of worship was soon provided which was thrown open to all Christian and philanthropic enterprises. The wholesome influence of this church was felt throughout the surrounding county. Mr. Kneeland extended his labors into Voluntown, Scotland and Preston. Aged men would journey many miles on Sunday to join in worship with this Baptist church and its earnest pastor. Laboring with such intensity, his life work was soon accomplished. A painful illness closed his life and ministry August, 1834. The immense crowd gathered at his funeral witnessed to the wide and deep impression made by this faithful Christian laborer."

CHAPTER XIV.

DESCENDANTS OF JOHN KNEELAND, ESQ.

(NOS. 842 TO 910.)

842. (770.) JOHN KNEELAND, ESQ.[17] (*Timothy*[16], *Joseph*[15], *Edward*[14], *Edward*[13], *Edward*[12], *John*[11], *William*[10], *James*[9], *Alexander*[8], *William*[7], *William*[6], *John*[5], *John*[4], *John*[3], *James*[2], *Alexander*[1]). Second son of Timothy Kneeland[16], b. at Gardner, Mass., April 7, 1776; m. in 1791, Polly, daughter of Israel Johnson, of Chesterfield, N. H., where he then resided; she d. April 25, 1842, æ. 66; he d. Feb. 9, 1850, æ. 83.

After marriage he located for several years in Vermont and then returned to Chesterfield where he spent his remaining life and where several descendants still reside. The first house erected by him at Chesterfield was a large frame building near the west village. It was built in 1790 and is owned and occupied by George Burnham, who married his granddaughter. From the porch of this house his brother, Rev. Abner Kneeland, then a Baptist minister, often preached. Although a builder by trade, he had a large farm which he owned and occupied for many years, and which has ever since been called the "Squire Kneeland farm." It is now occupied by C. P. Goodrich, Esq. John Kneeland was a Justice of the Peace, and held the office of "selectman" for the town of Chesterfield for sixteen years, a longer term than given to any other incumbent. He represented the town in the legislature during the years 1818, 1822 and 1825. Squire Kneeland was a country gentleman of the highest type, and his numerous descendants may well look back at his well-spent life with pride.

John Kneeland, Esq.[17].

Children of John and Polly (Johnson) Kneeland.

843.   (i.) POLLY[18], b. in Vermont, July 15, 1794; m. in 1817, to Joseph Clark; d. May 7, 1850 (see hereafter, 883).

844.   (ii). CYNTHIA KNEELAND[18], b. in Vermont, June 23, 1797; m. in 1820 to Levi Merrick, son of Constant Merrick. They settled in Bangor, N. Y. Have no record of their descendants.

845.   (iii.) ELECTA KNEELAND[18], b. in Chesterfield, Aug. 10, 1799; m. in 1820 to Ezra Titus; d. Feb. 26, 1869. They had one son, *Gen. H. B. Titus*, who was in the Civil War, ánd in 1888 was a lawyer in New York City. I have no trace of his present whereabouts or of his descendants.

846.   (iv.) LUCY KNEELAND[18], b. at Chesterfield April 26, 1803; m. in. 1828 to Josiah Higgins; d. Oct. 17, 1872. Children:

847.   (i.) *Mary M. Higgins*[19], b. July 28, 1829; m. William Holman, April 8, 1851; they reside in Chesterfield, N. H. Mrs. Holman has proved an indefatigable worker. It is only through her efforts that I have been able to secure this full report of the descendants of John Kneeland. May the angel of genealogists keep her from all harm and danger many, many "moons." Their children are:

848.   (i.) Mary R. Holman[20], b. at Chesterfield, May 5, 1853; m. E. Safford, Feb. 14, 1871. One child:

849.   *Grey F. Safford*[21], b. June 16, 1883.

850.   (ii.) Frank M. Holman[20], b. Dec. 30, 1854; unmarried.

851.   (iii.) Fred W. Holman[20], b. at Chesterfield, Sept. 30, 1856; m. Nellie Dunton, April 3, 1886. Children:

852.   (i.) *Margaret C. Holman*[21], b. May 20, 1889.

852A.   (ii.) *Wayne N. Holman*[21], b. July 18, 1890.

853.   (iv.) George A. Holman[20], b. Oct. 26, 1858, at Chesterfield; unmarried.

Mrs. Mary M. Holman

No. 847

854.   (v.) Helen L. Holman[20], b. March 6, 1861; d. Aug. 3, 1877.

855.   (ii.) *Arza A. Higgins*[19], b. at Chesterfield, N. H., March 13, 1831; m. (1) Sarah White; (2) Elsie Field; (3) Dora Crane. He now lives at Swanzey, Vt. Children:

856.   (i.) Lillian A. Higgins[20], b. April 28, 1876; m. Oct. 24, 1891, to Wm. F. Hammond, of Winchester, Vt.

857.   (ii.) Lydia Higgins[20], b. Jan. 29, 1886; lives at Swanzey, Vt.

858.   (iii.) *Henry H. Higgins*[19], b. at Chesterfield, N. H., May 16, 1835; m. Emma Whitcomb, about 1860; enlisted and was an officer in the war; was imprisoned in Libby prison; came home sick, and died Aug. 17, 1864.

859.   (iv.) *Sidney Baxter Higgins*[19], b. Sept. 27, 1841; enlisted in the army in 1862; was severely wounded and received several promotions for personal bravery; was discharged as first lieutenant. He was a merchant at Des Moines, Iowa, for about fifteen years; now resides at Masser, Neb. Married Alice Crook. Children:

860.   (i.) Edward Drake Higgins[20], b. at Des Moines, in 1878.

861.   (ii.) Alice Higgins[20], b. in 1888.

862.   (v.) ARZA KNEELAND[18], b. at Chesterfield, March 1, 1806; d. Aug. 4, 1825.

863.   (vi.) ABIAL KNEELAND[18], b. at Chesterfield, May 15, 1809; m. March 3, 1831, to Worcester Farr (of whom hereafter, 866).

864.   (vii.) ELIZA KNEELAND[18], b. at Chesterfield, Aug. 6, 1811; m. Archibald McCorkle, of Belton, Bell County, Texas; d. Dec. 4, 1893, æ. 82.

865.   (viii.) JOHN W. KNEELAND[18], b. at Chesterfield, July 23, 1814; m. Mary Austin, of Dexter, Me.; d. at Rogersville, Tenn., in 1855.

12

Abial Kneeland[18]

866. (863.) ABIAL KNEELAND[18] (*John[17]*, *Timothy[16]*,
        Joseph[15], *Edward[14]*, *Edward[13]*, *Edward[12]*, *John[11]*
        —*Alexander[1]*). Born at Chesterfield, N. H., May
        15, 1809; m. Worcester Farr, March 3, 1831.
    They always resided in Chesterfield, and had the follow-
ing children, all born at that place:

Children of Abial and Worcester (Farr) Kneeland.

867. (i.) LESTINA FARR[19], b. Sept. 2, 1831; m. Clark Covey,
        Feb. 1, 1852. They lived at Brattleboro, Vt., and
        afterwards went to Bloomington, Ill., and died
        there March 7, 1857. Children:
868.   (i.) *William G. Covey[20]*, b. at Brattleboro, Nov. 1,
            1852; m. Emma Martin and resided at Sullivan,
            Illinois.
869.   (ii.) *Arthur W. Covey[20]*, b. in 1856; had his name
            changed to De Forest; m. Emma Lawrence;
            resides in Hartford, Conn.
870. (ii.) GILBERT W. FARR[19], b. June 27, 1833; d. July
        17, 1838.
871. (iii.) CHESTER D. FARR[19], b. Aug. 21, 1834; d. Dec.
        28, 1838.
872. (iv.) FRANK H. FARR[19], b. Aug. 4, 1836; m. (1) Phila
        Prentice; she d. March 27, 1864; (2) Ellen J. Wilson,
        of Keene, N. H. They reside at Brattleboro, Vt.
873. (v.) IRA D. FARR[19], b. March 9, 1838; m. Mrs. Caroline
        S. Blood, daughter of Nelson Stowell, of Massena,
        N. Y. Lives at West Chesterfield, N. H.
874. (vi.) DENNIE W. FARR[19], b. Jan. 7, 1840; m. Mary H.
        Brown, daughter of Rev. Addison Brown, of
        Brattleboro, Vt. Enlisted in the Fourth Vermont
        Volunteers at the commencement of the war; was
        commissioned second lieutenant, and afterwards
        captain of Company C; was killed at the Battle of
        the Wilderness, on the fifth day of May, 1864.
        His body was brought to Chesterfield, N. H., and
        buried there with Masonic honors in the cemetery
        near the west village.

"And yet, and yet, we must not forget
That many brave boys must fall."

875. (vii.) JAMES E. FARR[19], b. June 24, 1843; d. Feb. 7, 1853.
876. (viii.) CHARLES M. FARR[19], b. June 7, 1845; m. (1) Mary T. Finnegan, of New York City; she d. May 4, 1875; (2) Mary Dwyer, of New York.
877. (ix.) BERNARD S. FARR[19], b. July 29, 1847; d. Feb. 6, 1833.
878. (x.) EDWIN W. FARR[19], b. Oct. 24, 1849; m. Abbie E. Smith, in August, 1874; lives at 26 Pier St., Cleveland, Ohio.
879. (xi.) HELEN E. FARR[19], b. Feb. 10, 1852; m. George F. Burnham, of Hartland, Vt., Nov. 1, 1875. They now reside at Chesterfield, N. H., in the house built by her grandfather, John Kneeland, in 1792. Their children are:
880. (i.) *Carl C. Burnham[20]*, b. July 14, 1877.
881. (ii.) *Chester M. Burnham[20]*, b. Aug. 28, 1883.
882. (iii.) *Marcie J. Burnham[20]*, b. June 11, 1885.
All born at Chesterfield.

883. (843.) POLLY KNEELAND[18] (*John[17]*, *Timothy[16]*, *Joseph[15]*, *Edward[14]*, *Edward[13]*, *Edward[12]*, *John[11]* —*Alexander[1]*). Eldest child of John Kneeland[17], b. in Dummerston, Vt., July 15, 1794; m. in 1817, to Joseph Clark. They had the following:

Children of Polly Kneeland[18] and Joseph Clark.

884. (i.) HENRY O. CLARK[19], b. June 1, 1819; m. Sept. 2, 1839, Hannah Willard. They resided at Walpole, N. H., for many years, he being a station agent of the Cheshire Railroad at that place. Afterwards he was transferred to Winchester, Mass., where he now resides. Their children, all born at Walpole, are:
885. (i.) *Hannah O. Clark[20]*, b. April 18, 1840; m. Theodore Parker.
886. (ii.) *Henry W. Clark[20]*, b. Jan. 11, 1842; served in the war, Comp. I, Ninth N. H. Vols.; m. Mary K. Farrar, of Winchester, Mass.; she d. March 10, 1886.

Polly Kneeland[18].

887.   (iii.) *Wallace R. Clark*[20], b. Nov. 11, 1844; d. Sept. 2, 1864.

888.   (ii.) ARZA KNEELAND CLARK[19], b. Feb. 9, 1823; m. Saphira S. Marsh, Nov. 6, 1845; d. Nov. 6, 1868. Children:

889.   (i.) *Arza H. Clark*[20], b. May 11, 1848; d. same month.

890.   (ii.) *Rosella S. Clark*[20], b. Jan. 1, 1849; m. Reuben A. Lewis. She is a widow; resides at Hinsdale, N. H. He d. Feb. 2, 1889.

891.   (iii.) *Arthur J. Clark*[20], b. Dec. 29, 1853; m. Belle C. Ellmore, of Hinsdale, Jan. 12, 1881; she d. Jan. 3, 1884. Children:

892.   (i.) Ralph A. Clark[21], b. June 4, 1882.
893.   (ii.) Marion B. Clark[21], b. Dec. 28, 1883.
                Married (2) Hattie E. Gallup, of Woodstock, Vt., April 5, 1893. No children.

894.   (iv.) *Charles W. Clark*[20], b. Oct. 25, 1863; unmarried.
                Arza H. Clark was a prominent citizen of Chesterfield; was "selectman" for four terms and town clerk for one term.

895.   (iii.) ELIZA ANN CLARK[19], b. Dec. 24, 1825; m. (1) Charles D. Carpenter, in 1843, who d. May 1, 1847; (2) Geo. S. Wilder, of Hinsdale, N. H.; she d. Feb. 11, 1868. Children by C. D. Carpenter:

896.   (i.) *Helen R. Carpenter*[20], b. July 8, 1844; m. in 1860, to Ogden A. Goodwin. Child:

897.   Claude[21], b. May 27, 1862; d. Sept. 6, 1862.
898.   (ii.) *Charles D. Carpenter*[20], b. Oct. 20, 1846; d. Oct. 4, 1849.
                Children by George S. Wilder:

899.   (iii.) *Fred G. Wilder*[20], b. Aug. 1, 1858; m. Abbie Holman, of Hinsdale, May 19, 1881. Children:

900.   (i.) Harold[21], May 11, 1883; d. March 24, 1885.
900A.   (ii.) Robert[21], b. April 23, 1886.
901.   (iv.) *Herbert M. Wilder*[20], b. Sept. 26, 1865; unmarried.

Hon. Wilder P. Clark[19].

902. (iv.) WILDER P. CLARK[19], b. Oct. 12, 1832 (of whom hereafter, 907).

903. (v.) HELEN M. CLARK[19], b. July 1, 1835; m. Spencer M. Leonard, of Westmoreland, April 18, 1855; resides at Westmoreland. Children:

904. (i.) *George Oliver Leonard*[20], b. Feb. 20, 1856; d. March 28, 1883.

905. (ii.) *Ida A. Leonard*[20], b. April 20, 1862; d. April 28, 1872.

906. (iii.) *Walter L. Leonard*[20], b. March 10, 1868; d. May 7, 1872.

907. (902.) HON. WILDER P. CLARK[19] (*Polly*[18], *John*[17], *Timothy*[16], *Joseph*[15], *Edward*[14], *Edward*[13], *Edward*[12], *John*[11]—*Alexander*[1]). Third son of Joseph and Polly (Kneeland) Clark, and grandson of John Kneeland, Esq. Born Oct. 12, 1832.

He received a liberal education and is a man of marked character and ability. He is a prominent manufacturer and wholesale dealer in wooden ware at Winchenden, Mass., and was a member of the legislature of Massachusetts during the years 1877, 1879 and 1883, serving on Finance and Insurance committees. In 1891 and 1892 he was a member of the Senate of Massachusetts and chairman of several important committees, and a member of the Senate Committee to represent the commonwealth at the opening of the World's Columbian Exposition, at Chicago. He married Mary C. Merrill, February 3, 1864, by whom he had the following children, who reside with him at Winchenden:

Children of Wilder P. and Mary C. Clark.

908. (i.) MURDOCK M. CLARK[20], b. at Belfast, Me., Dec. 9, 1867.

909. (ii.) MARY W. CLARK[20], b. in Winchenden, Mass., June 11, 1873.

910. (iii.) MAURICE L. CLARK[20], b. in Winchenden, July 13, 1875.

CHAPTER XV.

DESCENDANTS OF ASA KNEELAND.

(NOS. 911 TO 1187.)

911. (772.) ASA KNEELAND[17] (*Timothy*[16], *Joseph*[15], *Edward*[14], *Edward*[13], *Edward*[12], *John*[11], *William*[10], *James*[9], *Alexander*[8], *William*[7], *William*[6], *John*[5], *John*[4], *John*[3], *James*[2], *Alexander*[1]). Son of Timothy and Hannah (Stone) Kneeland, b. at Gardner, Mass., Sept. 20, 1771; m. Hannah Cheney, of Orange, Mass., Jan. 5, 1797.

They first settled in Newfane, Vt., where he was in partnership with his brother Abner, before the latter commenced his famous career in the pulpit and rostrum. He remained there until after the birth of his eldest son, John, in 1799, and then went into the unbroken forests of Canada, took up a plot of three hundred acres, built a log cabin and underwent the usual hardships of pioneer life. He afterwards erected a substantial frame house about fifty feet square and two stories high, with a stone chimney about fifteen feet square, running through the centre from cellar to roof. This chimney had fireplaces on each of its four sides and an immense bake oven in the kitchen. The writer was born in this old house and never will forget its roomy vastness and the comfort of lying on the rug in front of that kitchen fireplace with its cavernous depths lighted up by a back log about five feet long and eighteen inches thick. The old house has long since passed away, but the vision of that fireplace and the glow of that back log will be light and warmth to me as long as life is a reality.

Those who know the weight and size of a thousand shingles will have an adequate idea of the strength of Asa Kneeland when they learn the fact that he carried a full bunch on his shoulders up the ladder to the top of that house. He died

Asa Kneeland[17].

June 7, 1844, at the age of 67. His widow died Feb. 23, 1861, at the age of 83. She was a patient, perfect Christian. In memory of her love and tenderness to the writer, who was cast a motherless infant upon her care, I reproduce herewith, from an oil painting, the features of my dear old grandmother.

Hannah (Cheney) Kneeland was the daughter of Ebenezer and Hannah (Gould) Cheney, and was born Aug. 18, 1777, at Orange, Mass. Her father, Ebenezer Cheney, was the son of William and Joanna (Thayer) Cheney. He was born in Mendon, Mass., July 10, 1741, and served as Sergeant in Capt. Wen Jones' company in the French and Indian War, and was at Ticonderoga under Gen. Amherst. The gun, cartridge box and powder horn which he carried are now in the possession of one of his descendants—Hon. Henry E. Turner, of Lowville, N. Y. Upon the horn is cut "Ebenezer Cheney, Ticonderoga." He also served in the War of the Revolution, in Capt. Moses Harvey's company, of Col. David Wells' regiment, enlisting May 10, 1777. His father, William Cheney, was the last of five successive generations of William Cheneys, the first of which came to America from Stafford, England, prior to 1635.

According to Burke, the Stafford Cheneys are descendants of the Cheneys of Sherland, and have the same Coat of Arms, with the addition of the motto peculiar to their branch of the family, "Fato Prudentia Major." A sketch of the Sherley family, with a statement of their Coat of Arms, is given as follows in Burke's "Encyclopedia of Heraldry:"

"Tradition records that Sir John Cheney, of Sherland, an eminent soldier under the banner of Henry of Richmond, at Bosworth, personally encountering King Richard III, was felled to the ground by the monarch, had his crest struck off and his head laid bare. For some time he remained stunned, but recovering, he cut the skull and horns off the hide of an ox which chanced to be near, and fixing them upon his head to supply the upper part of the helmet, he returned to the battle and did such signal service that Henry, on being proclaimed king, assigned Cheney for crest the bull's horns, which his descendants still bear. Whatever credence may be given to this story, certain it is that Sir John Cheney was most instrumental in the successful issue of Richmond's cause, and was created by the monarch Baron Cheney, and made ' Knight of the Garter.'   Coat of Arms.—Az. six lions rampant, argent a canton erm.   Crest.—A bull's scalp.   Supporters.—Two greyhounds.   These were the arms of Sherland and adopted by the Cheneys on the marriage with the heiress.   To this must be added the most excellent motto of the Stafford family of Cheneys, ' Fato Prudentia Major.' "

I am indebted to Lewis Hall, of Jamestown, N. Y., who is the author of an unpublished work on the Cheney family, for much information in respect thereto.

Children of Asa and Hannah (Cheney) Kneeland.

912.   (i.) JOHN[18], b. in Newfane, Vt., March 4, 1799 (of whom hereafter, 925).

913.   (ii.) PHILENA[18], b. in Stukely, Canada, May 17, 1801 (of whom hereafter, 1,007).

914.   (iii.) HANNAH GOULD[18], b. in Stukely, Sept. 20, 1802 (of whom hereafter, 1,058).

915.   (iv.) MARIA[18], b. in Stukely, Dec. 6, 1803; m. Elisha G. White, Nov. 30, 1837.

916.   (v.) ASA[18], b. in Stukely, Dec. 25, 1804; m. and had four children:

916A.   (i.) *Agnes F.*[19].

917.   (ii.) *Albert*[19].

918.   (iii.) *Abigail*[19].

918A.   (iv.) *William*[19].

919.   (vi.) DULCINA[18], b. in Stukely, Aug. 26, 1806 (of whom hereafter, 1,099).

920.   (vii.) ABNER CHENEY[18], b. in Stukely, Nov. 17, 1807 (of whom hereafter, 1,112).

921.   (viii.) SARAH[18], b. in Stukely, Dec. 21, 1808 (of whom hereafter, 1,141).

922.   (ix.) LEONARD[18], b. in Stukely, Oct. 15, 1810 (of whom hereafter, 1,147).

923.   (x.) GARDNER[18], b. in Stukely, Nov. 23, 1814 (of whom hereafter, 1,188).

924.   (xi.) TIMOTHY AVERILL[18], b. Oct. 9, 1816 (of whom hereafter, 1,172).

HANNAH (CHENEY) KNEELAND

No. 911

925. (912.) JOHN KNEELAND[18] (*Asa*[17], *Timothy*[16], *Joseph*[15], *Edward*[14], *Edward*[13], *Edward*[12], *John*[11] —*Alexander*[1]). Eldest son of Asa and Hannah (Cheney) Kneeland, b. at Newfane, Vt., March 4, 1799; m. March 30, 1820, to Rebecca M. Brigham.

Like his father and grandfather and several of his brothers and sisters, he had eleven children. He died March 21, 1845. She died March 25, 1867.

Children of John and Rebecca M. (Brigham) Kneeland.

926. (i.) JOHN ALLEN[19], b. Jan. 5, 1821, at Stukely, Canada; he is unmarried; settled in Fulton County, Indiana, in 1844. In 1849 he settled at Humboldt Bay, Cal., and has resided in California ever since, his present residence being Arcata, Cal. He is a successful farmer and has always been content with digging potatoes for gold, instead of digging gold for potatoes.

927. (ii.) BENJAMIN MERRILL[19], b. Aug. 28, 1822, at Stukely.

928. (iii.) ALBERT CHENEY[19], b. June 27, 1824, in Stukely; d. March 12, 1845, in Rochester, Ind.

929. (iv.) HANNAH MARIA[19], b. April 27, 1826, in Stukely, Canada; m. (1) Abel Greenwood, Sept. 9, 1843, and (2) James Cornelius Feeley, Dec. 20, 1855. Children by Abel Greenwood:

930. (i.) *Laura Lovinia Greenwood*[20], b. June 16, 1844, in Stukely.

931. (ii.) *Abel Foster Greenwood*[20], b. Feb. 26, 1846, in Rochester, Ind.; m. Tida Butler, Jan. 18, 1869. Residence, Columbus, Ohio. Children:

932. (i.) Edward Foster Greenwood[21], b. Feb, 15, 1870.

933. (ii.) Margaret Minnie Greenwood[21], b. Jan. 4, 1872.

934. (iii.) John Greenwood[21], b. May 19, 1874.

935. (iv.) Laura Maria Greenwood[21], b. Nov. 7, 1879.

936. (v.) Charles Oliver Greenwood[21], b. Jan. 18, 1881.

937. (iii.) *Sarah Ellen Greenwood*[20], b. May 29, 1849, at Rochester, Ind.; d. Jan. 5, 1853.

John Kneeland[18].

By James C. Feeley:

938.   (iv.) *James Cornelius Feeley*[20], b. in Freeport, Ill.,
Dec. 6, 1856; m. Florence L. Avery. Resides
in Mason City, Iowa. Children:

939.   (i.) Florence May Feeley[21], b. May 4, 1878.
940.   (ii.) Harry James Feeley[21], b. March 15, 1883.
941.   (iii.) Myron Henry Feeley[21], b. Feb. 18, 1885.
942. (v.) SYLVIA[19], b. Nov. 15, 1828, in Stukely, Canada.;
m. Royal Kennedy, Aug. 22, 1849, who was b.
Oct. 25, 1822, and resides at Burr Oak, Kansas; a
farmer. She d. March 20, 1870, in La Porte
City, Iowa. Children:

943.   (i.) *Mandanie C. Kennedy*[20], b. June 27, 1850; m.
—— 17, 1867, in La Porte City, Iowa, to
Archibald M. Brinkerhoff. He is an under-
taker and resides at Garwin, Tama Co., Iowa.
Children:

944.   (i.) Emma Eldora Brinkerhoff[21], b. April 7,
1867; m. Edward Willard, of Oakland,
Cal., Sept. 9, 1888. Child:

944A.   (i.) *Archibald Edwin Willard*[22], b. July 1,
1870.

945.   (ii.) Etta Frances Brinkerhoff[21], b. Jan. 1, 1870;
m. Wells Fitzgerald, March 17, 1891. Child:

945A.   *Willard H. Fitzgerald*[22], b. June 27, 1895.
946.   (iii.) Almira C. B. Brinkerhoff[21], b. Oct. 19, 1878.
947.   (iv.) Jessie Garfield Brinkerhoff[21], b. Oct. 1, 1883.
948.   (ii.) *Cynthia Ellen Kennedy*[20], b. June 27, 1850; m.
Sept. 20, 1874, James Elden Blanchard. He is
an engineer and resides at Oakland, Cal.
Children:

949.   (i.) Edgar Cyrus Blanchard[21], b. June 1, 1875.
950.   (ii.) Royal Carter Blanchard[21], b. March 7, 1882.
951.   (iii.) Ethel Grace Blanchard[21], b. Sept. 16, 1886.
952.   (iii.) *Cyrus Milton Kennedy*[20], b. Feb. 2, 1857; m.
Laura Beal, in 1879. They reside in Hum-
phrey, Neb. Children:

953.   (i.) Edna Kennedy[21], b. Sept. 4, 1881.
954.   (ii.) Roy Kennedy[21], b, Jan. 3, 1885.

ANN B. KNEELAND.   GILBERT B. KNEELAND

No. 975

John Kneeland[18].

955.   (iii.) William May Kennedy[21], b. April 1, 1889.
956.   (iv.) Asa Kennedy[21], b. May 9, 1891.
957.   (iv.) *Edwin Almond Kennedy*[20], b. April 5, 1859. Reside at Jewell City, Kansas.
958.   (v.) *Laura Rebecca Kennedy*[20], b. Feb. 27, 1861 ; m. J. H. Euson. Reside at Stockton, Cal. Children :
959.   (i.) Erol Ray Euson[21], b. Sept. 4, 1889.
960.   (ii.) Inez Corinne Euson[21], b. March 26, 1894.
971.   (vi.) *Eva Sylvia Kennedy*[20], b. June 10, 1868. Residence, Jewell City, Kansas.
972.   (vii.) *Clara Bell Kennedy*[20], b. March 16, 1870; d. July 10, 1870.
973. (vi.) SARAH REBECCA[19], b. Jan. 20, 1831, in Stukely, Canada ; m. —— Abrams ; d. June 10, 1866, in Winterset, Iowa.
974. (vii.) ASA[19], b. Feb. 14, 1833, in Stukely ; d. March 7, 1845, in Rochester, Ind.
975. (viii.) GILBERT BAILEY[19], b. Jan. 9, 1835, in Stukely ; m. Nov. 5, 1860, in Dows Prairie, Cal., Betsy Ann Dilke, who was b. Sept. 10, 1845, in Jonesville, Mich. They reside at Arcata, Cal. Children :
976.   (i.) *Cynthia Ione*[20], b. Aug. 29, 1867, in Arcata ; m. Edwin A. Kennedy, Aug. 1, 1896. He is a carpenter and resides at Oakland, Cal.
977.   (ii.) *Lydia Leonie*[20], b. Aug. 16, 1869, in Arcata ; m. John B. Russell. Children :
978.   (i.) Mary Grace Russell[21], b. Feb. 27, 1887.
979.   (ii.) Anna Louise Russell[21], b. March 4, 1891.
980.   (iii.) *Oscar Eugene*[20], b. Nov. 17, 1871, in Arcata.
981.   (iv.) *Herman Melville*[20], b. Jan. 8, 1874, in Arcata.
982.   (v.) *Viola Kale*[20], b. April 3, 1877, in Arcata.
983.   (vi.) *Marion Mark*[20], b. Dec. 2, 1879, in Arcata.
984. (ix.) MANDANA PRATT[19], b. Sept. 9, 1837, in Stukely, Canada ; m. Oct. 30, 1860, at Dutch Flat, Cal., John Smith, who was b. Dec. 9, 1821, in Wheeling, Va. Reside at Arcata, Cal. Children :

John Kneeland[18].

985.   (i.) *Udella Smith*[20], b. July 19, 1861; m. Feb. 23,
           1879, Arthur P. Falor, who was b. Oct. 13,
           1839, in Rockville, Ill.   Residence, Maple
           Creek, Cal.   Children:
986.   (i.) Mito Pliny Falor[21], b. Dec. 14, 1879.
987.   (ii.) Elmer Eugene Falor[21], b. June 4, 1882.
988.   (iii.) George E. Falor[21], b. Jan. 10, 1884.
989.   (ii.) *Rebecca Elinor Smith*[20], b. April 3, 1865, in
           Colesburg, Ill.; m. Aaron Frederick Nelson,
           Dec. 25, 1884.   He was b. March 1, 1857, in
           Carlstadt,'Sweden.   They reside at Sciota, Cal.
           He is a lumberman.   Child:
989A. Sylvia Lorena Nelson, b. March 20, 1885.
990.   (iii.) *Lasa Kneeland Smith*[20], b. Feb. 4, 1867, in
           Dutch Flat, Cal.
991.   (iv.) *Ellis Seeley Smith*[20], b. May 18, 1869, in Ar-
           cata, Cal.
992.   (v.) *Byron Menefer Smith*[20], b. June 8, 1878.
993.   (x.) LYDIA LAWRENCE[19], b. Nov. 15, 1839, in Stukely,
           Canada; m. Dec. 22, 1859, Thomas Kennedy, who
           was b. Feb. 19, 1840, in Indiana.   They reside at
           Ingallston, Neb.   He is a cousin of Royal Kennedy,
           who m. Lydia's sister.   Children:
994.   (i.) *Gilbert Gilson Kennedy*[20], b. Oct. 24, 1860, in
           Plymouth, Ind.
995.   (ii.) *William Edwin Kennedy*[20], b. Oct. 31, 1862;
           m. Oct. 5, 1887, Effie Vervalin.   They reside
           at Ingallston, Neb.   Children:
996.   (i.) Nelly May Kennedy[21], b. July 26, 1888.
997.   (ii.) Roy E. L. Kennedy[21], b. May 5, 1890.
998.   (iii.) Ward Everet[21], b. June 23, 1892.
999.   (iv.) Henry William Kennedy[21], b. March 4,
           1894, d. Oct. 12, 1894.
1000. (v.) Edwina Olive Kennedy[21], b. June 12, 1895.
1001. (iii.) *Mary Eva Kennedy*[20], b. Feb. 9, 1867, in
           Plymouth, Ind.
1002. (iv.) *Endora Ellen Kennedy*[20], b. Dec. 14, 1872, in
           La Porte, Ind.; d. June 22, 1890.

1003. (v.) *Robert Leslie Kennedy*[20], b. May 16, 1875, in La Porte, Ind.; m. Charlotte D. Tracy, Sept. 8, 1894.

1004. (vi.) *Alta Elnora Kennedy*[20], b. May 16, 1875, in La Porte, Ind.; m. Peter M. Tracy, July 11, 1894.

1005. (vii.) *Udellins Elmer Kennedy*[20], b. Oct. 30, 1877, at La Porte, Ind.

1006. (xi.) LAURA ALMIRA[19], b. Dec. 6, 1841, in Stukely, Canada; d. Jan. 26, 1843.

1007. (913.) PHILENA KNEELAND[18] (*Asa*[17], *Timothy*[16], *Joseph*[15], *Edward*[14], *Edward*[13], *Edward*[12], *John*[11] —*Alexander*[1]). Eldest daughter of Asa and Hannah (Cheney) Kneeland, b. at South Stukely, Canada, May 17, 1801; m. Chase Fuller, Jan. 16, 1825.

He was a farmer, residing all his life at Bolton, Canada, where he was born May 16, 1802. Uncle Chase probably never saw a railroad or traveled fifty miles from his home farm. They were an honest, contented couple and had the usual Kneeland quota of eleven children.

Children of Chase and Philena (Kneeland) Fuller.

1008. (i.) ASA KNEELAND FULLER[19], b. May 1, 1826; d. in 1847.

1009. (ii.) DULCINA FULLER[19], b. Oct. 4, 1827; m. Nathan Morse Currier, March 1, 1852, who was b. Sept. 5, 1805, in Sandwich, N. H. They reside in Magog, Canada. Children:

1010. (i.) *Almus Nathan Currier*[20], b. Dec. 4, 1852; m. Mary Sweet. They reside in Newport, Vt., and have one child:

1011. Lulu May Currier[21], b. Sept. 7, 1887.

1012. (ii.) *Amanda Jane Currier*[20], b. June 25, 1855; m. April 4, 1882, to Walter Crosser; d. Sept. 18, 1887, in West Derby, Vt.

Philena Kneeland[18].

1013.   (iii.) *Maria Jane Currier*[20], b. Jan. 28, 1858; d. in infancy.

1014.   (iv.) *Ernest Nathan Currier*[20], b. Dec. 9, 1860; m. Oct. 2, 1886, in Magog, Eliza Tibbits, who was b. March 23, 1871.

1015.   (v.) *Jane Maria Currier*[20], b. Nov. 28, 1863; d. in infancy.

1016.   (vi.) *Laura Philena Alice Maude Currier*[20], b. Jan. 11, 1871.

1017.   (iii.) LEWIS FULLER[19], b. Sept. 20, 1829; m. Diana Temple Hoyt, who was b. Aug. 30, 1837; he d. Dec. 5, 1865, in Menomonse, Wis. Children:

1018.   (i.) *Miner Cheney Fuller*[20], b. Dec. 30, 1855; m. Mary Eliza Chamberlain, who was b. in Olta Springs, July 16, 1859. They reside in Reagan, Texas. Children:

1019.   (i.) Bertie Alleck Fuller[21], b. Nov. 22, 1878.

1020.   (ii.) Beryl Alice Fuller[21], b. May 12, 1880.

1021.   (iii.) Oscar Lewis Fuller[21], b. Dec. 17, 1881.

1022.   (iv.) Oneida L. Fuller[21], b. Jan. 21, 1884.

1023.   (v.) Osword Nathan Fuller[21], b. June 21, 1885.

1024.   (vi.) Angelo James Fuller[21], b. April 26, 1887.

1025.   (ii.) *Irvin Nason Fuller*[20], b. April 12, 1857; m. Mercy Malinda Manly.

1026.   (iii.) *Marian Philena Fuller*[20], b. Jan. 1, 1859; m. Dr. Samuel W. Rutledge, Aug. 26, 1877, who was b. Dec. 31, 1852. Residence, Grand Forks, Dakota. Child:

1027.   Ruby Rutledge[21], b. April 6, 1879, in Ross Creek, Minn.

1028.   (iv.) *Walter Van Dorn Fuller*[20], b. Jan. 10, 1861; m. Oct. 23, 1880, to Eliza Jane Stewart, who was b. Sept. 11, 1864. They reside in Aitken, Minn. Child:

1029.   Bertha Lucretia Fuller[21], b. March 15, 1882.

1030.   (v.) *Lewis Hoyt Fuller*[20], b. Dec. 9, 1862; m. Nov. 24, 1887, Della May Leech, who was b. Jan. 26, 1868. They reside in Wancoma, Iowa, and have no issue.

Philena Kneeland[18].

1031. (iv.) SABIA NELSON FULLER[19], b. Feb. 28, 1832; m. Stillman B. Copp, Jan. 10, 1860, who was b. Dec. 22, 1824; he d. Nov. 21, 1887, in George-ville, Canada. She resides on the home farm in Bolton. Children:

1032. (i.) *Sarton Fuller Copp*[20], b. Jan. 16, 1861; m. Sept. 12, 1881, Nellie Peckham, of Nashua, N. H. They reside at South Sudbury, Mass. Children:

1033. (i.) Grace Barr Copp[21], b. May 16, 1884.
1034. (ii.) Howard Gurton Copp[21], b. Aug. 25, 1885.
1035. (ii.) *Una Nelson Copp*[20], b. Nov. 22, 1862.
1036. (iii.) *Abba Lulella Copp*[20], b. July 1, 1864; m. April 7, 1885, to John Henry Bailey. They reside in Derby Line, Vt. No issue.
1037. (iv.) *George Fitch Copp*[20], b. Sept. 20, 1866.
1038. (v.) *Louis Stillman Copp*[20], b. March 6, 1869.
1039. (vi.) *Cheney Kneeland Copp*[20], b. Feb. 24, 1872.
1040. (vii.) *Lilly May Copp*[20], b. July 15, 1875.
1041. (v.) EBENEZER CHENEY FULLER[19], b. April 3, 1833; m. and settled in California.
1042. (vi.) THOMAS FULLER[19], b. Dec. 8, 1834; d. in 1851.
1043. (vii.) LAURA PHILENA FULLER[19], b. Sept. 5, 1838.
1044. (viii.) MANDLY NELSON FULLER[19], b. Sept. 29, 1839; m. in 1860 to Mary Elizabeth Ives. They remained on a farm in Bolton for ten years. In 1870 he went to Georgian Bay as a Methodist preacher. He returned to the Bolton farm, then went to Cali-fornia, in 1877. The next year he again returned to Bolton; three years later he was off to Cali-fornia; a year later went to Magog; from thence, in 1887, he returned to Bolton and was engaged in milling. He was there when last heard from. At this writing he may be in California or Japan. I hope my boyhood friend and cousin has at last gathered some moss from his "rolling stone," but I have my doubts. He is too honest to gather what he does not sow, and too good natured to keep what he gathers.

P. S.—The foregoing was written two months since. To-day I received a letter from him, sent from West Derby, Vt., where he is the pastor of a church. Verily, he is very much of a Kneeland. Their children are:

1045.   (i.) *James Richmond Fuller*[20], b. May 9, 1861.

1046.   (ii.) *Cheney Philander Fuller*[20], b. April 26, 1864; d. July 10, 1864.

1047.   (iii.) *Nellie Evelina Fuller*[20], b. Feb. 21, 1866.

1048.   (iv.) *Arthur Nelson Fuller*[20], b. Aug. 15, 1870; d. Nov. 9, 1880.

1049.   (v.) *Cora Elizabeth Fuller*[20], b. Nov. 5, 1878.

1050.   (vi.) *Francis Cheney Fuller*[20], b. Aug. 21, 1881.

1051.   (ix.) LOVEY MARIA FULLER[19], b. July 8, 1841; m. Levi Vincent, Nov. 8, 1861. Residence, Bolton, Canada. Children:

1052.   (i.) *Ella Edith Vincent*[20], b. Aug. 20, 1862.

1053.   (ii.) *Minnie Gertrude Vincent*[20], b. Sept. 11, 1866; d. Aug. 30, 1876.

1054.   (iii.) *Thatcher Theron Vincent*[20], b. Feb. 22, 1871.

1055.   (iv.) *George Symond Vincent*[20], b. Nov. 5, 1876.

1056.   (x.) MARY JANE FULLER[19], b. Feb. 10, 1843.

1057.   (xi.) ALPHONZO FULLER[19], b. March 17, 1844.

1058.   (914.) HANNAH GOULD KNEELAND[18] (*Asa*[17], *Timothy*[16], *Joseph*[15], *Edward*[14], *Edward*[13], *Edward*[12], *John*[11]—*Alexander*[1]). Second daughter and third child of Asa and Hannah (Cheney) Kneeland, b. at South Stukely, Can., Sept. 20, 1802; m. Dexter Parker, Jan. 1, 1822. He was b. Nov. 8, 1794, in Brattleboro, Vt., and d. April 14, 1873, in Bolton, Canada. She d. Oct. 3, 1873, at the same place.

Children of Dexter and Hannah Gould (Kneeland) Parker.

1059.   (i.) MATTHEW PARKER[19], b. March 27, 1825; d. March 30, 1825.

Hannah Gould Kneeland[18].

1060. (ii.) JAMES CORD PARKER[19], b. June 9, 1826; enlisted
          in the War of the Rebellion; killed at Newborn,
          N. C., March 20, 1862.   He m. Cynthia Morilla
          Wenon, at Athol, Mass., Nov. 29, 1849.   She was
          b. April 2, 1830, at Phillipston, Mass.   She d. Sept.
          18, 1864.   They resided at Athol, Mass., and had
          four children:

1061.   (i.) *Ella L. Parker[20]*, b. Dec. 10, 1850; d. Jan. 21,
          1869.

1062.   (ii.) *Ada L. Parker[20]*, b. Aug. 22, 1852; d. Sept.
          23, 1853.

1063.   (iii.) *May Aline Parker[20]*, b. March 28, 1854; m.
          Monroe F. Gage, of Athol, June 11, 1872.
          Children:

1064.   (i.) James Monroe Gage[21], b. May 19, 1877.
1065.   (ii.) Sarah Little Gage[21], b. Nov. 2, 1879.
1066.   (iii.) Ruth Winnifred Gage[21], b. Jan. 5, 1885;
          d. Jan. 11, 1885.

1067.   (iv.) *Harry Branscum Parker[20]*, b. April 29, 1856;
          m. Cora M. Hanes, of Holden, Mass., July 22,
          1880.   Children:

1068.   (i.) Harry Clarence Parker[21], b. July 6, 1881,
          at Dawsonville, Mass.

1069.   (ii.) Ernest Le Roy Parker[21], b. Aug. 10,
          1883, in Holden, Mass.

1070. (iii.) FLORA MARIA PARKER[19], b. Nov. 18, 1834; m.
          George Chase Bartlett, Dec. 26, 1853.   He was b.
          June 12, 1824, in Bethel, Canada.   Children:

1071.   (i.) *James Oscar Bartlett[20]*, b. Sept. 27, 1854; m.
          Mary Frances Bacon, of Boscobell, Canada.
          They reside in Cavour, Dakota.   Children:

1072.   (i.) Phoebe Ethel Bartlett[21], b. May 19, 1886.
1073.   (ii.) Florence Evelyn Bartlett[21], b. Jan. 29,
          1888.

1074.   (ii.) *Hannah Frances Bartlett[20]*, b. Aug. 11, 1856;
          m. Charles Ebenezer Kneeland (see No. 88).

1075.   (iii.) *Emily Eliza Bartlett[20]*, b. Feb. 10, 1859; m.
          Melvin F. Taylor, March 17, 1882, at Wabasha,
          Minn.; d. in 1888, at Yankton, Dakota.

13

Hannah Gould Kneeland[18].

1076.	(iv.) *Parker Coville Bartlett*[20], b. March 11, 1862.
1077.	(v.) *John Howard Bartlett*[20], b. April 11, 1873.
1078.	(vi.) *George Arthur Bartlett*[20], b. May 4, 1874.
1079.	(iv.) FRANCES MARION PARKER[19], b. Nov. 18, 1834; m. Oct. 14, 1851, Bethel Storrs Chamberlin, who was b. June 18, 1829. Their residence is in Bolton, Canada. P. O. address, South Stukely, Quebec. Children:
1080.	(i.) *Deforest Arlington Chamberlin*[20], b. July 16, 1853; killed Dec. 12, 1868, by falling of copper ore.
1081.	(ii.) *James Arthur Chamberlin*[20], b. Aug. 3, 1855; unmarried.
1082.	(iii.) *Lucy Angelia Chamberlin*[20], b. March 6, 1857; m. July 18, 1878, to Charles Young. He was b. in West Bolton, Nov. 11, 1854, and still resides there. Children:
1083.	(i.) Hattie Lelia Young[21], b. July 22, 1885.
1084.	(ii.) Martha Marion Young[21], b. Aug. 9, 1887.
1085.	(iv.) *Harley Eugene Chamberlin*[20], b. June 16, 1859; d. April 6, 1861.
1086.	(v.) *Hattie Moriah Chamberlin*[20], b. July 13, 1861; m. Jan. 4, 1877, to Mark Stanbridge, who was b. in England, Feb. 10, 1837. Residence, West Bolton. No children.
1087.	(vi.) *Alphonzo William Chamberlin*[20], b. Oct. 22, 1863; m. May 24, 1883, to Mary Martin, of Waterloo, Canada. They reside in North Shefford, Canada. Child:
1088.	Arthur Lincoln Chamberlin[21], b. Oct. 12, 1886.
1089.	(vii.) *Flora Lydia Chamberlin*[20], b. March 15, 1866; m. Nov. 28, 1883, at St. Albans, Vt., to John H. Odette, who was b. Sept. 21, 1864, at Clarenceville, Canada. They reside at St. Albans. Children:
1090.	(i.) Francis Marion Odette[21], b. Sept. 24, 1884.
1091.	(ii.) George William Odette[21], b. Oct. 7, 1886.
1092.	(viii.) *Rosepha Frances Chamberlin*[20], b. June 22, 1868; m. Nov. 18, 1885, Perrien Wesley Brown. Child:

Dulcinea Kneeland[18].

1093.   Jessie Rosepha Brown[21], b. April 18, 1886. Residence, Moss River, Quebec.

1094.   (ix.) *Sylvia Ella Chamberlin*[20], b. Aug. 6, 1871.

1095.   (x.) *Luke Arlington Chamberlin*[20], b. Sept. 23, 1873.

1096.   (xi.) *Bethuel Stone Chamberlin*[20], b. March 3, 1871; d. July 12, 1876.

1097.   (xii.) *Amanda Meral Chamberlin*[20], b. Dec. 9, 1877.

1098. (v.) JOHN M. PARKER[19], b. May 8, 1838; left home July 1, 1858, and never heard from since.

1099. (919.) DULCINEA KNEELAND[18] (*Asa*[17], *Timothy*[16], *Joseph*[15], *Edward*[14], *Edward*[13], *Edward*[12], *John*[11]—*Alexander*[1]). Fourth daughter and sixth child of Asa and Hannah (Cheney) Kneeland, b. in South Stukely, Canada, Aug. 26, 1806; m. first, Thomas Kendric Hill, Jan. 1, 1833; he d. Aug. 17, 1835. Married, second, Allen Bates, Dec. 1, 1840. He was b. in Vermont, April 10, 1796. During the first marriage she resided in Stanstead, Canada; after the second marriage, at Dunham, Canada.

Children of Dulcinea Kneeland, by Thomas Kendric Hill.

1100. (i.) THOMAS KENDRIC HILL[19], b. Nov. 5, 1833; d. March 10, 1842.

1101. (ii.) ARCHAELUS HILL[19], b. Feb. 22, 1835; d. March 8, 1835.

By Allen Bates.

1102. (iii.) MERRILL BATES[19], b. Sept. 14, 1843; m. April 28, 1869, Delilah Spears. She was b. in Dunham, March 26, 1849. They reside at Cowansville, Quebec, and have children:

1103.   (i.) *Candace Maranda Bates*[20], b. June 9, 1871.

1104.   (ii.) *George Leonard Bates*[20], b. Dec. 21, 1875.

1105.   (iii.) *Myron Merrill Bates*[20], b. Aug. 4, 1877.

1106. (iv.) THOMAS BATES[19], b. Jan. 22, 1845; d. March 20, 1845.

Abner Cheney Kneeland[18].

1107. (v.) GARDNER BATES[19], b. July 22, 1840; m. Sept. 2,
        1868, to Elizabeth Sanborn, of Brome, Canada.
        Children:
1108.   (i.) *Martha Dulcinea Bates[20]*, b. July 25, 1869.
1109.   (ii.) *Mary Ellen Bates[20]*, b. July 7, 1879.
1110.   (iii.) *Jessie Arthur Bates[20]*, b. Aug. 22, 1882.
1111.   (iv.) *Delilah Rosamond Bates[20]*, b. Nov. 30, 1886.

1112. (920.) ABNER CHENEY KNEELAND[18] (*Asa[17],
        Timothy[16], Joseph[15], Edward[14], Edward[13], Ed-
        ward[12], John[11]—Alexander[1]*). Third son of Asa
        and Hannah (Cheney) Kneeland, b. Nov. 17, 1807,
        in Stukely, Quebec; m. Tryphoena Gilson, of
        Proctorsville, Vt., Jan. 13, 1833.

He resided at different times at Stukely, Canada; Sherburne, Ludlow and Proctorsville, Vt.; Rochester and Indian-
apolis, Ind.; Humboldt Bay, Cal., and Owego, N. Y. He
was an intelligent, jovial, hardworking man. The good Lord
may possibly have made a truer friend and better neighbor,
but I do not believe he ever did. To him and his good wife
and equally good daughters, I am indebted for many a choice
bit of eatables and wearables while " soljering " in old Virginia.

Children of Abner and Tryphoena (Gilson) Kneeland.

1113. (i.) JAMES M. KNEELAND[19], b. Sept. 30, 1833, at
        Sherburne, Vt.; d. Sept. 27, 1835.
1114. (ii.) HANNAH SARETTE KNEELAND[19], b. Feb. 3, 1835,
        in Sherburne, Vt.; m. Sept. 19, 1854, in Proctorsville,
        Vt., Charles Martin Haywood, son of Luther Hay-
        wood and Hannah Pierce, and b. Aug. 16, 1833, in
        Ludlow, Vt. Residence (1887), Owego, N. Y.,
        42 Temple Street; dealer in monuments. Children:
1115.   (i.) *Myron Edgar Haywood[20]*, b. Feb. 26, 1860, in
            Bradford, Vt.; d. Feb. 20, 1863, in Owego, N.Y.
1116.   (ii.) *Arthur Vernon Haywood[20]*, b. July 14, 1861, in
            Bradford, Vt.; d. July 3, 1881, in Owego, N. Y.
1117.   (iii.) *Harry Clinton Haywood[20]*, b. Sept. 13, 1862, in
            Bradford, Vt.; m. E. Lena Goodrich. He has

succeeded to his father's marble business in Owego, where they reside. Children:

1118. (i.) Charles Martin Haywood[21], b. May 11, 1892.

1119. (ii.) Fannie Maria Haywood[21], b. Nov. 23, 1894.

1120. (iv.) *Alma L. Haywood*[20], b. March 7, 1875, in Owego, N. Y.

1121. (iii.) JOSIAH KNEELAND[19], b. March 4, 1836, at Sherburne, Vt.; d. Oct. 28, 1836.

1122. (iv.) MARGARET KNEELAND[19], b. Aug. 30, 1837, in Ludlow, Vt.; m. Nov. 11, 1861, in Proctorsville, Vt., George Hallett Knight, a native of Lancaster, N. H. George H. d. Aug. 4, 1878, in Owego, N. Y. Margaret resided, in 1887, in Binghampton, N. Y. Children:

1123. (i.) *Ernest Whitney Knight*[20], b. Nov. 1, 1862, in Proctorsville, Vt.; d. Jan. 25, 1869, in Owego, N. Y.; m. Sept. 17, 1882, in Candor, N. Y., Margaret Lydia Kyle. Residence, 1887, Shenandoah, Page County, Iowa. Children:

1124. (i.) Arthur Clinton Knight[21], b. March 18, 1885, in Candor, N. Y.

1125. (ii.) Edna Sylvia Knight[21], b. Nov. 24, 1886, in Candor, N. Y.

1126. (ii.) *Elizabeth D. Knight*[20], b. May 14, 1868; d. Jan. 25, 1869.

1127. (v.) JUDITH MARIA KNEELAND[19], b. May 31, 1839; m. Nov. 29, 1860, in Bradford, Vt., Jonathan Berry Witherill. Judith M. d. March 17, 1883, in Owego, N. Y. Children:

1128. (i.) *Infant son*[20], b. and d. 1866.

1129. (ii.) *Edith Irene Witherill*[20], b. June 16, 1868, in Owego, N. Y.; d. Jan. 7, 1869, in Owego, N. Y.

1130. (iii.) *Bertha Leone Witherill*[20], b. Jan. 30, 1870; in Owego, N. Y.; d. Jan. 3, 1887, in Owego, N. Y.

1131. (iv.) *Orville Emery Witherill*[20], b. Feb. 23, 1871, in Owego, N. Y.

1132. (v.) *Lester James Witherill*[20], b. Sept. 4, 1876, in Owego, N. Y.

Sarah Kneeland[18].

1133. (vi.) ESTHER LEWELLA KNEELAND[19], b. Sept. 6, 1840, in Rochester, Ind.; m. Dec. 23, 1867, in Big Rapids, Mich., John Martin Conner. Residence (1887) Big Rapids, Mich. Children:

1134. (i.) *James Cheney Conner[20]*, b. May 13, 1869, in Big Rapids, Mich.

1135. (ii.) *Vesta Conner[20]*, b. Oct. 15, 1871, in Big Rapids, Mich.

1136. (iii.) *Dallas Conner[20]*, b. Nov. 17, 1872, in Big Rapids, Mich.

1137. (vii.) VASHTI KNEELAND[19], b. July 22, 1842, in Rochester, Ind.; d. July 22, 1842.

1138. (viii.) MARY KNEELAND[19], b. July 22, 1844, in Rochester, Ind.; d. Oct. 6, 1845.

1139. (ix.) SYLVIA KNEELAND[19], b. Feb. 24, 1846, in Rochester, Ind.; still living; unmarried.

1140. (x.) GEORGE WASHINGTON KNEELAND[19], b. in Rochester, Ind., Jan. 28, 1849; d. June 19, 1865, at Ludlow, Vermont.

1141. (921.) SARAH KNEELAND[18] (*Asa[17]*, *Timothy[16]*, *Joseph[15]*, *Edward[14]*, *Edward[13]*, *Edward[12]*, *John[11]* —*Alexander[1]*). Fourth daughter and sixth child of Asa and Hannah (Cheney) Kneeland, b. Dec. 21, 1808, in South Stukely, Quebec; m. July 1, 1837, to Ezekiel Eastman. They are both dead.

Children of Ezekiel and Sarah (Kneeland) Eastman.

1142. (i.) HANNAH EASTMAN[19], m. Dan Bogue, of Enosburg, Vt. They both died without issue.

1143. (ii.) JOHN EASTMAN[19], m. Jane Graves. They both died, leaving three children:

1144. (i.) *Norman John Eastman[20]*, b. Feb. 6, 1876.

1145. (ii.) *Lillian Jane Eastman[20]*, b. March 3, 1878; adopted by Harris B. Kneeland (see No. 1201).

1146. (iii.) *Leslie Carroll Eastman[20]*, b. Aug. 16, 1883; adopted by Harris B. Kneeland (see No. 1202).

Asa L. Kneeland

No. 1153

1147. (922.) LEONARD KNEELAND[18] (*Asa*[17], *Timothy*[16], *Joseph*[15], *Edward*[14], *Edward*[13], *Edward*[12], *John*[11] —*Alexander*[1]). Fourth son of Asa and Hannah (Cheney) Kneeland, and grandson of Timothy Kneeland; b. in South Stukely, Quebec, Canada, Oct. 15, 1810; m. Nov. 28, 1833, in Orange, Mass., Sylvia Goddard, who was b. May 13, 1811. Leonard d. at Worcester, Mass., June 19, 1874.

Children of Leonard and Sylvia (Goddard) Kneeland.

1148. (i.) LUCY WRIGHT[19], b. at Athol, Mass., June 4, 1834; d. Jan. 25, 1842.

1149. (ii.) ELLEN MARIA[19], b. at Athol, Mass., June 2, 1837; m. first, William Thomas Atherton, May 13, 1856; he d. Jan. 13, 1857. She m. second, Warner H. Joslyn, of Ware, Mass., Dec. 30, 1857. He is a builder and resides at Worcester, Mass. No issue of either marriage.

1150. (iii.) ASA LEONARD[19], b. at Athol, Mass., Sept. 19, 1842 (of whom hereafter, 1153).

1151. (iv.) EBENEZER[19], b. at Athol, Mass., Aug. 31, 1844 (of whom hereafter, 1162).

1152. (v.) JONAS[19], b. at Athol, Mass., April 8, 1849 (of whom hereafter, 1168).

1153. (1150.) COL. ASA LEONARD KNEELAND[19] (*Leonard*[18], *Asa*[17], *Timothy*[16], *Joseph*[15], *Edward*[14], *Edward*[13], *Edward*[12], *John*[11]—*Alexander*[1]). Eldest son of Leonard and Sylvia (Goddard) Kneeland, and grandson of Asa Kneeland; b. at Athol, Mass., Sept. 19, 1842; m. Sarah Elizabeth Goddard, of Worcester, Dec. 25, 1869, and resides at 306 Park Avenue, in that city.

Col. Kneeland enlisted as a private in Company A, Thirty-second Mass. Volunteers, November 16, 1861; January 4, 1864, re-enlisted for a second term of three years. His regiment joined the Army of the Potomac, June, 1862, and

Col. Asa Leonard Kneeland[19].

remained with them until June 29, 1865. They were in the battles of the Army of the Potomac till Lee's surrender, including Antietam, Fredericksburg, Chancelorsville, Gettysburg, etc., and in the final struggle, beginning with Five Forks, April 1, 1865, and ending at Appomattox, April, 1865. Lieut. Kneeland's brigade—Second Brigade, First Division, Fifth Corps—was detailed to receive the formal surrender of the rebel army of Virginia. Col. Kneeland has in his possession two pieces of a Confederate flag which was torn to pieces at that time. While in front of Petersburg, every commissioned officer was absent from his company and he, then First Sergeant, commanded his old Company A for a month or two. A little later he was commissioned Second Lieutenant and assigned to Company H, and twelve days later was made First Lieutenant and put in command of Company F. His last day's duty was Acting Captain and officer of the day at Gallop's Island.

Since the war, being an enthusiastic member of the G. A. R., he was appointed aide-de-camp with the rank of Colonel, on the national staff, which rank he still holds. Mr. Kneeland has, since the war, been a builder and an extensive dealer in real estate, in the city of Worcester. At present he is the projector and general manager of the Wachusett Mountain Electric Railroad, twenty miles in length and requiring a capital of $500,000. He is a forceful public speaker and a solid, substantial business man.

Children of Asa L. and Sarah E. (Goddard) Kneeland.

1154. (i.) FRANCIS FALES KNEELAND[20], b. April 5, 1872, in Worcester, Mass.; m. Jennie Louise Whitney, of Worcester, Nov, 20, 1895.

1155. (ii.) CHARLES GODDARD KNEELAND[20], b. Dec. 15, 1874, in Worcester; d. an infant.

1156. (iii.) SARAH ELIZABETH KNEELAND[20], b. Nov. 26, 1875, in Worcester, Mass.

1157. (iv.) CLARA LOUISE KNEELAND[20], b. Sept. 22, 1878, in Worcester, Mass.

1158. (v.) IDA LUCY KNEELAND[20], b. July 1, 1880, in Worcester, Mass.

CLARA L KNEELAND

No. 1157

1159. (vi.) EMMA ENDORA KNEELAND[20], b. Aug. 9, 1883, in Worcester, Mass.
1160. (vii.) HERBERT LEONARD KNEELAND[20], b. Dec. 31, 1885, in Worcester, Mass.
1161. (viii.) LOUIS GROSVENOR KNEELAND[20], b. Dec. 31. 1885, in Worcester, Mass.
    A most lovely and loveable family.—ED.

1162. (1151.) EBENEZER KNEELAND[19] (*Leonard*[18], *Asa*[17], *Timothy*[16], *Joseph*[15], *Edward*[14], *Edward*[13], *Edward*[12], *John*[11]—*Alexander*[1]). Second son of Leonard and Sylvia (Goddard) Kneeland, and grandson of Asa Kneeland; b. at Athol, Mass., Aug. 31, 1844; m. first, Josephine Reynolds, at Athol, Jan. 28, 1864; m. second, Ada J. Palmer. at Lake Geneva, Wis., in June, 1877.

My personal acquaintance with cousin Eben lasted about five minutes. It is called to mind by the following extract from his communication of June 23, 1896: " I have not had the pleasure of meeting you since the battle of Spottsylvania Court House. Perhaps you remember the circumstance. I was coming off the field, wounded, and met the Eleventh Vermont, and enquired for Stillman Kneeland. You came and talked with me about five minutes and then went on into the battle. I shall never forget it." I have reason to remember it also, inasmuch as in the charge of the Vermont Brigade that followed it, I received a slight but exceedingly painful wound, and another cousin was killed. Ebenezer resides in Minneapolis, Minn., and is a successful contractor and builder.

Children of Ebenezer Kneeland, by Josephine Reynolds.

1163. (i.) EVERETT LINCOLN[20], b. in Athol, Mass., June 12, 1865 ; d. at Worcester, March 6, 1870.
1164. (ii.) FANNY WELLS[20], b. Feb. 12, 1867, at Hardwick, Mass.; m. at Hubbardston, June 22, 1888, to Frederick Mitchell Hastings, of North Grafton, Mass. He was b. March 17, 1862. Children :

1165.   (i.) *Ethel Estella Hastings[21]*, b. in North Grafton, Aug. 31, 1889.

1166.   (ii.) *Blanche Josephine Hastings[21]*, b. in North Grafton, May 30, 1892.

By Ada J. Palmer.

1167.   (iii.) BERTHA ADA[20], b. in Minneapolis, Minn., Dec. 3, 1883.

1168.   (1152.) JONAS GARDNER KNEELAND[19] (*Leonard[18], Asa[17], Timothy[16], Joseph[15], Edward[14], Edward[13], Edward[12], John[11] — Alexander[1]*). Youngest son of Leonard and Sylvia (Goddard) Kneeland, b. at Athol, Mass., April 8, 1849.

He learned the trade of carpenter and builder at a very early age and was foreman before he was eighteen years old. At twenty he was an extensive contractor and builder at Worcester, Mass., and erected many public and private buildings in that city and vicinity. At this time (1876) he was the architect and builder of the finest block of houses then erected in Fitchburg, and of a business block containing a hotel, stores, public hall and post office, at Upton, Mass, and many churches in neighboring towns. He now resides in Boston and has charge of the finishing department in one of the largest manufactures in the State of stair builders' supplies. On March 13, 1871, he married Mary Emerson Hill, daughter of Capt. Alfred and Phoebe (Emerson) Hill. Her mother, Phoebe Emerson, was a relative of Ralph Waldo Emerson, and the descendant, on the male side, of seven successive generations of clergymen. Notwithstanding this appalling fact, she is a sensible and charming lady. They reside in a beautiful cottage-villa in the suburbs of Boston, planned and erected by the husband.

Children of Jonas G. and Mary E. (Hill) Kneeland.

1169.   (i.) MARY EMERSON LILLIAN[20], b. Worcester, Mass., March 15, 1873. She resides with her parents, at 18 Elmont Street, Boston.

Jonas G. Knudsen

No. 1168

1170. (ii.) BERTHA MAUD[20], b. at Leominster, Mass., Feb.
17, 1876; m. at Boston, Oct. 3, 1894, to Walter
Billings, of that city. They have one child:
1171. *Dorothy Ella Billings*[21], b. July 5, 1895.

1172. (924.) TIMOTHY AVERILL KNEELAND[18] (*Asa*[17],
Timothy[16], *Joseph*[15], *Edward*[14], *Edward*[13], *Edward*[12], *John*[11]—*Alexander*[1]). Son of Asa Kneeland and Hannah Cheney, b. Oct. 9, 1816, in South
Stukely, P. Q.
He married twice and died in Dunham, P. Q., Sept. 5,
1861, age 45, the first death in grandfather's family. He was of
a refined temperament, a farmer and local preacher of considerable ability.

Children of Timothy A. Kneeland, by Anna Rexford.

She was b. Jan. 26, 1818, in Dunham, and d. there March
21, 1840; m. May 7, 1838.
1173. (i.) GEORGE AVERILL KNEELAND[19], b. in Stukely,
P. Q., April 29, 1839; *killed in the battle of the
Wilderness, May 6, 1864.* The first time I saw him
was at his father's funeral; the next time was on
the day of his death. My first battle was his last.
He was in all the battles fought by the old Vermont brigade to that time; I was in all thereafter.
My cousin and myself together completed the
record. Why his was the beginning and mine the
ending, instead of vice versa, God knows, and He
only.

By Sarah Bell.

She was born in Shefford, P. Q., July 8, 1823, and married
Timothy Kneeland, May 10, 1842.
1174. (ii.) LEANDER KNEELAND[19], b. in Stukely, P. Q., April
6, 1843; m. Nov. 8, 1865, at Athol, Mass., Mrs.
Mellissa Burbank Stevens, who was b. Dec. 4, 1829,
in Royalston, Mass., and died Sept. 14, 1868, at
Athol, Mass. Leander is now living at East
Jaffrey, N. H. They had one child:

Timothy Averill Kneeland[18].

1175. (i.) Infant son, unnamed; died with his mother on the day of his birth.

    Leander was married (2), September 4, 1880, to Lucy Ann Cutler, who was born July 13, 1851, in Mallon, N. H. They had one child:

1176. (ii.) *Mary Catharine Kneeland*[20], b. June 3, 1881, in Athol, Mass.

1177. (iii.) JAMES KNEELAND[19], b. in Shefford, P. Q., April 24, 1845; m. Marion E. Peck, in Dunham, Nov. 15, 1864. She was b. Oct. 13, 1846, in Enosburg, Vt. He is a farmer now residing at Johnson, Vt. They had four children:

1178. (i.) *Charles Henry Kneeland*[20], b. Nov. 13, 1865, in Dunham; m. in Hyde Park, Vt., Euleen Foss, July 10, 1887. She was b. Aug. 31, 1869, at Wolcott, Vt. They reside at Hyde Park, Vt.

1179. (ii.) *Elmer Merton Kneeland*[20], b. July 3, 1867, in Brome, P. Q.; m. April 24, 1886, in Denver, Col., Mary Jessie Wisnell. They reside in Johnson, Vt., and have one child:

1179A.   Grace Elmer Kneeland[21].

1180. (iii.) *Homer Erwin Kneeland*[20], b. July 31, 1869, in Fletcher, Vt.

1181. (iv.) *Frank Leslie Kneeland*[20], b. Jan. 25, 1877, in Johnson, Vt.

1182. (iv.) LUCY ALLEN KNEELAND[19], b. in Shefford, P. Q., April 11, 1847; m. George Wilson Badger, of Dunham, P. Q., who was b. Feb. 10, 1837, in Alburgh, Vt.; she d. Oct. 7, 1884, in Johnson, Vt. Children:

1182A. (i.) *James William Badger*[20], b. April 26, 1866; d. May 5, 1866.

1183. (ii.) *Ella Jane Badger*[20], b. May 17, 1868; now resides in Johnson, Vt.

1184. (iii.) *Alice Melissa Badger*[20], b. Dec. 13, 1875.

1185. (iv.) *Mattie Lucina Badger*[20], b. April 7, 1878.

1186. (v.) MARY KNEELAND[19], b. in Shefford, P. Q., March 25, 1849; d. Nov. 3, 1851, in Enosburg, Vt.

1187. (vi.) ALBERT CHENEY KNEELAND[19], b. in Montgomery, Vt., Sept. 15, 1853.

Gardner Kneeland.

No. 1188

CHAPTER XVI.

GARDNER KNEELAND AND HIS DESCENDANTS.

(NOS. 1188 TO 1238.)

1188. (923.) GARDNER KNEELAND[18] (*Asa*[17], *Timothy*[16], *Joseph*[15], *Edward*[14], *Edward*[13], *Edward*[12], *John*[11], *William*[10], *James*[9], *Alexander*[8], *William*[7], *William*[6], *John*[5], *John*[4], *John*[3], *James*[2], *Alexander*[1]). Sixth son and tenth child of Asa and Hannah (Cheney) Kneeland, eighth in descent from John Alden and Priscilla Molines, and ninth in descent from Degory Priest, of the Mayflower; b. in South Stukely, Quebec, Nov. 23, 1814; m. (1) Julia Ann Castle, in Waterloo, Quebec, Sept. 3, 1838; she d. July 30, 1845, leaving four sons, the youngest— myself—being about two months old.

She was the descendant in the male line of a noted London family of that name, whose Coat of Arms is thus given in Burke (see Burke's Heraldry, title "Castle"): "Az. on a bend or, three castles s. a. Crest.—A dexter arm couped and embossed fesse ways vested gu. cuffed or, holding a pennon of the second charged with a bee volant of the third, staff of the first." I wish I could herewith present, either from memory or through the aid of painter or photographer, a picture of the sainted mother who gave her life for mine; still greater, the wish that my life had been such that the sacrifice would have seemed less futile.

Gardner Kneeland, on the ninth of March, 1848, married (2) Susan Goddard, a daughter of Captain Ebenezer Goddard, of Orange, Mass., by whom he had one daughter and six sons, making in the aggregate the traditional Kneeland complement of eleven children, ten of whom are boys and all of whom at this writing (1897) are living. He succeeded his father, Asa Kneeland, on the old Kneeland farm in Stukely,

Gardner Kneeland[18].

much to the sorrow of the aforesaid ten sons, who grubbed its sterile soil. Later on he purchased an easier working farm in the valley and erected a cottage thereon where the couple lived alone for many years. They are now residing in the city of Montreal, where several of their children are located.

Gardner Kneeland is a man of sterling integrity and intellectual force. With different environments and more liberal educational facilities, he might have carved a mark high on the scroll of fame, but his duty to his parents confined him to the treadmill of farm life among the rocks and stiff clays of cold Canada. This epitaph I give unto my grand old father while, thank God, he yet lives: He filled his allotted line of life with a kindly grace, a rugged honesty, a neighborly fealty that endeared him to all his associates. He did what he could, not what he would, and what he did required not to be done over again. He inculcated into the very life of his children habits of industry, temperance and frugality, and impressed them with the value and dignity of true manhood and an orthodox but humanized Christianity. Insomuch as they may have come short of the perfect way is in spite, not in consequence, of his teachings. May the Indian summer of the present early old age of his life be prolonged many, many years, and the winter of death, if come it must, ripen quickly into an eternal spring.

Children of Gardner Kneeland, by Julia Ann Castle.

1189.   (i.) NELSON CASTLE KNEELAND[19], b. June 30, 1839, at South Stukely, Quebec; m. Feb. 9, 1863, in West Bolton, Quebec, to Azelia Maria Phelps. He is a farmer and carpenter. In his earlier years he had an intense desire to receive a thorough education, but fate seemed against him. He was always studious, but his earlier ambitions faded away as the time rolled on. After spending several years of married life in Bolton, he moved to Plainview, Minn., where he cleared and cultivated a large and beautiful farm. Several years since, for the purpose of providing better school privileges for his children, he moved to Owatonna, Minn.,

Harris. B. Kneeland

No. 1200

Gardner Kneeland[18].

where he still resides. Nelson is the very soul of honor. His own high ideals of manhood sometimes lead him to overconfidence in others, to his financial hurt. He has a lovely and loveable family, and possibly fate has been kinder to him than he gives her credit for. Children:

1190.   (i.) *Julia Maria[20]*, b. Aug. 5, 1864, in Bolton, Quebec; m. May 30, 1880, to Andrew William Ludwig Almquist, who was b. Oct. 17, 1832, in Sweden. They reside at Cokato, Minn. He is a hardware merchant. They had the following children:

1191.   (i.) Alice Charlotte Almquist[21], b. March 13, 1881; d. May 18, 1882.
1192.   (ii.) Arnold Walter Almquist[21], b. Oct. 12, 1882.
1193.   (iii.) Chester William Almquist[21], b. Sept. 4, 1886; d. Nov. 29, 1886.

1194.   (ii.) *Elbert Walter[20]*, b. May 25, 1866, in Bolton, Quebec.

1195.   (iii.) *Mary Azelia[20]*, b. May 16, 1874, in Plainview, Minn.

1198.   (iv.) *Oscar Arthur[20]*, b. July 27, 1880, in Cokato, Minn.

1199.   (v.) *Emma Beatrice[20]*, b. July 21, 1882, in Plainview, Minn.

1200. (ii.) HARRIS BRADLEY[19], b. Aug. 23, 1840, in South Stukely, Quebec; m. May 15, 1866, in Bolton, Mary Jerusha, daughter of Daniel W. and Maria (Pearl) Phelps, and sister of Azelia (Phelps) Kneeland. Harris is a model farmer; he has contended for many years against adverse soil and climate and has conquered the one and defied the other. I deem him one of nature's noblemen. He always has a kindly word and helping hand for any neighbor in distress or perplexity, and his idea of the term "neighbor" is as broad as that given in the gospel. They have no issue, but have adopted and made their own as closely as if theirs by natural right, the following:

Gardner Kneeland[18].

1201.   (i.) *Lillian Jane Kneeland[20]*, b. March 3, 1878.

1202.   (ii.) *Leslie Carroll Kneeland[20]*, b. Aug. 16, 1883. (See Nos. 1145-6.)

1203. (iii.) LEONARD JOHNSON[19], b. July 16, 1843, in South Stukely, Quebec; m. May 13, 1865, Emily J. Anderson. They reside in Cavour, Dakota. Leonard is a carpenter and builder, but has the Kneeland tendency to farming. He has done his share in fighting wolves, but has driven them permanently from the door of his prairie home, and may his last days be the best. He has six children, as follows :

1204.   (i.) *George Malcome[20]*, b. March 24, 1867, in Athol, Mass.

1205.   (ii.) *Ernest Gardner[20]*, b. Sept. 28, 1870, in West Brome, Canada.

1206.   (iii.) *Jennie Mary[20]*, b. May 2, 1873, in Plainview, Minn.

1207.   (iv.) *James Johnson[20]*, b. June 24, 1876, in Plainview.

1208.   (v.) *Cora Cathern[20]*, b. May 13, 1883, in Cavour, Dakota.

1209.   (vi.) *Julia Evertin[20]*, b. Aug. 3, 1886, in Cavour.

1210. (iv.) STILLMAN FOSTER[19], b. May 17, 1845, at South Stukely, Quebec (of whom hereafter, 1238).

By Susan Goddard.

1211.   (v.) LYDIA MARIA[19], b. Jan. 17, 1849, in South Stukely; m. May 12, 1870, to John Erastus Lawrence. In 1879, Mr. Lawrence—to me he will always be " Johnny "—was engaged as Principal of the Irene Training School, and Indian Agent for the Canadian Government, at Vermilion, on the Peace River, N. W. Territory. He has occupied this trust ever since. The station is about 3,000 miles from Montreal, 900 miles north of the Canadian Pacific Railroad and 600 miles from the nearest post office. This work he has performed by the aid of his able helpmeet with distinguished ability and success. This sheltered valley is nearly as fruitful as

ABNER W. KNEELAND, M.A., B C.L., PH.D.

No. 1221

other localities in the same longitude one thousand miles farther south. Mr. Lawrence is the gentleman, farmer, schoolmaster, minister, doctor and lawyer of that station. An absolute autocrat over a large settlement of Indians, whites and half-breeds, he rules alternately with a rod of iron and a wand of love. Children:

1212.   (i.) *Susan Hunt Lawrence, M.D.*[20], b. March 3, 1871, in South Stukely, Quebec; graduated at the Chicago Medical University, in 1894; m. July 24, 1896, to James Edward Skinner, who is also an M. D. They intend to locate in Japan or China as medical missionaries.

1213.   (ii.) *Orrin Cheney Lawrence*[20], b. May 29, 1873, in Brattleboro, Vt.; d. June 11, 1873.

1214.   (iii.) *Frederick Swan Lawrence*[20], b. Oct. 9, 1874, in Knowlton, Quebec.

1215.   (iv.) *Fenwick Norman Lawrence*[20], b. Jan. 11, 1878, in Sorel, Quebec.

1216.   (v.) *Clara Caroline Lawrence*[20], b. April 15, 1886, in Vermilion, Northwest Territory.

1217. (vi.) ALBERT JOEL[19], b. Dec. 12, 1850, in South Stukely, Quebec; m. (1) April 18, 1876, to Emma Ledora Butler; she d. Nov. 15, 1885. Married (2) April 7, 1896, to Harriet Jane Porter, of Waterloo, Quebec. Albert is a prominent builder and contractor residing and doing business at Montreal, Quebec, Canada. By his first wife he had three children, as follows:

1218.   (i.) *Nina Ellenor*[20], b. Jan. 7, 1877, in South Stukely.

1219.   (ii.) *Bertha Lillian*[20], b. Oct. 14, 1879, in South Stukely.

1220.   (iii.) *Myrtle Emma*[20], b. Feb. 7, 1882, in Plainview, Minnesota.

1221. (vii.) ABNER WINSLOW[19], M.A., B.C.L., PH.D., b. May 22, 1853, in South Stukely, Quebec; m. May 24, 1877, to Clara Florence Bedford, eldest daughter of Thomas Bedford, of Port Perry, Ont. Dr.

14

Gardner Kneeland[18]

Kneeland may well be considered one of the lead-ing educationalists of Canada. He was for many years Principal of the Panet Street school, in Mont-real, and is a member of the Council of Public Instruction for the Province of Quebec. He is now one of the Professors of the McGill Normal School, an institution connected with McGill Col-lege, Montreal. He was educated for the ministry and has at times filled nearly all the Protestant pulpits of that city. A throat difficulty, however, prevented him from following his chosen profession. He is a natural student, with a retentive memory, a ready flow of words, though given more to ideas than mere verbiage, and is gifted with indomitable pluck and stick-to-it-iveness. As a result he has already made his mark in the educational world, and is liable to carve it higher up before he dies. He was lately graduated with high honors in the Law Department of the McGill University. He resides at 51 Shaw Street, Montreal, and has three children:

1222.   (i.) *Edith Eliza*[20], b. Oct. 23, 1878, in Montreal.
1223.   (ii.) *Jessie Mabel*[20], b. May 24, 1880, in Montreal.
1224.   (iii.) *Arthur Franklin*[20], b. Feb. 6, 1886, in Montreal.
1225. (viii.) CHARLES EBENEZER[19], b. March 29, 1855, at Stukely; m. his cousin, Hannah, daughter of George C. and Flora (Parker) Bartlett, Oct. 31, 1877. Is foreman in the Royal Milling Co.'s mills, Great Falls, Montana, the largest flour mills in the State. Children:

1226.   (i.) *Howard Eben*[20], b. Aug. 23, 1879, at Plain-view, Minn.

1227.   (ii.) *Harry Bartlett*[20], b. July 25, 1884, at Cavour.
1228.   (iii.) *Charles Alfred*[20], b. Jan. 5, 1886, at Cavour.
1229. (ix.) JOHN ALLEN[19], b. Dec. 12, 1856, in Stukely; residence, Montreal, Quebec. He is a publisher and local missionary, a man of great power, height and influence among the poor of Montreal.

No. 1233

1230. (x.) WALTER GODDARD[19], b. at South Stukely, June
       2, 1859; m. Oct. 3, 1880, at North Fairfax, Vt., to
       Sarah Maria, daughter of Alfred and Mary A.
       (Page) Cochran. He resided in Montreal, Quebec,
       until May, 1897; now resides in Stukely. While
       in Montreal he was engaged in the building trade;
       he is now farming. He is a licensed preacher in
       the Methodist church and is quite a fluent speaker.
       While in Montreal he was leader of one of the city
       choirs. Children:

1231. (i.) *Lydia Abbie*[20], b. Oct. 6, 1882.

1232. (ii.) *Cora May*[20], b. Aug. 16, 1883.

1232A. (iii.) *Gardner Alfred*[20], b. May 30, 1886; d. June
       30, 1886.

1233. (xi.) WARREN ANDERSON[19], B.C.L., b. at South
       Stukely, July 5, 1861; the youngest and one of the
       brightest of the short dozen children of Gardner
       Kneeland. He has been for many years principal
       of what, under his tutelage, has become one of the
       largest institutions of learning in Montreal, known
       as the " Riverside " school, at Point St. Charles.
       Is Clerk of Session of St. Matthew's Presbyterian
       Church; elder in the Presbytery of Montreal and
       Synod of Montreal and Ottawa; many years Super-
       intendent of St. Matthew's Sunday School, and a
       lawyer by profession, though not by practice. He
       graduated at the Law Department of McGill Uni-
       versity, taking highest rank and the Elizabeth
       Torrance gold medal, although competing while
       attending to his duties as principal, against a large
       class of unfettered students. He has for three
       years been Secretary of the Teachers' Association
       of Montreal, and is sole agent for Canada for the
       Martha's Vineyard Summer Institute, at Cottage
       City, Mass., the largest institute for teachers in
       America. He m. July 5, 1882, at Rockburn, Que-
       bec, Sarah M., daughter of Rev. William A. John-
       ston, and granddaughter of Dr. William A. Johnston.
       She was b. Sept. 5, 1863, in Toronto, Ont., and d.
       July 30, 1896. Children:

Brig.-Gen. Stillman Foster Kneeland[19].

1234.   (i.) *Florence Minnie[20]*, b. May 12, 1884, in Rock-
          burn, Quebec.

1235.   (ii.) *Stanley Frederick[20]*, b. Feb. 22, 1887, in Mont-
          real, Quebec.

1236.   (iii.) *Clarence Russell Warren[20]*, b. March 29, 1895.

1237.   (iv.) *Ethel Louise[20]*, b. July 30, 1896.

1238. (1210.) BRIG.-GEN. STILLMAN FOSTER KNEE-
          LAND[19] (*Gardner[18], Asa[17], Timothy[16], Joseph[15],
          Edward[14], Edward[13], Edward[12], John[11]—Alex-
          ander[1]*). Fourth son of Gardner and Julia (Castle)
          Kneeland, b. at South Stukely, Quebec, May 17,
          1845; m. Nov. 29, 1871, Mary Stuart Wilson, a
          lineal descendant of Mary Stuart, Queen of Scots,
          and youngest daughter of James Wilson, Esq., the
          florist, who propagated the celebrated "Wilson's
          Albany," strawberry.

Inasmuch as the subject of this sketch is the writer of
the book, he inserts without comment, the biographical
notice contained in the National Cyclopedia of American
Biography (Vol. VII, p. 312), published by R. T. White & Co.,
of New York.

"KNEELAND, STILLMAN FOSTER, lawyer, author and
artist, was born at South Stukely, Quebec, May 17, 1845,
youngest son of Gardner and Julia Ann (Castle) Kneeland.
At the age of eleven he left his father's farm and became
apprenticed to the trade of printing. This he followed for
three years, pursuing meanwhile the preliminary studies for a
collegiate course. At the age of sixteen he passed the exami-
nations for entrance to McGill College, Montreal, but being an
ardent Federal he enlisted in the army and abandoned for the
time his educational ambition. He served in the Vermont
brigade during the last two years of the Civil War, and fought
in many battles, including the Wilderness, Coal Harbor, North
Anne, the preliminary contest before Petersburgh, and all
the valley fights under Sheridan. Returning with the Sixth
Corps to Petersburgh, he was severely wounded in a hand-to-
hand fight during the capture of that city, on account of which

"AFTER THE STORM"

Engraved from an oil painting by S. F. Kneeland

Brig.-Gen. Stillman Foster Kneeland[13].

- he received an honorary commission and discharge ' for wounds received in action.' He served many years in the National Guards of Vermont and New York, devoting special attention to rifle practice, being the author of a standard treatise on that subject and joint inventor of the celebrated ' Briggs-Kneeland ' rifle. After the war he studied law at Ludlow, with William H. Walker of Vermont, and in 1869 was graduated in the law department of Union University, then known as the Albany Law School. He commenced practice at Albany, N. Y., and soon acquired a very extensive commercial law business, in connection with which he wrote and published a treatise on ' Commercial Law,' which has since passed through many editions.

"In 1872 he removed to New York City, where he has since enjoyed an extensive and lucrative practice, and occupies the first rank among commercial lawyers. Many of his legal works are accepted as standard authority throughout the country; including ' Kneeland on Mechanics' Liens,' and Kneeland on Attachments.' He received the degree of LL. D. in 1886. Although best known as a lawyer, Mr. Kneeland takes high rank as an artist, examples from his brush having been exhibited throughout the country. He is also an extensive patron of art, and enjoys a house filled with examples of nearly all the modern and some of the ancient schools of painting.

"In 1894 he was Republican candidate for election to the legislature in a strong Democratic district in Brooklyn, and, running ahead of his ticket he received a majority of sixty-two votes. The returning-board, however, declared his opponent elected by the same majority. After a spirited contest the legislature declared him elected, and he took his seat late in the session. He was the author and secured the passage of a bill abolishing perpetual imprisonment for debt in the State of New York, which nearly depopulated the debtors' prisons. He is a member of the Union League and Montauk clubs; past vice-commander of the U. S. Grant Post, G. A. R.; first vice-president of the department of painting of the Brooklyn Institute of Arts and Sciences and chairman of the board of control of the Brooklyn Art Club; a charter member of

Brig.-Gen. Stillman Foster Kneeland[19].

the Order of Founders and Patriots of America, a member of the American Association for the Advancement of Science, and a member of the Sons of the American Revolution. In professional life he is noted for courtesy, brilliancy and for helpfulness to young lawyers. In January, 1897, he was appointed by Gov. Black, Judge-Advocate General on his staff, with rank of Brigadier-General."

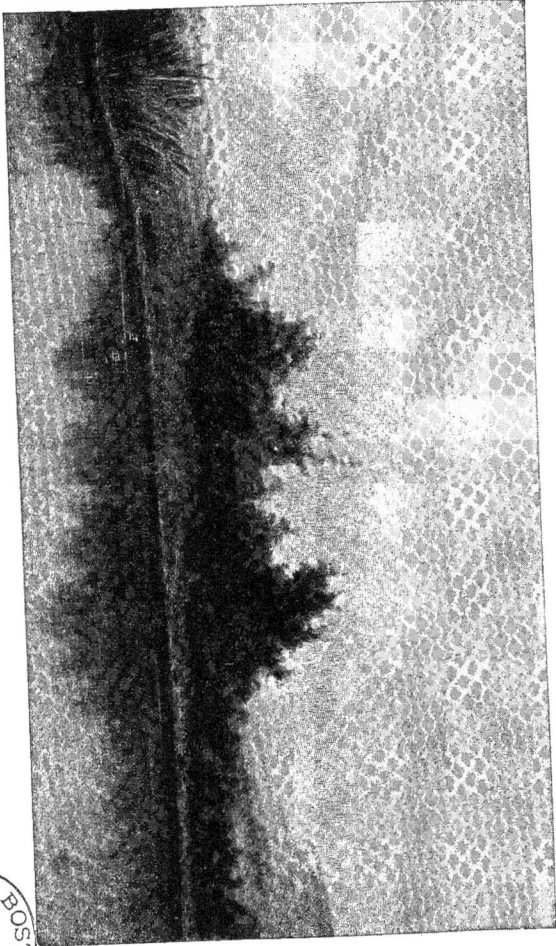

"MARSHLAND"

Engraved from an oil painting by S. F. Kneeland

CHAPTER XVII.

REV. ABNER KNEELAND.

(NO. 1239.)

1239. (773.) ABNER KNEELAND[17] (*Timothy*[16], *Joseph*[15], *Edward*[14], *Edward*[13], *Edward*[12], *John*[11]—*Alexander*[1]). Fourth son of Timothy and Martha (Stone) Kneeland. Probably the best known member of the Kneeland family.

Let those who think of him only as the founder of Pantheism in this country and of its journal, the Boston *Investigator*, remember that his work as a Christian minister and author lasted over a quarter of a century—1801 to 1830—before he became constrained to repudiate the doctrines of his forefathers. Abner Kneeland was born in Gardner, Mass., April 7, 1774. His father, Timothy Kneeland, was, during his early childhood, a soldier in the Revolution, and his earliest recollections must have been of "wars and rumors of wars." His youth was spent on the farm at Gardner, but gave evidence of coming intellectual ability. It is related that his father took him to hear a sermon in a new church built in the primitive style, showing the bare rafters. On his return home he was taken severely to task for having studied the structure of the building rather than listening to the sermon. In answer to this he repeated the text, and then point after point—gave almost *ver bata* the entire sermon. He then said, "Now, father, I can tell you just how many rafters there are in that church and how many mortises, how many holes without pins, how many with, and how many mistakes the carpenter made." This he did, showing the double working of his mind. I give herewith extracts from a biographical sketch written by Geo. Severance, of Tunbridge, Vt., and printed in the Boston *Investigator* of November 30, 1881.

Abner Kneeland[11].

[From the Boston *Investigator.*]

Abner Kneeland's early literary advantages were quite limited. He availed himself of the facilities of the common schools of Gardner, and had the benefit of only one academic term at Chesterfield, N. H. This was his literary equipment for public life, further than that he was self-taught.

About the time of attaining his majority, he and his brother Asa went to Dummerston, Vt., to work at the carpenter's trade. He was a resident of Dummerston about four years, and while there taught school more or less. At the age of twenty-three, April 9, 1797, he was married to a lady in the adjoining town of Putney, by the name of Waitstill Ormsbee, the daughter of Capt. Christopher Ormsbee. During his wedded life he was married four times. The second wife was Lucinda Mason, married June 11, 1806, a native of Wrentham, Mass. The third was Mrs. Eliza Osborn, of Salem,, near Boston, m. August 1, 1813; and the fourth was Mrs. Dolly L. Rice, born in Sudbury, Mass., but a resident of Billerica when married, which was December 25, 1834. He was sixty years of age when this marriage took place, and had four children thereafter, the youngest being born when he was sixty-eight years old.

Abner Kneeland was a resident of Dummerston, Vt., about four years. While a resident of this town' he was immersed by the Rev. Josiah Goddard, and became a member of the Baptist Church, of Putney, in due form. Soon after he began to exercise his talents as a preacher in the Baptist connection. His active connection with the Baptist church was brief. He has stated, prior to uniting with the Baptists, he had listened to the preaching of Rev. Elhannan Winchester, and was tinctured with his views of Universal salvation. This was not unknown to his Baptist friends, but it was thought by them he would outgrow any such tendencies.

Being on the point of leaving Dummerston for Alstead, N. H., he sought dismissal from the church at Putney. Some movement was made to deal with his heresy, but it simply resulted in an admonition. In going to Alstead it was his purpose to work at the carpenter's trade, for he claimed to be literally a carpenter and the son of a carpenter. In the month

Abner Kneeland

No. 1239

Copy of an oil painting in the possession of his daughter, Mrs. Boler.

of June, 1803, he was taken sick and did no work all summer. With his sickness his vocation as a carpenter was closed. As soon as he was able to ride he went to West Windsor, Vt., to visit a sister whose husband was a Universalist. There, being requested, he preached several discourses in an outspoken manner, fully disclosing his Universalist sentiments.

The news of this soon reached the Universalist Society at Langdon, an adjoining town to Alstead. The committee of the society soon waited upon him, and after preaching two Sundays he was engaged to preach out what money the society had to appropriate for this purpose. At that time the money for preaching was raised by a town tax and divided between the Universalists and the Congregationalists. When the Universalist portion had been expended, the Congregationalists engaged him to preach their portion. Before that time expired, a town meeting was called, and by a vote he was invited to settle as minister of the town. This invitation he accepted, but his ordination was postponed a year owing to the unfinished condition of the meeting-house.

At the Universalist convention, held at Winchester, N. H., 1803, Abner Kneeland was licensed as a Universalist preacher. This was the noted time when the Universalists put forth their profession of faith in order to avoid compulsory taxation to support orthodox Congregationalism. At this period Hosea Ballou was preaching in the small town of Barnard, Vt., and was preparing his famous work on the Atonement.

At length an ordination council met at Langdon, and on the 30th day of October, 1805, Abner Kneeland was solemnly ordained. Rev. Hosea Ballou preached the sermon and gave to Mr. Kneeland the right hand of fellowship; the introductory prayer was offered by Rev. Paul Dean; the ordaining prayer was by Rev. Zebulon Streeter, and the charge given by Rev. Ebenezer Paine.

Langdon is a little old farming town, and for years has dwindled in population. There never was a steeple attached to the church, though there was once two porticoes. It now stands, though in later years a pretty little church has been finished off in the upper story, the basement being used for a town house. If the building is properly cared for it will be serviceable for years to come. This much for the old structure where Rev. Abner Kneeland was ordained and stately preached for a series of years.

While settled at Langdon, Mr. Kneeland was elected representative to the legislature and served there as preacher nearly seven years. Near the close of his services at Langdon, the Universalists of Charlestown, Mass., erected a church, with the understanding that Mr. Kneeland was to be the preacher. He took charge of the Charlestown parish in 1811, and labored there nearly three years. Subsequently he married his third wife and opened a dry goods store in Salem, near Boston. He continued at this business about two years. About this period his mind was seriously exercised in regard to the divine authenticity of the scriptures. He made known his doubts to Rev. Hosea Ballou, which resulted in a friendly epistolary correspondence, which was printed in book form. For the time being, Mr. Kneeland's doubts were allayed, and he resumed his clerical labors in Whitestown, N. Y., in 1816.

The Rev. Stephen R. Smith in his "Historical Sketches," himself a Universalist preacher, thus alludes to Mr. Kneeland about this time: "He brought the experience of a number of years to bear upon the new field of labor, and the general reputation of his talents and acquirements above mediocrity, and certainly much above those who were now his fellow-laborers. Calm, courteous and gentlemanly in his deportment and intercourse, remarkably plain and intelligible in his discourses, he won the respect of opposers and enjoyed the highest confidence of his congregation. * * * And there were very few preachers then, in this connection, who would have thrown around them a greater number of salutary influences or given a more elevated tone to the Universalist ministry."

After a short ministry at Whitestown, in the autumn of 1818 we find Mr. Kneeland settled over the Lombard Street Universalist Society, at Philadelphia, Pa. Here he labored about seven years. While in Philadelphia he edited a Universalist periodical, "The Messenger," which was changed to "The Philadelphia Universalist Magazine and Christian Messenger—devoted to Doctrine, Religion and Morality." While in Philadelphia he published a volume of Universalist sermons which was re-published in a second edition. He also held a debate on the question of Universal salvation with the Rev. W. L. McCalla, a Presbyterian clergyman. This debate made a duodecimo of nearly 400 pages. In 1882 he published a version of the New Testament, double columns, in Greek and English, in which he followed Griesbach, with attempts at improvement from Campbell, Wakefield, Scarlett, McKnight and Thompson. Being studious in his habits Mr. Kneeland obtained a sufficient mastery of Hebrew, Greek and Latin for exegetical purposes.

The latter part of 1825 found him in New York City, in charge of the Prince Street Universalist Society. He then edited a paper known as "The Olive Branch." His doubts once more got the mastery of him, and he became quite outspoken. The Universalists refused longer to recognize him as an accredited preacher, and after some crimination, in May, 1829, Mr. Kneeland suspended himself from the order, as follows:

"WHEREAS, the circumstances which have attended my ministry in New York, and which have resulted from my labors in that place, are such as to produce a dissatisfaction in the minds of many, and to induce a belief that I am not what I profess to be, a real believer and defender of the Christian religion; and

"WHEREAS, this dissatisfaction and belief concerning me have become considerably extensive in other religions among Universalists, it is my desire that all associations and individual brethren of the order would allow me to suspend myself as to the fellowship of the order until I shall be able to give entire satisfaction that the cause of the world's Redeemer—of God, of truth, and righteousness—is the cause in which I am laboring and to which my talents are devoted. Wishing you success, brethren, in all that is good, I subscribe myself, yours affectionately in the bond of peace,

"ABNER KNEELAND."

Before leaving New York in the fall of 1829, in a series of lectures in "Broadway Hall," the Christian evidences were passed in review. These discourses were published in a

Abner Kneeland[17].

book. In 1830 we find Mr. Kneeland in Boston. That year
the *Investigator* was established, and it will, in a few months,
reach the age of fifty-one years, Messrs. Mendum and Seaver
having been the proprietor and editor of it for the past forty-
three years.

While at North Hartford, N. Y., Mr. Kneeland read for
the first time the works of Dr. Joseph Priestly. He avers
that in reading his "Disquisition on Matter and Spirit," he
became a Materialist in every and in the strictest sense of the
word. To quote from the *Investigator*, he says "Here the
scepticism of the editor began, and so far as we know, to this
cause, and this cause only, which gradually continued in spite
of all his efforts to prevent it, the whole fabric of Christian
evidence was completely demolished in his mind, without
leaving even a wreck behind."

Those who knew Mr. Kneeland best had no occasion to
accuse him of hypocrisy. If he doubted, he frankly expressed
his doubts. In defining his views in his latter years, he never
accepted the name Atheist. In his "Philosophic Creed,"
written in Hebron, N. H., in 1833, he emphatically calls himself a Pantheist. As a clergyman, all his energies were devoted
to textral exegesis. It is presumable he was not as extensively
read in the metaphysicians as some of his contemporaries were.
At that period Universalists were treated as semi-infidels.
Their preaching was almost entirely controversial. Their
mission seemed to be as far as possible to rid the Christian
world of the notion of endless hell torments. In view of
what has followed, their labor has not been in vain.

Mr. Kneeland made the first attempt in this country to
rid our orthography of all silent letters. He made a new
alphabet in the main and a character for each vowel sound.
He was the author of "A Child's First Book." He also published a defining spelling book of 200 pages. As editor of the
Investigator he encountered strong opposition. His indict-
ment, trial and imprisonment for sixty days in Leveritt Street
jail for the alleged crime of blasphemy, is no doubt fresh in
the minds of those who are posted in relation to the doings of
those stirring times. The Rev. Thomas Whittemore, editor
of the *Trumpet* (Universalist), called upon Mr. Kneeland to

Abner Kneeland

No. 1239

Copy of an oil painting in the Julian Hall, Boston.

Abner Kneeland[11].

define his position accurately in respect to the Divine existence. In averring that he did not believe in the God of the
Universalist, he was accused of ruling God out of existence. We all know the God of so-called Orthodoxy is not
God as Universalists define Him; and God, as defined by the
Pantheist, will not accord with the orthodox or Universalist
conception.

After seven years or more connection with the *Investigator*,
on going West in 1839, Mr. Kneeland's editorship closed.
After that time his future home was in Salubria, Iowa, till he
died, which was August 27, 1844. If now living he would be
107 years of age. At the time of his fatal sickness, it was
supposed to be the common bilious fever of the country.
When he seemed on the point of recovery, there was a sudden
relapse, and in two days his body was cold in death. When
first attacked his speech was so affected it was with difficulty
he could communicate with those around him. It was
thought he was not aware of his critical condition until it was
too late to give utterance to his thoughts. The day following
his decease, his family, friends and neighbors followed his
remains to the grave. A few brief remarks were made by a
friend. His body was deposited by the side of Capt. John
Kendall, an old friend.

The Farmington, Iowa, *Bee*, of November 6, 1880, thus
refers to the subject of this sketch: "On last Sabbath it was
our pleasure to visit the grave of the aged and celebrated
Pantheist, Abner Kneeland. This noted man established
himself two miles south of this city, in a small colony which
he called Salubria. In the month of August, 1844, he very
suddenly died. His grave is marked by a plain marble slab,
surrounded by some half dozen other mounds. Over the
sleeping-place is growing kenicanick and briars, the whole
surrounded by a field of green growing wheat, and in the
distance is still standing the house built by his hands. The
place is, indeed, salubrious and romantic. One standing upon
this beautiful spot cannot help being struck with the former
bravery and wisdom of the venerable sleeper."

Abner Kneeland[11].

[From the International Cyclopedia.]

"In 1830, when William Lloyd Garrison had sought in vain for a church or a hall in which to speak upon slavery, and was about to resort to the Common, Abner Kneeland and friends offered him the use of Julien Hall, then under their control, and there his lectures were delivered. In 1836 he was tried by the Supreme Court in Mass., for blasphemy uttered in his own paper. The words chiefly relied upon to support the charge were, "He believes in a God, which I do not," the words being taken as a denial of God's existence. Mr. Kneeland, in his defense, declared that the comma after the word "God" was erroneously inserted, and that all he meant to affirm was that he did not believe in the same God that his opponent did. At the first trial the jury stood eleven for conviction to one for acquittal, the dissentient being Charles Gordon Greene, of the *Morning Post*, which had been but lately established. A second trial resulted in conviction, and Mr. Kneeland was sentenced to imprisonment for a short term in the Boston jail. His conviction was disapproved by many earnest Christian men who thought it an infraction of the true liberty of speech and calculated to bring Christianity into reproach. The Rev. Dr. Channing and other eminent citizens united in a public protest against the prosecution. There has been no prosecution under the statute since that day, though hundreds of men have avowed their disbelief in God in terms far more offensive than those used by Mr. Kneeland. Public opinion upon the just limitation of the freedom of the press has greatly changed since that day."

We close this sketch with the following beautiful eulogium delivered by Oliver Wendell Holmes in an address before the Massachusetts Historical Society, in May, 1882 (see Vol. XIX, Mass. His. Soc., p. 306): "We have had revolutionary orators, reformers, martyrs; it was but a few years since that Abner Kneeland was sent to jail for expressing an opinion about the great First Cause; but we had nothing like this man with his seraphic voice and countenance, his choice vocabulary, his refined utterance, his gentle courage which, with a different manner, might be called audacity, his temperate statement of opinions which threatened to shake the existing order of thought like an earthquake."

CHAPTER XVIII.

DESCENDANTS OF REV. ABNER KNEELAND.

(NOS. 1240 TO 1284.)

Children of Abner Kneeland by Waitstill Ormsbee, of Putney, Vt., whom he married April 9, 1797; she died Feb. 2, 1806:

1240. (i.) HARRIET WAITSTILL KNEELAND[18], b. in Putney, Vt., in 1798; d. in Eastondale, Mass., June 21, 1889, æ. 91 (of whom hereafter, 1279).

1241. (ii.) SOPHRONIE KNEELAND[18], b. in Putney, Vt., Oct. 5, 1799; d. in Franklin, N. H., June 23, 1876, æ. 77 (of whom hereafter, 1258).

1242. (iii.) JOHN STONE KNEELAND[18], b. in Putney, Vt., Oct. 5, 1799; unmarried; d. at Salubria, Iowa, Feb. 2, 1881, æ. 81.

1243. (iv.) CHRISTOPHER KNEELAND[18], b. in 1801; d. in infancy.

By Lucinda Mason,

of Wrentham, Mass. She died at Langdon, N. H., aged 32.

1244. (v.) LUCINDA KNEELAND[18].

1245. (vi.) ABNER ORMSBEE KNEELAND[18]. He was a farmer residing at Alstead, N. H. He died in February, 1895, leaving one son:

1245A. *Tyler Kneeland*[19], who was a teacher, and had four sons and one daughter. I have no record of their names or ages.

Abner Kneeland[11].

By Mrs. Dolly L. Rice.

1247.   (ix.) SUSAN RICE[18], b. at Boston, Dec. 15, 1835 (of whom hereafter, 1272).

1248.   (x.) A son, b. at Boston, April 27, 1838; d. in infancy, unnamed.

1249.   (xi.) ALBERT ALPHONSO[18], b. at Salubria, Iowa, April 11, 1840; m. Ellen Tabor Pierson, June 15, 1869, at Denver, Col. They resided at Denver. She d. at Watsonville, Cal., in 1877. He was a successful miner and stockman, one of the pioneers of the great West, and known always as "Brave Bert Kneeland." He fought in the Civil War and later under Gen. Halliday in the raid on the Indians after the massacre at Sand Creek. As an accomplished horseman, a clear, cool-headed fighter, a business man and a true, warm-hearted friend, he had no superior among the "Fifty-niners" in Colorado. He died at his beautiful home in Denver, April 3, 1884, leaving as successor, his only child:

1249A   *Josephine Marion Kneeland*[19], b. at Denver, Sept. 27, 1872. She resides at present in New York City, where she is completing her vocal studies under an eminent teacher. With her full soprano voice and dramatic ability, she is liable to achieve as signal a success as that of her celebrated grandfather, Abner Kneeland.

1250.   (xii.) MARY MORIAH[18], b. at Salubria, Aug. 26, 1842; m. George D. Johnson, of that place, March 27, 1862. They had seven children:

1251.   (i.) *Bertha Kneeland Johnson*[19], b. at Salubria, Sept. 1, 1863.

1252.   (ii.) *Emma L. Johnson*[19], b. at Salubria, Dec. 20, 1864.

1253.   (iii.) *Frank H. Johnson*[19], b. at Farmington, Iowa, Jan. 15, 1866; d. at Kansas City, Nov. 16, 1873.

1254.   (iv.) *Herder M. Johnson*[19], b. at Chillicothe, Mo., Oct. 15, 1868; d. at Kansas City, Aug. 22, 1871.

1255.   (v.) *Hugh M. Johnson*[19] b. at Salubria, Aug. 11, 1874.

JOSEPHINE M. KNEELAND

No. 1249A

1256. (vi.) *Yzixy M. Johnson[19]*, b. at Salubria, Oct. 14,
       1876.
1257. (vii.) *Jennie B. Johnson[19]*, b. at Olath, Kas., Dec. 2,
       1878.

1258. (1241.) SOPHRONIE KNEELAND[18] (*Abner[17]*,
       Timothy[16], *Joseph[15]*, *Edward[14]*, *Edward[13]*, *Ed-
       ward[12]*, *John[11]—Alexander[1]*). Second daughter
       of Rev. Abner Kneeland, b. at Putney, Vt., Oct.
       5, 1799; m. Rev. William Morse, Dec. 25, 1825, a
       talented Universalist preacher then located at
       Philadelphia, Pa., and afterwards quite intimately
       associated with Abner Kneeland. She died June
       23, 1876, aged 77. They had children as follows:

Children of Sophronie Kneeland[18] and Rev. Wm. Morse.

1259. (i.) WILLIAM PITT MORSE[19], b. at Nantucket, Mass.,
       April 26, 1826; d. June 24, 1826.
1260. (ii.) SOPHRONIE KNEELAND MORSE[19], b. at Nantucket,
       Mass., Sept. 10, 1827; d. April 29, 1828.
1261. (iii.) AMELIA MORSE[19], b. in Quincy, Mass., Feb. 25,
       1834; m. Hon. Daniel Barnard, of Franklin, N.
       H., Nov. 8, 1854. Mrs. Barnard was the only sur-
       viving child (of whom hereafter, 1262).

1262. (1261.) AMELIA MORSE[19] (*Sophronie[18]*, *Abner[17]*,
       Timothy[16], *Joseph[15]*, *Edward[14]*, *Edward[13]*, *Ed-
       ward[12]*, *John[11]—Alexander[1]*). Born in Quincy,
       Mass., Feb. 25, 1834; m. Hon. Daniel Barnard, of
       Franklin, N. H.

Mr. Barnard was born in Orange, N. H., Jan. 23, 1827; d.
in Franklin, N. H., Jan. 10, 1891. For forty years he was
identified in the interests of his native State. When twenty-
one years of age he was sent to the legislature from Orange
and represented the town for four successive years. At different times he represented Franklin; was President of the
Senate; member of the Governor's Council and County Solic-
tor for several years. In 1887 he was nominated for Congress,
lacking a very few votes of being elected. At the time of his
death he was Attorney-General of the State of New Hampshire.

15

Susan Rice Kneeland[18].

Children of Amelia Morse[19] and Hon. Daniel Barnard.

1263. (i.) WILLIAM M. BARNARD[20], b. Jan. 10, 1856; d. April 15, 1886. He was a young lawyer of great prominence and in partnership with his father at the time of his death.

1264. (ii.) EMMA S. BARNARD[20], b. Dec., 1857; m. Samuel Pray, of Newtonville, Mass., and now resides there. She has one daughter:

1264A.   *Dorothy Pray*[21], b. Dec. 11, 1893.

1265. (iii.) MARY AMELIA BARNARD[20], b. Aug. 30, 1860; m. Frederick H. Daniell. They reside at Franklin Falls, N. H., and have two children:

1266.   (i.) *William Barnard Daniell*[21], b. April 1, 1890.

1267.   (ii.) *Marguerite Daniell*[21], b. April 27, 1892.

1268. (iv.) JAMES E. BARNARD[20], b. Jan. 29, 1863. He is a lawyer, practicing at Franklin, N. H. Married Maude Redwood.

1269. (v.) DANIEL BARNARD, JR.[20], b. June 22, 1865; d. March 15, 1866.

1270. (vi.) CHARLES D. BARNARD[20], b. April 18, 1868; in the railroad business at Chicago; m. Jennie Anderson.

1271. (vii.) FRANK EUGENE BARNARD[20], b. Feb. 17, 1871; is unmarried; a member of the bar of great promise, now practicing in Boston, Mass.

1272. (1246.) SUSAN RICE KNEELAND[18] (*Abner*[17], *Timothy*[16], *Joseph*[15], *Edward*[14], *Edward*[13], *Edward*[12], *John*[11]—*Alexander*[1]). Eldest daughter of Rev. Abner Kneeland and Dolly L. Rice, b. at Boston, Mass., Dec. 15, 1835, and now resides at Farmington, Iowa, with her husband, Thomas B. Boler, whom she married at Salubria, March 8, 1855.

She is the oldest living child of Abner Kneeland, and went with him to Salubria, Farmington, Iowa, and shared his voluntary exile at that place until his death. They had the following children:

Children of Susan Rice Kneeland[18] and Thomas B. Boler.

1273. (i.) GEORGE EDWIN BOLER[19], b. at Athens, Mo., Feb. 6, 1856; m. Carrie Neff, of Memphis, Tenn., Sept. 27, 1885, and resides at 123 High St., in that city.

1274. (ii.) OZION KNEELAND BOLER[19], b. at Athens, Mo.,
July 2, 1860; m. Effie Alder, of Milton, Iowa,
Sept. 7, 1877, and resides at 1902 Palean Street,
Keokuk, Iowa.

1275. (iii.) MARY MARGARET BOLER[19], b. in Athens, Mo.,
Oct. 27, 1865; m. Frank D. Carr, Dec. 15, 1892, at
Farmington, Iowa.

1276. (iv.) ELLIS RICE BOLER[19], b. in Fort Madison, Iowa,
June 14, 1868; m. Marie Livezey. One daughter:

1276A. *Frances L. K. Boler*[20], b. April 7, 1896.
They live at 2436 Tracy Avenue, Kansas City.

1277. (v.) SAMUEL D. BOLER[19], b. in Fort Madison, Iowa,
Aug. 10, 1874; Pacific & U. S. Express Co., Fort
Worth, Texas.

1278. (vi.) GRACE HELEN BOLER[19], b. at Weaver, Iowa,
March 17, 1878.

1279. (1240.) HARRIET WAITSTILL KNEELAND[18]
(*Abner*[17], *Timothy*[16], *Joseph*[15], *Edward*[14], *Edward*[13], *Edward*[12], *John*[11]—*Alexander*[1]). Eldest
child of Rev. Abner Kneeland and Waitstill Ormsbee, b. at Putney, Vt., in 1798; d. at Eastondale,
Mass., June 21, 1889, æ. 91. She married, first,
John Newell, of Charlestown, Mass. They had one
son:

1280. (i.) JOHN NEWELL[19], he died at the age of 18.
She married, second, George Goodridge, of Charlestown, Mass. They had one daughter:

1282. (ii.) HARRIET NEWELL GOODRIDGE[19], b. Nov. 14, 1837;
d. in Eastondale, Mass., May 8, 1895. She m. first,
William Baldwin, and had two children:

1283. (i.) *Herbert Kneeland Baldwin*[20]. He now lives
in British Columbia.

1284. (ii.) *Frank H. Baldwin*[20]. He lives in Cazedena,
Col.; has three children.
She married, second, David Howard, of Eastondale, Mass., where they now reside.

CHAPTER XIX.

DESCENDANTS OF SILAS KNEELAND.

(NOS. 1285 TO 1347.)

1285. (777.) SILAS KNEELAND[17] (*Timothy*[16], *Joseph*[15], *Edward*[14], *Edward*[13], *Edward*[12], *John*[11]—*Alexander*[1]). Youngest son of Timothy Kneeland and Moriah Stone, born at Gardner, Mass., Feb. 2, 1793; located at Fayston, Vt., and married June 8, 1817, to Martha Laws, who was born of English parents, in Temple, N. H., Jan. 23, 1796. He had ten children, and died at Waitsfield, Vt., Aug. 27, 1862, æ. 69. She died Dec. 16, 1868.

Children of Silas and Martha (Laws) Kneeland.

1286. (i.) LEVI HOWARD[18], b. May 12, 1818; d. same day.
1287. (ii.) LUCY[18], b. June 5, 1819; m. Geo. McGoon; she d. Dec. 30, 1880.
1288. (iii.) MORIAH[18], b. May 1, 1821; married Ebenezer Chapin. Children:
1289. (i.) *Oscar Eugene*[19], b. July 13, 1845.
1290. (ii.) *Milton Schuyler*[19], b. Mar. 18, 1847; d.
1291. (iii.) *Elmer Newton*[19], b. March 8, 1849.
1292. (iv.) *Martha Alice*[19], b. Oct. 18, 1853.
1293. (iv.) JOEL[18], b. Oct. 13, 1823 (of whom hereafter, 1325).
1294. (v.) NANCY[18], b. Jan. 16, 1826; m. Cyrus G. Howard. Resides at Manhattan, Kansas. Children:
1295. (i.) *Darius H. Howard*[19], b. Dec. 10, 1850; d. May 6, 1851.
1296. (ii.) *Walter C. Howard*[19], b. May 16, 1852; m. Cassie J. Moore, May 1, 1878.
1297. (iii.) *Jasper M. Howard*[19], b. Oct. 16, 1856; m. Vernelia J. Yarrington, Mar. 19, 1879. Children:

Silas Kneeland[17].

1298.   (i.) Maud Howard[20], b. Feb. 18, 1881.
1299.   (ii.) Cassie Howard[20], b. May 27, 1883.
1300.   (iii.) John Howard[20], b. Deç. 23, 1887.
           They reside at 80 E. Ohio St., Indianapolis, Ind.
1301.   (iv.) *Arthur Howard*[19], b. Dec. 24, 1858; d. Mar. 5, 1865.
1302.   (v.) *Dr. Giles P. Howard*[19], b. Nov. 5, 1862 (of whom hereafter).
1303.   (vi.) IRA RICHARDSON[18], b. July 30, 1828; d. July 18, 1832.
1304.   (vii.) MARTHA[18], b. Oct. 24, 1830; d. July 21, 1832.
1305.   (viii.) ABEL ALONZO MCDELLA[18], b. Feb. 2, 1834: m. Clarissa L. Stoddard, May 14, 1857. They had three children:
1306.   (i.) *Doric Abel*[19], b. Mar. 30, 1858. To whom and his good mother I am indebted for this genealogy of the descendants of Silas Kneeland. He is a bachelor, but will not be much longer if I can get him down to New York.
1307.   (ii.) *Clara Serena*[19], b. Dec. 5, 1859; d. Sept. 26, 1882.
1308.   (iii.) *Alice Lincoln*[19], b. March 4, 1865; m. June 11, 1885, to C. E. Greason; d. April 23, 1886.
1309.   (ix.) GEORGE WASHINGTON STEARNS[18], b. Feb. 3, 1837; m. Nov. 22, 1860, to Mary Eliza Morril Stoddard. Children:
1310.   (i.) *Ira Duane*[19], b. April 10, 1862.
1311.   (ii.) *Athrea Maria*[19], b. May 17, 1868; m. Clarence Pagé, Dec. 24, 1894. They have one child:
1311A.   Clarence A. Page[20], b. June 3, 1896.
1312.   (iii.) *Levi Stoddard*[19], b. Feb. 28, 1874; d. May 31, 1875.
1313.   (iv.) *Flora Isabella*[19], b. Sept. 10, 1875; m. Elmer A. Heliot, Nov. 28, 1895.
1314.   (v.) *Clarissa Abia*[19], b. Nov. 17, 1878.
           This entire family live at Topolo Campo, Sinaloa, Mexico.
1315.   (x.) MARY AMELIA[18], b. Oct. 9, 1842; m. Dec. 1865, William F. Turner. Children:

Joel Kneeland[18].

1316.   (i.) *Frank Le Roy*[19], b. Oct. 20, 1866; m. Emma Baughman, Nov. 13, 1890.

1317.   (ii.) *Mary Hannah*[19], b. Aug. 3, 1868.

1318.   (iii.) *Ina Martha*[19], b. July 7, 1869; m. Edward E. Bruce, May 4, 1893. One son :

1319.   Robert E. Bruce[20], b. March 20, 1894.

1320.   (iv.) *George Llewellyn*[19], b. Nov. 28, 1871; m. Mary Bertie Payne. Child :

1321.   John Ellsworth Turner[20], b. May 29, 1893.

1322.   **(v.)** *Elbert Alonzo*[19], b. Jan. 19, 1875; m. **Lona E.** Fleming, 1892. Children :

1323.   (i.) Donald Francis[20], b. in 1893.

1324.   (ii.) A daughter, b. in 1894.

1325.   (1293.) JOEL KNEELAND[18] (*Silas[17], Timothy[16], Joseph[15], Edward[14], Edward[13], Edward[12], John[11] —Alexander[1]*). Second son of Silas and Martha (Laws) Kneeland, b. Oct. 13, 1823; m. Sept. 12, 1847, Enceba H. Goodell. She was b. Nov. 11, 1824, and d. April 20, 1891. He d. Nov. 13. 1875.

Children of Joel and Enceba (Goodell) Kneeland.

1326.   (i.) JULIA MARIA[19], b. June 27, 1848; m. George W. Eddy, Oct. 12, 1866. They reside at Oakland, Cal. Children :

1327.   (i.) *Meda A. Eddy*[20], b. Dec. 24, 1867.

1328.   (ii.) *Bert Wallace Eddy*[20], b. Sept. 1, 1869; d. Aug. 22, 1884.

1329.   (iii.) *Benjamin Franklin Eddy*[20], b. Feb. 3, 1871.

1330.   (iv.) *Charles Eugene Eddy*[20], b. April 19, 1877.

1331.   (v.) *Maud Elva Eddy*[20], b. June 30, 1878.

1332.   (ii.) GEORGE EDWARD[19], b. Feb. 23, 1850; d. March 31, 1854.

1333.   (iii.) JOHN WESLEY[19], b. Dec. 19, 1851.

1334.   (iv.) EDMOND JAMES[19], b. June 2, 1854; d. Oct. 21, 1862.

1335.   (v.) ALFRED EUGENE[19], b. May 21, 1856; d. Sept. 25, 1857.

Joel Kneeland[13].

1336. (vi.) JOEL LORA[19], b. May 18, 1858; d. same day.

1337. (vii.) MARY EVA[19], b. March 20, 1861; m. first, Jan. 5, 1876, Fitz Roy Caley; he d. March 25, 1878. Married, second, Aug. 14, 1880, Herbert Philo Cary. Children:

1338.   (i.) *Charles Lewis Cary*[20], b. Jan. 21, 1882; d. Jan. 23, 1882.

1339.   (ii.) *Frank Herbert Cary*[20], b. March 12, 1883.

1340.   (iii.) *Jessie Linn Cary*[20], b. May 2, 1886; d. Aug. 10, 1888.

1341.   (iv.) *Ralph Bradford Cary*[20], b. Jan. 23, 1890.

1342.   (v.) *Chester Howard Cary*[20], b. Nov. 25, 1891.

1343.   (vi.) *Ethel Clarisse Cary*[20], b. Nov. 22, 1894.

1344. (viii.) CHARLES EDGAR[19], b. March 6, 1864; m. and resides in the Indian Territory. They have one daughter, aged about seven years.

1345. (ix.) WILLIAM HENRY[19], b. Feb. 20, 1866. He resides at Oklahoma; m. and has a son, born about 1890.

1346. (x.) BENJAMIN FRANKLIN[19], b. April 6, 1868.

1347. (xi.) JAMES MUNROE[19], b. Feb. 29, 1872.

CHAPTER XX.

THE STEARNS FAMILY.

(NOS. 1348 TO 1427.)

1348. (774.) LUCY KNEELAND[17] (*Timothy*[16], *Joseph*[15], *Edward*[14], *Edward*[13], *Edward*[12], *John*[11]—*Alexander*[1]). Daughter of Timothy and Maria (Stone) Kneeland, b. at Gardner, Mass., Nov. 8, 1776— Independence year; d. at Reading, Vt., Feb. 2, 1875, æ. *98 years, 2 months and 26 days.*

She was the sister of Rev. Abner Kneeland, and although a devout Christian, believed absolutely in her famous brother. She was also the sister of Asa Kneeland, the grandfather of the writer. I often visited her after she was 90 years of age and found her bright, cheerful and very youthful in disposition and heart. I shall never forget a pair of woolen socks she knit for me in those days; they were soft, and warm and cheerful, and about No. 14 in size. Verily, the people of her younger days were framed on liberal foundations. She left her home in Gardner at the age of eighteen and took up her residence with her brother, John Kneeland, Esq., of Chesterfield, N. H. After completing her education at the Chesterfield Academy, she traveled all the way to West Windsor, Vt., on horseback, through the woods and without a companion. She there met, at the home of her brother-in-law Josiah Nichols, her future husband, Paul Stearns. He was a young widower with an infant child. She took pity on them both, married the father, cared for the child, and added ten more children thereunto. Some of the children are still living, although the marriage took place at the birth of the present century. Mrs. Stearns was one of those strong, steadfast, sterling women that formed the stability of the country in its earlier stages of existence. It is true that she smoked a pipe; her sister-in-law, my grandmother, did the same. Was it for this reason that their lives were cut short at the respective ages of 98 and 99?

Children of Lucy Kneeland[17] and Paul Stearns.

1349. (i.) TIMOTHY KNEELAND STEARNS[18], d. in infancy.

1350. (ii.) LUCY STEARNS[18], b. in 1804; m. John Gilson (of whom hereafter, 1400).

1351. (iii.) GRACE STEARNS[18], b. in 1806; m. Almon Davis; d. in 1863, without issue.

1352. (iv.) THOMAS STEARNS[18], b. in Sept., 1808; d. at the age of 18.

1353. (v.) JOHN MILTON STEARNS[18], b. Dec. 13, 1810. He is a lawyer and an LL.D., residing in Brooklyn, N. Y., a man of strict integrity and high moral character; the author of several publications and an authority on matters relating to real estate titles. He was married three times and has two children—a daughter who married Hon. Homer A. Nelson, and a son, J. Milton Stearns, who resides in Brooklyn, N. Y.

1354. (vi.) SARAH STEARNS[18], b. Dec. 14, 1812; d. Feb., 1867; m. Samuel Lamb, of Bridgewater, Vt. (of whom hereafter, 1371).

1355. (vii.) BENJAMIN FRANKLIN STEARNS[18], twin of

1355A. (viii.) GEORGE WASHINGTON STEARNS[18], b. Dec. 25, 1814; resides at Felchville, Vt. Has two sons:

1356. (i.) *Oscar H. Stearns[19]*, b. 1842; attorney-at-law; resides in Brooklyn, N. Y.

1357. (ii.) *Frank Stearns[19]*, b. at Chester, Vt.

1358. (ix.) PAUL W. STEARNS[18], b. March 4, 1817; d. in 1878. Children:

1359. (i.) *Elwin Stearns[19]*, an attorney-at-law; resides at Manchester, Iowa.

1360. (ii.) *Dora Stearns[19]*, m. Dr. Pettigrew.

Sarah Stearns[18].

1361. (x.) HONESTUS STEARNS[18], b. July 22, 1820; m. first, July 17, 1845, to Leonora D. Matthews; she was b. Feb. 29, 1820.   Married, second, Dec. 4, 1850, to Marietta McGill, who was b. Sept. 20, 1825, and d. Sept. 11, 1873.   Married, third, Oct. 18, 1874, Emeline Brown Lovell, of Pittsfield, Vt.; she d. July 26, 1884.   Children, by Leonora D. Matthews:

1362. (i.) *Helen Minerva Stearns[19]*, b. March 26, 1846; m. at Bethel, Vt., to Dr. Geo. W. Nichols.
By Marietta McGill:

1363. (ii.) *George Gill Stearns[19]*, b. in Nov., 1851; m. Dec. 24, 1879, to Mattie J. Amos, of Ironton, Ohio; he d. Feb. 15, 1889, at Reading, Vt. she d. about 1884.   They had one child:

1364. Lillian E. Stearns[20], b. about Jan. 1, 1881; she lives with her grandparents at Ironton.

1365. (iii.) *Kate Maria Stearns[19]*, b. June 13, 1853; m. Aug. 16, 1882, to Oscar F. Rice, of Weathersfield, Vt.; he d. about 1892.   They had four children, of which the following are living at Felchville:

1366. (i.) Ethel Rice[20].
1367. (ii.) Stella Rice[20].
1368. (iii.) Karl Rice[20].
1369. (iv.) *Marietta Lucilla Stearns[19]*, b. Jan., 1859; m. Oscar G. Randall, May 9, 1880.   They had four children, of whom three survive and reside at Brattleboro, Vt.

1370. (v.) *Cora Theodosia Stearns[19]*, b. July 16, 1863; m. George L. Whitcomb, Nov. 8, 1883.   They reside at West Lebanon.

1371. (1354.) SARAH STEARNS[18] (*Lucy Kneeland[17], Timothy[16], Joseph[15], Edward[14], Edward[13], Edward[12], John[11]—Alexander[1]*).   Daughter of Paul and Lucy (Kneeland) Stearns, b. in Reading, Dec. 14, 1812; m. Samuel Lamb, of Bridgewater, Vt., May 29, 1838.   They resided at Bridgewater, and had eight children.   She d. Feb. 1, 1867.

Children of Samuel and Sarah (Stearns) Lamb.

1372. (i.) THOMAS H. B. LAMB[19], b. Aug. 1, 1840. He was a man of rare intellect, and if he had been possessed of sufficient educational advantages and length of life he would have been "a giant in the land." As it was, his light went out with thousands of others in the War of the Rebellion. He was appointed a local preacher, and every Sabbath found him filling a pulpit preaching with great power and success. He enlisted in 1862 and died in the army, without issue.

1373. (ii.) ELLEN GRACE LAMB[19], b. Dec. 16, 1841; m. J. P. Lewis, Feb. 25, 1859. They had eleven children, as follows:

1374.   (i.) *Laura Annetta Lewis*[20], b. Sept. 10, 1860; m. Ora Chamberlain, Jan. 1, 1879.

1375.   (ii.) *Frank Arthur Lewis*[20], b. Dec. 10, 1861; d. July 20, 1871.

1376.   (iii.) *Ruth Ellen Lewis*[20], b. Feb. 16, 1864; m. Gilman Robinson, Feb. 21, 1885.

1377.   (iv.) *Milo Jonathan Lewis*[20], b. March 20, 1866; m. Nannie Cobb, Feb. 19, 1888.

1378.   (v.) *Lucy L. Lewis*[20], b. July 26, 1868; m. Edward J. Curtis, April 22, 1881; d. April 10, 1893.

1379.   (vi.) *Edith Jane Lewis*[20], b. Oct. 10, 1871; d. May 17, 1873.

1380.   (vii.) *Robin Jay Lewis*[20], b. Nov. 4, 1873.

1381.   (viii.) *Ethel Marie Lewis*[20].

1382.   (ix.) Son, b. and d. Aug. 10, 1878.

1383.   (x.) *Edith S. Lewis*[20], b. July 8, 1880.

1384.   (xi.) *Claire Lewis*[20], b. Sept. 23, 1883.

NOTE.—Mrs. Robinson and Mrs. Cobb live in Woodstock, Vt.; all the other children at Bridgewater, Vt. They are all farmers.

1385. (iii.) BETSY STEARNS LAMB[19], b. Sept. 2, 1843; m. Philip Royce, Jan. 5, 1863. They reside at Brownsville, Vt., and have five children, all living. I am indebted to Mrs. Royce for this statement of the descendants of her mother. Children:

Lucy (Stearns) Gilson[18].

1386.	(i.) *Charles Sylvester Royce[20]*, b. May 3, 1864; m. first, Annie Lyman; she d. Feb. 22, 1890. Married, second, Jennie Maloy, Sept. 23, 1891. He is a druggist and resides at Malvern, Iowa.

1387.	(ii.) *Sarah Grace Royce[20]* (A.B., Smith, '90), b. Feb. 25, 1866. She is a teacher of Latin and Greek at the Binghampton, N. Y., High School.

1388.	(iii.) *Bertha Lulu Royce[20]*, b. May 25, 1878. She is a graduate of Woodstock High School, and entered Smith College, Sept. 23, 1896.

1389.	(iv.) *Clayton Elbert[20]*, b. Dec. 20, 1886.

1390.	(iv.) SARAH JANE LAMB[19], b. April 26, 1845; m. Wm. W. Webb, June 4, 1869. They reside at East Barnard and had two children, viz.:

1391.	(i.) *Myrtle Ione Webb[20]*, b. Jan. 16, 1873; m. Edward J. Curtis, April 20, 1895.

1392.	(ii.) *Lucina Eloise[20]*, b. Nov. 11, 1880; d. Sept. 30, 1884.

1393.	(v.) ASENATH W. LAMB[19], b. Feb. 25, 1848; d. June 29, 1891, without issue.

1394.	(vi.) SAMUEL H. LAMB[19], b. Dec. 30, 1850; m. Ellen R. Sanborn, Jan. 1, 1879. They reside at East Barnard, and have one child:

1395.	*Benton H. Lamb[20]*, b. Jan. 29, 1881.

1396.	(vii.) LUCY ANN LAMB[19], b. Feb. 15, 1852; m. Lyman B. Robinson, a lawyer of Belle Plain, Iowa, Oct. 2, 1879. They have two children and reside at Avoca, Iowa.

1397.	(i.) *Melvin Harold Robinson[20]*, b. Feb. 3, 1886.

1398.	(ii.) *Rodney Potter Robinson[20]*, b. March 15, 1890.

1399.	(viii.) MELVIN C. LAMB[19]; b. March 25, 1854; d. Sept. 24, 1881.

1400.	(1350.) LUCY (STEARNS) GILSON[18] (*Lucy Kneeland Stearns[17]*, *Timothy[16]*, *Joseph[15]*, *Edward[14]*, *Edward[13]*, *Edward[12]*, *John[11]—Alexander[1]*). Eldest daughter of Lucy Kneeland and Paul Stearns, granddaughter of Timothy Kneeland and niece of

Rev. Abner Kneeland; b. at Reading, Vt., March 29, 1805; m. to John Gilson, by Rev. Samuel C. Loveland, March 31, 1824. They resided in Reading and had thirteen children, seven of whom are still living (1896).

John Gilson was born in Rindge, N. H., July 1, 1798. He was a member of one of the oldest families in the country. The first of the name was William Gilson, who resided in the town of Scituate, Mass., as early as 1631. Savage, in his Gen'l History of N. E. (Vol. II., p. 259), speaks of him as follows: "A man of good powers of mind and property. He built the first mill in the colony for grinding corn. In 1633 only four persons in the colony were rated higher for the purposes of taxation. He was on four separate occasions elected an assistant to the government." He died without issue, his property passing to the children of a deceased sister. We have not the relationship existing between him and the ancestors of John Gilson, but we can trace the latter line fully 350 years. The earliest ancestor in that line was Thomas Gilson. He came over in "The Alexander," which arrived May 2, 1635. He was then twenty-one years of age. He settled in Chelmsford, and had several children, the second son being Joseph Gilson, who was one of the founders of the town of Groton, Mass., and one of the thirty "original proprietors" of the common lands of that town (p. 27, Hist. of Groton). He remained in Chelmsford until his marriage hereinafter set forth. From Savage's Gen'l Hist. of N. E. and the History of Groton, we trace the line from him down to Abel Gilson, father of the John Gilson under consideration. It runs as follows:

JOSEPH GILSON[2], m. Mary Caper, Nov. 18, 1660, and moved to Groton. He had three children, the youngest being:

JOHN GILSON[3], b. in Groton, Feb. 23, 1674; m. Sarah ———; d. Sept. 10, 1707. They had five children, the eldest being:

JOHN GILSON[4], b. in Groton, March 2, 1697; m. Mary Shattuck, Dec. 8, 1722. They had nine children, the eldest son being:

JOHN GILSON[5], b. in Groton, May 12, 1726; d. at Rindge,

N. H., May 10, 1804; m. first, Hannah ———, by whom he had three children.   Married, second, Prudence Lawrence, Jan. 19, 1764, by whom he had two children, the eldest being:

ABEL GILSON[6], b. in Everton, Mass., June 14, 1764 (the Bible record makes it June *11*, 1764).   He lived in Rindge, N. H., until about 1870 and then moved to Reading, Vt.   He married Margaret Carey, of Attleboro, Mass.   Their youngest son was:

JOHN GILSON[7], b. July 1, 1798, who married Lucy Stearns, as hereinbefore stated.   The entire list of children of Abel Gilson are as follows:

Abel Gilson, Jr., b. at Rindge, H. H., April 20, 1790.

Hepzibah Gilson, b. at Rindge.

Josiah Gilson, b. at Rindge; settled in Proctorsville, Vt. "Squire Gilson" was Justice of the Peace for the town of Cavendish over fifty years, and was respected and esteemed by all.

Prudence Gilson, b. at Rindge, N. H.

John Gilson, b. at Rindge, N. H.

Betsy Gilson, married Surrey Ross, who settled in Proctorsville, Vt.   She was "Aunt Betsy" to almost every one—at any rate, she was to the writer.   He will never forget the kindness received from her family and from her brother, Josiah, and sister, "Aunt" Tryphena (Gilson) Kneeland.

Tryphena Gilson, b. at Reading, Vt.; m. Abner Kneeland, the nephew of Rev. Abner Kneeland.

Judith Gilson, b. at Reading, Vt.

Mary Gilson, b. at Reading, Vt.

Children of John and Lucy (Stearns) Gilson.

1401.   (i.) LUCY ANN GILSON[19], b. at Reading, Vt., April 8, 1825; d. Aug. 4, 1843.

1402.   (ii.) ABEL SOBEISKA GILSON[19], b. at Reading, Vt., Oct. 31, 1826; m. Mrs. Elizabeth (Noxon) Pixley, in 1851.   They resided in New Carlisle, Ind., and had three daughters and one son, as follows:

1403.   (i.) *Sophia W. Gilson*[20], b. at Proctorsville, Vt., Jan. 31, 1852; m. Jan. 15, 1878, to George Milton

ELLA A. GILSON   NELLIE C. GILSON   MIDGE M. GILSON

Lucy (Stearns) Gilson[18].

Valentine, of Pulaski, N. Y. They reside at Benton Harbor, Mich., where he is in the practice of the law. Children:

1404.   (i.) Edson Blaine Valentine[21], b. Jan. 27, 1879.

1405.   (ii.) George Lawrence Valentine[21], b. May 5, 1886.

1406.   (ii.) *William N. Gilson*[20], b. May 25, 1853; d. June 17, 1853.

1407.   (iii.) *Marion Elizabeth Gilson*[20], b. Oct. 1, 1854; m. Oct. 16, 1879, Marshall F. White, of New Carlisle, Ind.; she d. Feb. 22, 1884, leaving one daughter:

1407A.   Mary Angela White[21], b. June 1, 1881.

1408.   (iv.) *Mary Madeline Gilson*[20], b. Sept. 7, 1856; unmarried. Resides with her father, at New Carlisle.

1409. (iii.) MARY GILSON[19], unmarried and lives with her parents.

1410. (iv.) Infant daughter, b. Feb. 27, 1828; d. March 2, 1828.

1411. (v.) EMILY LORETTE GILSON[19], b. at Reading, Jan. 31, 1829; d. Feb. 11, 1851.

1412. (vi.) CHARLES PARKMAN GILSON[19], b. at Reading, Sept. 3, 1830; m. Sarah Ward, of Plymouth, Vt. They live at 123 South Third St., Brooklyn, E. D., and have three children, as follows:

1413.   (i.) *Ella A. Gilson*[20].

1414.   (ii.) *Nellie C. Gilson*[20].

1415.   (iii.) *Midge M. Gilson*[20].

    This trinity is one of the most charming among the descendants of the clan. They are accomplished musicians and instructors of music and art.

1416. (vii.) ELLEN VIOLA GILSON[19], b. July 17, 1832; m. first, Leavitt C. Wood, May 12, 1853. After his death, m. second, George A. Petty, and lives at Rutland, Vt. No issue.

1417. (viii.) WILBUR JOSIAH GILSON[19], b. May 23, 1835; married and lives in Rutland, Vt. Has one daughter living. His wife and infant son are dead.

Lucy (Stearns) Gilson[18].

1418. (ix.) THOMAS STEARNS GILSON[19], b. at Reading, Aug. 17, 1837. He lives in Rutland, Vt. Married twice and has three daughters and one son living:

1419.   (i.) *Agnes Gilson[20].*

1420.   (ii.) *Helen Gilson[20].*

1421.   (iii.) *Mary Gilson[20].*

1422.   (iv.) *Thomas Gilson[20].*

1423. (x). EDSON PTOLEMY GILSON[19], b. at Reading, Oct. 5, 1839; m. Anna C. Clement, of Rutland, Vt.

1424. (xi.) HENRY HARRISON GILSON[19], b. at Reading, Vt.. July 4, 1842; d. March 20, 1844.

1425. (xii.) CLEORA ANN GILSON[19], b. at Reading, Vt., March 27, 1845; m. Augustus Slack, Oct. 8, 1873. They live at 67 Pine Street, Rutland, Vt., and have one son living:

1426.   *Waldo Henry Slack[20]*, b. July 14, 1878.

1427. (xiii.) MARY LUCRETIA GILSON[19], b. Sept. 4, 1848; d. Feb. 1, 1849.

PART VII.

JONATHAN KNEELAND'S FAMILY.

(NOS. 1428 TO 1782.)

DEDICATED TO

Dr. JONATHAN KNEELAND,

TO WHOM

THE CLAN IS LARGELY INDEBTED FOR THE SUGGESTION OF

THIS BOOK AND FOR MUCH OF THE WORK

PERTAINING TO

THIS BRANCH OF THE FAMILY.

16

CHAPTER XXI.

JOHN AND JONATHAN.

(NOS. 1428 TO 1588.)

1428. (682.) JOHN KNEELAND[15] (*Benjamin*[14], *Edward*[13], *Edward*[12], *John*[11], *William*[10], *James*[9], *Alexander*[8], *William*[7], *William*[6], *John*[5], *John*[4], *John*[3], *James*[2], *Alexander*[1]). Second son of Benjamin Kneeland[14], b. at Framingham, Mass., June 6, 1710 (see Temple's Hist. of Framingham).

He followed his father in his devious wanderings up the Connecticut Valley, and became one of the founders of Marlboro, Conn. He afterwards located in East Haddam, where several of his children were born. He married Mehitable Lord, a member of a large and influential family residing in that place. He was a good deacon, a man of strong religious and political views and liberally educated for those early days.

Children of John and Mehitable (Lord) Kneeland.

1429. (i.) JONATHAN[16], b. March 4, 1737, at Colchester, Conn.; "died Apriell ye 6th, 1740" (Colchester Records).

1430. (ii.) JOHN[16], b. at Colchester, "January ye 4th, 1739."

1431. (iii.) MEHITABLE[16], b. at Colchester, Feb. 6, 1742.

1432. (iv.) JONATHAN[16], b. at East Haddam, Conn., Aug. 26, 1744 (of whom hereafter, 1436).

1433. (v.) BENJAMIN[16], b. at East Haddam, Nov. 21, 1746 (of whom hereafter, 1441).

1434. (vi.) JEMIMA[16], b. Jan. 17, 1749 (of whom hereafter, 1560).

1435. (vii.) ICHABOD[16], b. Dec. 14, 1753; m. Cynthia Fillmore.

Benjamin Kneeland[16].

1436. (1432.) JONATHAN KNEELAND[16] (*John[15], Benjamin[14], Edward[13], Edward[12], John[11]—Alexander[1]*). Third son of Deacon John Kneeland[15], one of the founders of Marlboro, Conn.; b. in Marlboro, Aug. 26, 1744; m. Mary Spencer, and settled in East Haddam, about 1768. They had four sons and one daughter. Jonathan was a soldier in the Revolution and died soon after its close.

Children of Jonathan and Mary (Spencer) Kneeland.

1437. (i.) JOHN[17], b. at East Haddam, May 10, 1769; m. Sally Benson and had twelve children; d. 1821 (of whom hereafter, 1589).

1438. (ii.) WARREN[17], b. at East Haddam, Nov. 2, 1771; d. in 1868, æ. 97; m. Elizabeth Fitzgerald, and had eight children (of whom hereafter, 1631).

1439. (iii.) ASA[17], b. at East Haddam, 1773; d. in 1842, æ. 69; m. Hannah Green, and had twelve children (of whom hereafter, 1676).

1440. (iv.) AMASA[17], b. at East Haddam, Sept. 7, 1776; d. April 22, 1845, æ. 68; m. Charlotte Kidder, and had eleven children (of whom hereafter, 1700).

1440A. (v.) POLLY[17], b. 1777; m. Thomas Jones, had ten children—two daughters and eight sons; d. in 1871, æ. 94.

1441. (1433.) BENJAMIN KNEELAND[16] (*John[15], Benjamin[14], Edward[13], Edward[12], John[11]—Alexander[1]*). Fourth son of John[15], and Mehitable (Lord) Kneeland, b. at East Haddam, Conn., Nov. 21, 1746. The only information I have received of his immediate descendants is through letters sent by his grandson, the late Ozias H. Kneeland, written in 1888 to his cousin, Dr. Jonathan Kneeland. Ozias was an octogenarian, but his letter was remarkably clear in statement and written in a firm hand.

Benjamin Kneeland[16].

Children of Benjamin and Mehitable (Lord) Kneeland.

1442. (i.) MEHITABLE[17]. She m. Ozias Hewett, and had two children:
1442A.   (i.) *Chauncey B. Hewett[18].*
1442B.   (ii.) *John Kneeland Hewett[18].*
1443. (ii.) JOHN[17]. He lived to manhood and died a bachelor.
1444. (iii.) SIMEON[17], b. Oct. 23, 1779 (of whom hereafter, 1474).
1445. (iv.) SALLY[17], m. Augustus Kent. Children:
1446.   (i.) *John Kent[18].*
1447.   (ii.) *Sabria Kent[18].*
1448.   (iii.) *Mary Ann Kent[18].*
1449. (v.) CYNTHIA[17], m. Isban Eaton. Children:
1450.   (i.) *Betsy Eaton[18].*
1451.   (ii.) *Amanda Eaton[18].*
1452.   (iii.) *John K. Eaton[18].*
1453.   (iv.) *Julius Eaton[18].*
1454.   (v.) *Phoebe Eaton[18].*
1455.   (vi.) *Hiram Eaton[18].*
1456. (vi.) BETSY[17], m. Isaac Eaton. Children:
1456A.   (i.) *Benjamin Kneeland Eaton[18]*, m. Huldah Cady, and had six children, as follows:
1457.   (i.) Huldah C. Eaton[19].
1458.   (ii.) Ebenezer Eaton[19].
1459.   (iii.) Edgar Eaton[19].
1460.   (iv.) Hiram Eaton[19].
1461.   (v.) Rosalfa Eaton[19].
1462.   (vi.) John K. Eaton[19].
           They reside at Bartonville, N. Y.
1463.   (ii.) *Joseph Eaton[18].*
1464.   (iii.) *Adaline Eaton[18].*
1465.   (iv.) *Chauncey B. Eaton[18].*
1466.   (v.) *Hiram Eaton[18].*
1467. (vii.) ANNA[17], m. Ebenezer Cady. They had six children (which seems to be the magic number in this family) as follows:
1468.   (i.) *Huldah Cady[18].*
1469.   (ii.) *Joseph Cady[18].*

Simeon Kneeland[17].

1470.	(iii.) *Betsy Cady*[18].
1471.	(iv.) *Patty Cady*[18].
1472.	(v.) *Tanna Cady*[18].
1473.	(vi.) *Edwin Cady*[18].

1474. (1444.) SIMEON KNEELAND[17] (*Benjamin*[16], *John*[15], *Benjamin*[14], *Edward*[13], *Edward*[12], *John*[11]—*Alexander*[1]). Second son of Benjamin Kneeland[16], b. Oct. 23, 1779; d. Nov. 13, 1846; m. Prudence —— and had nine children:

1475. (i.) OZIAS H.[18], b. Oct. 31, 1808 (of whom hereafter, 1496).

1476. (ii.) SIMEON C.[18].   Children:

1477.   (i.) *Edwin H. Kneeland*[19].   He lives at Eau Claire, Wis.

1478.   (ii.) *Addison H. Kneeland*[19].

1479.   (iii.) *Lovina Kneeland*[19].

1480.   (iv.) *Mercy Kneeland*[19].

1481.   (v.) *William H. Kneeland*[19].

1482.   (vi.) *Charlotte Kneeland*[19], now lives in St. Paul, Minn.

1483.   (vii.) *Ann Kneeland*[19].

1484. (iii.) AMANDA M.[18], b. Nov. 4, 1813.

1485. (iv.) JOHN D.[18], b. March 20, 1815.

1486. (v.) BENJAMIN L.[18], b. Oct. 14, 1816.

1487. (vi.) LOVINA[18], b. Nov. 24, 1820; m. —— Brown; living at Elizabethtown, N. Y.

1488. (vii.) ABNER D.[18], b. Oct. 30, 1823; d. Feb. 10, 1883; has two children, residing at Eau Claire, Wis.

1489.   (i.) *Sarah*[19].

1490.   (ii.) *Benjamin*[19].

1491. (viii.) HULDAH A.[18], b. Feb. 11, 1826; m. Frank M. Joy, of Eau Claire, Wis.

1492. (ix.) PRUDENCE C.[18], b. July 12, 1828; m. Edwin K. Spencer.   They reside at Geneva, Ohio, and have three children:

1493.   (i.) *Warren Spencer*[19].

1494.   (ii.) *Simeon Spencer*[19].

1495.   (iii.) *Nettie L. Spencer*[19].

OZIAS H. KNEELAND

No. 1496

Ozias H. Kneeland[18].

1496.   (1475.) OZIAS H. KNEELAND[18] (*Simeon*[17], *Benja-min*[16], *John*[15], *Benjamin*[14], *Edward*[13], *Edward*[12], *John*[11]—*Alexander*[1]). Born in Charleston, Montgomery County, N. Y., Oct. 31, 1808; moved to Battle Creek, Mich., in 1883, where he lived a retired life until his death, July 26, 1895, at the good old age of 87.

I am indebted to him for much of the history as to Benjamin Kneeland and his descendants, and to his granddaughter, Fannie J. Kneeland, for a completion and correction thereof. He married Phebe J. Ford, April 1, 1829, by whom he had the following:

Children of Ozias H. and Phebe J. (Ford) Kneeland.

1496A.   (i.) ORVILLE[19], b. Feb. 4, 1830; m. Jane A. Ruff. Children:

1497.   (i.) *Charles J.*[20], b. July 8, 1857; d. June 27, 1876.

1498.   (ii.) *Hattie B.*[20], b. March 16, 1856. She is a teacher in the High School, at Elgin, Ill.

1499.   (iii.) *Willis C.*[20], b. July 20, 1860: is a prominent physician in Denver, Col.; m. Florence Edna Stephenson. Children:

1500.   (i.) Elizabeth Isabella[21].

1501.   (ii.) William Gilbert[21].

1502.   (iv.) *Carrie M.*[20], b. Dec. 4, 1863.

1503.   (v.) *Howard L.*[20], b. Sept. 15, 1867. He is a merchant at Battle Creek, Mich.; m. Lida B. Carl. One child:

1504.   Blanch Lillian[21].

1505.   (vi.) *Emma A.*[20], d. in 1870.

1506.   (ii.) SALLY MORIAH[19], b. May 8, 1833; married John Jeffers, Oct., 1855. They reside at Mariaville, N. Y. Children:

1507.   (i.) *Amanda Viola Jeffers*[20].

1508.   (ii.) *William O. Jeffers*[20].

1509.   (iii.) *Maggie B. Jeffers*[20].

1510.   (iv.) *Warren B. Jeffers*[20].

1511.   (v.) *Zinnie D. Jeffers*[20].

1512.   (vi.) *James D. Jeffers*[20].

Jemima Kneeland[16].

1513.   (vii.) *John Jeffers[20].*

1514.   (viii.) *Freeman M. Jeffers[20].*

1515.   (iii.) JUDITH ANN[19], b. July 24, 1837; m. Warren
         Blinn. They reside at Charlotte, N. C., and had
         the following children:

1516.   (i.) *Cora B. Blinn[20].*

1517.   (ii.) *Joseph W. Blinn[20].*

1518.   (iii.) *Philo K. Blinn[20].*

1519.   (iv.) *Grace Blinn[20].*

1520.   (v.) *John J. Blinn[20].*

1521.   (vi.) *Mabel Blinn[20].*

1522.   (iv.) PRUDENCE ADALINE[19], b. May 27, 1839; m. J. C.
         Dougall, in 1863. They reside at Oil City, Pa.
         Children:

1523.   (i.) *James L. Dougall[20].*

1524.   (ii.) *Lizzie Dougall[20].*

1525.   (v.) TRYPHENA JANE[19], b. Feb. 28, 1846; m. W. H.
         Mason. They reside at Battle Creek, Mich. Had
         one child:

1526.   *Cora B. Mason[20].*

1527.   (vi.) AMANDA MALVINA[19], b. Dec. 19, 1852; d. Nov.
         17, 1856.

1528.   (vii.) EDGAR O.[19], b. Dec. 2, 1854; m. Charlotte S.
         Clute, Oct. 5, 1876. They reside at Battle Creek,
         and have one child:

1529.   *Fannie J. Kneeland[20]*, who has kindly rendered
         much assistance to me in this work.

1560.   (1434.) JEMIMA KNEELAND[16] (*John[15], Benja-
         min[14], Edward[13], Edward[12], John[11]—Alexander[1]*),
         youngest daughter of John Kneeland[15], b. at Marl-
         boro, Conn.; m. Cyrus Fillmore, a great-uncle of
         President Millard Fillmore.

They settled at Manlius, Onondaga County, N. Y., when
it was a wilderness. He cleared up a farm and resided on it
till their family of eight children had grown up. When the
hive had swarmed he sold out and went to live with their
youngest daughter, at Catarangus, and died there. He lived
to be 94 years of age. She died some years younger.

HATTIE BELLE KNEELAND

No. 1498

William Fillmore[17].

Children of Jemima Kneeland[16] and Cyrus Fillmore.

1561. (i.) HENRY FILLMORE[17].

1562. (ii.) LUTHER FILLMORE[17], represented Wayne in N. Y. Legislature, in 1824.

1563. (iii.) WILLIAM FILLMORE[17] (of whom hereafter, 1569).

1564. (iv.) ICHABOD FILLMORE[17]. No further record.

1565. (v.) CYRUS FILLMORE[17]. No further record.

1566. (vi.) PHEBE FILLMORE[17].

1567. (vii.) LAVINIA FILLMORE[17].

1568. (viii.) BETSEY FILLMORE[17]. The latter three all married and went West. No further record.

1569. (1563.) WILLIAM FILLMORE[17] (*Jemima Kneeland*[16], *John*[15], *Benjamin*[14], *Edward*[13], *Edward*[12], *John*[11]—*Alexander*[1]).

He lived in the town of Manlius, N. Y., during his entire span of 94 years. He was twice married. By his first wife he had twelve children. I have not dared to enquire as to his second experiment.

Children of William Fillmore.

1570. (i.) EDWIN G. FILLMORE[18], a farmer residing at Fayetteville, N. Y.; m. Harriet Wing and had seven children:

1571. (i.) *George Washington Fillmore*[19], General Superintendent of the Southern Pacific Railroad System.

1572. (ii.) *William C. Fillmore*[19].

1573. (iii.) *Jerome A. Fillmore*[19].

1574. (iv.) *Wing H. Fillmore*[19].

1575. (v.) *Edwin L. Fillmore*[19].

1576. (vi.) *Nancy Fillmore*[19], m. M. Shelton and lives in Idaho.

1577. (vii.) *Mary Fillmore*[19], unmarried; is a teacher at Fayetteville. All of the sons are in the railroad business in the West.

1578. (ii.) LUTHER FILLMORE[18], lives in California.

1579. (iii.) FRANK FILLMORE[18], of Scranton, Pa.

William Fillmore[17].

1580.   (iv.) HENRY C. FILLMORE[18], b. in Manlius, in 1820,
          and died there in 1884.   His children were:

1581.   (i.) *Henry B. Fillmore[19]*, d. July 6, 1860, æ. 8 years.

1582.   (ii.) *Charles A. Fillmore[19]*, d. Aug. 10, 1872, æ.
          15 years.

1583.   (iii.) *Fred. J. Fillmore[19]*, d. March 19, 1876, æ. 15
          years.

1584.   (iv.) *Flora O. Fillmore[19]*, d. May 23, 1880, æ. 19
          years.

1585.   (v.) *Frank B. Fillmore[19]*, now living at Fayette-
          ville, N. Y., m. Julia Boyd.   Children:

1586.   (i.) Flora B. Fillmore[20].
1587.   (ii.) Mary E. Fillmore[20].
1588.   (iii.) Harry J. Fillmore[20].

I have no record of the other of the twelve children of
William Fillmore[17], except that one of the sons, while on a
trip to California with his wife, was suffocated in their sleeping-
room at the Palmer House, Chicago.   Both died from the
result, the wife instantly and the husband within ten days.   I
surmise that he "blew out the gas," though history is silent
on that point.

(NOS. 1589 TO 1630.)

1589. (1437.) JOHN KNEELAND[17] (*Jonathan*[16], *John*[15], *Benjamin*[14], *Edward*[13], *Edward*[12], *John*[11], *William*[10], *James*[9], *Alexander*[8], *William*[7], *William*[6], *John*[5], *John*[4], *John*[3], *James*[2], *Alexander*[1]). Oldest son of Jonathan Kneeland, b. at East Haddam, Conn., May 10, 1769.

As he is always described as "Deacon," I assume that he was one who upheld the tradition of the John Kneeland[12] who came to this country with a sword in one hand and a Bible in the other, prepared to do battle by the one for the other. He married Sally Benson and had twelve children, each of whom lived to a ripened age, and some of whom are still living with much more than three score and ten to their credit. They resided in Livingston County, N. Y. In the year 1833, the five sons moved to Livingston County, Mich., then an unbroken wilderness; the rest of the children followed the next year, but the father remained in New York State and died there at a ripe old age.

Children of John and Sally (Benson) Kneeland.

1590. (i.) ICHABOD[18]. He m. first, Anna Prentice, of Skaneateles, N. Y., by whom he had four children, all born at Skaneateles. She d. at that place and he went to Livingston County, Mich., and married Sophronia Dunks, by whom he had one daughter and perhaps other children. The children by the first wife I find recorded at p. 119 of "The Prentice Family," as follows:

John Kneeland[17].

1591.   (i.) *Francis Kneeland*[19].
1592.   (ii.) *Prentice Kneeland*[19].
1593.   (iii.) *Lorinda Kneeland*[19].
1594.   (iv.) *Elizabeth Kneeland*[19].
1595.   His daughter by his second wife m. Eli Benjamin,
         and resides at Flushing, Mich.
1596.   (ii.) WARREN[18]. He m. Fanny Hyde, of Livingston
         County, N. Y. (Of whom hereafter, 1617.)
1597.   (iii.) AMASA[18]. Went to Michigan and afterwards to
         Wisconsin, and died there without issue.
1598.   (iv.) WHITFIELD[18], m. Sarah Fry; settled in Lansing,
         Mich., and died there in 1870, without issue.
1599.   (v.) NATHAN[18], went to Michigan and afterwards to
         California, and died there without known issue.
1600.   (vi.) JOHN B.[18], b. in 1812; m. Lucina Sickles, in 1845;
         they had three children:
1601.   (i.) *Frank E.*[19], b. in 1846; he m. Hannah Ella
             Whitney, 1866; they had three children:
1602.   (i.) Cora M.[20], b. in 1869; now living in
                 Toledo, Ohio.
1603.   (ii.) Frederick B.[20], b. in 1876.
1604.   (iii.) Eva D.[20], b. in 1885.
1605.   (ii.) *Lillian C.*[19], b. May 28, 1852; m. Joseph B.
             Davidson, May 5, 1870. Children:
1606.   (i.) John W. Davidson[20], b. at Bannister,
                 Mich., Dec. 14, 1871.
1607.   (ii.) Frank E. Davidson[20], b. at same place,
                 Nov. 9, 1873.
1608.   (iii.) *Jay B.*[19], b. June 19, 1861; m. Della A.
             Teeter, July 25, 1888; they reside in Owosso,
             Mich. Have one child:
1609.   Lyle A.[20], b. at Owosso, Sept. 2, 1893.
1610.   (vii.) CLARINDA[18], m. Ben Howe, in New York State;
         moved to Iona County, Mich., and have one son:
1611.   *Franklin Howe*[19], still living there.
1612.   (viii.) PHILENA[18], d. in 1879, unmarried.
1613.   (ix.) MINERVA[18], m. and lived in Walled Lake, Mich.;
         both dead; no descendants.
1614.   (x.) MARY[18], m. Daniel D. Y. Chandler.

1615. (xi.) ZIPPORAH[18], unmarried; lives at Walled Lake, Oakland County, Mich.

1616. (xii.) SARAH[18], unmarried; d. at Whitfield's home, in Michigan.

1617. (1596.) WARREN KNEELAND[18] (*John*[17], *Jonathan*[16], *John*[15], *Benjamin*[14], *Edward*[13], *Edward*[12], *John*[11]—*Alexander*[1]). Second son of Deacon John Kneeland[17]; m. Fanny Hyde in Livingston County, N. Y.; located in Howell, Livingston County, Mich. He d. in 1846, and his wife in 1876. They had seven children, as follows:

Children of Warren and Fanny (Hyde) Kneeland.

1618. (i.) SARAH[19]. She m. J. J. Bennet, of Perry, Mich., and had two sons and three daughters.

1619. (ii.) DEWITT CLINTON[19], m. Augusta Walker; d. July 23, 1876, leaving one daughter:

1620. *Maude Kneeland*[20]. She lives at Howell, Mich., with her husband, Chas. E. Gagh, whom she married Feb. 24, 1893. He is in partnership with her uncle, A. D. Kneeland (following) under the name of "D. C. & A. D. Kneeland Stock Farm."

1621. (iii.) AMASA DANA[19], b. ———— ————. It is to him that I am indebted for one of the most clearly written and comprehensive of all the letters received for the compilation of this work. It covers all the descendants of his grandfather, Deacon John Kneeland. If I ever try a law-suit in that vicinity again I shall feel constrained to board with him a week in token of my appreciation of his valued services in behalf of our family. He still lives at Howell, Mich., but don't all call on him at once. As he has not given the names of his wife and children, I assume that he is either unduly modest or a bachelor.

1622. (iv.) MINERVA[19], m. Dr. Leland Walker. He is dead and she lives with her two sons, at Howell, Mich.

Warren Kneeland[18].

1623. (v.) HARRIET[19], m. James Hearse; they live at Pinckey, Mich.   No children.

1624. (vi.) LEWIS BENSON[19], m. and lives at Orleans, Iona County, Mich.

1625. (vii.) CLARA[19], m. Miner J. Hosley; lives at Oak Grove, Mich.; have two daughters and one son.

CHAPTER XXIII.

DESCENDANTS OF WARREN KNEELAND.

(NOS. 1631 TO 1675.)

1631. (1438.) WARREN KNEELAND[17] (*Jonathan*[16], *John*[15], *Benjamin*[14], *Edward*[13], *Edward*[12], *John*[11], *William*[10], *James*[9], *Alexander*[8], *William*[7], *William*[6], *John*[5], *John*[4], *John*[3], *James*[2], *Alexander*[1]). Second son of Jonathan[16], b. in East Haddam, Conn., Nov. 2, 1771; m. first, Elizabeth Fitzgerald, Jan. 3, 1809; she died in 1818. Married, second, Rachel R. Sherman, *nee* Rachel Randell, widow of Garner Sherman. She died in Illinois with her son Harmon, about 1860.

Warren was a teacher for nearly thirty years in Saratoga and Onondaga Counties, N. Y.; was also a farmer, a man of decided religious views, and a worthy successor of his Puritan forefathers.

Children of Warren Kneeland, by Elizabeth Fitzgerald.

1632. (i.) JOEL[18], b. Jan., 1810; was thrown from a horse and killed during a violent thunderstorm, on June 10, 1837; unmarried.

1633. (ii.) JONATHAN[18], b. Feb. 10, 1812 (of whom hereafter, 1640).

1634. (iii.) DAVID F.[18], b. in 1811; d. at the age of four months.

1635. (iv.) NANCY[18], b. June 27, 1814 (of whom hereafter, 1652).

By Rachel (Randell) Sherman.

1636. (v.) ELIZABETH[18].

1637. (vi.) ANDREW JACKSON[18], b. March 20, 1823 (of whom hereafter, 1659).

Dr. Jonathan Kneeland[18].

1638. (vii.) CYNTHIA[18], b. about 1825; she m. A. Nostrand,
and had three children, two sons and a daughter.
The sons enlisted in the war and both died in a
military hospital. The mother and sister are also
dead.

1639. (viii.) WARREN H.[18], b. in 1831; m. and settled in
El Paso; afterwards went to Oakland, Cal., where
he now resides.

1640. (1633.) DR. JONATHAN KNEELAND[18] (*Warren[17],
Jonathan[16], John[15], Benjamin[14], Edward[13], Edward[12], John[11]—Alexander[1]*).

This is one of the star characters of the race. He is a
typical Kneeland. To longevity, temperance, sterling honesty,
ability, self-assertiveness and wit, add the fact of being grounded
and permeated with true religious instincts, and the sum total
is Dr. Jonathan Kneeland. He is the second son of Warren
Kneeland, the Yankee schoolmaster, and the father of the Rev.
Dr. M. D. Kneeland. Being thus sandwiched, it is easier to
believe the statement that at the age of six he received a
prize for having read the Bible through by course. While we
can sympathize with his struggles over some of the chronological chapters, we must admire the patience and perse-
ance of the lad, which argued well for his future success in
life. He was born Feb. 12, 1812, and is at this writing (1897)
eighty-five years old.

Fortunately, it has not been left to me to write the history
of his life. It was told in a most humorous but pathetic
manner at his semi-centennial celebration, a few years since.
I insert the entire record of that meeting from a Syracuse
paper, as best showing the character of the man and the
esteem of his associates:

HALF-CENTURY BANQUET.

**The Doctors Make Merry over a Memorable Occasion—Dr. H. D. Di-
dama tells a few Funny Anecdotes about Dr. Jonathan Kneeland—
Witty Remarks by the Practitioners.**

At the banquet by the Onondaga Medical Society at the
Vanderbilt House yesterday afternoon, in honor of Dr. Jonathan Kneeland, who has completed his fiftieth year as a

Jonathan Kneeland M.D.

No. 1640

Dr. Jonathan Kneeland[18].

member of the society, Dr. H. D. Didama read the following sketch of the venerable doctor's life: " Dr. Jonathan Kneeland was born February 10, 1812, in a log cabin, in Marcellus Township, between Skaneateles and Otisco lakes. His father, Warren Kneeland, was an accomplished Yankee schoolmaster, who taught in district schools for twenty years, in Saratoga and Onondaga Counties—training, in 1798-9, the twigs of genius which grew into sturdy trees on Pompey Hill. When but eleven years of age he was apprenticed to learn the art of healing to Jeremiah Bumbus Whiting, of Sempronius. Bumbus was a college graduate and he agreed to reward Kneeland for faithful services in ten years, with a horse and saddle-bags. This delightful experience and prospect was rudely ended by the relapse of the learned Whiting to his old but relinquished habit of quaffing the flowing bowl. Jonathan returned to his father's log house, left home without leave when but fifteen years old, attended district, select and academic schools, and taught for two winters at the encouraging remuneration of $10 and $18 a month. After this he went to Lane Seminary, where he taught for a while and then entered the Collegiate department a year in advance, under the able Presidency of Dr. Lyman Beecher. Purposing about this time to go as a medical missionary to Persia, China or Burmah, he attended medical lectures at the Ohio Medical College. This was in 1832, the year when the great epidemic of Asiatic cholera devastated the country. Jonathan was sent to Cincinnati to study the disease and came back to care for his fellow students at Lane Seminary, working day and night without undressing, and witnessing the death of ten of his associates. Then he was attacked himself by the dire disease, and under the eminent treatment of the learned Doctors Eberle and Drake, he became an altered man, his shrinking nature manifesting itself to such an extent that his weight came down from 140 pounds to 71. The doctor was brought home to Marcellus, a distance of 900 miles, to die. For nine long years he was an invalid. His intellect during all this time, and ever after, remained clear and unclouded. He regained and, with four relapses, has exercised delightfully ever since, his faculty of fluent speech. In 1841 he gave up his life plans and devoted himself

17

Dr. *Jonathan Kneeland*[18].

to the practice of medicine in his native land.   He opened an office in Vesper, then removed to Thornhill, where he remained twelve years.

"Dr. Kneeland has received the honorary degree of M. D. from the Regents of the University of New York and also from the Ohio Medical College.   These were conferred for well-known merit and were unsought by the deserving doctor. In all the years of an extensive and successful practice, the doctor has sought to keep abreast with the best members of his profession, not only by the careful study of journals and books but by attending repeated courses of lectures in Philadelphia and New York, and by service in hospitals and dispensaries.   Dr. Kneeland faithfully attended at the various county, State and national medical societies to which he belonged.   He was a delegate to the State Medical Society for four years and an active member for twenty years, serving many times as censor.   He has been for thirty-five years a member of the American Medical Association.   At the meetings of these societies, as at our own county society, which honors itself to-day by honoring him, he has never furnished any evidence that his faculty of speech was ever impaired. Bright, witty, humorous, learned and instructive, he has often awakened a dull and prosy meeting into one of vigorous activity.

"He has contributed to various medical journals articles of great merit, some of them having been translated into foreign tongues.   More than forty years ago he published, at the request of the eminent Dr. Frank Hamilton, a paper on 'Angina Pectoris,' which attracted marked attention at home and abroad.   Other articles on 'Rupture of the Bladder,' 'Diphtheria,' 'Unknown Death,' 'Cancer,' 'Sanitary Condition of Onondaga Indians,' and 'Common Sense *versus* Medication in Treatment of Chronic Diseases,' have appeared in different journals, the last two in the Transactions of the New York State Medical Association, of which he was one of the founders.   Dr. Kneeland has held the office of Coroner eighteen years; was Superintendent of the Onondaga Indian School twenty-five years, and ten years physician to the Indians.   He has had what he always deserved, a host of devoted friends and not one enemy. He did valuable work during the war as a volunteer surgeon, and his services were appreciated and honored by Secretary Stanton and Governor Morgan.

" Dr. Kneeland himself attributes his success as a physician and man to what he calls the ability to guess correctly; to his acute, quick sympathy with humanity and, indeed, with all life; and to his earnest effort to square his conduct with the Golden Rule rightly interpreted: 'Whatsoever ye ought to desire others to do unto you, do ye so to them.' His ability to guess is clearly shown in the readiness with which he solves enigmas. His sympathy with all animated nature is manifested in the affection displayed towards him by women and children, and even by cats and dogs—an affection which he heartily reciprocates.

" The faithful observance of the Golden Rule in his daily intercourse with his fellows, has not always brought money to his coffers, but it has secured what is infinitely more precious than gold or gems, an approving conscience void of offense towards God and man. And, somehow, in this world, as Burns expresses it:

> " 'A correspondence fixed with heaven
> Is sure a noble anchor.'

" But our friend will permit us to express the opinion that what he calls ability to guess correctly, is really the exercise of perceptive faculties naturally keen and sharpened by close and persevering observation.

> " ' A primrose by the river's brim
> A yellow primrose is to him.'

" But it is something more; and this something more is an outcome of a love for and study of nature. And that long and relentless attack of illness combined with poverty, illness so severe that voice became quenched into utter silence and flesh so melted away that the poor skeleton required a suit of plaster of Paris to hold it upright, would have crushed into dumb despair any faith less faltering, and broken down any will less invincible than those which buoyed up and carried through to triumphant success the venerable brother whom we

delight to honor to-day.   God bless and preserve to us and his
worthy family for many more happy years, Dr. Jonathan
Kneeland."

Dr. Kneeland then responded happily.   He said that he
ought to compress his speech in two letters: N.C., "nuff said."
In his opinion Dr. Didama had used the whitewash brush too
freely, but he would retaliate by telling a few stories of his
friend's earlier days, and this he did, causing considerable
merriment.   Dr. Kneeland said that he had met at fifty
annual meetings of the society, thirty-eight semi-annual meetings, and ninety-eight quarterly meetings.   He spoke pleasantly
of the days gone by, and of the old members of the society,
some of whom had long ago been called to their Maker.

As Dr. Kneeland was about to take his seat, a member
of the society asked him to tell about his experience with
the Cardiff giant.   The doctor said, in reply, that he knew the
giant was a sham and said so when he found under it a penny
of the date of 1858.   He thought it was a sham then, and felt
sure of it now.

Dr. Sears then read a letter from Dr. Elsner, in which
the latter expressed his regret at his inability to be present at
the banquet and extended his congratulations to Dr. Kneeland.

Dr. Totman was called upon to respond to the toast, "The
Clergy."   He said that he did not know what relation they
could bear to the doctors gathered there, but supposed if the
ministers were there they could tell.   The speaker continuing
spoke of Dr. Kneeland's long connection with the society and
recalled a few amusing stories.

Dr. Van Duyn said that he joined the medical society
twenty-one years ago.   When he went back to that time there
was one figure that arose preëminently above all others, and
that was the man in whose honor the banquet was given.   It
seemed to him that there was something in Dr. Kneeland's
life that impressed him more than anything else, and that was
his ready knowledge of medicine, theology, literature and
almost every other subject.   It showed that a physician could
have knowledge beside that which he learned of medicine.

Dr. W. W. Munson responded to the toast, " The Country
Doctor."   He said that Dr. Kneeland was the first physician

Dr. Jonathan Kneeland[18].

who called on him when he began the practice of medicine on the hill. Dr. Kneeland was the man who took his diploma when he asked for admittance to the society. That was almost twenty years ago, and it made the speaker feel as though he was growing old too. It did not seem possible to him that Dr. Kneeland was 79 years old, for he knew of no man who could take as many steps to the minute in walking across the country.

The banquet was brought to a close with three rousing cheers for Dr. Kneeland.

He married Miriam Dwelle, Feb., 7, 1845, to whom three children were born, all of whom are living.

One of the ambitions of Dr. Kneeland's later life has been to see, in " sure enough " print, this Kneeland genealogy. As he devoted much labor to its preparation, I have been trying to make myself believe that the contest between his pertinacity and my procrastination has preserved his life. Having won the contest, may he enjoy both the book and the life for many, many years.

Children of Dr. Jonathan and Miriam (Dwelle) Kneeland.

1641.   (i.) FRANK JOEL[19], b. Dec. 10, 1845 ; m. Etta Edwards, of Whitehall, Wis., Dec. 5, 1883. They have two children :

1641A.   (i.) *Martin Dwelle[20]*, b. July 14, 1885.

1641B.   (ii.) *Frank Edwards[20]*, b. in 1891.

1642.   (ii.) MARTIN DWELLE[19], b. September 24, 1848 (of whom hereafter, 1646).

1643.   (iii.) STELLA[19], b. Feb. 20, 1854 ; graduated in 1875 from Mount Holyoke Seminary ; was a teacher for five years in Syracuse High School ; m. Frederick Colburn Eddy, Cashier of the First National Bank, of Syracuse, where they now reside. Have three children :

1644.   (i.) *Marjorie Kneeland Eddy[20]*, b. April 8, 1887.

1645.   (ii.) *Frederick C. Eddy[20]*, b. July 30, 1894 ; d. Aug. 19, 1894.

1645A.   (iii.) *Helen Miriam Eddy[20]*, b. in 1896.

1646.   (1642.) REV. MARTIN D. KNEELAND, D.D.[19](*Jona-*
than[18], *Warren*[17], *Jonathan*[16], *John*[15], *Benjamin*[14],
Edward[13], *Edward*[12], *John*[11]—*Alexander*[1]).   Second son of Dr. Jonathan Kneeland, was b. in
Onondaga County, N. Y., Sept. 24, 1848.

He went from the district school to Onondaga Valley
Academy, then to Cazenovia Seminary, and was graduated
at Hamilton College in 1869, with the literary oration and a
Phi Beta Kappa key.   The year after his graduation he was
Principal of Southold Academy, Long Island, N. Y.   Having
chosen the ministry as his life work, he studied at Auburn
Theological Seminary, from which he was graduated in 1873.
He was settled immediately over the Presbyterian church of
Waterloo, N. Y., where he remained nearly ten years.   He
was called from this old and important church to become
pastor of the Presbyterian church of Fredonia, N. Y., where
he remained until December, 1887.   During these years Mr.
Kneeland edited a local temperance and religious paper, called
The Fredonia Presbyterian, which exerted a decided influence
upon the community.   This was his first experience in enlisting the power of the press in connection with the pastorate,
and it proved so successful that it became a strong feature in
his after ministry.

At the commencement of 1887 his alma mater honored
him with the degree of D.D., and shortly after he was called
to Titusville, Pa., to assume charge of one of the strongest
Presbyterian churches in the oil regions.   He remained here
but three years, when he was called to the Roxbury Presbyterian Church, Boston, Mass.   He undertook this enterprise
when a very small audience was worshipping in a hall, but
when he resigned this pastorate five years later, he left a
church numbering 325 communicants and worshipping in a
beautiful stone edifice erected only by strenuous efforts and
many sacrifices.   Dr. Kneeland gave up the pastorate to
become the secretary of the New England Sabbath Protective
League, an inter-denominational work presenting greater possi-
bilities of usefulness and a much broader field of labor than
any he had before occupied.   In addition to presenting the
necessity of a day of rest upon platform and pulpit, he edits

REV. MARTIN D. KNEELAND, D.D.

No. 1646

The Defender, the only organ in the interest of Sabbath observance published in New England.

Dr. Kneeland has held important offices in connection with the institutions from which he was graduated and has been sent as a commissioner to six General Assemblies of the Presbyterian church. He was also sent, in 1888, as a delegate to the International Missionary Conference, in London, England. Mr. Kneeland married Sarah A. Lord, a daughter of Rev. William H. Lord, D.D., of Montpelier, Vt., and granddaughter of President Nathan Lord, of Dartmouth College, on Oct. 27, 1875. He resides at Roxbury, Mass.

Children of Martin D. and Sarah A. (Lord) Kneeland.

1647. (i.) ELIZABETH LORD[20], b. April 8, 1877.
1648. (ii.) FRANK JONATHAN[20], b. May 30, 1879.
1649. (iii.) WILLIAM AIKEN[20], b. Aug. 9, 1884.
1650. (iv.) PAUL DWELLE[20], b. March 2, 1887.
1651. (v.) RUTH STELLA[20], b. Nov. 7, 1888.

1652. (1635.) NANCY KNEELAND[18] (*Warren*[17], *Jonathan*[16], *John*[15], *Benjamin*[14], *Edward*[13], *Edward*[12], *John*[11]—*Alexander*[1]).

She was the only daughter of Warren Kneeland, and sister of Dr. Jonathan Kneeland; m. in 1833, Rev. Jeremiah B. Evarts, a Baptist clergyman, who died in 1846 and by whom she had three children. She married a second time, in 1852, to Minard Lafever, a famous architect of New York City. After his death, in 1854, she was for many years one of the leaders in work for the Home for the Friendless, in that city. Afterwards she went to her daughter's home, in Highland, Ill., where she still resides. As she is again a widow I dare not give her age, but in view of the fact that she is two years younger than her brother Jonathan, some of the inquisitive, the mathematical or the aspiring may be able to spell it out for themselves.

Children of Nancy Kneeland[18] and Rev. J. B. Evarts.

1653. (i.) THEODORE[19], d. in the army, in 1863, without children.

Andrew Jackson Kneeland[18].

1654.   (ii.) MARY[19], d. in 1858; unmarried.
1655.   (iii.) MARTHA[19], m. Albert Holden, to whom were
            born three children, who, with their mother, are
            now living:
1656.   (i.) *Annie Holden[20].*
1657.   (ii.) *Marjorie Holden[20].*
1658.   (iii.) *Hoyt Holden[20].*

    Mrs. Holden lived in Illinois, and was a writer
    of celebrity, whose *nom de plume* of "Amber"
    made her widely and favorably known.   She was a
    member of the Chicago Press Club and died in 1896.

1659.   (1637).   ANDREW JACKSON KNEELAND[18](*War-*
            ren[17], *Jonathan*[16], *John*[15], *Benjamin*[14], *Edward*[13],
            Edward[12], *John*[11]—*Alexander*[1]).   Fourth son of
            Warren and Rachel (Sherman) Kneeland, b. in the
            town of Marcellus, Onondaga County, N. Y.,
            March 20, 1823.

Went to Binghamton a short time before the birth of his
son Harmon, and remained there; engaged as a contractor and
builder till 1867, when he removed with his family to Augusta,
Oneida County; purchased the interest of the other heirs in the
family homestead above mentioned, and became a successful
farmer.   His death occurred there on April 17, 1886, from an
injury received in the woods by falling from the limb of a tree;
m. at Augusta, Jan. 31, 1850, to Lucy Adaline Parker.   Her
paternal grandfather, Amos Parker, was for seven years a soldier
in the War of the Revolution, taking an active part for our
country in that sanguinary conflict, serving some of the time
under General Lafayette.   At the close of the war he settled
in Augusta, Oneida County, N. Y., where he was a pioneer on
some land ceded to him by the government for faithful services.   A part of this land since brought under cultivation and
improvement is now the family homestead.   Mrs. Kneeland's
father, Harmon Parker, son of Amos, was also a farmer, and
was a man of considerable enterprise.

Harmon J. Kneeland

No. 1661

Harmon Jackson Kneeland[19].

Children of Andrew J. and Adaline (Parker) Kneeland.

1660. (i). VIRGIL GAIUS,[19], b. Dec. 15, 1850, d. Sept. 2, 1851.

1661. (ii). HARMON JACKSON[19], b. Nov. 21, 1852. He attended school in Binghamton, and later at Augusta Academy and at Whitestown Seminary, near Utica, N. Y., where he was salutatorian of his class on the day of graduation. While at Binghamton he carried daily newspapers for two or three years, and afterward while at Augusta, he worked on the homestead farm and for other farmers in that neighborhood, at farm labor and carpenter work. He also taught school in Oneida and Ulster Counties, in New York State, and thus acquired the means for obtaining his education, which was further continued at Hamilton College, Clinton, N. Y. He was also local editor of the *Oriskany Falls News*, while he was teaching in that village in Oneida County, that being the name of the paper of that village of that time. He was always proficient in his studies and ranked high in his classes, and was at all times, except during school hours, ready to enjoy the sports of the campus with his fellow schoolmates, being an athletic youth of good physique and health. While obtaining his education he had decided upon the profession of the law, to which he began to turn his attention in 1877, reading most of the time with A. D. Wales, Esq., a distinguished lawyer of Binghamton, with whom he boarded most of the time while reading, and studying law preparatory for his admission to the bar. He made rapid progress in the study of law, and was admitted to the bar in May, 1880, at the general term of the Supreme Court held at Ithaca, N. Y.

He then entered upon the active practice of his profession at Binghamton, N. Y., where he has since remained. Having a natural aptitude for his calling, and being well furnished with legal lore, he has succeeded in reaching and maintaining an enviable position at the Broome County Bar. Binghamton

Harmon Jackson Kneeland[19].

being a city of about 45,000 inhabitants and being the county seat of Broome County and well supplied with lawyers, the business of a lawyer there naturally drifts into a general practice, and so Mr. Kneeland's practice is of a general nature although he may be said to be especially gifted in collections, Surrogate's Court practice, mortgage foreclosure, conveyancing, real estate, etc.

He is a good trial lawyer. He thoroughly prepares his cases before going into court and always struggles hard to win them, having faith in the justice of his client's cause and his clients having faith in him. He does not stoop to the tricks and technicalities of the pettifogger, but having mastered the details, he has what may be called a natural instinct to discover the weak points in the case of the opposition and he makes his attacks at those points with an unyielding courage and perseverance, and tenaciously works to win with a persistent determination that yields to no obstacle. In all office work, in which he is an adept, he is very careful to have every matter entrusted to him, correct and right before it leaves his office. He is noted as a careful and thorough practitioner, and as one who can be trusted with any business placed in his charge. He is one of those lawyers to whom business naturally comes because of the way in which he does it and because of the way in which he settles with his clients after the business is concluded.

While not an active politician in the sense of being an office seeker, as a firm believer in the principals of the Republican party and an earnest worker in its ranks, Mr. Kneeland is a patriotic citizen, and greatly interested in the public weal. He has been a member of the county and city republican committee, a worker and speaker during different campaigns, and a considerable power in the politics of the county. He is interested to some

CASSIUS L. KNEELAND

No. 1668

Cassius Lee Kneeland[19].

extent in real estate, and is treasurer and secretary of the Shinhopple wood acid works. In the Masonic Order he belongs to Otseningo Lodge, Binghamton Chapter and Malta Commandery. He is also a member of Anawan Tribe of Red Men, having filled all the chairs in said tribe, and is also President of the Red Men's Mutual Benefit Association of Binghamton, and is an honorary member of the Twentieth Separate Company, having served six years, a part of the time as sergeant.

He was married June 14, 1893, to Miss Seddie M. Bonnell, of Binghamton, a charming and accomplished young lady. Mr. and Mrs. Kneeland are members of the First Presbyterian Church of Binghamton. They have a beautiful residence at No. 123 Chapin Street, Binghamton, where they enjoy a delightful home life and exercise a generous and graceful hospitality.

1662. (iii.) CHILDIS BIRD D.[19], b. at Bimghamton, Dec. 23, 1854; he now resides an Rome, N. Y.; is a law student of much promise.

1663. (iv.) LILLIE J.[19], b. at Binghamton, N. Y., July 8, 1857; m. May 13, 1885, at Augusta, N. Y., to William O. Caire. Has two children living:

1664.   (i.) *Elsie Adeline Caire[20]*, b. in 1888.
1665.   (ii.) *Victor Kneeland Caire[20]*, b. in 1891.

1666. (v.) MARY A.[19], b. in Binghamton, Jan. 27, 1860; m. George A. Lyon, of Solsville, N. Y., Oct. 23, 1889; d. at Solsville, April 13, 1894, leaving one child:

1667.   *Stella Lyon[20]*, b. in 1892.

1668. (vi.) CASSIUS LEE[19], b. at Binghamton, Broome County, N. Y., on the 11th day of November, 1861. He attended the common schools of Binghamton, and Augusta, N. Y., and was fitted for college by an academical education at the latter place. At the age of nineteen he entered the business college of W. G. Chaffee, at Oswego, N. Y., as a student, but in less than four months was appointed one of the principals of that Phonographic Institute, which

Cassius Lee Kneeland[19].

position he held until he was graduated in the fall of
the same year in which he entered, having passed
a successful business course of studies, including
phonography. His progress while in school, like
that of all his brothers and sisters, was marked with
much studiousness and rapid and brilliant work,
and his rhetorical skill, coupled with his business
perception and ability, soon secured him a position
as private secretary and amanuensis for Lieut.-
Governor Jones, which position he filled with great
efficiency until he received a position as correspondent and stenographer for the Household Sewing
Machine Company, a large manufacturing corporation of Providence, R. I. With this company he
remained until January, 1891, when he gave it up
with the intention of devoting the remainder of his
life to the study and practice of the law. In March,
1891, he was admitted to practice law in all the
State and county courts of Rhode Island, after
passing a most successful examination, and on the
15th day of April of the same year, his shingle
first appeared as an attorney and counselor-at-law,
at 19 College street, Providence, R. I.

From the first he was successful in this new
avocation, and in a short time had built up a good
practice which, by his integrity, ability and assidu
ous labors, coupled with his natural tendencies in
this peculiar field and his high moral qualifications, has grown to an extensive and highly remu-
nerative practice. He has always taken a deep
interest in the advancement of young men, and
has for years been identified in one way or another
with the Young Men's Christian Association. He
is at the present time an active member of the
lyceum connected with that association in Providence, and the records there show that in the
winter of 1895 and 1896 he was twice elected
President of that organization, which has a large
membership composed of lawyers, doctors, colle-

Andrew Delos Kneeland

No. 1669

Andrew Delos Kneeland[19].

gians and business men. On October, 16, 1893, Mr. Kneeland was married to Florence Linfield Allen, the daughter of a prosperous business man—a carriage manufacturer—of the city of Providence, and there he has apparently settled down for the remainder of his life to practice his chosen profession, the law.

1669. (vii.) ANDREW DELOS[19], b. at Binghamton, May 6, 1863 ; m. April 21, 1887, at Rome, N. Y., to Martha Hutchinson Seymour. Has two children :

1670.   (i.) *Joy Pauline[20]*, b. April 1, 1891, at Rome.

1671.   (ii.) *Belle Genevieve[20]*, b. July 16, 1893.

    My friend Delos is also a lawyer. The fact that there are only five lawyers in this family is due to the further fact that the remaining members were girls. Had Virgil Gaius survived his name he would possibly, by virtue thereof, have been the greatest lawyer of them all. It is to this member of the family and his uncle Jonathan that I am indebted for valuable information relating to the descendants of John Kneeland, of Marlboro, Conn. He has held many positions of trust and is an honor to the profession and our race.

1672. (viii.) VIRGIE ELLA[19], b. at Binghamton, May 20, 1865; now (1897) at Geneseo Normal School. Her residence is at Rome, N. Y., and she is a teacher.

1673. (ix.) LUCY STELLE[19], b. in Augusta, N. Y., Nov. 15, 1867. She is unmarried and lives in P—— ——nce, R. I., with her sister, Flora Belle.

1674. (x.) FLORA BELLE[19], b. in Augusta, N. Y., Feb. 15, 1870. She is unmarried and lives in Providence, R. I.

1675. (xi.) JESSIE ADEL[19], b. in Augusta, N. Y., March 20, 1872 ; d. in Utica, N. Y., Dec. 17, 1893.

CHAPTER XXIV.

DESCENDANTS OF ASA KNEELAND.

1676. (1439.) ASA KNEELAND[17] (*Jonathan*[16], *John*[15], *Benjamin*[14], *Edward*[13], *Edward*[12], *John*[11], *William*[10], *James*[9], *Alexander*[8], *William*[7], *William*[6], *John*[5], *John*[4], *John*[3], *James*[2], *Alexander*[1]). Third son of Jonathan and Mary (Spencer) Kneeland, b. in 1774, at East Haddam, Conn.

His father was in the war and he must have had early recollections of the revolutionary times. He married Hannah Green in the year 1800, and although there were eleven children born to them there is but one male descendant to carry down the name, the grandson of his son Edward. He (Asa) died in 1818. His business is thus quaintly stated in a letter of his daughter, Henrietta, which gives his genealogical tree: "Here begins the third book of 'Chronicles.' The second book ends with a command for some one to build a house. Now, my father built many a house and knew all the architectural details by which a good one should be builded, yet I never really enjoyed living in one of his buildings."

Children of Asa and Hannah (Green) Kneeland.

1677. (i.) EDWARD[18], b. Jan. 15, 1801; m. Mary Thompson. They had one son:

1678.   *Edward*[19], who married and had one son:

1679.   Edward[20]. This is the only male descendant of Asa Kneeland.

1680. (ii.) CHARLES[18], b. in 1802; d. same year.

1681. (iii.) SARAH[18], b. in 1803; m. Joseph Berry; d. in 1853, without issue.

1682. (iv.) HORACE[18], b. May 12, 1806 (he was a twin brother of Hector, hereafter). I have been intensely interested in this particular Kneeland without knowing him. His counterpart has been in my house for years. It is an oil painting by the celebrated artist, Charles L. Elliot. As a work of art it is worth well up in the thousands and it is a picture with a history. It was, in the early days of the National Academy of Design, exhibited by the artist. The committee hung it "above the line." Elliot was so angry at what he considered a slur both upon himself and his sculptor friend, Horace Kneeland, whose portrait it was, that he deliberately cut it from the frame and carried it off, leaving the frame hanging on the wall. This created a great commotion, resulting in a legal fight to test the right of a national academician over his picture while on exhibition in the academy. After the death of Horace it was sold as one of the best examples of the greatest portrait painter this country ever produced. It thus came into the possession of an art collector, from whom I purchased it both for its artistic merit and because of its title, "Portrait of Kneeland." It was supposed at the time of purchase to have been a portrait of Rev. Abner Kneeland. Since then, however, its history was told to me by James M. Hart, N. A., who exhibited one of his pictures at the same time. He knew all the parties and saw the picture cut out. He said that it was painted as a present to Horace Kneeland, the New York sculptor, who was a great friend of Elliot.

Horace at one time bid fair to take the highest rank in art. A severe and lingering illness, however, terminated his life in 1875, leaving a wife but no children. The New York Directory from 1840 to 1850, gives his address: " Horace Kneeland, Sculptor, 280 Broadway." In the Registrar's office, August 7, 1875, are filed letters of adminis-

Asa Kneeland[17].

tration granted to Lucy Ann Kneeland on the estate of her late husband, Horace Kneeland. The next of kin, to whom notices were sent, were: " Hector Kneeland, brother, San Francisco, Cal.; Angeline Southwick, sister, Shullsburg, Wis.; Henrietta Mann, sister, St. Paul, Minn., and the three children of his deceased sister, Cornelia Baker, St. Paul, Minn." This corresponds with the descendants of Asa Kneeland, as the widow understood them to exist in 1875, and, of course, fixes his position in the Kneeland family. Horace had one child, but it must have died prior to 1875, as it is not mentioned in the probate proceedings. He had a mangificent physique, a large head, full black beard, a strong face, with bright blue eyes and the high cheek bones that are a prominent feature in all the race. I present herewith a photographic reproduction of the painting. I wish I could give Elliot's magnificent color scheme and his exquisite brush work.

1683.   (v.) HECTOR[18], twin brother; b. May 12, 1806; m. Maria Smith, and had one daughter:

1684.   *Helen Kneeland[19].* She resides in San Francisco, and her father was living there in 1890, æ. 84, but has since passed away.

1685 and 1686.   (vi. and vii.) CHARLES[18] and CATHARINE[18], twins, b. June 8, 1808. Charles m. Catharine Horo; he d. in 1847, without issue. Catharine m. Alonzo Meachem; they lived at Davenport, Iowa, and had two children and three grandchildren.

1687.   (viii.) ANGELINE[18], b. June, 1810; d. April 1, 1880, æ. 70; m. first, Fred Knickerbocker, by whom she had four children; m. second, Daniel Southwick, of Shullsburg, Wis., by whom she had three children.

1688.   (ix.) ALMIRA[18], b. Sept. 10, 1812; d. June, 1838.

1689.   (x.) CORNELIA[18], b. March 7, 1816; m. Daniel Baker, of St. Paul, Minn., by whom she had three children:

1690.   (i.) *Daniel Baker[19].*

1691.   (ii.) *Asa Baker[19].*

HORACE KNEELAND

No. 1682

Asa Kneeland[17].

1692.   (iii.) *Cornelia Baker*[19]. Cornelia died prior to the death of her brother Horace, in 1875.

1693.   (xi.) HIRAM[18], b. March 27, 1818; d. Sept., 1840.

1694.   (xii.) HENRIETTA[18], b. Jan. 6, 1822; m. first, James M. Goodhue, by whom she had four children:

1695 and 1696.   (i. and ii.) *James*[19] and *May*[19], twins, b. March 4, 1847.   May m. Charles A. Moore; no children; she d. in 1874.   James m. Helen Kimball; no children.

1697.   (iii.) *Edward*[19], b. June 23, 1848; d. Nov., 1849.

1698.   (iv.) *Eve*[19], b. July 4, 1851; m. first, Morris Lampney, by whom she had five children; m. second, Jasper Tarbox; both living; no children.

1699.   (v.) *James*[19].

Henrietta is still living and I am indebted to her in part for this history of her father's descendants.

18

CHAPTER XXV.

DESCENDANTS OF AMASA KNEELAND.

(NOS. 1700 TO 1782.)

1700. (1440.) AMASA KNEELAND[17](*Jonathan*[16], *John*[15], *Benjamin*[14], *Edward*[13], *Edward*[12], *John*[11], *William*[10], *James*[9], *Alexander*[8], *William*[7], *William*[6], *John*[5], *John*[4], *John*[3], *James*[2], *Alexander*[1]). Fourth son of Jonathan Kneeland, of East Haddam, Conn., b. Sept. 7, 1776, a year of saintly memories.

His father was a soldier in the Continental army. With such a genesis, can it be wondered that his was a true, patriotic, noble life? No one of all the race has been more blessed in his children and descendants. They include divines, lawyers, doctors, merchants, legislators, soldiers, sailors and tillers of the soil. Each representative added new honors and dignity to his chosen profession. To this true summary it need only be added that for sixty years his eldest child was engaged in missionary work, and died with the harness on in " India's coral strand."

He married Charlotte Kidder, in 1807, and spent his remaining days at Spafford and Thorn Hill, town of Marcellus, Onondaga County, N. Y. Amasa Kneeland and each of his eleven children were school teachers in the old days when teaching meant something.

Children of Amasa and Charlotte (Kidder) Kneeland.

1701. (i.) STELLA[18], b. Jan. 13, 1808 (of whom hereafter, 1713).
1702. (ii.) ELLEN[18], b. April 2, 1809 (of whom hereafter, 1756).
1703. (iii.) HON. SAMUEL STILLMAN[18], b. April 2, 1811 (of whom hereafter, 1765).
1704. (iv.) PERSIS[18], b. in 1813; d. in 1844; unmarried.

Stella Kneeland[18].

1705.   (v.) AMASA SPENCER[18], b. Oct. 22, 1815 (of whom hereafter, 1770.)

1706.   (vi.) MARY[18], b. Aug., 1817; d. Oct. 8, 1882, æ. 65.
She m. Geo. Sessions, and resided at Jefferson, Col.

1707.   (vii.) JOHN KIDDER[18], b. in April, 1819; m. and lives
at Cadilac, Mich.

1708.   (viii.) HON. A. JUDSON[18], b. May 5 ,1821 (of whom
hereafter, 1782).

1709.   (ix.) JANE ANN[18], b. March 30, 1823; m. Martin Spencer, and resides at Galva, Ill.

1710.   (x.) BENJAMIN TURNBULL[18], b. June 3, 1825; m. Harriet Mills.   Resides at Dalton, N. Y.

1711.   (xi.) DOLPHAS BENNETT[18], b. in 1827; m. Miranda
Charles, and lives at Ionia.

1713.   (1701.) STELLA KNEELAND[18] (*Amasa*[17], *Jonathan*[16], *John*[15], *Benjamin*[14], *Edward*[13], *Edward*[12],
John[11]—*Alexander*[1]).

Perhaps the best summary of her wonderful life is contained in the following clipping from the *Rangoon News*.   It
is from the inspired pen of an associate in missionary work,
Dr. F. D. Phinney:

ENTERED INTO REST,

**Rangoon, September 30, 1891, Mrs. Stella Kneeland Bennett, Aged 83
Years—For 61 Years a Missionary to Burmah.**

"Born January 13, 1808; sailed from Philadelphia, May,
1829; arrived at Moulmein, January 14, 1830; removed to
Tavoy, 1837; returned to Moulmein, 1855; removed to Rangoon, 1862; died September 30, 1891.   These dates are but
the distance points in the picture of a completed life, beautiful in its Christlikeness, wonderful in the measure of its blessing, seldom equalled in length or in fulness in missionary
service.   Would that a worthy artist might reproduce the
picture.   Who, even of those nearest to her, can estimate the
blessing to others of this long life-time, or say when her works
shall cease to follow her?

"Possessed of superior mental endowments, she became a
thorough student, not only mastering the Burman and Sgau

Stella Kneeland[18].

Karen languages, but at the same time keeping abreast with the literature of the day and with the progress of science, and coupling keenness of perception with breadth of view, her judgment was appealed to, both by a multitude of natives and by her missionary associates as well. Admired for her characteristics of mind, she was the more beloved for her qualities of heart. To speak of her as loving wife and mother is not to use an idle phrase, certainly to that large number who at different times have enjoyed the hospitality of her home, or been nursed back to health by her tender, thoughtful, kindly ministrations. With a sympathy broad enough to cover all who might come to her in trouble, and with a patient interest which extended to the minutest items of sorrow, she was constantly appealed to for aid or consolation, and none worthy ever left her presence without being the better for her advice or comfort, or more material aid. And withal so modest, never telling of the good she did or the money she gave, forbidding those who helped her in carrying out her plans from making known the giver, it will be impossible to estimate the good she has done until the great book shall be opened and the treasures laid up in heaven shall be revealed.

"Whether we look at her in her school work or after the duties of the day are done, reading with straining eyes the dim Burman palm leaves, or later on correcting all the proofs from the Press in both Burmese and Karen, or taking charge of the Press during Mr. Bennett's absence from the country, or instructing and sending forth her Bible women and preachers, or in personal entreaty with the impenitent, or caring for the wants of the needy and sorrowful, it requires no gift of prophecy to hear even now the 'Well done, good and faithful servant, enter thou into the joy of thy Lord.'"

Stella Kneeland Bennett, the daughter of Amasa and Charlotte Kneeland, was born in Thorn Hill, town of Marcellus, Onondaga County, N. Y., being the eldest of twelve children. Stella began her education at the district school the summer after she was three years old, and finished her school life at the then somewhat famous Cortland Academy, Homer, N. Y. Her interest in missions dated from the sailing of Dr. Judson and his companions, when she was four years

Stella Kneeland [18].

old. She was converted at twelve years of age in a series of Methodist revival meetings, but did not publicly acknowledge her hope in Christ till several years later.

She was married to Cephas Bennett, January 10, 1826, the marriage taking place in Thorn Hill, after which the young couple went immediately to Utica, N. Y., where Mr. Bennett was established in the publishing business. But his interest in missions did not allow his mind to be at rest, and his wife's interest only strengthened his determination to give his life to the latter work. On May 19, 1829, Mr. and Mrs. Bennett sailed from Philadelphia in the brig Mary, bound for Calcutta. Long and weary was the voyage. On July 30 the Cape of Good Hope was rounded, and for three days and nights they were at the mercy of a fearful storm; but weathering this, after two months more they arrived in Madras, where they were kindly received by a Christian family, and a life-long and intimate acquaintance was begun. Another month and they reached Calcutta, and after unavoidable delays they at length embarked for Maulmein, and arrived at Amherst January 13, 1830, *eight months* after leaving America. In 1836 there was distributed from their printing press between three and four thousand Burman, two thousand English and fourteen hundred temperance tracts. Mrs. Bennett was an invaluable helper to her husband in the press work, reading proof in several different languages. She also translated into the Burmese, Gallaudet's "Child's Book on the Soul," and Dr. Alcott's "The House I Live In," which is still a standard text book in both mission and government schools.

Mr. and Mrs. Bennett celebrated the fiftieth anniversary of their marriage in Rangoon, Burmah, the first golden wedding in mission circles, which was duly noted. In 1882, after fifty years of service, Mr. Bennett was relieved from the work of the press by the arrival of Mr. Phinney from America, who took charge. Mr. Bennett fell asleep on November 16, 1885, aged 81, and on September 30, 1891, Mrs. Bennett followed, aged 83. Hers was a sweet, useful, unselfish life, loved by all missionaries and natives alike. She was "Mamma" Bennett to all and, like her Master, was most happy when ministering to others.

Stella Kneeland[18].

Children of Stella Kneeland[18] and Cephas Bennett.

1714. (i.) ELSINA STELLA BENNETT[19], b. April 29, 1828, in Utica, N. Y.; m. James Northrup, April 29, 1847. They resided and she still resides at Homer, N. Y. He was b. March 3, 1823, and d. at Homer, N. Y., Aug. 6, 1884. Children:

1715. (i.) *Mary Stella Northrup*[20], b. Sept. 3, 1849; d. March 1, 1870.

1716. (ii.) *Ellen Maria Northrup*[20], b. June 7, 1851; d. March 9, 1869.

1717. (iii.) *Charles B. Northrup*[20], b. May 12, 1853; drowned July 18, 1864.

1718. (iv.) *Elizabeth N. Northrup*[20], b. May 2, 1855; d. May 2, 1875.

1719. (v.) *Charlotte Kidder Northrup*[20], b. May 25, 1857; d. Aug. 31, 1873.

1720. (vi.) *Sarah Eliza Northrup*[20], b. July 15, 1859; m. Aug. 4, 1880, to Augustus A. Lines. They reside in Homer, N. Y.

1721. (vii.) *Cephas Moses Northrup*[20], b. April 20, 1862.

1722. (viii.) *Alfred Bennett Northrup*[20], b. April 3, 1864; d. Nov. 29, 1884.

1723. (ix.) *Edward James Northrup*[20], b. Nov. 11, 1867.

1724. (ii.) MARY ELODIA BENNETT[19], b. at Calcutta, India, Nov. 1, 1829; m. first, Daniel Whittaker; he d. Aug. 18, 1857; m. second, Thomas S. Ranney, Dec. 14, 1858; he d. May 13, 1886. Mrs. Ranney now resides at 3032 South Park avenue, Chicago. Children:

1725. (i.) *Cephas Bennett Whittaker*[20], b. in Maulmein, Burmah, Nov. 10, 1853; d. April 15, 1857.

1726. (ii.) *Mary Stella Whittaker*[20], b. in Maulmein, Burmah, Feb. 2, 1855; residence, Chicago, Ill. Married; is Secretary of the American Home Missionary Society.

1727. (iii.) *Ruth Whittaker*[20], b. in Toungor, Burmah, Feb. 24, 1857; resides in Rangoon, Burmah; unmarried; has been a missionary in Rangoon since 1884.

1728. (iii.) WILLIAM PALMER BENNETT[19], b. in Burmah, Oct. 17, 1831 (of whom hereafter, 1736).

1729. (iv.) ANNA MARIA BENNETT[19], b. in India, Aug. 1, 1833 (of whom hereafter, 1746).

1730. (v.) ELLEN MATILDA BENNETT[19], b. in India, June 8, 1835; m. Capt. G. F. Wells, Sept. 11, 1857; they now reside at Kyverdale Road, Stoke Newington, London, N., England. He was a commander and captain in the Honorable East India Company Service. After the mutiny, was transferred to the British naval establishment; d. about 1890. Have two children living:

1731.   (i.) *Edward Bennett Wells*[20], Manager of the Gordon Steamship Co.

1732.   (ii.) *George Frederich Wells*[20], Cashier of the London County Bank, of London.

1733. (vi.) SARAH JANE BENNETT[19], b. in Burmah, June 16, 1837; m. Jas. R. Grieve; they now reside at Miller School, Virginia. No issue.

1734. (vii.) EDWARD CEPHAS BENNETT[19], b. in Burmah, Oct. 1, 1842; d. Dec. 1, 1854, in Michigan.

1735. (viii.) ALFRED HENRY BENNETT[19], b. in Burmah, Nov. 11, 1845; d. in Burmah, Sept. 25, 1848.

1736. (1728.) WILLIAM PALMER BENNETT[19] (*Stella [Kneeland] Bennett*[18], *Amasa*[17], *Jonathan*[16], *John*[15], *Benjamin*[14], *Edward*[13], *Edward*[12], *John*[11]—*Alexander*[1]). Born in Maulmein, Burmah, Oct. 17, 1831.

At the age of nine he was brought by his parents to the United States and placed in the home of Mr. Philander Gorton, at Woodstock, N. Y. Received a good education at the academies of Woodstock, Cazanovia and Groton, all in New York State. At age of seventeen, taught school at Groton and subsequently practiced that Kneeland trade for several winters at Dryden, N. Y., and in Michigan. Was married in Groton, N. Y., Oct. 5, 1850, to Miss Lovisa Brokaw. In 1851, removed to Jackson County, Mich., and in 1852 settled in Marcellus Township, Cass County, Mich., then almost a primeval wilderness. Was for ten years supervisor of Marcellus

William Palmer Bennett[10].

township. In 1868, was elected Judge of Probate of Cass
County, and removed with his family to Cassopolis, the county
seat. Occupied that office until his death, being elected to it
at seven consecutive Presidential elections. Was a member—
often chairman—of the school board of Cassopolis for at least
twenty years, and served several years as President of the
village. He died June 11, 1896. The following extracts from
obituary notices published in the Cassopolis newspapers show
that his characteristics were essentially those of the Kneeland
race:

"The Judge was an unflinching and aggressive partisan,
in politics opposed to the writer of this paragraph, and it has
frequently fallen to our lot to oppose his election somewhat
vigorously, notwithstanding which our personal relations have
always been of the most friendly character, and we have
always entertained for him a sincere admiration for his sturdy
and manly independence, outspoken sentiments and hatred of
all shams and humbugs whatsoever. His painstaking care
and devotion to the accurate performance of the details of
his office have been conspicuous through his whole career, and
have made a record for his remaining relatives to be proud
of."—*National Democrat*, June 18, 1896.

"He was always at his place with ready ear and wise
counsel for all honest and needy comers. He was the attorney of the poor and the staunch champion of the widow and
the fatherless, standing always between them and those who
would profit unfairly by their inexperience and helplessness. He
was the friend and adviser of those in all sorts and conditions
of life who sought to share their burdens with him and relied,
with reason, upon his strength, wisdom and disinterested judgment. He was sometimes impatient with the technicalities
of the law, when they were sought to be brought into play to
hinder or defeat justice, but he was rarely mistaken in the
equities and, if what was proposed appeared to be right, meas-
ured by his accepted standards, 'he followed right because
right is right, in scorn of consequence.'

"He never admitted craft or indirection among his methods. His principles and prejudices were fixed and known to
all, and no emergency could shake the courage of his convic-

William Palmer Bennett[19].

tions. He was true to his friends and treated his enemies all too fairly. He lived for others—as had his forefathers for generations—and was possessed with an exaggerated idea of the claims of duty upon him. His conception of the service rightfully required because of his office, led him to unremitting work of exhaustive character, but it saved to the estates of Cass County untold thousands of dollars, gained many re-united families and saved for good citizenship and useful lives many ill-started children. The statutes of the State are bettered through his recommendations in matters pertaining to probate courts and the care of dependent and delinquent children.

"His service and counsel in village matters have ever been of value toward substantial progress, and no work under-taken or urged by him has failed of final approval. During his long service on the School Board he was able to contribute very much to the elevation of the curriculum and, more than any other, toward placing the system upon its present high plane. His own rare literary culture and wide-ranged reading had been largely self-acquired, and he strove to place before the children of his poorest neighbors better opportunities than his own had been."—*Cassopolis Vigilant,* June 18, 1896.

Children of William P. and Lovisa (Brokaw) Bennett.

1737. (i.) JOHN ALTON BENNETT[20], b. Jan. 27, 1853; d. Oct. 5, 1854.

1738. (ii.) ALTON W. BENNETT[20], b. May 30, 1855; gradu-ated from the Law Department, University of Michigan (Ann Arbor), in 1877, and has practiced his profession since in Big Rapids, Mich.; has been, or is now, Circuit Court Commissioner, Justice of the Peace, member of Board of Education and alderman of the city of Big Rapids; is Grand Master-at-Arms of the Grand Lodge of Michigan, Knights of Pythias. Was married Sept. 3, 1878, at Big Rapids, to Miss Mary M. Roben, and has had issue as follows:

1739. (i.) *Alton R.*[21], b. February 4, 1882.

1740. (ii.) *Nellie*[21], b. June 13, 1885; d. Oct. 24, 1886.

William Palmer Bennett[19].

1741.   (iii.) *Mary L.*[21], b. Sept. 15, 1887.

1742.   (iii.) FRANK M. BENNETT[20], b. May 7, 1857; gradu-
ated from the U. S. Naval Academy, Annapolis,
Md., in 1879, and has since been an officer of the
engineer corps of the navy.   Is now Past Assistant
Engineer with rank corresponding to naval lieutenant—relative rank of captain in the army.   Has
seen service at sea in North and South America,
Europe, Asia, Africa and Oceanica; was detailed by
Navy Department as instructor in Chicago Manual
Training School, 1885–1887; was Chief Engineer
of the government's naval exhibit at the World's
Columbian Exposition; for about four years was
assistant to the chief of the Bureau of Steam
Engineering in the Navy Department; is a member
of the Society of Sons of the American Revolution,
by virtue of military services rendered by two
great-great-grandfathers—Asa Bennett and Jonathan Kneeland; author of "The Steam Navy of the
United States" (8 vo., 900 pp., 1896).   Was. married Sept. 2, 1885, to Miss Nettie N. Read. daughter of S. T. Read, of Cassopolis, Mich.   To them
was born, July 7, 1886, a daughter:

1742A.   (i.) *Stella Kneeland Bennett.*
Nettie .Read Bennett died July 22, 1887.
Frank M. was married again, June 14, 1893, to
Miss Mary Henderson Eastman, of Washington,
D. C., daughter of the late Major Robert Eastman,
Fifth U. S. Infantry.   One child has resulted from
this union:

1743.   (ii.) *Mary Dorothy*[21], b. Sept. 8, 1894.

1744.   (iv.) STELLA M. BENNETT[20], b. March 30, 1859; graduated from the Cassopolis High School, in 1875;
taught in the same school the following year.   Has
been a member of the W. C. T. U. since its organization, in which she has held various local, district
and State offices.   At the age of 27 was elected a
member of the Board of Education of the city of
Big Rapids, Mich., and held that office four years,

FOUR GENERATIONS IN THE BENNETT FAMILY

STELLA (KNEELAND) BENNETT
No. 1713

HON. WM. P. BENNETT
No. 1736

FRANK M. BENNETT, P. A. Eng. U.S. N.
No. 1742

MARY D. BENNETT
No. 1743

Anna Maria Bennett[19].

being the only woman ever so honored in that city. Is an active member of the Presbyterian church and has for many years been prominently identified with the various charitable, benevolent and educational enterprises of her city and State. Was married at the age of seventeen, in December, 1876, to Lieut. Douglas Roben, U. S. Navy, and has had issue as follows:

1744A.   *Donald Bennett Roben*[21], b. July 17, 1878.

1744B.   *Pansie Roben*[21], b. May 14, 1882; d. March 26, 1883.

1744C.   *Lovisa Blanche Roben*[21], b. October 3, 1884.

1744D.   *Douglas Bennett Roben*[21], b. Sept. 20, 1891.

1745.   (v.) In addition to the above, William P. and Lovisa (Brokaw) Bennett had a daughter, born Nov. 8, 1868, who died about four weeks later and was never named. The stone above her grave bears this inscription:

> " Whom the angels name Lenore.
> Nameless here for evermore."

1746.   (1729.) ANNA MARIA BENNETT[19] (*Stella*[18], *Amasa*[17], *Jonathan*[16], *John*[15], *Benjamin*[14], *Edward*[13], *Edward*[12], *John*[11]—*Alexander*[1]). Third daughter of Cephas and Stella (Kneeland) Bennett, was born in Rangoon, Burmah, on Aug. 1, 1833; took the long ocean voyage to America with her parents at the age of seven; was educated at Utica, N.Y., and in Philadelphia, Pa.; then taught for nearly three years near Philadelphia and in Georgia Female College, at Madison, Ga.; was married to Dr. George W. Burton, a graduate of the University of Pennsylvania and at that time a medical missionary to China, on Nov. 3, 1853, at Madison, Georgia.

After a visit to her husband's family, at Murfreesboro, Tenn., went on a four months' bridal trip in a sailing vessel from New York around the Cape of Good Hope to Shanghai, China. A seven years' residence in China followed, and the homeward voyage with her three little boys; then thé Civil

Anna Maria Bennett[19].

War—Dr. Burton coming home and taking his family and his
mother from Murfreesboro, Tenn., and the track of war down
into Georgia and himself serving as a surgeon in the Confederate army; after the war, a quiet life in Kentucky. Such has
been Mrs. Burton's varied experience.

When her parents, Cephas and Stella (Kneeland) Bennett,
returned to their missionary work in India, Miss Persis Kneeland, Mrs. Bennett's sister, took charge of the home place in
Utica, N. Y., and of Anna and two of the other little girls.
The children for three years spent the vacations at the homes
of their grandparents, Amasa Kneeland and Alfred Bennett, in
the country. What love of nature was fostered by the many
rambles about those country places! What memories of the
old homes little brown-eyed Anna has carried through all the
years! Dr. Burton is an active practitioner in Louisville, Ky.,
and at their home is a tiny city garden with blue grass, grape
vines, two or three trees, a wealth of roses, zinnias, sweet peas
and other flowers, where the twittering of the sparrows can be
heard at dawn and where, a little later in the evenings, Mrs.
Bennett can usually be found when the weather permits. She
enjoys her flowers thoroughly, but never more than when
giving them to brighten some one else. Of great refinement
and culture, well read, liberal and active in the cause of foreign
missions, sympathetic, thoughtful for others, yet, perhaps,
Mrs. Burton's most striking characteristics are her deep, un-
feigned piety and strict conscientiousness. She is a home-
maker, "the heart of her husband doth safely trust in her
always," and her children "rise up and call her blessed."

Children of Dr. George W. and Anna M. (Bennett) Burton.

1747. (i.) FRANK BURTON[20], b. March 3, 1855, at Shanghai,
China; d. Dec. 7, 1861, at Murfreesboro, Tenn.

1748. (ii.) HARDY BURTON[20], b. Sept. 22, 1856, at Shanghai,
China; attended Berthel College, Russellville, Ky.;
formerly of the firm of Caldwell & Burton, real
estate, Louisville, Ky.; Manager of real estate
department of Louisville Trust Co., Louisville, Ky.
Married, Nov. 14, 1882, Finette Bagby. Children:

1749. (i.) *Eugene Burton[21]*, b. Aug. 28, 1883.

MRS. ANNA MARIA BURTON

No. 1746

Ellen Kneeland[18].

1750. (ii.) *Hardie May Burton*[21], b. Oct. 14, 1888.
1751. (iii.) *Annie B. Burton*[21], b. Aug. 6, 1894.
1752. (iii.) GEORGE BURTON[20], b. Oct. 3, 1858, at Shanghai, China; d. Nov. 30, 1861, at Murfreesboro, Tenn.
1753. (iv.) STELLA[20], b. Dec. 19, 1864, at Macon, Ga.; d. July 9, 1865, at Macon, Ga.
1754. (v.) FINIE MURFREE[20], b. July 3, 1866; graduate of Louisville Female Seminary and of Training Class of Louisville Free Kindergarten Association; assistant training teacher of Louisville Free Kindergarten Association.
1755. (vi.) GEORGE LEE[20], b. April 17, 1868; graduate of University of Virginia; formerly Professor of Greek, Louisville Male High School; graduate (B.L.) of Louisville Law School; lawyer, Louisville, Ky.

1756. (1702.) ELLEN KNEELAND[18] (*Amasa*[17], *Jonathan*[16], *John*[15], *Benjamin*[14], *Edward*[13], *Edward*[12], *John*[11]—*Alexander*[1]). Second daughter of Amasa and Charlotte (Kidder) Kneeland, b. in Onondaga County, N. Y., April 2, 1809; m. Seymour Tracy. He was b. Dec. 17, 1804, and d. Dec. 8, 1886; she d. Dec. 3, 1888. They resided at Junction City, Mo., and had the following children:

Children of Ellen Kneeland[18] and Seymour Tracy.

1757. (i.) WILLIAM CHARLES TRACY[19], b. May 21, 1839; m. Della Gould. Children:
1758. (i.) *Albert Tracy*[20].
1759. (ii.) *Mary Tracy*[20].
1760. (iii.) *John Tracy*[20].
1761. (ii.) MORGAN DOLPHUS TRACY[19], b. Sept. 19, 1840; m. Lucy Emma Morris. They reside at Penn Yan, N. Y. Children:
1761A. (i.) *Lucy E. Tracy*[20], b. Sept. 20, 1871.
1761B. (ii.) *Emma I. Tracy*[20], b. July 27, 1873; m. Eli Shelden.
1761C. (iii.) *Morris Tracy*[20], b. Dec. 19, 1886.

Hon. Samuel Stillman Kneeland[18].

1762.   (iii.) STELLA KNEELAND TRACY[19], b. June 27, 1842.
1763.   (iv.) SEYMOUR SPENCER TRACY[19], b. July 25, 1844.
1764.   (v.) JOHN RICE TRACY[19], b. June 6, 1848.

1765. (1703.) HON. SAMUEL STILLMAN KNEELAND[18]
    (*Amasa*[17], *Jonathan*[16], *John*[15], *Benjamin*[14], *Edward*[13], *Edward*[12], *John*[11]—*Alexander*[1]). Eldest
    son of Amasa and Charlotte (Kidder) Kneeland,
    b. at Spafford, Onondaga County, N. Y., April 2,
    1811; d. at Skaneateles, N. Y., æ. 85 years; m.
    Cordelia Wright, of Morallus, N. Y., Oct. 17, 1848;
    was a member of the New York Legislature in
    1853, and was Supervisor of his town from 1857 to
    1860.

It is somewhat singular that two of the three Kneelands in
the legislature of this State bore the cognomen of Stillman,
the writer, Stillman Foster[19], being a member of Assembly in
1894. It is. doubtful whether either of them was really a
"Still-man." I extract the following obituary from a local
journal:

HON. S. STILLMAN KNEELAND.

"Last Friday morning our citizens were shocked and
pained to learn that S. Stillman Kneeland had suddenly
passed to the repose of death. About nine months ago Mr.
Kneeland suffered a stroke of paralysis from the effects of
which he never recovered, although during the last few weeks
of his illness there was a marked improvement in his condition,
and the day before his death he was able to take a short ride
in his wheel chair. At four o'clock in the morning his daughter Frances, who was in the room with him, heard a heavy
and unusual breathing and hastened to his bedside, but the
other members of the family had hardly time to reach his
room before he had passed peacefully away, at the ripe age of
84 years, 6 months and 2 days.

"In the death of Mr. Kneeland, all who had the pleasure
of an intimate acquaintance with him feel that theirs is a
personal bereavement and they deeply sympathize with the
sorely afflicted family. Previous to his partial blindness,
which had been coming upon him for the past ten years or

Samuel Stillman Kneeland

No. 1765

Rev. Amasa Spencer Kneeland[18].

more, Mr. Kneeland had been a great reader, and being possessed of a remarkably retentive memory and the happy faculty of expressing his thoughts, and together with his fund of pat anecdotes and his spontaneous flashes of wit, he was a man to whom it was a rare pleasure to listen. To say that his was a noble manhood and spotless character is but to repeat what is said by all who knew him.

"Samuel Stillman Kneeland was born in the town of Marcellus (now Spafford) near Borodino, April 2, 1811, where he lived until twenty-two years ago, when he came to this village, where he has since resided. By occupation he was a farmer and a school teacher. He was elected to several town offices—school inspector, supervisor, assessor, etc., and in 1852 he was chosen to represent the second assembly district of Onondaga County, in all of which offices he served his constituency intelligently and with fidelity. Since the organization of the Republican party, in 1856, he has been a staunch Republican and never failed to cast his vote at the State and national elections.

> ' " The sweet remembrance of the just
> Shall flourish when he sleeps in dust.' "

Children of Samuel Stillman and Cordelia (Wright) Kneeland.

1766.   (i.) FRANCES[19], b. in 1850; unmarried.
1767.   (ii.) ELLEN[19], b. in 1851 ; m. Mr. Thorne.
1768.   (iii.) JESSIE F.[19], b. in 1856; unmarried.
1769.   (iv.) GRACE KNEELAND[19], d. at the age of seven. All the others living.

1770. (1705.) REV. AMASA SPENCER KNEELAND[18] (*Amasa*[17], *Jonathan*[16], *John*[15], *Benjamin*[14], *Edward*[13], *Edward*[12], *John*[11]—*Alexander*[1]). Second son of Amasa Kneeland, b. Oct. 22, 1815, at Thorn Hill, Onondaga County, N. Y.

When twenty years of age, he went to Western Michigan, where he rapidly rose in the estimation of his associates on account of superior ability to plan and execute business schemes. He was clear-sighted and laid a foundation for a

Rev. F. Wayland Kneeland[19].

fortune. During the winter of his twenty-fifth year he was converted and immediately gave up all thoughts of business, entering, instead, upon a preparation for the ministry. He preached in Western New York for forty years, and was eminently successful. He sought first to know the truth and then to express it, both from the pulpit and as a man among the people. In all philanthropic enterprises he was an enthusiast, and before the war he was a thorough abolitionist. He was always deeply interested in missions and lived to witness the completion of the life-work of his eldest sister, Stella (Kneeland) Bennett, who served a term of sixty years of mission work in India. He also lived to see his two sons firmly established as ministers of the gospel and his daughter an instructor of great merit and influence. There is no necessity of saying more, as his face presented herewith is his best eulogy. Like all of his race, he had a keen sense of humor, and to this was added a devout love of all that was noble and Christ-like. This combination enabled him easily to win and control men. He died at Galva, Ill., May 12, 1892, while on a visit to his youngest sister, Ann Spencer. He married Almira B. Foote, and had the following children:

Children of Rev. Amasa Spencer and Almira (Foote) Kneeland.

1771. (i.) ELIZABETH PERCIS[19], b. at Strykersville, N. Y., Jan. 2, 1855; now living at Galva, Ill. She is still a Kneeland and a teacher of distinguished ability, with a wide circle of friends.

1772. (ii.) F. WAYLAND[19], b. at Strykersville, N. Y., Sept. 15, 1856 (of whom hereafter, 1774).

1773. (iii.) I. SPRAGUE KNEELAND[19], b. at Strykersville, N. Y., April 19, 1859 (of whom hereafter, 1778).

1774. (1772.) REV. F. WAYLAND KNEELAND[19] (*Amasa*[18], *Amasa*[17], *Jonathan*[16], *John*[15], *Benjamin*[14], *Edward*[13], *Edward*[12], *John*[11]—*Alexander*[1]), b. at Strykersville, N. Y., Sept. 15, 1856.

He received his collegiate education at the University of Rochester, N. Y., receiving the degree of A.B., June, 1880,

REV. AMASA SPENCER KNEELAND

No. 1770

and graduated at the Theological Seminary, May, 1887, and settled immediately in the Baptist pastorate at East Haddam, Conn., officiating in the Central Baptist Church, at that place, until November, 1890, when he received a call from the First Baptist Church, at Newark, N. Y., which he has since filled. He married Anna Randolph, of Rochester, Dec. 27, 1881, and had three children, as follows:

Children of Rev. F. Wayland and Anna (Randolph) Kneeland.

1775.   (i.) PAUL S.[20], b. at Angelica, N. Y., Dec. 3, 1882.

1776.   (ii.) LLOYD R.[20], b. in Angelica, N. Y., Oct. 18, 1884.

1777.   (iii.) MARJORIE B.[20], b. in Moodus, Conn., Jan. 19, 1888.

1778.   (1773.) REV. IRA SPRAGUE KNEELAND[19] (*Amasa*[18], *Amasa*[17], *Jonathan*[16], *John*[15], *Benjamin*[14], *Edward*[13], *Edward*[12], *John*[11]—*Alexander*[1]).

Youngest son of Rev. Amasa Spencer Kneeland[18], was b. at Strykersville, Wyo. County, N.Y., April 19, 1859. Graduated at Colgate Academy, class of '80; University of Rochester, class of '84; Rochester Theological Seminary, class of '87. Formerly pastor of Baptist churches at Dell Rapids, S. D., Rochester and Buffalo, and is now located at Springville, N.Y. He married Emma Greenwald Conklin, and is now, to use his own expression in a recent letter, "the happy dad (when they are asleep) of three very lively boys; so the race is not likely to become extinct just yet." I print this bit of unconscious humor without his knowledge or consent, so that these same children, reading it hereafter when they are intensely awake, may make it still more lively for the "dad."

Children of Rev. Ira S. and Emma G. (Conklin) Kneeland.

1779.   (i.) CAREY CLIFFORD KNEELAND[20].

1780.   (ii.) ROY CONKLIN KNEELAND[20].

1781.   (iii.) ROSS SPENCER KNEELAND[20].

1782.   (1708.) HON. A. JUDSON KNEELAND[18] (*Amasa*[17], *Jonathan*[16], *John*[15], *Benjamin*[14], *Edward*[13], *Edward*[12], *John*[11]—*Alexander*[1]). Fourth son of Amasa and Charlotte (Kidder) Kneeland, b. May 5, 1821.

19

Hon. A. Judson Kneeland[18].

His life is so well summed up by the following obituary notice in a local paper that I leave it there, adding simply the fact that he married Esther Griswold, and always lived at Homer, Cortland County, N. Y.   They had no issue.

DEATH OF HON. A. J. KNEELAND.

" The glory of a village is in the fair fame of its citizens, and I ask a place in your columns for a few words upon the character of one whose recent death has been the cause of general grief in the community.   A. Judson Kneeland possessed in a marked degree certain stern and unbending virtues as a citizen, a lawyer and a magistrate which are too uncommon to go unnoticed in these days of bowing and creeping for place and favor.   It is difficult, in speaking of the dead whose traits of character we admire, to entirely avoid the language of extravagant eulogy, but your correspondent remembers too well the expressions of disapprobation from the deceased at the display of indiscriminate praise to write of him other than as he was, or to claim for him any exemption from the weakness which, in some form, beset all that is human.

" Mr. Kneeland studied law with the Hon. Ira Harris, of Albany, and was admitted to practice in 1848.   He was a lawyer of the old school, thoroughly versed in the fundamental principles of civil and criminal jurisprudence, and imbued with the lofty sentiment which animated that class of older lawyers as to the usefulness, the dignity and the honor of the profession.   As a magistrate he had that love of right and hatred of wrong, that clear insight of human nature and that practical knowledge of affairs combined with sound judgment and common sense, that enabled him to get at the truth and made him a terror to evil doers.   But it is not as a lawyer that Mr. Kneeland displayed those marked characteristics which are most worthy of homage.   His fearlessness as a citizen and clean, pure, public life commanded the deeper reverence of those who knew him well.   You could rest assured without inquiry that his wholesome nature and moral sense would carry him to the right side of every political and moral question.   He was upright and downstraight, and every question found him occupying pronounced and uncompromis-

Francis Wayland Kneeland.

No. 1774

Hon. A. Judson Kneeland[18].

ing ground upon one side or the other. 'If you are right you cannot be too radical' was the motto on which he acted. He hated wickedness, chicanery and fraud, and |to his credit it can be said that bad men knew this almost instinctively and did not unfold their wicked plans to him.

"His elevation above evil, his hatred for wickedness, led superficial observers to think that he was cold and misanthropic, but in his heart there was no hatred of men but only the deepest and warmest of kindness; he only hated the evil which made human life miserable and hindered its growth in light and goodness. While he was sensitive to public opinion, it was not his master, but he rather took counsel of his own judgment and tested results by his own sense of right. Although he had been for seven years assistant assessor of internal revenue and always an ardent political worker, still he kept himself clean and unspotted. The abhorrence in which he held a former public man who sought to get money from him for the pretended purpose of purchasing votes after his nomination as Assemblyman, was well known to his friends. As a member of Assembly, although not known upon the floor as a debater, he was a conscientious and able worker in the committee room, and he commanded the respect and esteem of his fellow-members.

"Educated at the common schools, he so improved the after years of his life that his mind was replete with valuable information. He enjoyed most the works of Dickens and Thackeray, and the trial of an action was a pleasure to him whenever it brought forth some quaint, eccentric character wherein he might find similarities to the odd creations of Dickens. Thackeray was his favorite author, and it might be said of Mr. Kneeland, as it was said of Thackeray, that he had 'the keenest satire and the kindliest heart.' The natural tendency of political life is downward, and the hope of political reform rests in men like Mr. Kneeland who have self-respect, courage and loyalty to the right. Society is not apt to appreciate the extent of its obligation to such men.

"The autopsy disclosed the fact that vital organs had been affected for a considerable period of time. Through years of pain Mr. Kneeland, with heroic courage and patient

Hon. A. Judson Kneelana[18].

endurance, faithfully performed his duties as a lawyer and a magistrate, making friends of his clients and a debtor of the community. Heroism in the more obscure affairs of life is not heralded as when met in the momentous sweep of battle. To win the grand old name of gentleman, and while suffering from the tortures of malignant disease to carry it through all the avenues of life unsoiled, is heroic.

> " Life may be given in many ways,
> And loyalty to truth be sealed,
> As bravely in the closet as the field ;
> So bountiful is fate."

—F. Pierce, in the Homer Republican.

Ira Sprague Kneeland.

No. 1778

PART VIII.

DR. HEZEKIAH KNEELAND'S FAMILY.

(NOS. 1783 TO 1853.)

DEDICATED TO

DR. HEZEKIAH KNEELAND,

ONE OF THE HEROES OF A HEROIC AGE.

Russel A. Kneeland.

No. 1812

CHAPTER XXVI.

DR. HEZEKIAH KNEELAND AND MERCY PEPOON.

1783. (687.) DR. HEZEKIAH KNEELAND[15] (*Benjamin*[14], *Edward*[13], *Edward*[12], *John*[11], *William*[10], *James*[9], *Alexander*[8], *William*[7], *William*[6], *John*[5], *John*[4], *John*[3], *James*[2], *Alexander*[1]). Sixth son of Benjamin Kneeland[14], b. at Hebron, Conn., June 26, 1722, after his father had ceased his wanderings and found a place "where the sole of his foot" could rest with ease.

Dr. Kneeland was the first member of this branch of the family to adopt one of the liberal professions. We have no record of his early life or studies. The first record (outside of his birth) that we find of his name, is a statement in the "History of Colchester," that he was the first physician in Marlboro, Conn. His name appears in the Revolutionary records of Connecticut as one of the private surgeons who, without pay, was, during the entire struggle, most assiduous in caring for the sick and wounded patriots. From the "speech of the people" comes the story that he was a wonderfully gifted surgeon and was called to aid in difficult cases over fifty miles from home in the old days when the round trip occupied five days. Marvelous legends are told of the ingenious devices used by him to overcome the difficulties in the profession that are now obviated by remedies and appliances since discovered. He married, Oct. 22, 1847, Mercy Pepoon, a lady of great personal beauty and accomplishments and of royal descent. The name is Anglicised from the French "Pepin." It was originally a given name, but adopted as a family name by the

Dr. Hezekiah Kneeland[15].

descendants of Pepin, who was king of Aquitania, 817–838. He was the second son of Louis I.—"le Débonnaire"—and grandson of Charles the Great.

Three members of the family came to this country in the seventeenth century to escape the persecution of the French fanatics. One went to North Carolina and was the ancestor of the celebrated southern family of that name. The other two were brothers and made extensive voyages of discovery from Quebec. They became thoroughly versed in Indian dialects, habits and methods of warfare. Among other discoveries made by them was a lake in the Mississippi Valley which was named for them, Lake Pepin. It lies about forty miles southeast of St. Paul, and was formerly claimed as a part of the French possessions. A fort was built there under Count—afterwards Governor—Frontenac. The Pepin brothers at this time were officers under Frontenac and acted as interpreters for his army. The following is the first reference to our branch of the family: "*Jacques Pepin*, sent to Massachusetts by his father, who is an elder in the Protestant church in Rochelle, France, petitions for and obtains leave to settle here." (Mass. Archives, 15 A 7. See also 41 N. E. Gen'l Reg., p. 81.) This is under date of July 12, 1665.

From the records of Colchester, Conn., we find that Joseph Pepoon, the son of John (Jacques) and Mercy Pepoon (Pepin), married Mary Dibell "December y[e] 11th, 1717." This Joseph was the youngest son of the Jacques Pepin above mentioned. The children of this marriage were:

1. JOSEPH PEPOON, b. May 20, 1719; d. Oct. 20, 1725.
2. MARY PEPOON, b. April 18, 1721; d. Oct. 3, 1725.
3. SILAS PEPOON, b. Jan. 5, 1723; d. Jan. 5, 1723.

Mary, first wife of Joseph Pepoon, d. Feb. 23, 1724. He married, second, Mary Thomas, Jan. 13, 1725 (of whom hereafter). The children of this marriage were:

4. ELIZABETH PEPOON, b. Oct. 20, 1725.
5. MERCY PEPOON, b. Sept. 25, 1727; m. Dr. Hezekiah Kneeland.

6 and 7. SARAH and RUTH, twins, b. Dec. 30, 1728.

Mary Thomas, mother of Mercy Pepoon, and grandmother of the children of Dr. Hezekiah Kneeland, was also

Russel Austin Kneeland

No. 1814

Dr. Hezekiah Kneeland[15].

of a distinguished family, of which I give the following sketch:

HON. WILLIAM THOMAS[1], b. in Wales, in 1574; settled in Plymouth in 1630 and made a freeman of the colony, March 17, 1642, and chosen assistant to Gov. Bradford in that year, which office he held the remainder of his days; died in August, 1651. Among his children were:

CAPT. NATHANIEL THOMAS[2], b. in 1600. Prior to 1643 he was designated as Lieut. Thomas, and commanded the watch at Green Harbor against the Indians. In that year he was appointed by the court, town Captain. He died in 1678. His son and heir was:

CAPT. NATHANIEL THOMAS[3], b. in 1643; m. Deborah, daughter of Nicholas Jacob. He was a captain in King Philip's War and wrote, on June 25, 1675, a very interesting report thereof, which is preserved (see p. 55, of Miss Thomas' History of Marshfield). He had ten children, including:

NATHANIEL THOMAS, ESQ.[4], who married Mary Appleton, in 1694. They had several children, including:

MARY THOMAS[5], b. Oct. 10, 1705, who m. Joseph Pepoon, and was the mother of Mercy Pepoon, as hereinbefore stated (see Colchester Records by Charles M. Taintor, p. 93).

This much of Mercy Pepoon, whose rich olive complexion and black eyes often crop out among the fair sex of her descendants. The inheritance thereof is very much prized even to this day by the happy recipients. Dr. Hezekiah Kneeland died of heart disease at the age of 57.

Children of Dr. Hezekiah and Mercy (Pepoon) Kneeland.

From Colchester Records:

1784. (i.) MERCY[16], b. at Colchester—afterwards changed to Marlboro—Conn., Aug. 17, 1748; d. Aug. 30, 1748.

1785. (ii.) RACHEL[16], b. at Colchester, Dec. 27, 1749; m. Mr. Loveland.

1786. (iii.) MERCY[16], b. at Colchester, Nov. 25, 1751; m. her cousin, David Kneeland, son of Isaac, at Hebron, Oct. 10, 1771 (of whom hereafter).

1787. (iv.) DOROTHY[16], b. at Colchester, Dec. 3, 1753; d. Jan. 16, 1764.

Elizabeth Kneeland[16].

1788.   (v.) SAMUEL[16], b. at Colchester, May 16, 1755.   He
          served seven years in the Continental army, was
          severely wounded and drew a pension.   He was
          never married.   He went with his mother and
          sisters to Geneseo, N. Y., and resided there until
          his death.   He was buried in Temple Hill Ceme-
          tery, at that place.   The inscription on the grave-
          stone is, "Samuel Kneeland, died Feb. 19, 1828,
          aged 73."

1789.   (vi.) DOLLY[16], b. at Colchester, March 2, 1760; m.
          Deacon Beach, of Geneseo.

1790.   (vii.) LIZZIE[16], b. at Colchester, June 7, 1762; d. April
          10, 1767.

1791.   (viii.) LUCINDA[16], b. at Colchester, Oct. 6, 1764; d.
          June 8, 1766.

1792.   (ix.) SYLVIA[16], b. at Colchester, March 22, 1767; d.
          April 5, 1767.

1793.   (x.) ELIZABETH[16], b. at Colchester, Feb. 2, 1768 (of
          whom hereafter, 1795).

1794.   (xi.) TIMOTHY PEPOON[16], b. at Marlboro, Conn., March
          4, 1770 (of whom hereafter, 1796).

While the foregoing are found in the Colchester Records,
Dr. Hezekiah and his family lived in Marlboro.   The clerk's
office, however, remained in Colchester until about 1780, Marlboro being formed from that and adjoining towns about 1740.

1795.   (1793.) ELIZABETH KNEELAND[16] (*Dr. Heze-
          kiah[15], Benjamin[14], Edward[13], Edward[12], John[11]
          —Alexander[1]*).   Sixth daughter of Dr. Hezekiah
          and Mercy (Pepoon) Kneeland, b. at Marlboro,
          Feb. 2, 1768; m. Robert Chappel who, like her
          mother, Mercy Pepoon, was of French descent.

One of their children, ELIZABETH[17], married Rev. Dr.
Jeremiah Porter, who was a chaplain in the U. S. Army for
over fifty years.   During the war she remained in the field
service with her husband and was superintendent of the
hospital nurses in Sherman's army.   An incident in their
history shows the foresight and confidence of Gen. Sherman.
When they arrived at Lookout Mountain, Dr. and Mrs.

Thomas Tracy Kneeland

No. 1815

Porter were sent to New York City under sealed orders. These, they discovered to be directions to fully equip the hospital service with sanitary stores for use at Atlanta. The stores were procured and they boarded a steamer and arrived in front of Atlanta just two days before Sherman got there. As a result, everything was made ready for the reception of the wounded as soon as the army came. She died after the war, at the age of 80, respected and loved by thousands of army boys and by all who knew her. I wish I could create an epitaph here for this one of the many heroic women who did so much for the boys in blue in the dark days that "tried men's souls."

CHAPTER XXVII.

DESCENDANTS OF TIMOTHY P. KNEELAND.

(NOS. 1796 TO 1853.)

1796. (1794.) TIMOTHY PEPOON KNEELAND[16] (*Dr. Hezekiah*[15], *Benjamin*[14], *Edward*[13], *Edward*[12], *John*[11], *William*[10], *James*[9], *Alexander*[8], *William*[7], *William*[6], *John*[5], *John*[4], *John*[3], *James*[2], *Alexander*[1]). Youngest child of Dr. Hezekiah and Mercy (Pepoon) Kneeland, b. at Marlboro, Conn., March, 1770.

He was educated for his father's profession of medicine, but before he was ready to practice he fell in love and that settled it and him. He went to New York State and spent the remainder of his days on a farm. One winter, while living at Ogden, there had been no provision made for a teacher, and rather than have the children of the place go without the usual schooling, he volunteered to fill the position without pay, and did so to the general satisfaction of everyone. He was, for many years Town Clerk and Treasurer, and was recognized as a man of unblemished reputation and of the highest character. His hospitality to guests and generosity to neighbors was boundless. Though not a member of any church he was much interested in religious matters and was one of four men who each gave $100 toward the building of the first church in Ogden. He served the church as clerk, and his house was the rendezvous for all the clergy. His daughter remembers—with a shiver, I surmise, though she does not admit it—when six ministers were guests at one time of her father's home, one of whom stayed there for six months. He married, first, Nabby Griswold Tracy, daughter of Thomas and Lucy (Sprague) Tracy, of Lenox, Mass. They moved to Franklin, N. Y., where his brother had previously settled. From there he went to Geneseo, and, in 1814, to Ogden, N. Y., where his wife died March 1, 1819. The following year he married Elizabeth

Henry Tracy ...

No. 1818

Yale, of Lee, Mass., a daughter of "Squire" Josiah and Ruth (Tracy) Yale. She was a niece of his first wife. She bore him no children. He died Dec. 22, 1826, at Ogden, N. Y.

Children of Timothy P. and Nabby (Tracy) Kneeland.

1797. (i.) TIMOTHY[17], b. at Franklin, N. Y., May 6, 1802 (of whom hereafter, 1804).

1798. (ii.) SAMUEL[17], b. at Geneseo, N. Y., June 19, 1804; d. at Ogden, N. Y., April 11, 1832.

1799. (iii.) THOMAS TRACY[17], b. at Geneseo, N. Y., Aug. 4, 1806 (of whom hereafter, 1815).

1800. (iv.) ELISHA YALE[17], b. at Geneseo, N. Y., June 17, 1810 (of whom hereafter, 1822).

1801. (v.) CYRUS FRANKLIN[17], b. at Geneseo, N. Y., March 30, 1812; d. Sept. 14, 1856.

1802. (vi.) MERCY LUCY[17], b. at Ogden, Jan. 17, 1816; d. in childhood.

1803. (vii.) SARAH ELIZABETH[17], b. at Ogden, Sept. 14, 1820 (of whom hereafter, 1838).

1804. (1797.) TIMOTHY KNEELAND[17] (*Timothy P.*[16], *Dr. Hezekiah*[15], *Benjamin*[14], *Edward*[13], *Edward*[12], *John*[11]—*Alexander*[1]). Eldest son of Timothy Pepoon and Nabby (Tracy) Kneeland and grandson of Dr. Hezekiah and Mercy Kneeland, b. at Franklin, N. Y., May 6, 1802; m. Oct. 3, 1827, to Anna Austin, of Goshen, Conn. Timothy Kneeland died at Ogden, April 22, 1846. She died at Clarendon, Vt., Oct. 15, 1876.

Children of Timothy and Anna (Austin) Kneeland.

1805. (i.) RUSSEL AUSTIN[18], b. at Ogden, N. Y., May 3, 1830 (of whom hereafter, 1812).

1806. (ii.) ALBERT TRACY[18], b. at Ogden, July 28, 1832; d. Nov. 26, 1857.

1807. (iii.) EMMA[18], b. at Ogden, June 6, 1836; m. Nov. 14, 1860, to Arima D. Smith. They reside at Elm Hill Farm, Clarendon, Vt., and have the following children :

Russel Austin Kneeland[18].

1808.   (i.) *Alfred Kneeland Smith*[19], b. Sept. 8, 1861.

1809.   (ii.) *Anna Kneeland Smith*[19], b. Nov. 25, 1867; she
            m. David N. Haynes, May 3, 1888.

1810.   (iv.) TIMOTHY[18], b. at Ogden, Dec. 31, 1839; d. Aug.
            1, 1840.

1811.   (v.) GILBERT HATHAWAY[18], b. at Ogden, Sept. 30,
            1841.

1812.   (1805.) RUSSEL AUSTIN KNEELAND[18] (*Tim-
            othy*[17], *Timothy P.*[16], *Dr. Hezekiah*[15], *Benjamin*[14],
            Edward[13], *Edward*[12], *John*[11]—*Alexander*[1]). Eld-
            est son of Timothy and Anna (Austin) Kneeland.
            He was b. in Ogden, N. Y., May 3, 1830, and d. at
            Geneseo, N. Y., Feb. 9, 1889.

In the town of Geneseo, Mr. Kneeland at various times
held the offices of Justice of the Peace, Assessor, Highway
Commissioner and Supervisor. In the years 1872 and 1873 he
was Superintendent of the Genesee Valley Canal. Politically
he had been, from its organization, a member of the Republican
party and a firm believer in and supporter of its doctrines.
In all the transactions of his somewhat varied career, he was
emphatically a square man and possessed the utmost confidence of all who knew him. He was a good neighbor and a
firm friend. He was a member of the Masonic Order and had
been for many years. He took the Blue Lodge degrees at
Spencerport, and became master of the lodge; took the
chapter degrees at Rochester, and while a resident of Batavia,
became a member of Batavia Commandery. On removing to
Geneseo, he became affiliated with that lodge, assisted in the
organization of a chapter, and became the High Priest of the
latter. He loved the institution and was a firm supporter of
its customs, and had often, to his intimates, expressed a desire
that when the occasion came to him, he should be buried with
the ceremonies of the Order. He was married, Feb. 6, 1855,
to Mary Abby Hamilton, at Ogden, N. Y. Of this marriage
two children were born:

1813.   (i.) ALBERT HAMILTON TRACY KNEELAND[19], who d.
            at the age of sixteen years.

Frank Gilbert Kneeland

No. 1819

Thomas Tracy Kneeland[17].

1814.   (ii.) RUSSEL AUSTIN KNEELAND[19], b. in Ogden, June 13, 1860, and graduated from the Geneseo State Normal School, in 1879; was for five years Principal of Union schools; was elected School Commissioner of the Northern District of Livingston County, in 1884, and reëlected in 1887. Has been located in Rochester since 1890, and is a representative of the American Book Company, of New York City. He married Fanny Munger, of Bergen, N. Y., Nov. 19, 1884.

1815.   (1799.) THOS. TRACY KNEELAND[17] (*Timothy P.*[16], *Dr. Hezekiah*[15], *Benjamin*[14], *Edward*[13], *Edward*[12], *John*[11]—*Alexander*[1]). Eldest son of Timothy P. and Nabby (Tracy) Kneeland, b. at Geneseo, N. Y., Aug. 4, 1806; m. Sarah Brown, at Ogden, N. Y., Oct. 1, 1834.

He went to Michigan, in 1833, and made a government location at Tecumseh, to which he returned the following year with his bride. They settled in Tecumseh, where he started a foundry and plow factory. The next year (1835) he brought to his new works the first steam engine operated in that State outside of Detroit and Monroe. He continued the foundry business up to 1848, when his health failed. The following year, 1849, he made the overland trip to California and dug out of the sands what was better than gold—health. With this he returned to his old home the next year and engaged in mercantile business, and managed, also, a couple of farms up to 1874, when he built the first steam grist mill in Tecumseh. His wife dying in September, 1885, he removed to St. Louis, Mo., where he has since resided with his son, Frank G. He is now ninety years of age, hale and hearty.

Children of Thos. Tracy and Sarah (Brown) Kneeland.

1816.   (i.) SARAH[18], d. in infancy.
1816A. (ii.) MARY[18], d. in infancy.
1817.   (iii.) SAMUEL MILES[18], b. at Tecumseh, Mich., in 1836; educated at the University of Michigan and commenced the practice of law; married in 1862, to Mary Augusta Nicholson and immediately entered

Elisha Yale Kneeland[17].

the army—18th Mich. Vols. He was promoted to
First Lieutenant, and served until the close of the
war on the staff of Major-Gen. Gordon Granger.
After the war closed he was appointed as Register
of the U. S. land office, at Springfield, Mo., and
died there in 1870, without issue.

1818.   (iv.) HENRY TRACY[18], b. at Tecumseh, Mich., Nov. 6,
1848; went to Colorado, in 1873; was for some
years in mercantile business in Leadville; was
twice married—first, to Katharine O'Donnell; second, to Josephine Godderly, of Warsaw, Ill.; no
issue by either wife. He is now living in Aspen,
Col., being extensively engaged in mining, smelting
and cattle raising.

1819.   (v.) FRANK GILBERT[18], b. at Tecumseh, Mich., Nov.
13, 1853; educated at High School there and later
pursued special studies in the Seminary; removed
in 1876 to St. Louis, Mo., where he has since lived;
is engaged in loans and real estate business. Married, Nov. 21, 1882, to Helen Lovell Dodge, only
daughter of Alexander W. Dodge, of Ionia, Mich.
Children:

1820.   (i.) *Dorothy Kneeland*[19], b. at St. Louis, June 1,
1887.

1821.   (ii.) *John Tracy Kneeland*[19], b. as St. Louis, Mo.,
Sept. 7, 1889; d. there, June 30, 1894.

1822.   (1800.) ELISHA YALE KNEELAND[17] (*Timothy
P.*[16], *Dr. Hezekiah*[15], *Benjamin*[14], *Edward*[13], *Edward*[12], *John*[11]—*Alexander*[1]). Fourth son of
Timothy Pepoon and Nabby (Tracy) Kneeland, b.
at Geneva, N. Y., June 17, 1810; m. first, Nov. 6,
1834, Charlotte Ball, at Ogden, N. Y. After her
death he married, second, Catharine F. Hotchkins;
she died Dec. 1, 1896. He died Oct. 27, 1891.

He was of a very inventive turn of mind and an expert
mechanical engineer. He founded the celebrated New York
Novelty Co. and spent a fortune in bringing it to a paying basis.
Unfortunately, for the want of sufficient funds, it slipped into

No. 1822

Children of Harriet Eliza Kneeland and Conway W. Ball.

(When the text of page 305 was printed, I was under the impression that Harriet Eliza—No. 1823—had but one child, Kneeland Ball. The correct information was received just prior to publication, and is as follows):

(i.) HENRY KNEELAND BALL[19], married in 1885 to Netta Crissey. They reside at 318 West Washington avenue, Elmira, N. Y, Their children are:
(i.) *Crissey Kneeland Ball*[20].
(ii.) *Louise Ball*[20].
(iii.) *Samuel Seymour Ball*[20].
(iv.) *Netta Ball*[20].

(ii.) EMMA BALL[19], married Henry J. Wilkes, of Buffalo. Children:
(i.) *Stewart Ball Wilkes*[20].
(ii.) *Warren Ball Wilkes*[20].
(iii.) *Gordon Wilkes*[20].
(iv.) *Miriam Wilkes*[20].
(v.) *Kneeland Wilkes*[20].

(iii.) ROBERT BALL[19], deceased.

(iv.) FANNY HARRIET BALL[19], married Frank J. Underwood, of Buffalo. Children:
(i.) *Harold Underwood*[20].
(ii.) *Orison Cheney Underwood*[20].
(iii.) *Florence Underwood*[20].

(v.) CHARLOTTE BALL[19].

(vi.) KNEELAND BALL[19].

(vii.) VIRGINIA BALL[19].

the hands of others, who reaped the benefit of his brains and business acumen, the concern being now rated in the millions. He subsequently settled in Buffalo, where he was extensively engaged in the construction of elevators. He had an intense admiration for and belief in the Kneeland race, and both personally and by letter assisted the writer in untangling some of the kinks in the chain of descent, which service I had hoped to repay in kind.

Children of Elisha Yale and Charlotte (Ball) Kneeland.

1823.   (i.) HARRIET ELIZA[18], b. Oct. 22, 1837; m. Conway W. Ball. He is one of the officers of the Board of Trade, in Buffalo, and they reside in that city. They have one son:

1824.   *Kneeland Ball*[19].

1825.   (ii.) HENRY TIMOTHY[18], b. Sept. 14, 1839; d. March 27, 1892. He was the head of the well-known commission house of Henry T. Kneeland & Co., now Kneeland & Co., of the Produce Exchange, and was the originator of the grading system that has made heavy dealings in grain a possibility. On his death he was succeeded in business by his son Yale. The other active partner was his brother, Franklin E. Kneeland, who still remains in the firm. He had six children, all of whom are living, viz.:

1826.   (i.) *Yale*[19], who graduated at Yale College in 1890, and is now a member of the firm of Kneeland & Co., and resides on Gramercy Park, in the city of New York.

1827.   (ii.) *Alice*[19].

1828.   (iii.) *Jessee*[19].

1829.   (iv.) *Henry Timothy*[19].

1830.   (v.) *Edith*[19].

1831.   (vi.) *Vida*[19].

1832.   (iv.) JOSEPH BALL[18], b. Jan. 13, 1844; d. Jan. 1, 1846.

1833.   (v.) FRANKLIN EDWARD[18], b. June 5, 1846; m. Mary Emma Anderson, at Brooklyn, Dec. 18, 1877. He is a broker in the Produce Exchange and a member

20

Sarah Elizabeth[17].

of the firm of Kneeland & Co.   He resides in
Brooklyn.   They have a family of two children :

1834.   (i.) *Franklin E., Jr.*[19].
1835.   (ii.) *Mary Margaret*[19].
1836.   (vi.) JOHN TRACY[18], b. July 17, 1848; d. Aug. 7, 1849.
1837.   (vii.) SARAH ANNA[18], b. May 2, 1851; d. Dec. 29, 1871.
1837A.   (viii.) JULIA MARIA[18], b. March 1, 1856; d. April 15,
1859.

1838.   (1803.) SARAH ELIZABETH[17] (*Timothy P.*[16], *Dr.
Hezekiah*[15], *Benjamin*[14], *Edward*[13], *Edward*[12],
John[11]—*Alexander*[1]).   Youngest child of Timothy
Pepoon and Nabby (Tracy) Kneeland, b. at Ogden,
N. Y., Sept. 14, 1820; m. in July, 1841, to Col.
Gilbert Hathaway, of Rochester, N. Y.

Children of Sarah E. Kneeland[17] and Col. Gilbert Hathaway.

1839.   (i.) ANNIE ELLEN HATHAWAY[18], b. in 1845; m. Mr.
Lynch, of Laporte, Ind.   They had four children,
as follows :
1840.   (i.) *Annie Elizabeth Lynch*[19]; b. Oct. 26, 1875.
1841.   (ii.) *Georgiana Augusta Lynch*[19], b. Oct. 16, 1876;
m. Jasper F. Lynch, Jan. 18, 1895.   They have
one child :
1841A.   Robert Jasper P. Lynch[20], b. Oct. 22, 1895.
1842.   (iii.) *Hylton Hathaway Lynch*[19], b. April 16, 1878.
1843.   (iv.) *Charles Jasper Lynch*[19], b. Sept. 17, 1879.
Hylton and Charles are at college in Ontario,
Canada.
1844.   (v.) *Gilbert Mark Lynch*[19], b. March 13, 1883.
Resides at Dover, Ontario, Canada.
1845.   (ii.) CURTIS GILBERT HATHAWAY[18], born in 1848.   He
is a banker, and resides at Colorado Springs, Col.
1846.   (iii.) SARAH ROSE HATHAWAY[18], and
1847.   (iv.) ELIZABETH LILY HATHAWAY[18], twins, b. in 1850.
Sarah is unmarried and lives at Laporte, Ind.
Elizabeth married Mr. Watson, and has one child :
1848.   *Lily Rose Watson*[19], b. Aug. 21, 1876.

SARAH E. (KNEELAND) HATHAWAY

No. 1838

Sarah Elizabeth[17].

1849. (v.) ALFRED T. HATHAWAY[18], b. in 1858; m. and resides at Salida, Col. They had four children, as follows :

1850.   (i.) *Ralph Hathaway*[19], b. Oct. 9, 1877.

1851.   (ii.) *Alfred Hathaway*[19], b. May 15, 1879.

1852.   (iii.) *Gilbert Hathaway*[19], b. Dec. 25, 1881.

1853.   (iv.) *Bessie Hathaway*[19], b. June 16, 1883 ; d. Sept. 18, 1885.

PART IX.

THE DAVID KNEELAND FAMILY.

(NOS. 1854 TO 2086.)

DEDICATED TO

MRS. ELLA (KNEELAND) GREGORY,

WHOSE KINDLY ASSISTANCE

SUPPLIED TO THE AUTHOR MUCH OF THE

MOST VALUED MATTER OF THIS PART.

SARAH KNEELAND KING

No. 1949

The flower of the David Kneeland family

THE THREE DAVIDS.

(NOS. 1854 TO 1888.)

This family is illustrious both in its ancestry and its descendants. The senior David Kneeland stood midway between the religious fervor, the constant dangers, the fierce struggles of the early Colonial period, and the ambitions, the ardent pulse-throbs, the accumulated harvest of the later days. Out of this double heritage may there not now come the blessings of the peace that follows the storm; a pause when the refinements of art, the ease and polish of civilization and the higher life of true religion may have sway and domination. Descended from the heroes of the Mayflower through their best representatives, the Fullers (see Chap. XIII.), from the Colonial warriors through Capt. and Surgeon-Gen. Matthew Fuller, Edward Kneeland and the Rowleys, and from the Revolutionary patriots through Isaac Kneeland, who served at Lexington and Bunker Hill and sent three sons to the army, it is not strange that David Kneeland and his descendants were firm and brave in the prosecution of private rights, and patriotic in their relations to the government. With this generalization we proceed to the subject of our chapter.

1854. (745.) DAVID KNEELAND[16] (*Isaac*[15], *Benjamin*[14], *Edward*[13], *Edward*[12], *John*[11], *William*[10], *James*[9], *Alexander*[8], *William*[7], *William*[6], *John*[5], *John*[4], *John*[3], *James*[2], *Alexander*[1]). Sixth son of Isaac and Content (Rowley) Kneeland, of Marlboro, b. April 23, 1752 (see Hebron Records). He married, Oct. 10, 1771, his cousin, Mercy Kneeland, daughter of Dr. Hezekiah and Mercy (Pepoon) Kneeland (see Chap. XXVII). She was b. Nov. 25, 1751 (see Colchester Records).

David Kneeland[16].

They remained in Marlboro for several years after his marriage, and then moved to East Hampton, Conn., where they joined the Congregational church by letter from the Marlboro church. From thence, about 1809, they went to the beautiful Genesee valley, in New York, where several of their kinsmen had already congregated. From the records of the Presbyterian church we find the following: "The first Congregational church in Geneseo was constituted and regularly organized on the fifth day of May, 1810, by the Rev. Daniel Oliver, a missionary from a mission society in Massachusetts for propagating the gospel *among the Indians* and others in North America." Here follow twenty-one names, constituting the original membership, among which we find "David Kneeland, Mercy Kneeland, Silvia Kneeland and Nabby S. Kneeland." Silvia was the sister of Mercy Kneeland, and Nabby was the wife of her brother, Timothy Pepoon Kneeland. They had established their residence here some years before and it was probably through them that David located at Geneseo. The records of this church contain, under the heading of baptized children, the names and dates of birth of David's children. These children were all born long prior to the establishment of the church. Although these dates were possibly inserted under the direction of the family, I give, in preference, the town records, some of which materially differ therefrom. David was an educated, ambitious and successful farmer. His three sons, David, Benjamin and James, were all of age and married before he located at Geneseo. Inasmuch as he was then nearly 70 years old, it is evident that instead of clearing up a farm on his own account, he purchased one already well under way. David Kneeland died Feb. 24, 1834, aged 82. Mercy died Jan. 9, 1834, aged 82.

Children of David and Mercy Kneeland.

The data as to David Jr., Jerusha and Anna are from Hebron records and the remainder from the church records of East Hampton, where they were born and baptized.

1855.   (i.) DAVID[17], b. at Marlboro, Conn. (formerly Hebron),
           Aug. 23, 1772 (of whom hereafter, 1863).

RESIDENCE OF JAMES KNEELAND

No. 1980a

David Kneeland, Jr.[17].

1856. (ii.) JERUSHA[17], b. at Marlboro, March 13, 1774; m. Mr. Loomis; settled in Elba, Genesee County, N. Y., and died there.

1857. (iii.) ANNA[17], b. at Marlboro, May 29, 1776; bapt. at East Hampton, Oct. 22, 1776. She was unmarried and went with her parents to Geneseo. She lived to a ripe old age and died at Medina, N. Y.

1858. (iv.) CAROLINE[17], b. Jan. 17, 1778, at East Hampton, Conn.; m. first, Mr. Sage, who died soon after, leaving one daughter:

1859. *Caroline Sage*[18], as the only issue. She died at the age of ten.

Caroline married, second, Dr. Bennett, of Le Roy, N. Y. They resided there until her death.

1860. (v.) BENJAMIN[17], b. at East Hampton, Conn.; bapt. Sept. 17, 1782 (of whom hereafter, 2000).

1861. (vi.) JAMES[17], b. at East Hampton; bapt. April 17, 1785 (of whom hereafter, 2056).

1862. (vii.) SYLVIA[17], b. Jan. 1, 1789, at East Hampton; m. Mr. Barnes; settled and died at Medina, N. Y.

1863. (1855.) DAVID KNEELAND, JR.[17] (*David*[16], *Isaac*[15], *Benjamin*[14], *Edward*[13], *Edward*[12], *John*[11]—*Alexander*[1]). Eldest son of David and Mercy Kneeland, grandson on the father's side of Isaac Kneeland and Content Rowley, and on the mother's side, of Dr. Hezekiah Kneeland and Mercy Pepoon; b. at Marlboro (formerly Hebron), Aug. 23, 1772; m. first, Statira Williams, in 1797. She was b. April 10, 1777, and d. in 1811.

She was a descendant of one of the oldest American families. Her father, Lieut. Thomas Williams fought in the battles of Lexington and Bunker Hill, and throughout the entire War of the Revolution. His brother, Lieut. Charles Williams, was killed in the battle of Long Island. Statira's grandfather, Charles Williams, was born in Hadley, Mass., in October, 1691, and was the son of Charles Williams of that place, and the great-grandson of Thomas Williams, of Plymouth, who married Elizabeth Tait, Nov. 30, 1638 (see Vol. I. of

David Kneeland, Jr.[17].

Plymouth Records, p. 103). He shared in the distribution of meadow lands, in 1633 (id., p. 15), and served in the war against the Pequins in 1637 (id., p. 61). It is believed that he was the son of Thomas Williams, who came over in the Mayflower. The latter died during the first terrible winter, but it is believed that John and Thomas Williams, who formed a part of the early history of the Puritans, were his children, and came over in a later ship. The great-grandmother of Statira Williams, wife of Charles Williams, was Mary Robinson. She was a lineal descendant, through Isaac Robinson, of Rev. John Robinson, who was rightly designated "the father of the Mayflower." Out of his church came the original Puritans. He was the very spirit and essence of the movement that made New England a possibility. Dr. Savage designates the father and son as follows: "Isaac Robinson, Plymouth, 1630, son of blessed John, the apostle of Leyden, came, probably, with his mother in the Wyth, 1630." Thus, while through his grandmother, Content Rowley, David Kneeland, Jr., was a descendant of the Mayflower Puritans, his wife, Statira Williams, descended from one who is entitled to that superior honor which the Creator bears to the created—a goodly double crown of heritage, and well has it been up-borne by their descendants.

Children of David Kneeland, by Statira Williams.

1864.   (i.) STATIRA[18], b. Jan., 1799; d. Oct. 20, 1818; unmarried.

1865.   (ii.) JULIA[18], b. Nov. 17, 1800; m. John Clifford. They lived in Buffalo, and she died in Canada, in 1863, while en route to Milwaukee, Wis., to visit her brothers. They had two children:

1866.   (i.) *Julia Amanda Clifford*[19], b. 1823, in State of New York; d. Oct. 11, 1847, in Watertown, Wis.; buried first at Forest Home Cemetery, Milwaukee; removed, 1885, to Brandon, Vt. She m. Levi F. Jackson; they had one child, a daughter.

RESIDENCE OF NORMAN L. KNEELAND

No. 1917

David Kneeland, Jr.[17].

1867. (ii.) *John C. Clifford*[19], b. 1833; m. Lily Brown, a daughter of William O. Brown, a prominent and successful banker of Buffalo, N. Y. They had a large family of children.

1868. (iii.) SYLVESTER W.[18], b. May 27, 1803 (of whom hereafter, 1889).

1869. (iv.) JOEL[18], b. Jan. 19, 1805; m. Cornelia Phoebe Hurlburt, who was born Feb. 23, 1810, and d. June 11, 1881. Joel died in Milwaukee, Nov. 21, 1859. He was a man of unerring judgment, not only in business matters but on policies advocated by public men of his day. All political schemes he seemed able to probe at once, sifting all men and their policies in church and state with an unbiased and also unsparing hand and oftentimes most just, as he lived at a formative period of a great era, which led to the opening of the Civil War. He predicted the war in 1857—thought it might occur after the election for 1860. His insight and strategy proved him the master mind, and he was the great factor in winning a celebrated land case of ten years' litigation, called the Brown suit, in Milwaukee, Wis. He had but a general education, but was given to study. He was a natural cartoonist. In that calling he would have been a master, certainly as a great caricaturist, his conceptions grand and his remarks witty and comprehensive. He had an ever ready wit and was always pleasant socially, with the metaphysical insight that we see in the writings of Hawthorne and George Eliot. So, he was a delightful companion, and as a traveling companion always had something original and interesting about men and nature, being a child-like companion of nature and her true interpreter. About 1830–31 he, with his brother, Moses Kneeland, went to the Rideau Canal, Upper Canada, where their brother-in-law, John Clifford, had taken contracts. He remained about a year and then returned to Le Roy, N. Y., and for some years

David Kneeland, Jr.[17].

purchased and sold farms, and returned to Milwaukee about 1847. His name is in the city directory, 1847-8, "Joel Kneeland, land owner and land agent, No. 8 Spring." His partner was his brother, Moses Kneeland. After some five years they dissolved partnership, and until his death in 1859 he was alone in caring for his property and adding to it.   Children:

1870.   (i.) *Cornelia Sybil*[19], b. Oct. 19, 1850, at Milwaukee, Wis.

1871.   (ii.) *Joel Hurlburt*[19], b. April 6, 1852.

1872.   (v.) OLIVIA[18], b. April 3, 1807; m. Consider Warner, about 1826.   He was b. in Chesterfield, Mass., Feb. 14, 1791, and resided, at the time of his marriage, in the town of Stafford, Genesee County, N. Y. They afterwards settled in the town of Le Roy. Olivia died there, April 30, 1831, and her husband in December, 1870.   They had one son:

1873.   *James K. Warner*[19], b. Sept. 6, 1829, at Le Roy, N. Y.; m. Elizabeth J. Griffin, Nov. 16, 1863, at Black Lake, St. Lawrence County, N. Y.; they resided in Milwaukee, Wis.   They removed to Atlanta, Ga., in 1870, and have since resided there.   They have one son:

1874A.   James William Warner[20], b. at Marietta, Ga., Feb. 3, 1871; he m. Susan E. Clark, at Shelby, Ala., Nov. 27, 1894.   They have one son:

1874B.   *James Clark Warner*[21], b. Dec. 26, 1895, at Atlanta, Ga.

1875.   (vi.) MOSES[18], b. April 2, 1809 (of whom hereafter, 1957).

1876.   (vii.) PHILA[18], b. Oct. 27, 1810 (of whom hereafter, 1981.)

David Kneeland, Jr., married for a second wife, Mrs. Catherine Hanna, who was born Catherine Pierson.   She was the oldest daughter of Joseph Pierson, one of the first settlers in Hartford (now Avon), Livingston County, N. Y., and a descendant of Henry Pierson, one of the founders of Southamp-

JAMES P. KNEELAND

No. 1883

ton, L. I., in 1640, and brother of Rev. Abraham Pierson. They came from Yorkshire, England, to Lynn, Mass., in 1639. Rev. Abraham Pierson, first President of Yale College, was also of this family, as was also Col. Abraham Pierson, who was "a paymaster in Washington's army, the pay-roll being still preserved in the family; and in the time that tried men's souls, when our fortunes and finances were at a low ebb, he paid the soldiers from his own private purse" (Pierson Genealogy). Catherine Pierson was the granddaughter of two Revolutionary patriots. Her mother was Sarah Waterhouse, a descendant of Jacob Waterhouse, who settled in Wethersfield, Conn., in 1630, and who was a descendant of Sir Edward Waterhouse, of Lindsay County, England. She was also a descendant of John Clark, one of the founders of Saybrook, Conn. He was one of the patentees chosen by Gov. Winthrop of the royal charter granted to Connecticut, April 20, 1662.

Mrs. Kneeland was a woman of superior intelligence, great force of character and rare graces of person and mind. Her matrimonial experiences were unique, in that, after the death of Mr. Kneeland, she married the third time and lived to celebrate the fiftieth anniversary of this marriage with her husband. The celebration took place in the old homestead at Avon, built in 1812, which she had inherited from her father and which is still in possession of her descendants.

By Catherine (Pierson) Hanna.

1877. (viii.) JAMES[18], b. Feb. 12, 1816, at Le Roy, N. Y. (of whom hereafter, 1980A.)

1878. (ix.) DAVID PIERSON[18], b. Nov. 10, 1818, at Le Roy, N. Y.; m. Almira A. Lawrence, Feb. 13, 1842 (of whom hereafter, 1880).

1879. (x.) CAROLINE CATHERINE[18], b. June 24, 1821; d. Aug. 13, 1836.

1880. (1878.) DAVID PIERSON KNEELAND[18] (*David[17]*, *David[16]*, *Isaac[15]*, *Benjamin[14]*, *Edward[13]*, *Edward[12]*, *John[11]* — *Alexander[1]*). Son of David Kneeland, Jr., by his second wife Catherine (Pier-

David Pierson Kneeland[18].

son) Hanna, b. at Le Roy, Nov. 10, 1818; m. Almira
A. Lawrence, in Waukegan, Ills., Feb. 13, 1842,
and d. in Le Roy, N. Y., on his thirty-fifth birthday, Nov. 10, 1853. Almira, his wife, died in Le
Roy, N. Y., Jan. 5, 1875.

While a young man he was hopefully converted under the
ministry of the Rev. Gilbert Crawford, and in March, 1846,
united with the Presbyterian church, in Le Roy. Though
reared to the art of tilling the soil, and prosecuting it with a
skill, energy and success rarely equalled till within a few days
of his death, he had not neglected the cultivation of personal
piety—to lay up treasures in heaven. Such was his growth in
"knowledge and grace," so sound in doctrine and consistent
in a life of practical godliness, that in the early part of that
year he was elected and ordained to the eldership in that
church. He gave largely of his means to support the institutions of the gospel at home and abroad. He was a man held
in the highest esteem by all who knew him and was noted for
his good business qualifications, good, clear judgment and
straightforward, honest dealings. His death was deeply
lamented by the community.

Children of David P. and Almira (Lawrence) Kneeland.

1881.　(i.)　CATHARINE VIRGINIA[19], b. May 22, 1843, at Le
Roy, N. Y.; m. Prof. William M. Gabb, of Philadelphia, Pa., Geologist for the U. S. Government,
July 14, 1869; d. at Las Vegas, Santo Domingo,
Aug. 21, 1870. Prof. Gabb was sent to San
Domingo by the U. S. Government as a geologist
in charge of a party to make surveys and geological
discoveries for the benefit of American archives.
He was absent on official business when his wife
was taken dangerously ill, and word was sent to
him. Upon receiving the message he immediately
sprang upon a saddled horse and never left the
saddle for thirty-six hours, except for the purpose
of changing horses, and though he returned with
all speed, found her dead and buried. Her remains
were, a year later, taken up, removed to Le Roy,

MARY D. (KNEELAND) VAN DEUSEN

No 1885

N. Y., and found a resting-place in the family burying plot in Macpelah Cemetery. Prof. Gabb died in Philadelphia some eight years later. having never re-married. Virginia was a great student and lover of art and nature. She graduated at Ingham University, in Le Roy, with the highest honors. She was gifted with rare conversational powers, a remarkable memory, together with a charm of man-ner, making her beloved by a large circle of friends and acquaintances.

1882. (ii.) JULIA AUGUSTA[19], b. at Le Roy, N. Y., April 23, 1845; m. first, Henry B. Olmsted, of Le Roy, N.Y., Sept. 8, 1871; he d. Oct. 2, 1872. Married, second, Lucien E. Hallock, of Batavia, N. Y., March 20, 1884; he d. July 28, 1884. She now resides in Kansas City, Mo.

1883. (iii.) JAMES PIERSON[19], b. at Le Roy, N. Y., Sept. 8, 1847; m. Julia A. Pardee, daughter of the late Hon. Tracy Pardee, of Batavia, N. Y., Sept. 30, 1884. They now reside in Brooklyn, N. Y. He is an assistant to his cousin, Sylvester H. Kneeland, the well-known broker and promoter of New York City.

1884. (iv.) GRACE MARIA[19], b. April 9, 1850, at Le Roy, N. Y.; m. Arthur Pennell, a civil engineer, of London, England, in Le Roy, N. Y., Sept. 28, 1878; d. in Kansas City, Mo., Oct. 24, 1891, and buried at Re Roy. A true Christian, with gentle ways and a worthy life, taking an active interest in church matters, especially the Episcopal church, of which she was a member. An ever true friend, she died beloved by all who knew her.

1885. (v.) MARY DAVID[19], b. Feb. 23, 1853, at Le Roy, N. Y.; m. John R. Van Deusen, of Brooklyn, N. Y., Sept. 6, 1875. He d. at Kansas City, Mo., April 10, 1894. He had been connected with the Island of Santo Domingo, W. I., in a business way for several years, when, in the fall of 1876, he was induced to go there to reside permanently. Both he and his

David Pierson Kneeland[18].

wife had formerly spent some time on the Island, and had consequently acquired some knowledge of the Spanish language, which, with the mild tropical climate and curious customs of the people, all conduced to make their life there very pleasant and interesting. The following year, however, political disturbances arose, and the country was soon divided into three separate parties—the red, blue, and green. The red was then in power, but the wholesale robberies of these officials caused such great dissatisfaction, that it ultimately resulted in a general revolution and riot. The town of Puerto Plata appeared to be the headquarters for all disturbances. The soldiers had gathered upon the borders of the town, and begun firing upon the fort in which the government soldiers had safely bestowed themselves. Cannon balls and bullets were flying in all directions, and the residents were obliged to take refuge in the thick stone warehouses for protection. All fresh provisions from the country were devoured by the soldiers, and the people were forced to depend upon the small supply of canned goods of the merchants. Starvation and sickness and suffering were soon apparent among all classes of people. Finally, at the end of ten weeks, the marauders managed to gain possession of the government buildings and fort, and peace was declared. Mrs. Van Deusen found, upon returning to her home, that a cannon ball and several bullets had gone through her house, but otherwise nothing was disturbed. She returned to her northern home some few months afterward, as she found that the sweet, balmy breezes of the Carribean, and the curious mode of tropical life, had ceased their fascination.

SYLVESTER W. KNEELAND

No. 1889

DESCENDANTS OF SYLVESTER W. KNEELAND.

1889. (1868.) SYLVESTER W. KNEELAND[18] (*David*[17], *David*[16], *Isaac*[15], *Benjamin*[14], *Edward*[13], *Edward*[12], *John*[11], *William*[10], *James*[9], *Alexander*[8], *William*[7], *William*[6], *John*[5], *John*[4], *John*[3], *James*[2], *Alexander*[1]). Eldest son of David Kneeland, Jr., was born in Hartford, Conn., May 27, 1803, and died in Eagle Harbor, N. Y., May 26, 1875.

When about two years of age he was taken by his parents to the celebrated Genesee Valley, in Western New York, where they resided for several years, in Geneseo, Livingston County. In the year 1815, with his father's family of six children, he moved to Le Roy, Genesee County, where he remained until he reached his majority. On April 5, 1827, at the age of 24, he married his step-sister, Sarah Hanna, a daughter of Matthew and Catherine (Pierson) Hanna. He and his bride of seventeen possessed what was considered a fortune in those days— fifteen hundred dollars each. Together they bought a farm in Bergen, Genesee County, upon which they erected a good log house, and in which three of their children were born. In 1832 they sold their farm and bought a larger one in Barre, Orleans County, and which has ever since been owned by their descendants, and where are now living their great-grandchildren. At one time their eight children were stricken with the measles. Their dearly beloved eldest son, David, a most promising young man, did not recover from the disease, but died Feb. 13, 1849. Two years later, Oct. 23, 1851, the third

21

Sylvester W. Kneeland[18].

son, Moses, an earnest and close student, died of congestion of the brain.   Almost heartbroken, a new home was purchased some miles distant from the scene of their sad losses—at Eagle Harbor, where they remained to the end of their days.

Mrs. Kneeland was a woman of a sweet and gentle nature, rarely seen away from her own home, which she always made one of open hospitality.   She was a great reader, being especially interested in all political events of the day, ever enjoying thoroughly a good speech.   She died Jan. 16, 1866.   Mr. Kneeland was a successful farmer, and a practical business man. He gave his children the best educational facilities in his power.   He was for several years Justice of the Peace, playing the rôle of country Squire, and trying small cases with honor to himself and satisfaction to his townsmen.   He helped with his advice and means many deserving young men as they were starting out in life for themselves.

Children of Sylvester W. and Sarah (Hanna) Kneeland.

1890.   (i.) ALMIRA[19], b. July 1, 1828, at Bergen, Genesee County, N. Y.   (Of whom hereafter, 1898).

1891.   (ii.) DAVID[19], b. July 28, 1830, at Bergen, N. Y.; d. Feb. 13, 1849.

1892.   (iii.) NORMAN L.[19], b. Feb. 6, 1832, at Bergen, N. Y. (Of whom hereafter, 1917).

1893.   (iv.) MOSES J.[19], b. Aug. 30, 1833, at Barre, Orleans County, N. Y.; d. Oct. 23, 1851.

1894.   (v.) SARAH J.[19], b. Jan. 16, 1836, at Barre, N. Y.   (Of whom hereafter, 1946).

1895.   (vi.) JAMES PIERSON[19], b. Feb. 27, 1838, at Barre, N. Y.   (Of whom hereafter, 1952).

1896.   (vii.) SYLVESTER HANNA[19], b. April 20, 1840, at Barre, N. Y.   Is a successful banker and broker, residing and doing business in the city and State of New York.   He is unmarried.

1897.   (viii.) ELLA A.[19], b. March 27, 1846, at Barre, N. Y.; m. Arnold Gregory, Nov. 6, 1884, in Milwaukee, Wis.

Norman L. Kneeland

No. 1917

Almira Kneeland[19].

1898. (1890.) ALMIRA KNEELAND[19] (*Sylvester W.*[18], *David* [17], *David* [16], *Isaac*[15], *Benjamin*[14], *Edward*[13], *Edward* [12], *John*[11]—*Alexander*[1]). Eldest child of Sylvester W. and Sarah (Hanna) Kneeland, b. July 1, 1828, at Bergen, Genesee County, N. Y. She received a thorough education and married Arnold Gregory, at Barre, Orleans County, N. Y., and had five children. She d. June 16, 1881.

Children of Almira Kneeland[19] and Arnold Gregory.

1899. (i.) CHARLES KNEELAND GREGORY[20], b. July 15, 1850, at Batavia, N. Y.; d. Dec. 3, 1875.

1900. (ii.) MOSES WILLIS GREGORY[20], b. Feb. 10, 1852, at Batavia, N. Y.; m. Mary E. Porter, of Albion, N. Y., Nov. 1, 1875. Their children are:

1901. (i.) *Le Roy Porter Gregory*[21], b. Feb. 28, 1878, at Ridgeway, N. Y.

1902. (ii.) *Herbert Arnold Gregory*[21], b. Dec. 5, 1879, at West Albion, N. Y.

1903. (iii.) *Grace Edith Gregory*[21], b. Jan. 11, 1881, at West Albion, N. Y.

1904. (iv.) *Welles Arthur Gregory*[21], b. Aug. 4, 1882, at Ridgeway, Knowlesville, N. Y.

1905. (v.) *Mildred Gregory*[21], b. Aug. 22, 1885, at Ridgeway.

1906. (vi.) *Frank A. Gregory*[21], b. July 6, 1888, at Ridgeway; d. April 25, 1889.

1907. (vii.) *Willis Earle Gregory*[21], b. Nov. 24, 1891, at Ridgeway.

1908. (iii.) SARAH SOPHIA GREGORY[20], b. Aug. 19, 1855, at Barre, Orleans County, N. Y.; m. Dan S. Root, Nov. 16, 1875, at Albion, N. Y. Children:

1909. (i.) *Charles G. Root*[21], b. Aug. 13, 1876, at Milville, Orleans County, N. Y.

1910. (ii.) *Orpheus Arnold Root*[21], b. June 7, 1882, at Milville.

1911. (iii.) *Dan Samuel Root*[21], b. Dec. 15, 1888, at Milville, N. Y. He had a twin brother, who died Jan. 19, 1889, unnamed.

1912.   (iv.) GRACE E. GREGORY[20], b. Nov. 29, 1865, at Barre, d. Jan. 24, 1879.

1913.   (v.) CATHARINE ISABEL GREGORY[20], b. Oct. 3, 1867, at Barre, N. Y.; m. Edward E. Hill, March 29, 1888, at Barre, N. Y.   Children:

1914.   (i.) *Almira G. Hill*[21], b. Feb. 21, 1890, at St. Thomas, Ontario, Canada.

1915.   (ii.) *William Parmaly Hill*[21], b. April 16, 1892, at Ridgeway, Knowlesville, N. Y.

1916.   (iii.) *Ruth Mercedes Hill*[21], b. Feb. 28, 1894, at Ridgeway.

1917.   (1892.) NORMAN L. KNEELAND[19] (*Sylvester W.*[18], *David*[17], *David*[16], *Isaac*[15], *Benjamin*[14], *Edward*[13], *Edward*[12], *John*[11]—*Alexander*[1]).   Second son of Sylvester W. Kneeland, b. Feb. 6, 1832, at Bergen, Genesee County, N. Y.; m. Carrie A. Baker, March 11, 1856, at Albion.

Mr. Kneeland obtained his first knowledge of books in Knowlesville, attending, later, the Albion Academy and Genesee College. After reaching manhood he engaged in the manufacturing business in St. Catharines, Canada. Shortly after the breaking out of the War of the Rebellion he enlisted in Company D, 151st N. Y. Volunteers. His regiment was assigned to garrison duty at Baltimore, Md., Gen. Wool being commandant of the forces. After a year of service Mr. Kneeland found he could not endure the physical hardships of army life, as his health became seriously affected. He asked for and received a discharge on account of disability. In 1865 he decided to go West, and started in November, by way of the great lakes, for Milwaukee, Wis. Arriving there and liking the country, he located upon a farm of ninety acres, about two miles from the city, which had been owned for fifteen years by his father and uncle. He soon after bought the farm, and cultivated it for many years, in the meantime building for his family a comfortable home. The city grew too rapidly in his direction to suit his comfort as a farmer, and finally, when a system of electric railways to the

O. S. Kneeland.

No. 1919

outlying suburban towns was inaugurated, a corner of the farm was cut off by one of the railways passing through it.

About that time the Park Commissioners purchased a number of beautiful tracts of land in different localities, to form a belt of parks around the city, to be ultimately connected by boulevards. Mr. Kneeland's farm was added to one of the largest and loveliest of these, which is known as the West Side Park. Where formerly were Mr. Kneeland's orchards and gardens are now picturesque lakes, around which are magnificent drives, and in which are imbedded, like jewels, beautiful wooded islands. With their sloping banks covered with flowering shrubs and edged with iris, and a variety of water-plants, are a series of lily ponds. Their surfaces are covered here and there with the broad, dark green of the lily pads, nestling among which the many colors of the rich blooms are half hidden. In 1889 Mr. Kneeland moved to one of Milwaukee's finest suburbs, Wauwatosa, and built for himself a home, one of the most attractive and handsomest in the place, where he and his devoted wife now reside, enjoying the evening of their lives. He is a Son of the American Revolution.

Children of Norman L. and Carrie A. (Baker) Kneeland.

1918. (i.) ELLA A.[20], b. Jan. 7, 1857, at St. Catharines, Can.

1919. (ii.) OTIS SYLVESTER[20], b. Aug. 5, 1859, at Eagle Harbor, N. Y.; m. Margaret Frame, April 3, 1884. They reside in Lewiston, Mich. Their children are:

1920.   (i.) Son, unnamed; b. Jan. 3, 1885, at Wauwatosa, Wis.; d. Jan. 7, 1885.

1921.   (ii.) *Grace Margaret*[21], b. Jan. 18, 1886, at Wauwatosa.

1922.   (iii.) *Sarah Louise*[21], b. Feb. 18, 1888, at same place.

1923.   (iv.) *Sylvester Frame*[21], b. Feb. 12, 1890, at Wauwatosa.

1924.   (v.) *Norman Livingston*[21], b. May 31, 1892, at Everett, Washington.

1925.   (vi.) *Helen Hortense*[21], and

1926   (vii.) *Walter Everett*[21], twins, b. Sept. 13, 1895, at Everett.

Norman L. Kneeland[19].

1927. (iii.) DAVID M.[20], b. Feb. 28, 1861, at Eagle Harbor, N. Y.; m. Cornelia Buttles, at Milwaukee, Wis., June 24, 1884. He is an active, energetic business man, the General Manager and Treasurer of the Michelson and Hanson Lumber Co. The mill is one of the largest in the State, and was built under the supervision of Mr. Kneeland. He lives at Lewiston, Mich. Children:

1928.   (i.) *Bessie K.*[21], b. Nov. 20, 1885, at Wauwatosa, Wis.; d. Nov. 12, 1886.

1929.   (ii.) *Frances Sarah*[21], b. Aug. 14, 1887, at Milwaukee, Wis.

1930.   (iii.) *David Russell*[21], b. March 24, 1889, at Grayling, Mich.; d. Jan. 30, 1890.

1931.   (iv.) *James*[21], b. July 15, 1892, at Grayling, Mich.

1932.   (v.) *Matthew Pierson*[21], b. Feb. 8, 1894, at Lewiston, Mich.

1933. (iv.) ANNA M.[20], b. July 29, 1864, at Eagle Harbor, N. Y.; m. Charles A. Carpenter, Sept. 25, 1885, at Milwaukee, Wis. They live at Faribault, Minn. Children:

1934.   (i.) *Kathryn Anna Carpenter*[21], b. Aug. 5, 1886, at Faribault, Minn.

1935.   (ii.) *Marion Esther Carpenter*[21], b. Oct. 9, 1888, at same place.

1936.   (iii.) *Thomas Kneeland Carpenter*[21], b. Sept. 9, 1890, at same place; d. Nov. 15, 1890.

1937.   (iv.) *Charles Kneeland Carpenter*[21], b. Aug. 18, 1891, at same place.

1938. (v.) SARAH L.[20], b. March 9, 1866, at Milwaukee, Wis., m. William Allen Godfrey, June 16, 1892, at Wauwatosa, Wis., where they now reside. Children:

1939.   (i.) *Russell Kneeland Godfrey*[21], b. April 2, 1893, at Wauwatosa, Wis.

1940.   (ii.) *Norman Edward Godfrey*[21], b. Aug. 15, 1895, at same place.

1941. (vi.) ROSE B.[20], b. Aug. 19, 1872, at Milwaukee, Wis.; m. Byron Brown Farries, Jan. 5, 1892, at Wauwatosa, Wis. They reside in Lewiston, Mich. Children:

David M Kneeland

No. 1927

James Pierson Kneeland[19].

1942.   (i.) *Miriam Eleanor Farries*[21], b. March 17, 1893, at Wauwatosa, Wis.

1943.   (ii.) *Carolyn Jean Farries*[21], b. Jan. 22, 1895, at Wauwatosa, Wis.

1944.   (vii.) JAMES RALPH[20], b. July 11, 1880, at Milwaukee, Wis. He is now a student of Lawrence University, at Appleton, Wis.

1945.   (viii.) FRANK[20], b. April 19, 1883, at Milwaukee, Wis.; d. Aug. 10, 1883.

1946.   (1894.) SARAH J. KNEELAND[19] (*Sylvester W.*[18], *David*[17], *David*[16], *Isaac*[15], *Benjamin*[14], *Edward*[13], *Edward*[12], *John*[11]—*Alexander*[1]). Second daughter of Sylvester W. and Sarah (Hanna) Kneeland, b. Jan. 16, 1836, at Barre, Orleans County, N. Y.; m. Henry S. Danolds, December 30, 1851; she d. Dec. 22, 1875, at Avon, N. Y. They had one child only:

1947.   MARTHA KNEELAND DANOLDS[20], b. May 26, 1858, at Eagle Harbor, N. Y.; m. Feb. 21, 1883, William F. King, a member of the firm of Calhoun, Robbins & Co., of New York City. They had four children, as follows:

1948.   (i.) Son, unnamed, b. and d. Dec. 3, 1883.

1949.   (ii.) *Sarah Kneeland King*[21], b. Nov. 22, 1884, at No. 55 East Sixty-fourth street, New York.

1950.   (iii.) *Martha Elliot King*[21], b. Feb. 5, 1886, at No. 60 West Fiftieth street, New York.

1951.   (iv.) *Hildegarde King*[21], b. Aug. 28, 1892, at Tuxedo, N. Y.

1952.   (1895.) JAMES PIERSON KNEELAND[19] (*Sylvester W.*[18], *David*[17], *David*[16], *Isaac*[15], *Benjamin*[14], *Edward*[13], *Edward*[12], *John*[11]—*Alexander*[1]). Fourth son of Sylvester W. and Sarah (Hanna) Kneeland, b. at Barre, Orleans County, N. Y., Feb. 27, 1838; m. Alice Peaslee, Oct. 16, 1861. She was b. July 3, 1842.

James Pierson Kneeland[19].

Children of James P. and Alice (Peaslee) Kneeland.

1953. (i.) FRANCES OLIVIA[20], b. Aug. 30, 1866, at Milwaukee, Wis.; m. Harry O. Bradley, Dec. 15, 1885, at Yates, N. Y.; d. Jan. 6, 1887, at Cedar Rapids, Iowa.

1954. (ii.) SYLVESTER HANNA[20], b. Jan. 7, 1874, at Cedar Rapids, Iowa. He resides in Nebraska.

1955. (iii.) ALICE[20], b. April 25, 1876, at Fairfield, Neb.; m. John R. Kerr, July 10, 1895. They have one son:

1956. *John Kneeland Kerr[21]*, b. July 31, 1896.

Moses Kneeland

No. 1957

CHAPTER XXX.

DESCENDANTS OF MOSES KNEELAND.

(NOS. 1957 TO 1980.)

1957. (1875.) MOSES KNEELAND[18] (*David*[17], *David*[16], *Isaac*[15], *Benjamin*[14], *Edward*[13], *Edward*[12], *John*[11], *William*[10], *James*[9], *Alexander*[8], *William*[7], *William*[6], *John*[5], *John*[4], *John*[3], *James*[2], *Alexander*[1]). Son of David Kneeland, b. in New York State, April 2, 1809, and d. in Milwaukee, Wis., on the 21st day of January, 1864; m. Ellen Clarinda Martin, Sept. 20, 1836.

He was an early pioneer of Milwaukee, going there in 1842, when the population was only 2700. From the time of his arrival there he was identified with all public enterprises of importance, and worthily held offices of honor and trust during nearly all the period of his residence. He was one of the trustees under the old village charter, was alderman from the Fourth Ward at the first organization of the city government, and was successively elected to that office for a number of years. He also served on the Board of Supervisors and in the Board of Councilors, of which body he was a member representing the Seventh Ward at the time of his death. In all of these offices he proved himself an industrious and faithful representative of the interest of the people. Through his enterprise and business sagacity he had accumulated a handsome fortune, and whenever any work of public importance was to be done he was ever foremost with his means as well as his energies to aid its accomplishment. He was a heavy stockholder and a director in the Fond du Lac & Green Bay Railroad Company, and when the consolidation of that road with the La Crosse Railroad took place, in 1854, he became Vice-President of the new organization, which position

he held until 1857, when he resigned.   After the road passed
from the control of the old company and a new one had been
formed under the name of the Milwaukee & Minnesota Railroad Company, he was elected President, which position he
held until his death in 1864.

Children of Moses and Ellen Clarinda (Martin) Kneeland.

1958.   (i.) SARAH OLIVIA[19], b. March 18, 1838; m. Walter
S. Chandler, May 16, 1859, who d. Dec. 27, 1896.
She resides at Milwaukee, Wis.   Children:

1959.   (i.) *Ralph*[20], b. July 16, 1861; m. Louise Eldred,
Oct. 18, 1893.   Resides at Milwaukee, Wis.

1960.   (ii.) *Cornelia Burwell*[20], died in infancy.

1961.   (iii.) *Ellen Clarinda Kneeland*[20], died in infancy.

1962.   (iv.) *Burr Kneeland*[20], b. Oct. 22, 1872, and resides
at Milwaukee, Wis.

1963.   (ii.) ELLEN CLARINDA[19], b. April 12, 1839; m. James
Lester Sexton, Oct. 17, 1860, who d. June 1, 1883.
She resides at Charlotte, N. C.   Children:

1964.   (i.) *Frances Kneeland*[20], b. Jan. 23, 1864; m.
Henry Buik, Oct. 27, 1892, and resides at
Harvey, North Dakota.   Children:

1965.   (i.) Ellen Clarinda[21], b. July 26, 1893.

1966.   (ii.) Henry Kirkwood[21], b. July 20, 1895.

1967.   (ii.) *Emma*[20], b. Feb. 19, 1865; m. Stanton E.
Taylor, Jan. 29, 1889.   Resides at Winona,
Minn.   Children:

1968.   (i.) Marjorie Helen[21], b. April 23, 1890.

1969.   (ii.) James Sexton[21], b. Aug. 3, 1894.

1970.   (iii.) Cornelia Katherine[21], b. March 26, 1896.

1971.   (iii.) *Lester*[20], b. July, 1866; d. Aug. 20, 1867.

1972.   (iv.) *James Lester*[20], b. Dec. 11, 1869.   Resides at
Charlotte, N. C.

1973.   (iii.) FRANCES[19], b. April 7, 1842; m. John Gardiner
Flint, Jan. 4, 1865, who d. March 24, 1896.   She
resides at Milwaukee, Wis.   Children:

1974.   (i.) Infant daughter, b. and d. Sept. 2, 1865.

1975.   (ii.) *John Gardiner*[20], b. Jan. 3, 1867; d. Aug.
20, 1867.

Wyman Kneeland Flint.

No. 1980

Wyman Kneeland Flint[20].

1976. (iii.) *Wyman Kneeland*[20], b. March 4, 1868; m. Jennie Louise Ray, June 2, 1897 (of whom hereafter, 1980).

1977. (iv.) *Francis Gardiner*[20], b. April 27, 1870; d. Aug. 8, 1870.

1978. (v.) Infant son, b. and d. Jan. 23, 1874.

1979. (iv.) MOSES BURR[19], b. Nov. 27, 1848; d. July 2, 1875.

1980. (1976.) WYMAN KNEELAND FLINT[20] (*Frances*[19], *Moses*[18], *David*[17], *David*[16], *Isaac*[15], *Benjamin*[14], *Edward*[13], *Edward*[12], *John*[11], *William*[10], *James*[9], *Alexander*[8], *William*[7], *William*[6], *John*[5], *John*[4], *John*[3], *James*[2], *Alexander*[1]). Son of John Gardiner, and Frances (Kneeland) Flint, b. in Milwaukee, March 4, 1868.

Was educated at Markham Academy, Milwaukee; graduated from there in 1886. In 1887 he entered the freshman class at Harvard College, receiving the degree of Bachelor of Arts, *Cum laude*, in 1891. He also received honorable mention in the fine arts at the time of taking his degree. In the fall of 1891 he entered the Harvard Law School and continued there until 1893. During his course at the law school he was clerk of the court of the Austin Law Club, one of the oldest and best known law clubs in the school. In the summer of 1893 he entered his father's business and has continued in the active management until the death of J. G. Flint, at Chihuahua, Mexico, March 24, 1896, and is now conducting the business under his father's name. Mr. Flint has been a great traveler, having visited every State in the Union, including Alaska, having been many times abroad and also to Mexico and Cuba. In Milwaukee he is a member of the Milwaukee Club, Milwaukee Country Club, Deutscher Club, Harvard Club of Milwaukee, and Club Français, and in addition to these is a member of the Colonial Club of Cambridge, Mass., and of the Harvard Club of New York. He is also a member, through direct lineal descent, of the Society Sons of the American Revolution, Society of Colonial Wars, Society of the War of 1812, the Order of Founders and Patriots of America, and the Society of Mayflower Descendants, as well as the Folk-Lore Society of the United States.

CHAPTER XXXI.

HON. JAMES KNEELAND, OF MILWAUKEE.

(NO. 1980A.)

1980A. (1871.) JAMES KNEELAND[18] (*David*[17], *David*[16], *Isaac*[15], *Benjamin*[14], *Edward*[13], *Edward*[12], *John*[11], *William*[10], *James*[9], *Alexander*[8], *William*[7], *William*[6], *John*[5], *John*[4], *John*[3], *James*[2], *Alexander*[1]). Son of David and Catharine Pierson (Hanna) Kneeland, b. in Le Roy, Genesee County, N. Y., Feb. 12, 1816, and is now (1897) living in Milwaukee, Wis.

He belongs to several of the city clubs, notably the Pioneer Club. He is a Son of the American Revolution; a charter member of the Wisconsin Society of Colonial Wars, and a member of the Society of Mayflower Descendants, and of The Founders and Patriots of America. His stately and beautiful mansion, a glimpse of which is herewith given, is presided over by his niece, Mrs. Ella Kneeland Gregory, who has lived with him almost continuously since her childhood. The early years of Mr. Kneeland's life were spent upon a farm. The educational facilities of that region and that period were limited, but Mr. Kneeland had a capable instructor in his mother, who, in the midst of manifold household duties, found time to devote to his intellectual and moral training. He had a genius for the easy acquisition of knowledge, and had mastered the ordinary English branches at an age when most boys have only made a beginning. His perceptions were unusually quick, and nature seemed to have endowed him with the happy faculty of making the best of every opportunity which presented itself for his advancement in life. In practical affairs he was no less apt than in acquiring an education, and when he was fourteen years of age he entered into a contract with his stepfather, by whom he was

James Kneeland

James Kneeland[18].

treated with loving consideration, under which he took charge
of the farm, at a salary of one hundred and fifty dollars a
year, with the privilege of going to school three months each
winter. At sixteen, his thorough education and first-class
business qualifications had attracted to him the attention of
prominent men of the community, and a year later he accepted
a clerical position with the firm of M. P. Lampson & Co.,
general merchants, of Le Roy. The senior member of this
firm was a brother of Sir Edward Lampson, head of the noted
seal skin curing and dyeing establishment, of London. He
was an intelligent and enterprising merchant, and when young
Kneeland entered his employ—at the expiration of the time
which he had contracted to remain with his stepfather—he was
given an opportunity for rapid development of the commercial
instinct which he possessed.

In the business experience of his boyhood, he was remarkable for the precision with which he discharged all his
duties, his ready grasp of situations presenting themselves
in the ordinary course of business, and the ease and celerity
with which he met all demands made upon him. His employers' interests he regarded as his own, and whatever he could
do to promote those interests he did without stopping to
enquire whether he had stipulated to render such services, or
whether the compensation which he received justified extra
labor or effort on his part. His methods were such as to win
the full and implicit confidence of his employers, and in a
comparatively short time his capacity, good judgment and
genius for trade made him their counselor and advisor, and
established a friendship which lasted many years after their
paths in life had become divergent.

Naturally enough, a young man whose ability, energy and
enterprise were apparent in his every movement, could not
long be content to remain in the employ of others when he
felt conscious of his own resources and was fully cognizant of
the fact that he lived in a country of magnificent opportunities.
Having come into possession of what was considered in those
days a considerable amount of capital for a young man—
means which came to him in part through inheritance and in
part through accumulated earnings—like his immediate ances-

334 THE DAVID KNEELAND FAMILY.

tor he sought for this capital a new field of investment. In the fall of 1837, in company with another young man, he started West on an exploring expedition, making the long journey from New York State to Illinois in what was known in the parlance of those days as a "Democrat wagon." On this trip the young men traversed portions of Pennsylvania, Ohio, Indiana and Michigan, and finally came to a temporary halt in McHenry County, Illinois, where they remained during the winter of 1837-38. Here they purchased a squatter's claim to lands then unsurveyed and "staked out" the town of Richmond, now a place of considerable consequence. Disposing of his interest in this enterprise, Mr. Kneeland continued his trip through Illinois, visiting Chicago, Springfield, Ottawa, Joliet and other towns then in the infantile stage of their existence. While coming up the Illinois river on this trip, he had the unique experience, during a terrific storm accompanied by a flood of water, of being aboard a small river steamer which lost her bearings and steered into a forest, from which she extricated herself with much difficulty and loss of time.

At that time the Illinois and Michigan Canal, that great waterway which was designed by its promoters to connect the waters of the Mississippi river with those of the lakes, and which had aroused the enthusiastic anticipation of all classes of people along the line of the proposed improvement, was in process of construction. One or two friends of Mr. Kneeland, who had come out from the East, were in some way identified with the work, and he concluded to pay them a visit. The result of this visit was that he took one of the heaviest contracts on the canal and carried the work to completion. The work which he undertook was at what is now the village of Lemont, where a deep cut had to be made through solid rock. The section of which he and his associates took charge was the heaviest of these "rock cuts," and was the only one of these sections ever fully completed according to contract.

Although Mr. Kneeland had had no previous experience in the construction of public works, his ability to adapt himself to any occupation or circumstances was made manifest in the success with which he managed the enterprise. His keen

James Kneeland[18].

intelligence was brought to bear on the situation, and where old and experienced contractors wasted, he saved; where they labored at a disadvantage, he managed to work to advantage; where they used man power, he introduced horse power and steam power, and young as he was in the business of canal construction he was the first to introduce the steam drill on the line of the canal. No legitimate agency which could be made to contribute to the success of the enterprise was overlooked. His employés were treated with kindness and consideration, while perfect discipline was at all times maintained among them, and the result of his thoroughly systematic operations was success where others failed. The compensation which he and his associates received for their work amounted in the aggregate to more than two hundred thousand dollars, and when the financial resources of the State of Illinois began to show signs of impairment, Mr. Kneeland was one of the few who closed up their affairs in time to escape serious loss.

Closing out his interest in the canal contract January 1, 1841, he made a trip to Springfield and St. Louis, enjoying a season of rest and recreation and availing himself at the time of an opportunity to convert the bank currency and State securities which he had taken in part payment for his canal work into safe and available assets. He spent considerable time in Springfield in the winter of 1840-41, finding the society of the capital city peculiarly agreeable, and forming the acquaintance of many men afterwards famous in public life, among them Abraham Lincoln and Stephen A. Douglas. While there Mr. Kneeland and the late John S. Wright, of Chicago, gave a famous sleighing party to the élite young people of the city, in an eight-horse sleigh improvised for the occasion, and among the gentlemen of that party were six who were afterwards United States Senators. Stephen A. Douglas, Gen. James Shields, who at different times represented in the senate the States of Illinois, Minnesota and Missouri, Judge Lyman Trumbull, Isaac P. Walker, one of the first senators from Wisconsin, Gen. James McDougal, one of the early senators from California, and Col. Edward D. Baker, who represented Oregon in the senate when the Civil War began and who was killed in the battle of Ball's Bluff a

few months later, were all of this party.   Lincoln was not of
the party, for the reason, as Mr. Kneeland sometimes laugh-
ingly explains, that it was a very select company of invited
guests, and Lincoln was not looked upon in those days as
quite fit to enter the charmed circle of Springfield's best
society.

After remaining some time in Springfield he went to St.
Louis, where he made an advantageous exchange of Illinois
State bonds for New Orleans sugar, and then visited banks at
various points which had temporarily resumed specie payment,
to effect the redemption in coin of currency which he had in
his possession.   A strong box was the only protection which
he had for several thousand dollars' worth of coin
brought back with him, and for which he paid only a passen-
ger's rate of transportation on the stages by which he traveled
much of the time.

In the spring of 1841 he decided to establish himself in
business in Milwaukee, and a portion of the stock of sugars
which he had contracted for in St. Louis was in due course of
time shipped by river, freight wagons and lakes to this point.
He also made a trip to the East for the purchase of other
goods, and early in the summer opened a general store, which
soon became famous throughout this region as a complete
trade emporium.   Whatever the public demanded he sought
to supply, and the immigrants who were then coming there
in constantly increasing numbers to settle on the fertile lands
of Wisconsin, found in Mr. Kneeland's store a complete out-
fitting establishment.   If they brought with them foreign
coin he purchased the coin at its market value, and whatever
they needed to begin life with as pioneers, he was ready to
furnish them.   So accustomed did the people become to finding everything they had occasion to ask for at his place of
business, that amusing tests of his capacity to meet any emergency were sometimes made.   On one occasion the people of
West Troy, who had joined together to build a union church,
called on him to supply all the material needed for its construction.   Everything having been supplied but the pulpit, one of
the members of the congregation wagered that Mr. Kneeland
would supply this on demand.   The order for the pulpit came

James Kneeland[18].

in the regular course of business, and half an hour later it had been filled, Mr. Kneeland having fortunately observed that morning that a pulpit in one of the little churches of Milwaukee was about to be discarded—taking advantage of this circumstance to accommodate his customer. On another occasion one of his customers, who had settled on a farm near Rock river, having been supplied with farm implements, household utensils and everything necessary to his comfort and convenience, wrote that he needed a wife. Mr. Kneeland promptly replied that the commission was a somewhat delicate one, but if his customer would visit Milwaukee he would undertake to fill the order to his entire satisfaction. The invitation was accepted and in due course of time the young farmer married the young woman to whom Mr. Kneeland introduced him.

For ten years or more Mr. Kneeland continued in the mercantile business, and while thus engaged in trade sought to promote in every way possible the social, moral and material advancement of this city. He was among those who interested themselves most actively in the first movement made toward securing telegraphic communication with the outside world; he aided in the publication of the first city directory; served as an officer of the first artillery company organized here, and was a promoter of the first social club. His business operations extended outside the field of merchandising, and his investments in State and local securities and real estate were extensive. The deed for land on which the town of West Bend is now located, came to him direct from President Polk, and was presented by him some years since to the Old Settlers' Club, of Washington County. The schooner "Fur Trader," which was probably the first sailing vessel on Lake Superior, was sent from here to its destination by Mr. Kneeland, and as he sometimes facetiously observes, it had to be sent overland. That is to say, it had to be taken overland around the Falls of Sault St. Marie, which, although the distance to be traversed was not great, was considerable of an undertaking.

In 1844 a most unsatisfactory condition of the financial affairs of the territory of Wisconsin, induced Mr. Kneeland to

22

James Kneeland[18].

become a candidate for member of the Territorial Legislature, his object being to secure such legislation as would insure the payment of territorial obligations and build up the public credit.   He was elected easily to the legislative council, and in the sessions of 1844-5 and 1845-6 was one of the acknowledged leaders of that body.   Without delay he framed and introduced a bill providing for a territorial tax levy and, in a slightly modified form, secured its passage.   This enactment fixed the rate of taxation on all the taxable property of the territory at one and one-half mills, and brought in revenue enough to liquidate all outstanding obligations and leave a surplus, which was passed to the credit of the new State government in 1848.   The wisdom of this legislation has since been manifest to all who have given the subject any consideration, but at that time, owing to conflicting systems of local taxation, skillful management and the exercise of much diplomacy were required to bring about the desired result.   Mr. Kneeland not only proved himself an able financier, but an equally able and competent legislator on other subjects, and reference to the legislative journals of 1844-5 and 1845-6 establishes the fact that of the bills which were passed during the session of those years, a larger number were formulated and introduced by him than by any other member; among other notable enactments of which he was the author being that under which the city of Milwaukee received its first charter, and also that under which the public school system of Milwaukee was built up.

The period of his service in the legislature was a critical period in the history of the territory, then just budding into statehood.   Mr. Kneeland was one of the pioneers who realized that certain legislation was of vital importance to the prospective commonwealth, and he set out to secure this legislation.   He became a member of the legislature with well defined purposes in view, and he failed in none of his undertakings.   Some of the controversies of the session were of a heated character, and one in which he engaged led to his being challenged to fight a duel.   He accepted the challenge with the nonchalance of one brought up to believe in "the code duello," and named "pistol with bowie knife attached"

James Kneeland[18].

as the weapon to be used, stipulating, also, that the fight should be to a finish. The harsh terms had the effect of cooling the ardor of his adversary, and a reconciliation was effected which developed later into a warm friendship.

About 1846 Mr. Kneeland, believing that the development of the interior of the territory would be greatly facilitated by the building of a railroad which should connect Lake Michigan with the Mississippi river, began, with others, the agitation of a project to build such railway. When the Milwaukee & Waukesha Railroad Company was organized, and later merged into the Milwaukee & Mississippi Railroad Company, he served as a director and vice-president of this company, and rendered especially valuable services to the enterprise in securing legislation essential to its success. His admirable discretion, keen foresight and *suaviter in modo* enabled him to accomplish what some of his contemporaries and associates despaired of accomplishing, and to him the city of Milwaukee is indebted in large measure for its first railroad. Having become a large owner of real estate, for some years after he retired from merchandising, his time and attention were given mainly to the improvement of his realty holdings and to railway and other public enterprises. The shading of streets and beautifying of the city in other ways also engrossed a share of his attention as early as 1842, and it is not probable that any other citizen of Milwaukee has contributed so much toward making the shaded drives, now regarded as one of its most beautiful and attractive features. Surveying the situation carefully, he early made up his mind that the shipping interests of the city must ultimately seek the Menomonee river for harbor and dock facilities, and for eighteen years he labored to secure legislative authority for the straightening and improvement of this river. His labors were rewarded at last and in pursuance of the plan adopted he entered upon another era of canal building, which involved an immense expenditure of money but brought rich returns in the increased value of abutting property, while this development of the canal and dockage system has been vastly beneficial to the city of Milwaukee.

In 1867-68 he served as tax commissioner of Milwaukee

and in this capacity was called upon to deal with some exceedingly troublesome and vexatious matters of taxation and finance. Owing to certain legislative enactments changing the methods of taxation, controversies had arisen which had blocked the collection of taxes and caused serious embarrassment. The banks of the city, for instance, had not paid taxes for two years, and persistently refused to accommodate themselves to the new order of things. Taking hold of this matter in the systematic way which has been characteristic of all his undertakings, Mr. Kneeland formulated a plan under which there was a readjustment of assessments. The banks consented to pay three years' taxes in one year, and a vastly improved condition of affairs was the immediate result. A bitter warfare was waged against his methods in the start, but persistent effort on his part brought about the desired result and he had the satisfaction, within a few years, of having his course endorsed by an entire community which had been hostile to him in the beginning.

A Democrat of the old school, he has, when he has cared to do so, wielded an important influence in his party, but caring nothing for political preferment he has sought public office only when he felt that certain public interests which he deemed specially inportant might be promoted through his efforts. An Episcopalian in his religious affiliations, he was one of the organizers of St. James' parish, in the summer of 1850, was for many years a vestryman and warden of the parish, and is still an honored member of St. James' Church. He was one of the purchasers of the land on which the present church stands, personally having supervised the building of the beautiful stone edifice, and when it was partially destroyed by fire some years since, the task of rebuilding it mainly devolved upon him.

Mr. Kneeland married Anna Maria Foster, native of Watertown, N. Y., a lady whose charming grace of manner, sympathetic nature, kindly and Christian acts during her long residence in Milwaukee, endeared her to an unusual degree, not only to the domestic circle, but to all those who enjoyed her friendship or acquaintance. Mrs. Kneeland died in 1875, a year or two before the completion of the beautiful home

James Kneeland[18].

which they had planned to erect on the site selected for the purpose many years earlier. In carrying forward a work thus planned Mr. Kneeland found one of the sweetest pleasures of his later life, and few American homes evince a more highly cultivated taste, or more intelligent supervision of its appointments. Some one has aptly observed that "a home is that house which partakes of the individuality of its owner." Viewing it in this light, the residence of Mr. Kneeland is, in the fullest and broadest sense of the term, a home. In all the details of its arrangement and furnishings it evidences careful and intelligent consideration. The spacious grounds by which it is surrounded typify his breadth of view, as their ornamentation typifies his love of the beautiful in nature. Not less charming than the home and its surroundings, is the hospitality of its owner, and some of the notable social events of the city have taken place there, chief among them, perhaps, being a reception tendered to the wife of President Cleveland some years since, which will long be remembered by those who met the "first lady of the land" under those favorable auspices.

To say that Mr. Kneeland has been an eminently successful man in all his undertakings, is easy; to explain the secret of it is not so easy. In viewing his long and eventful career, one finds no record of the failure of an enterprise for the conduct of which he has been personally responsible, and the ease and facility with which he has accomplished results evoke wonder and surprise. A careful analysis of his character, however, furnishes a key to the solution of the problem. Tact, diplomacy and perceptions unusually quick and keen, were among the chief favors which nature bestowed upon him. As he grew to manhood, a rule of his life, of which he was, perhaps, himself unconscious, might have been formulated in these words: "Whatever is worth doing is worth an intelligent thought." And so it came about that he has never done anything haphazard. Everything he has done has been intelligently considered in advance, and quick perceptions have enabled him to see and do the right thing promptly. What has seemed to come to him as fortune's favors, has in reality come to him as the result of deliberate calculations, made with unerring precision sometimes years in advance of their culmin-

James Kneeland[18].

ation.   Acquiring a complete mastery of himself in early life,
his counsels have been his own, and his placid and immobile
face has seldom betrayed the workings of his mind.   Suave in
manner, polished, courteous and genial in his intercourse with
all classes of people, possessing a sort of personal magnetism
which seems to influence even the lower animals and causes
them to do his bidding, he has seemed to encounter but few
of the storms of life, while his career has been prolific of
good results.   Verily, a worthy representative of the original
James Kneeland, "wha hae wi' Wallace bled."

BENJAMIN F. KNEELAND

No. 2000

DESCENDANTS OF PHILA (KNEELAND) WARNER.

(NOS. 1981 TO 1999.)

1981.   (1876.) PHILA KNEELAND[18] (*David*[17], *David*[16], *Isaac*[15], *Benjamin*[14], *Edward*[13], *Edward*[12], *John*[11], *William*[10], *James*[9], *Alexander*[8], *William*[7], *William*[6], *John*[5], *John*[4], *John*[3], *James*[2], *Alexander*[1]). Youngest child of David, Jr., and Statira (Williams) Kneeland, was born Oct. 27, 1810, it is supposed, at Geneseo, N. Y.

Her mother went with her a babe of a few months old to Franklin County, N. Y., to visit a sister. A fever was epidemic in the place, the mother was stricken and died. Phila K. Warner died at Linden, Mich., March 12, 1875. She married Parley Warner (b. Dec. 27, 1807, at Norwich, Hampshire County, Mass.; d. Sept. 6, 1892), in 1830, at Le Roy, N. Y. Parley was nephew of Consider Warner, who m. Olivia, fifth child of David, Jr., and Statira Kneeland. Their wedding tour, the day after, was to their home in Bergen, N. Y., behind an ox team in a drizzling rain storm. In 1837 Mr. Warner bought his farm on which he died in Linden, of the government, at Detroit, and the next spring moved upon it with his wife. They made the journey from Detroit in a wagon, into what was almost a wilderness, as the railroad was not built through to Linden until 1855. Church services were held in their first school house and the congregation rode on horseback to them.

Children of Phila Kneeland[18] and Parley Warner.

Two children were born to them :

1982.   (i.) OLIVIA[19], b. Sept., 1840; lived to be only two days old, and

1983.   (ii.) SILAS KNEELAND WARNER[19], b. March 23, 1846.

1984. (1983). SILAS K. WARNER[19] (*Phila Kneeland*[18], *David*[17], *David*[16], *Isaac*[15], *Benjamin*[14], *Edward*[13], *Edward*[12], *John*[11]—*Alexander*[1]). Only son of Parley and Phila (Kneeland) Warner, b. at Linden, Mich., March 23, 1846; m. first, Fannie M. Clark, Jan. 1, 1868; she d. July 30, of the same year. Married, second, Celia A. Sage, March 8, 1870. To them were born fifteen children, all at Linden, Mich., at the old home.

Children of Silas Kneeland Warner and Celia A. Sage.

1985. (i.) PAUL D. WARNER[20], b. Aug. 12, 1871; d. in Chicago, Feb. 18, 1896.

1986. (ii.) JULIA ANNA WARNER[20], b. Feb. 18, 1873; m. James Jameson, Feb., 1895. They reside in Detroit.

1987. (iii.) FRED WARNER[20], b. March 25, 1874.

1988. (iv.) SAGE K. WARNER[20], b. June 9, 1875.

1989. (v.) MARY ELIZABETH WARNER[20], b. Nov. 9, 1876.

1990. (vi.) ALTHEA GERTRUDE WARNER[20], b. Jan. 2, 1878.

1991. (vii.) JOB H. WARNER[20], b. July 18, 1880; d. Sept. 7, 1880.

1992. (viii.) LEVI P. WARNER[20], b. Sept. 9, 1881; d. Oct. 29, 1881.

1993. (ix.) RUTH EMELINE WARNER[20], b. July 20, 1883.

1994. (x.) RACHEL MARIA WARNER[20], b. July 3, 1884; d. Aug. 10, 1884.

1995. (xi.) KATE C. WARNER[20], b. July 17, 1885.

1996. (xii.) JAMES K. WARNER[20], b. May 14, 1886.

1997. (xiii.) ROSE EVANGELINE WARNER[20], b. April 2, 1887.

1998. (xiv.) ADAH C. WARNER[20], b. March 20, 1888; she d. Sept. 15, 1888.

1999. (xv.) SILAS K. WARNER[20], b. Nov. 9, 1889; d. March 12, 1891.

Silas K. Warner, the father, died Oct. 30, 1889.

Edwin Kneeland.

No. 2010

CHAPTER XXXIII.

DESCENDANTS OF BENJAMIN AND JAMES.

(NOS. 2000 TO 2084.)

2000. (1760.) BENJAMIN KNEELAND[17](*David*[16],*Isaac*[15], *Benjamin*[14], *Edward*[13], *Edward*[12], *John*[11], *William*[10], *James*[9], *Alexander*[8], *William*[7], *William*[6], *John*[5], *John*[4], *John*[3], *James*[2], *Alexander*[1]). Second son of David and Mercy Kneeland, bapt. at East Hampton, Sept. 15, 1782; accompanied the rest of the family to New York State; m. Hannah Barnes, of Geneseo, Livingston County, N. Y., and settled for life on one of those beautiful valley farms. He d. Jan. 10, 1821. They had six children, all born in Geneseo, as follows:

Children of Benjamin and Hannah (Barnes) Kneeland.

2001. (i.) BELA[18], b. Aug. 17, 1810. No further record.

2002. (ii.) EVELINE[18], b. Jan. 17, 1812; married· and located in Dakota, and died there in March, 1894.

2003. (iii.) LORENZO P.[18], b. July 16, 1813; married and settled in Davenport, Iowa. He d. in 1895, leaving two children, who reside there:

2004. (i.) *Mary*[19], m. Giles Guy, of Davenport.

2005. (ii.) *Jane Eveline*[19], a teacher.

2006. (iv.) MATILDA[18], b. May 10, 1816; married and lives in California.

2007. (v.) BENJAMIN F.[18], b. Dec. 31, 1817 (of whom hereafter 2009).

2008. (vi.) PHILO NELSON[18], b. Aug. 5, 1819 (of whom hereafter, 2050).

Benjamin F. Kneeland[18].

2009.   (2007.) BENJAMIN F. KNEELAND[18] (*Benjamin[17], David[16], Isaac[15], Benjamin[14], Edward[13], Edward[12], John[11]—Alexander[1]*). Farmer; eldest son of Benjamin Kneeland, b. at Geneseo, Livingston County, N. Y., Dec. 31, 1817; he m. Oct. 8, 1840, at Geneseo, Catharine Weller.

In 1843 he located in Bengal, Mich., bought a farm of 400 acres and remained on it for forty years and until he had enough cash in bank to retire upon. He still owns the farm, but since 1883 has lived with his wife at St. Johns, Mich. In his letter, written in February, 1896, to Chas. L. Kneeland, of Lansing, Mich., he says: "I think the Kneeland tribe are thoroughbreds. There is a strong resemblance in all I ever knew of the name, both in look and disposition—all proud and haughty. The majority of my acquaintances of that name are farmers. They are thrifty, have plenty of property for all the necessaries and some of the luxuries of life. They are honest. I never knew of one being in jail." He had three sons and three daughters.

Children of Benjamin and Catharine (Weller) Kneeland.

2010.   (i.) EDWIN[19], b. Dec. 29, 1844; m. first, Oct., 1872, to Sarah Gannon; second, Nov., 1895, to Frances Gaskel. No children.

2011.   (ii.) MELISSA[19], b. June 10, 1846; m. June 10, 1869, to Joel Stanton Wolcott, a retired farmer of St. Johns, Mich. Children:

2012.   (i.) *Archie Paul Wolcott[20]*, b. Aug. 31, 1870; m. Oct. 10, 1892, to Cora May Putnam. He is a law student at St. Johns, Mich.

2013.   (ii.) *Stella May Wolcott[20]*, b. Nov. 4, 1873. She is a teacher in the High School at St. Johns.

2014.   (iii.) *Lewis Gould Wolcott[20]*, b. July 31, 1875; he was a druggist; d. Jan. 18, 1897.

2015.   (iv.) *Helen Louise[20]*, b. Aug. 4, 1890.

2016.   (iii.) LINDA[19], b. Dec. 19, 1851; m. Murrett Frink, Dec. 16, 1875. Children:

2017.   (i.) *Elmo Frink[20]*, b. Dec. 19, 1882; now at High School.

Horace Barnes Kneeland

No. 2019

Philo Nelson Kneeland[18].

2018.   (ii.) *Edna Frink[20]*, b. Dec. 10, 1886; now at Adrian College.

2019.   (iv.) HORACE ·BARNES[19], b. Oct. 4, 1853; m. Amelia Fink, April 5, 1876. He is a farmer residing near St. Johns. Children:

2020.   (i.) *Dow[20]*, b. Feb. 21, 1878. He is attending the High School at St. Johns.

2021.   (ii.) *Katie Whitlock[20]*, adopted (see No. 2026).

2022.   (v.) DELLA[19], b. Jan. 22, 1856; m. Dec., 1879, to James Whitlock. Their children are :

2023.   (i.) *Althea Whitlock[20]*, b. Sept. 29, 1880.

2024.   (ii.) *Bert Whitlock[20]*, b. Jan. 10, 1884.

2025.   (iii.) *Earl Whitlock[20]*, b. July 14, 1886.

2026.   (iv.) *Katie (Whitlock) Kneeland[20]*, b. Jan. 12, 1889; adopted by H. B. Kneeland (see No. 2021).

2027.   (vi.) BENJAMIN[19], b. Jan. 15, 1868; d. Feb., 1877.

This entire family lives in or near St. Johns, Mich., except Edna Frink, who is in college at Adrian, and Stella May Wolcott, who is teaching at Morenci, Mich. At least that is the way of it at this writing—April, 1897. When this is read fifty years from now, the fact that grandfather "*is* at High School," etc., will be amusing literature. I am indebted to Mrs. Wolcott for this sketch of the descendants of Benjamin F. Kneeland. They insist on spelling it "Benjiman." A man should have the pleasure of spelling his name as he sees fit, but I put it down in the good old orthodox fashion. When his grandson, Archie, is a Judge, I will argue the matter out before him.

2050.   (2008.) PHILO NELSON KNEELAND[18] (*Benjamin[17], David[16], Isaac[15], Benjamin[14], Edward[13], Edward[12], John[11]—Alexander[1]*). Hardware merchant, doing business at Detroit, Mich.; b. at Geneseo, N. Y., Aug. 5, 1819; youngest child of Benjamin and Hannah (Barnes) Kneeland[17]; m. Anna Wellwood, Oct. 9, 1851.

Children of Philo Nelson and Anna (Wellwood) Kneeland.

2051.   (i.) ANNA MATILDA[19], b. July 7, 1853; unmarried; lives with her father, at Detroit.

2052. (ii.) WILLIAM PHILO[19], b. Feb. 18, 1855 ; m. Elizabeth Schafer, and resides at Kansas City, Mo. They have two children :

2053.   (i.) *Anna M.*[20], b. at Kansas City.

2054.   (ii.) *Ida Jane*[20], b. at Kansas City.

2055. (iii.) IDA JANE[19], b. March 18, 1858; unmarried; resides with her father, at Detroit.

2056. (1761.) JAMES KNEELAND[17] (*David*[16], *Isaac*[15], *Benjamin*[14], *Edward*[13], *Edward*[12], *John*[11]—*Alexander*[1]). Son of David Kneeland, Sr., b. at East Hampton, Conn.; bapt. April 17, 1785 ; m. Hannah C. Austin, Nov. 13, 1817, at Geneseo, N. Y.

She was a descendant of Gov. Catlin, of Connecticut. They resided at Hartland, Niagara County, N. Y., where he died Oct. 22, 1851, and she died in 1855. He was a prominent and influential citizen, and held among other positions the office of Sheriff of Niagara County.

Children of James and Hannah C. (Austin) Kneeland.

2057. (i.) MARY ANN[18], b. at Geneseo, Sept. 16, 1818; m. Philander W. Howe, Nov. 8, 1839, and d. May 1, 1845. They had one son :

2058.   *Henry W. Howe*[19], b. April 20, 1845, at Caryville, N. Y. He resides in Cedar Rapids, Iowa.

2059. (ii.) EDWIN[18], b. at Geneseo, Aug. 21, 1820 ; m. Fidelia Leland, Aug. 5, 1847, and d. Sept. 25, 1877. They had two children :

2060.   (i.) *Gertrude*[19], b. Sept., 1850; d. Aug., 1873.

2061.   (ii.) *Lorenzo Dow*[19], b. July 17, 1857 (of whom hereafter, 2084).

2062. (iii.) JAMES H.[18], b. Sept. 28, 1822 ; d. Sept. 12, 1837, Elba, Genesee County, N. Y.

2063. (iv.) JOSEPH A.[18], b. at Geneseo, April 22, 1825 ; m. Susan E. Pratt, Oct. 12, 1847 ; d. at Hartland, N.Y., July 15, 1850. They had one son :

2064.   *Austin Lay Kneeland*[19], b. in Hartland, N. Y., Oct. 11, 1848. He is unmarried and lives at Sabitha, Kansas.

DOW KNEELAND

No. 2020

2065.   (v.) CLARISSA[18], b. April 5, 1828, at Geneseo, N. Y.;
m. Darwin Edmunds, Dec. 22, 1847. He was b. at
Hartland, Nov. 20, 1826; d. at Prescott, Iowa, Jan.,
1897. They had the following children:

2066.   (i.) *Florence M. Edmunds*[19], b. at Hartland, N. Y.,
Oct. 28, 1848; m. James A. Helin, Jan. 29,
1873; residence, in Missouri.

2067.   (ii.) *James R. Edmunds*[19], b. May 30, 1850; m.
Jane E. Edmunson, Sept. 22, 1874. Resides
in Washington.

2068.   (iii.) *Clara Edith Edmunds*[19], b. May 26, 1852; m.
C. S. Crowre, Nov. 19, 1873. Resides in Pres-
cott, Iowa.

2069.   (iv.) *Abbie E. ¦Edmunds*[19], b. Dec. 14, 1859; m.
J. W. Foy, Feb. 23, 1879. Resides in Prescott.

2070.   (v.) *Mary Elma Edmunds*[19], b. Dec. 17, 1867; d.
July 4, 1881.

2071.   (vi.) JOHN N. KNEELAND[18], b. at Avon, N. Y., Aug.
10, 1832; m. at Hartland, N. Y., E. Amanda Shaw,
Sept. 14, 1852; d. Aug. 31, 1893. In 1864 he
moved from Hartland, N. Y., to Burr Oak, Mich.,
and was engaged in the hardware business at that
place until 1878. In 1884-5 he was in charge of
an exhibition at New Orleans, and also at the
World's Fair, in Chicago, in 1893. His widow still
resides at Burr Oak. They had the following
children:

2072.   (i.) *Albert E.*[19], b. Aug. 11, 1853; m. Frankie
Mills, Nov. 2, 1876; she d. in 1886. They had
one daughter:

2073.   Ethel M.[20], b. Aug. 19, 1878, at Alma, Kas.

2074.   (ii.) *Minnie*[19], b. July 5, 1855; d. Sept. 8, 1882.

2075.   (iii.) *Alice*[19], b. Nov. 3, 1857; m. Sept. 18, 1878,
to W. H. Wallace. Residence, Topeka, Kas.
Their children are:

2076.   (i.) Ina Ruth Wallace[20], b. at Burr Oak, Feb.
7, 1880.

2077.   (ii.) Frank Wilson Wallace[20], b. Sept. 4, 1882.

2078.   (iii.) Minnie Electa Wallace[20], b. Oct. 14,
1885, at Eskridge, Kansas.

Lorenzo Dow Kneeland[19].

2079.   (iv.) Elinor Alice Wallace[20], b. April 21, 1892, at Topeka, Kansas.

2080.   (iv.) *Frank Wilson[19]*, b. Feb. 9, 1860; m. March 18, 1887, in Council Grove, Morris County, Kansas, to Maggie J. Hunter. Child:

2081.   Frank Wilson[20], b. Dec. 21, 1890. They reside in Admire, Kansas, where he is in the hardware business.

2082.   (v.) *Electa[19]*, b. March 29, 1863; m. May 31, 1887, to Chas. Caldwell. They reside at Mason, Mich.

2083.   (vi.) *Albertus[19]*, b. April 12, 1865; unmarried. Resides at Jackson, Mich.

2084.   (2061.) LORENZO DOW KNEELAND[19] (*Edwin[18], James[17], David[16], Isaac[15], Benjamin[14], Edward[13], Edward[12], John[11], William[10], James[9], Alexander[8], William[7], William[6], John[5], John[4], John[3], James[2], Alexander[1]*). Only son of Edwin and Fidelia (Leland) Kneeland, b. July 17, 1857.

His early boyhood was spent amid usual surroundings, near Middleport, Niagara County, New York. The Erie canal ran alongside of the homestead, and possibly the subsequent taste for transportation and railways was begun at that time. One of the first practical results was a sequestration of a sufficient amount of fine whitewood lumber from the home stock, highly prized by the senior, with other material, to construct a flatboat to sail upon the canal. The boat was built in very good form, and no little skill and finish, the Kneelands being "handy" with tools. It is needless to add that our subject was not only a proud boy of twelve, but a very happy one for the moment. A few days thereafter the senior discovered the loss of the whitewood, nails, etc., and Lorenzo was given an opportunity to study other uses, rather than for boats, to which whitewood could be adapted. To accentuate the bitterness of the situation, the sun's rays had, in a few days, drawn the boat almost out of the canal, where it was tethered—in fact the shortness of the rope was said to have been the only thing restraining the boat from traveling overland into the next county.

Phil. H. Kneeland

No. 2050

Lorenzo Dow Kneeland[19].

Young Kneeland left his home at fourteen years of age, going to Chicago alone, and entered the employ of one of the large railways operating west of that city; later on, holding positions of responsibility, and learning the best of all lessons, careful business habits. In later years, investments and actual personal experience in mining and real estate operations, resulted in generous financial returns. One of the most important suburbs of Chicago owes its foundation and successful development to his management. A large tract of land, consisting of nearly a thousand acres, situated near Pullman, was purchased by Mr. Kneeland and associates, some of whom were leading business men of Chicago, Boston and other New England cities. The territory was improved with all city conveniences. Large factories were located and put in operation, many fine houses sprung up almost magically, churches, schools, newspapers, fire and police departments followed closely, until that which in the beginning of 1892 was but a tract of farm land, is at the close of 1896 a flourishing town of six thousand people, and may be said to have only begun its career. The tract has recently been annexed to, and is now an important part of the great city of Chicago.

It is an interesting study of what brains, courage and capital so frequently accomplish in our splendid civilization. Something like five millions of dollars in capital was employed, but who shall adequately measure the *brains and courage* part? Great achievements have an air of *easy to accomplish* to the multitude, but only they who have had *to do* know of the fiery furnaces. It is probably a truism that most of the enterprises of the centuries would have been abandoned, ere they were begun, could their projectors have had conception of the difficulties attendant. But "to him that *hath* shall be given, and from him that hath not shall be taken away," and again we all remember what befell the foolish servant who hid the talent in a napkin.

Mr. Kneeland became an active member of the Board of Trade and many of the leading clubs, the Union League being the most prominent. In politics he was ever an ardent Republican. Twice married, first to the younger daughter of Judge Calvin DeWolf, one of the pioneers of Chicago and

Lorenzo Dow Kneeland[19].

first of the abolitionists who, on more than one occasion, suffered in behalf of the cause. Mrs. Kneeland was much beloved by all who knew her, but lived only a little over four years after marriage, dying at the birth of a daughter, which followed its mother after a short life of six months' duration. Six years later Mr. Kneeland married the only daughter of Joseph T. Moulton, of Chicago, one of the most celebrated grain elevator designers and builders of his time. The Moultons are of old colonial stock and occupied important positions in New Hampshire in those and succeeding times.

The mother of Lorenzo D. was of the Leland family, now one of the most celebrated families in our country, Sir Thomas Leland having settled in Massachusetts soon after the arrival of the Mayflower. The paternal grandmother of Mr. Kneeland was Hannah Austin, a direct descendant of Gov. Catlin, of Connecticut, and thus was united some of the best blood of New England. It is known that peculiarly unfortunate and unhappy conditions attended the early boyhood of Lorenzo, surrounded by which many would have succumbed, but the blood of hardy ancestors brought with it some valuable characteristics, and those who care to look into the life of this man may find ample examples of what a boy with the "right sort of stuff" in him can make of himself. The Kneelands reside in Chicago, winters, but usually spend the summers at their country seat, "The Oaks," on the Rock river, Ogle County, Ills. The natural scenery at this point is said to be the most beautiful in the State. Many artists seek this locality. The region is also noted for its legendary lore. Margaret Fuller, some years prior to her death, spent a season along the Rock river in this vicinity, and some of her most charming sketches were written at that time, and relate to local features, one of the principal islands in the river having been named Margaret Fuller Island.

No. 2084

PART X.

LOCAL BRANCHES OF THAT ILK.

(NOS. 2087 TO 2141.)

The earliest known member of the clan that settled in New York City was Seth Rowley Kneeland, a veteran of the War of the Revolution and a lineal descendant of Dr. Samuel Fuller and Edward Fuller, of the Mayflower. His mother, Sarah Rowley, was a younger sister of Content Rowley, the wife of Isaac Kneeland. Their lineage from the Mayflower has been fully considered elsewhere (see Chap. XIII.). Seth R. Kneeland was joined in New York a few years later by his nephew, Henry Kneeland, the eldest son of his brother, Ebenezer. Seth's eldest son was named Henry Ebenezer for this father and nephew. The families drifted apart later, insomuch that none of the present generation knew of the relationship existing between them. It was through Mrs. Mitchill, the youngest daughter of Seth, that I first learned that Henry was his nephew. My first impression was that the latter was identical with the grandson of Samuel Kneeland, who bore the same name. I treat in this chapter only the descendants of Seth Kneeland. The descendants of Henry, I reserve for a separate chapter (see Chap. XLI.).

2087. (718.) LIEUT. SETH ROWLEY KNEELAND[16] (*Ebenezer*[15], *Benjamin*[14], *Edward*[13], *Edward*[12], *John*[11], *William*[10], *James*[9], *Alexander*[8], *William*[7], *William*[6], *John*[5], *John*[4], *John*[3], *James*[2], *Alexander*[1]). Youngest child of Ebenezer and Sarah (Rowley) Kneeland, b. at Hebron, Conn., April 29, 1757.

He married Eunice Bacon, of Berlin, Conn., and settled at East Hartford, Conn., and enlisted from there April 22,

D. Austin Taylor[18].

1777, "for the war," in Capt. Wells' Company, Connecticut Line. Was promoted to Sergeant and was with Wolcott's Regiment at the siege of Boston, and promoted Lieutenant for bravery in battle on that occasion. After the close of the war he settled in New York City, where he resided until his death, in 1827. I have no information as to the exact time of his arrival in New York, but we know that it was prior to 1789, for Valentine's Manual of the Common Council of New York for 1854, at p. 152, has a facsimile of his membership certificate for that year in the "Volunteer Aid" Fire Company. We also find in the Manual for 1866, at p. 792, a statement that in 1793 he was assistant foreman of Engine No. 2. He purchased a house in New York in 1792 and his name appears in the first directory, issued in 1793, together with that of Henry Kneeland. In the directory he was designated as "house carpenter" prior to 1800. From that time until 1812 he is put down as "inspector of lumber." The first recorded deed from him is dated May 12, 1794. It covered property on Cherry street purchased January 25, 1792. The grantors are "Seth Rowlee Kneeland and Eunice his wife," this being the first reference to her in the New York records. She survived her husband for several years. His will was filed in 1828. It specially mentions his daughter Ann and his grandson Seth.

Children of Seth Rowley and Eunice (Bacon) Kneeland.

2088. (i.) HENRY EBENEZER[17]. He died without issue.
2089. (ii.) SUSAN DODGE[17], m. Gad Taylor. They had six children, as follows:
2090.   (i.) *Mary DeForest Taylor*[18], m. Rev. D. Clark, Rector of Christ Church, Waterbury. She is now dead.
2091.   (ii.) *George Frederick Taylor*[18], m. Mary Hinchman, and has since died.
2092.   (iii.) *Susan Emily Taylor*[18], died unmarried.
2093.   (iv.) *Henry Taylor*[18].
2094.   (v.) *D. Austin Taylor*[18]. He married and died. No further record.

SETH R. KNEELAND

No. 287

Reproduction of a medallion in the possession of his daughter, Mrs. Mitchill.

2095.   (vi.) *Louisa Taylor*[18], died unmarried.
2096.   (iii.) EFFIE[17] (first), d. in infancy.
2097.   (iv.) EFFIE[17] (second), d. in infancy.
2098.   (v.) LAWRENCE[17], b. Dec. 7, 1792 (of whom hereafter, 2126).
2099.   (vi.) MARIA[17], m. Grover C. Furman. They had one child :
2100.   *Aldine Furman*[18], who m. W. G. Anderson.
2101.   (vii.) ANN ELIZA[17] (first), d. in infancy.
2102.   (viii.) ANN ELIZA[17] (second), m. Dec. 7; 1830, to Samuel L. Mitchill, nephew, namesake and heir of the celebrated Samuel Latham Mitchill, who was one of the founders of the New York Hospital and the Academy of Sciences. She resides in the city of New York and I hold myself indebted to her and to her daughter, Anna Maria Mitchill, for genealogical data relating to this branch of the family. She and all her descendants are entitled to membership in the Mayflower Society, through her grandmother, Sarah (Rowley) Kneeland, who was a lineal descendant of Samuel and Edward Fuller, of the Mayflower. They are also eligible to the Society of Colonial Dames through the same person and also through their ancestor, Captain and Surgeon-General Matthew Fuller, a distinguished physician who was an officer in the Colonial army for thirty years ending with King Philip's War. They are also entitled to membership in the Sons and Daughters of the American Revolution, through Lieut. Seth Rowley Kneeland. They had eleven children as follows :
2103.   (i.) *Adeline Mitchill*[18], m. to Edwin L. Post. They had the following children :
2104.   (i.) S. L. M. Post[19], m. Mary Allen.
2105.   (ii) E. T. Post[19], m. Evelyn Baker.
2106.   (iii.) Alice Adeline Post[19], m. Wm. B. Scott.
2107.   (iv.) Sarah R. Post[19], m. George H. Allen.
2108.   (ii.) *Samuel Latham Mitchill, Jr.*[18], m. Helen Smith, deceased.

Furman Lawrence Kneeland [18].

2109. (iii.) *Cornelius Mitchill* [18], m. Helen E. Reed. Children:

2110. (i.) Neille Reed [19], m. Agnes Lewis.

2111. (ii.) Helen Reed [19], m. Frank Jackson, M.D.

2112. (iii.) Edith Reed [19], m. Henry Brellwitz.

2113. (iv.) *Annie Maria Mitchill* [18], unmarried.

2114. (v.) *Mary Louise Mitchill* [18], m. to John Van Dusen Reed. Children:

2115. (i.) Marie L. Reed [19], deceased.

2116. (ii.) Eleanor Florence Reed [19].

2117. (iii.) Gertrude Georgeana Reed [19].

2118. (vi.) *Margaret Eliza Mitchill* [18], unmarried.

2119. (vii.) *Almira Mitchill* [18], m. Edwin C. Sturges. Children:

2120. (i.) Anne Kneeland Sturges [19].

2121. (ii.) Theodore Sturges [19].

2122. (iii.) Edwin C. Sturges, Jr [19].

2123. (viii.) *Helene Mitchill* [18], d. in infancy.

2124. (ix.) *Edwin Burr Mitchill* [18], d. young.

2125. (x.) *Bleecker Neilson* [18], m. to Laura Van Lieun. They have no issue.

2125A. (xi.) *George Mitchill* [18], d. in infancy.

2126. (2098.) LAWRENCE KNEELAND [17] (*Seth Rowley* [16], *Ebenezer* [15], *Benjamin* [14], *Edward* [13], *Edward* [12], *John* [11]—*Alexander* [1]). Second son of Seth Rowley and Eunice (Bacon) Kneeland, b. in the city of New York, Dec. 7, 1792; m. Martha Clayton Chevers, Sept. 10, 1817; d. Aug. 3, 1824.

Children of Lawrence and Martha (Chevers) Kneeland.

2127. (i.) SETH ROWLEY [18], b. at New York City, Oct. 19, 1818. He was unmarried and died in California.

2128. (ii.) WILLIAM CHEVERS [18], b. at New York City, Aug. 3, 1820; m. Mary Hinman; d. at New York, in November, 1877.

2129. (iii.) FURMAN LAWRENCE [18], b. at New York City, Dec. 12, 1823; m. Cornelia A. Van Pelt, Oct. 3,

Marjorie Dodd[20].

1850. He resided in Brooklyn in the later years of his life and died there, May 30, 1844. Children:

2130.   (i.) *Cornelia*[19], b. at New York City, Sept. 2. 1856. She resides in Brooklyn, and is unmarried.

2131.   (ii.) *Lawrence*[19], b. at New York City, Sept 3, 1858; m. Louisa A. Winzel, April 28, 1886. He is a member of the legal profession, high in esteem personally and professionally and a member of the well-known firm of Black & Kneeland, of 44 Pine street, New York. They reside in Brooklyn and have the following children

2132.   (i.) Eleanor[20], b. at Brooklyn, N. Y., Feb. 22, 1887.

2133.   (ii.) Marjorie[20], b. at Brooklyn, July 7, 1888.
2134.   (iii.) Hildegarde[20], b. at Brooklyn, July 10, 1889.
2135.   (iv.) Natalie[20], b. at Brooklyn, May 7, 1892.

2136.   (iii.) *Clayton*[19], b. at New York, March 8, 1860; m. Fannie V. Schuff, March 18, 1890. Child:

2137.   Elmer Clayton[20], b. at Brooklyn, Feb. 20, 1891; d. Dec. 25, 1895. This was the last male heir in the fourth generation of Seth R. Kneeland.

2138.   (iv.) *Furman Lawrence*[19], b. at Brooklyn, Oct. 6, 1866; m. Annie Adele Otis, April 25, 1893. Child:

2139.   Helen[20], b. at Brooklyn, Feb. 18, 1894.

2140.   (v.) *Agnes*[19], b. in Brooklyn, Oct. 7, 1867; m. Ernst H. Dodd, Feb. 4, 1890. Child:

2141.   Marjorie Dodd[20], b. July 27, 1891.

CHAPTER XXXV.

THE NORTHAMPTON FAMILY.

(NOS. 2142 TO 2247.)

This branch of the Kneeland family receives its name and localization from the fact that one of its most prominent members, Fred. N. Kneeland, the Cashier of the First National Bank of Northampton, resides in that beautiful New England city of homes. If these chapters were separately dedicated, there would come in my mind a contest between him and his sister Hattie as to the place of honor. I have received much aid and sympathy from each of them.

2142.   (688.) EDWARD KNEELAND[15], (*Benjamin*[14], *Edward*[13], *Edward*[12], *John*[11], *William*[10], *James*[9], *Alexander*[8], *William*[7], *William*[6], *John*[5], *John*[4], *John*[3], *James*[2], *Alexander*[1]).   Youngest son of Benjamin Kneeland[14], b. Feb. 23, 1724, after his father had ceased his wanderings and settled finally at Colchester, Conn.

Edward married Deborah Martin and continued to reside in Colchester until about 1769, when he took up a tract of land in Royalton, Vt., which he cleared and built thereon a substantial house for the bride of his eldest son, Joseph, who was married in 1778. There was destined to be, however, a terrible awakening from the dream of happiness in that household. Two years after the marriage came the " Royalton Massacre." Edward, then broken down by sickness and hard work, aged before his time, and his two sons, Joseph and Edward, Jr., the latter a youth of thirteen, were captured.

Hall, in his History of Eastern Vermont, referring to the

massacre, says (p. 385): "Advancing silently and with great caution, the Indians next entered the dwelling of Mr. Joseph Kneeland which was about a half a mile distant from Havens. Here they made prisoners of Kneeland and his aged father, also of Simeon Belknap, Giles Gibbs and Jonathan Brown." Again (at p. 390), the same author, speaking of the Indian retreat, says: "Taking one of the prisoners named Kneeland, an aged man, they sent him to the Americans with the information that they would put all the captives to death should an attack be made. To Giles Gibbs and Joseph Kneeland the rage of the savages had already proved fatal. The former, expecting that his friends would relieve him and his companions, had refused to march. He was afterwards found with a tomahawk buried deep in his skull. The latter was killed and scalped to avenge the death of the Indian who had been shot by the Americans. As soon as the old man Kneeland had been sent to the camp of the pursuers, the Indians resumed their flight with the utmost expedition." Edward, Jr., was never re-captured. He was adopted by a chief and lived with him for eight years, following them in their wanderings through Vermont and Canada, and at one time tramped all the way from the mouth to the source of the Connecticut. He became expert in woodcraft and in the use of the rude weapons of the Indian. After the death of the chief, he was sold, in Canada, to a Frenchman and permitted by him to return to his old home, where he married and became the head of a numerous family.

Children of Edward and Deborah (Martin) Kneeland.

2143. (i.) DEBORAH[16], b. at Colchester, Conn., Aug. 10, 1757.
2144. (ii.) JOSEPH[16], b. at Colchester, Conn., May 15, 1759; m. at Royalton, Vt., in 1778, and had one child:
2145. *Joseph[17]*.
The father was killed by the Indians at the Royalton massacre, in 1780.
2146. (iii.) LUCINDA[16], b. at Colchester, Oct. 17, 1766.
2147. (iv.) EDWARD[16], b. at Colchester, March 19, 1767 (of whom hereafter, 2148).

2148. (2147.) EDWARD KNEELAND[16](*Edward*[15], *Benjamin*[14], *Edward*[13], *Edward*[12], *John*[11]—*Alexander*[1]).
We have given a history of his early life in connection with that of his father, Edward. On his return from captivity he married Elizabeth Peck, of Rehoboth, Mass. He settled in Hadley and became the father of a little brood of twelve children. He died in 1829, at the age of 66.

Children of Edward and Elizabeth (Peck) Kneeland.

2149. (i.) JOSEPH[17] (of whom hereafter, 2161).

2150. (ii.) SAMUEL[17], m. and settled at Lockport, N. Y., with his family.

2151. (iii.) EDWARD[17], died in infancy.

2152. (iv.) EDWARD[17], b. March 24, 1807 (of whom hereafter, 2224).

2153. (v.) HARNEY[17], died young.

2154. (vi.) HANNAH[17], m. Nathaniel Porter. No children.

2155. (vii.) BETSEY[17], m. first, Wm. Lebeveau; second, Caleb Wright.

2156. (viii.) LUCINDA[17], m. Wm. W. Bliss. No children.

2157. (ix.) LYDIA[17], m. Walter Day. No children.

2158. (x.) ELECTA[17], m. Theodore Bellows. No children.

2159. (xi.) EMILY[17], m. Ebenezer Nutting (of whom hereafter 2236).

2160. (xii.) CLARISSA[17], m. Nathaniel Porter after her sister Hannah died.

2161. (2149.) JOSEPH KNEELAND[17] (*Edward*[16], *Edward*[15], *Benjamin*[14], *Edward*[13], *Edward*[12], *John*[11] —*Alexander*[1]). Eldest son of Edward Kneeland, of Royalton fame.
He married Lydia Champion (see History of Champion Family) and settled at West Springfield, Mass. His wife died about 1830 and he married her sister, Lora Champion.

Children of Joseph Kneeland, by Lydia Champion.

2162. (i.) JOSEPH CHAMPION[18], b. Jan. 19, 1816 (of whom hereafter, 2183).

Josephine Kneeland[18].

2163. (ii.) HARVEY LYMAN[18], b. Jan. 18, 1818 (of whom hereafter, 2189).

2164. (iii.) ISAAC NEWTON[18], b. April 1, 1820 (of whom hereafter, 2198).

2165. (iv.) LYDIA AMORETTE[18], b. March 26, 1822 (of whom hereafter, 2216).

2166. (v.) BENJAMIN FRANKLIN[18], b. March 8, 1825; m. first, Lorinda Allen, of Holyoke, Mass.; no children. Married, second, Cordelia Cort, of Huntington, Mass. Children:

2167.   (i.) *Emma*[19], b. April 24, 1854; m. Irving Graus, of Northampton. Two children:

2168.   (i.) Bertha Graus[20].

2169.   (ii.) Robert Graus[20].

2170.   (ii.) *Hattie*[19], b. April 24, 1854; m. Lewis Cowles, of Amherst. They had one child:

2170A.   Mabel Cowles[20].

2171. (vi.) LAURIETTE[18], b. in 1827; d. same year.

2172. (vii.) LAURIETTE[18], b. Aug. 12, 1829; m. Dwight Russell, of Amherst, Mass. Children:

2173.   (i.) *Edward Champion*[19], b. April 18, 1851; d. Jan., 1893, unmarried.

2174.   (ii.) *Frederick Lyman*[19], b. Feb. 22, 1853.

2175.   (iii.) *Clarence Kneeland*[19], b. June 1, 1856.

2176.   (iv.) *Lilla Champion*[19], b. April 22, 1858.

2177.   (v.) *Jennie Lauriette*[19], b. Dec. 23, 1860.

2178.   (vi.) *Martin Dwight*[19], b. Jan. 10, 1863.

2179.   (vii.) *George H.*[19], b. Oct. 15, 1865.

2180.   (viii.) *Ida Josephine*[19], b. March 4, 1868.

2181.   (ix.) *Robert Strong*[19], b. Nov. 28, 1872.

By Lora Champion.

2182. (viii.) JOSEPHINE[18], b. July 25, 1833; m. Moses Judson Stone, in 1820. He d. June 1, 1879. His widow resides in Brooklyn.

Harvey Lyman Kneeland[18].

2183.   (2162.) JOSEPH CHAMPION KNEELAND[18] (*Jo-
          seph*[17], *Edward*[16], *Edward*[15], *Benjamin*[14], *Ed-
          ward*[13], *Edward*[12], *John*[11]—*Alexander*[1]).   Eldest
          son of Joseph Kneeland[17] and grandson of Ed-
          ward[16], of Royalton fame.

He resided at Northampton, Mass., married Harriet
Strong, daughter of Seth Strong, of Northampton, and had
five children, two of whom are living.   He was killed August
21, 1895, on the tracks of the Boston & Maine Railroad, at the
Holyoke street crossing, in Northampton.   He was called a
"character," and that he was, though not in the commonplace
sense.   He was a character among characters and a really
wonderful genius for invention, which brought him fame and
substance.   Several of these inventions and improvements
relating to printing and paper making machinery have proved
practical and almost invaluable.   He was self educated and had
a knowledge of the world and men which many of the college
educated would envy.   He had a wide acquaintance with
noted men, his business taking him often to Washington and
the large cities.   He was a man of perception and taste, a
great admirer of Robert Burns, and could quote largely from
that author.

Children of Joseph C. and Harriet (Strong) Kneeland.

2184.   (i.) EDWARD[19], b. Oct. 20, 1839; m. Ellen M. Puslin,
          of Malone, N. Y., Aug. 26, 1862.   Have one child:
2184A.   *Alice Winifred*[20], b. July 9, 1866.
2185.   (ii.) HENRY[19], b. July 18, 1841; d. Dec., 1854.
2186.   (iii.) ELLEN[19], b. Dec. 22, 1844; unmarried.
2187.   (iv.) GEORGE[19], b. March, 1848; d. June, 1855.
2188.   (v.) JOSEPH[19], b. July, 1853; d. July, 1854.

2189.   (2163.) HARVEY LYMAN KNEELAND[18] (*Jo-
          seph*[17], *Edward*[16], *Edward*[15], *Benjamin*[14], *Ed-
          ward*[13], *Edward*[12], *John*[11]—*Alexander*[1]).   Born
          at Springfield, Mass., Jan. 18, 1818; m. first, Jane
          Marshall, of Brookfield, Mass., by whom he had
          two children.   He d. April 24, 1878.   His widow,
          Rebecca T. Kneeland is now living at Springland,
          Long Island.

HARVEY LYMAN KNEELAND
No. 2189

WILLIAM L. KNEELAND
No. 2193

ELWOOD V. W. KNEELAND
No. 2194

Children of Harvey Lyman and Jane (Marshall) Kneeland.

2190. (i.) JENNIE EMMA[19], b. Jan. 1, 1845, at Parkman, Ohio, m. John Thos. Dunn, May 22, 1863. Children:

2191.   (i.) *Edward Marshall Dunn[20]*, b. Sept. 1, 1864; drowned while skating, Dec. 2, 1876.

2192.   (ii.) *Edwin Saxon Dunn[20]*, b. Aug. 17, 1866; d. Jan. 15, 1895.

2193. (ii.) WILLIAM LEARNED[19], b. Oct. 20, 1852, at Albany, N. Y.; m. Sarah Hewlett Van Wyck, June 16, 1879. Children:

2194.   (i.) *Elwood Van Wyck[20]*, b. Jan. 2, 1883.

2195.   (ii.) *Florence Adele[20]*, b. July 4, 1889.
    Wm. L. is now in business in New York and resides in Brooklyn.

Harvey Lyman married, second, Rebecca Tice, of Brooklyn, N. Y., June 3, 1868, by whom he had:

2196. (iii.) HARVEY TICE[19], b. Sept. 25, 1869; m. Emillie B. La Moree, Nov. 22, 1893. Resides on Long Island. They have one child:

2197.   *Harvey Lyman[20]*, b. Oct. 13, 1894.

2198. (2164.) ISAAC NEWTON KNEELAND[18](*Joseph[17]*, *Edward[16]*, *Edward[15]*, *Benjamin[14]*, *Edward[13]*, *Edward[12]*, *John[11]—Alexander[1]*). Third son of Joseph and Lydia (Champion) Kneeland; m. in 1841 to Frances M. Strong, a sister of his brother Joseph's wife. He died in 1860. Mrs. Kneeland resides with her son, Frederick Newton Kneeland, at Northampton, Mass. They had seven children, as follows:

Children of Isaac Newton and Frances (Strong) Kneeland.

2199. (i.) MARY LOUISE[19], b. Sept. 25, 1842; m. Sept. 25, 1865, George M. Harlow, of Northampton. They had six children, as follows:

2200.   (i.) *Sadie Gertrude Harlow[20]*, b. March 9, 1867; m. Charles Warren, March 9, 1886.

2201.   (ii.) *George Frederic Harlow[20]*, b. Sept. 7, 1872.

2202.   (iii.) *Arthur Bradford Harlow[20]*, b. March 29, 1875.

Frederick Newton Kneeland[19].

2203.   (iv.) *Annie Mabel Harlow[20]*, b. Aug. 13, 1878.
2204.   (v.) *Grace Evelyn Harlow[20]*, b. Dec. 22, 1880.
2205.   (vi.) *Ralph Harlow[20]*, b. May 21, 1884.
2206.   (ii.) EMILY JANE[19], b. July 31, 1845 ; d. July 23, 1847.
2207.   (iii.) CHARLES STRONG[19], b. Nov. 18, 1847; d. July 23, 1849.
2208.   (iv.) FREDERICK NEWTON[19], b. Sept. 8, 1850; m. Dec. 9, 1879 (of whom hereafter, 2212).
2209.   (v.) HARRIET JOSEPHINE[19], b. Aug. 1, 1852. She resides with her brother Frederick, at Northampton, and I am indebted to her for much of the information relating to this branch of the family.
2210.   (vi.) LILIAN FRANCES[19], b. April 18, 1856; d. Feb., 1858.
2211.   (vii.) ANNIE ISABEL[19], b. Oct. 4, 1859; d. June 21, 1862.

2212.   (2208.) FREDERICK NEWTON KNEELAND[19] (*Isaac N.*[18], *Joseph*[17], *Edward*[16], *Edward*[15], *Benjamin*[14], *Edward*[13], *Edward*[12], *John*[11]—*Alexander*[1]). Second son of Isaac Newton and Frances M. (Strong) Kneeland, b. Sept. 8, 1850; m. Dec. 9, 1879, to Adelaide Frances Dyer.

He resides on Paradise Road in Northampton, Mass., and has a most charming home and family. We present herewith a picture of his residence made from one of his photographs. He is cashier and principal manager of the First National Bank of Northampton, and is known as one of the leading bankers of the East. To show that he has the versatility emblematic of the race, I give herewith a clipping from the anniversary number of the Northampton *Gazette*.

F. N. KNEELAND.
Artist, Publisher and Banker.

" We all think we know our own city well enough not to need a guide book, but after we have read Kneeland's ' Drives in Northampton and Vicinity' we see that we are mistaken. This work is by F. N. Kneeland, cashier of the First National Bank, where he has worked twenty-seven years. The authorship of this and his other work, ' Northampton, the Meadow City,' makes Mr. Kneeland one of the leading authors of the

FREDERICK NEWTON KNEELAND

No. 2212

RESIDENCE OF FREDERICK NEWTON KNEELAND.

No. 2212

Lydia Amorette Kneeland[18].

city. The first book, issued in 1888, is a small, narrow page, pocket width book, containing two small maps and directions for taking 118 drives. The book is still sold and is in special demand by the college girls, who occasionally consult the author for advice on longer routes than are outlined in his book.

" The second book, published last year, is the most artistic work ever issued for any town. It describes and illustrates with numerous pictures, the beauties of Northampton, and contains several articles of great literary and statistical merit. Bishop Huntington, Prof. Tyler, George W. Cable, Mrs. Prof. Emerson and others, contributed historical or descriptive articles, and there are accounts of the educational and charitable institutions of the city, written generally by the persons in charge.

" Some of the pictures are worth framing and possess great merit from an artistic view. Mr. Kneeland took the pictures for his work, and is one of the best amateur photographers in the State. His literary work is all well done, his first care being to have all the facts well established, and he is equally painstaking in the mechanical details of his publications. We are pleased to pay honor to our townsman who has given us two valuable publications."

Mr. Kneeland has had three children, as follows:

Children of Frederick N. and Adelaide F. (Dyer) Kneeland.

2213.　(i.) MARY FRANCES[20], b. Jan. 2, 1882.
2214.　(ii.) ROBERT STRONG[20], b. April 26, 1883.
2215.　(iii.) DORRIS[20], b. Dec. 6, 1889; d. May 6, 1891.

2216.　(2165.) LYDIA AMORETTE KNEELAND[18] (*Joseph*[17], *Edward*[16], *Edward*[15], *Benjamin*[14], *Edward*[13], *Edward*[12], *John*[11]—*Alexander*[1]). Daughter of Joseph and Lydia (Champion) Kneeland, was b. in West Springfield, Mass., March 26, 1822, and d. in Cambridge, Mass., April 7, 1889.

She married Joseph Kennard, July 13, 1844. He was the son of William Kennard and the grandson of Dimond Kennard, of Elliot, Mass., who was a captain in the Revolutionary War. His mother was Margaret Leighton, of Kittery, Me.,

Edward Kneeland[17].

who was b. May 9, 1788, and was a descendant of Capt. Leighton, of the Colonial Wars. She died in Cambridge, April 8, 1829. They had the following children, all born at Cambridge, Mass.:

Children of Lydia A. Kneeland[18] and Joseph Kennard.

2217. (i.) MARION ISABEL KENNARD[19], b. June 15, 1845.

2217A. (ii.) BENJAMIN CHAMPION KENNARD[19], b. May 31, 1849 (of whom hereafter, 2221).

2218. (iii.) CHARLES IRVING KENNARD[19], b. Sept., 1852; lived 5 years and 6 months.

2219. (iv.) EVA JOSEPHINE KENNARD[19], b. Dec., 1855; lived 1 year and 4 months.

2220. (v.) ELIZABETH JOSEPHINE DANA KENNARD[19], b. May 10, 1858. Lives at Cambridge, Mass.

2221. (2217.) BENJAMIN CHAMPION KENNARD[19] (*Lydia A. Kneeland[18], Joseph[17], Edward[16], Edward[15], Benjamin[14], Edward[13], Edward[12], John[11] —Alexander[1]*). Eldest son of Joseph and Lydia A. (Kneeland) Kennard, b. in Cambridge, Mass., May 31, 1849; m. at Meriden, Conn., Oct. 20, 1875, to Justina C. Baldwin (Baldwin Gen., No. 2071, p. 584).

Mr. Kennard is a prosperous business man of Meriden, Conn., and an officer in the Edward Miller & Co. Manufacturing Corporation. He is now serving his third term in the Common Council of Meriden, having served both as alderman and councilman, and is now chairman of the Finance Committee.

Children of Benjamin C. and Justina C. (Baldwin) Kennard.

2222. (i.) HELEN MAY KENNARD[20], b. Oct. 18, 1876.

2223. (ii.) BENJAMIN LEIGHTON KENNARD[20], b. Dec. 22, 1878.

2224. (2152.) EDWARD KNEELAND[17] (*Edward[16], Edward[15], Benjamin[14], Edward[13], Edward[12], John[11] —Alexander[1]*). This is the last of the direct line of Edward Kneelands. He married, Nov. 7, 1835, Samantha Day, by whom one son and three daughters were born. He died Aug. 26, 1877.

Benj. C. Kennard

No. 2221

Children of Edward and Samantha (Day) Kneeland.

2225. (i.) FRANCES A.[18], b. Sept. 20, 1836; m. Willis Van Wagenen, of Sharon, N. Y., Dec. 26, 1865. They had two children:

2226.   (i.) *Loraine*[19], b. at Scoharie, N. Y., Sept. 11, 1866.

2227.   (ii.) *Willis, Jr.*[19], b. at Dedham, Mass., Feb. 17, 1874.

2228. (ii.) MILTON M.[18], b. May 29, 1838; m. Abbie Buel, Dec., 1871. They had a daughter:

2228A.   *Grace B.*[19], b. Sept. 25, 1872, who m. Thue Eldred, Oct. 23, 1895. They reside at Troy, Mich.

2229. (iii.) ELLEN D.[18], b. Dec. 23, 1840; unmarried.

2230. (iv.) PHOEBE J.[18], b. May 30, 1847; m. Charles C. Judd, of Northampton, May 28, 1874. They had five children, as follows:

2231.   (i.) *Clymene L. Judd*[19], b. Sept. 18, 1875.

2232.   (ii.) *Annie C. Judd*[19], b. Sept. 29, 1877.

2233.   (iii.) *Helen A. Judd*[19], b. July 21, 1881; d. March 19, 1883.

2234.   (iv.) *Charles Judd*[19], b. Jan. 7, and d. Jan. 9, 1883.

2235.   (v.) *Edward S. Judd*[19], b. Aug. 27, 1886.

2236. (2159.) EMILY KNEELAND[17] (*Edward*[16], *Edward*[15], *Benjamin*[14], *Edward*[13], *Edward*[12], *John*[11] —*Alexander*[1]). Eleventh child of Edward and Elizabeth (Peck) Kneeland, b. in Hartley, Mass., March 14, 1805; m. Ebenezer Nutting, Jan. 1, 1827.

He was a farmer and local preacher of the M. E. Church. He died April 30, 1886, aged 82 years and 5 months. She died Oct. 12, 1892, aged 87 years, being the last survivor of the family of Edward Kneeland[16].

Children of Emily Kneeland[17] and Ebenezer Nutting.

2237. (i.) EDWARD PORTER NUTTING[18], b. May 23, 1828. He was in the 27th Mass. during the late war and died in the army in 1863. He married and had one son:

24

George Wesley Nutting[18].

2237A.   *George W. Nutting*[19].   He married and had three
           children, all now living, as follows:
2238.   (i.) Porter Nutting[20].
2239.   (ii.) Grant Nutting[20].
2240.   (iii.) Mabel Nutting[20].
2241.   (ii.) CLARISSA ELIZABETH NUTTING[18], b. July 18, 1831;
           m. Levi Dickinson, and d. at the age of 30, leaving
           one child:
2241A.   *Clara Dickinson*[19], who d. in 1893.
2242.   (iii.) EMILY LUCINDA NUTTING[18], b. May 4, 1834; m·
           Henry D. Nutting, and had three children:
2243.   (i.) *Jennie Nutting*[19].
2244.   (ii.) *Mary Nutting*[19].
2245.   (iii.) *Fred. Nutting*[19].
           They are all living at Faribault, Minn., except
           Mary, who died at the age of 20.
2246.   (iv.) EBENEZER FREEMAN NUTTING[18], b. June 27,
           1837.   He was with his father in the 27th Mass.,
           but survived him through the entire war.   He was
           severely wounded at Petersburg, June 18, 1864,
           and now lives in Florence, Mass.   I received this
           data from him.
2247.   (v.) GEORGE WESLEY NUTTING[18], b. June 23, 1840;
           d. April 6, 1845.

CHAPTER XXXVI.

THE CONNECTICUT FAMILY.

(NOS. 2248 TO 2420.)

2248. (744.) JOSEPH KNEELAND[16] (*Isaac*[15], *Benjamin*[14], *Edward*[13], *Edward*[12], *John*[11], *William*[10], *James*[9], *Alexander*[8], *William*[7], *William*[6], *John*[5], *John*[4], *John*[3], *James*[2], *Alexander*[1]). Son of Isaac and Content (Rowley) Kneeland, b. at Hebron (afterwards Marlboro), Conn., Aug. 13, 1749; m. Nov. 5, 1772, to Ruth Pratt, who was born at Colchester, Conn., March 25, 1754.

They had eleven children, all of whom were born at Hebron and Marlboro, where he resided all his life and ended his days Sept. 7, 1799, in the fifty-first year of his age. He was a wealthy farmer, gave all his children a liberal education for those early days, and grounded in them the elements of pure Christianity and honest methods of living. His descendants now reside in nearly every State of the Union—a godly, honorable race, filling all the professions and most of the trades, but with a strong mother-love for the farm and country. All these are lineally descended from the Mayflower through the Fullers and Rowleys (see Chap. XIII.)

Children of Joseph and Ruth (Pratt) Kneeland.

2249. (i.) RUTH[17], b. at Hebron, Conn., May 21, 1773 (of whom hereafter, 2260).

2250. (ii.) MOLLY[17], b. at Hebron, Dec. 28, 1774. She married and resided in Livingston County, Ohio.

2251. (iii.) JOSEPH[17], b. at Hebron, March 3, 1776 (of whom hereafter, 2273).

2252. (iv.) BENJAMIN[17], b. at Marlboro, Conn., Oct. 21, 1777 (see Daniel[17], Chap. XXXVIII.).

2253.   (v.) DANIEL[17], b. at Marlboro, March 2, 1781 (of whom hereafter, Chap. XXXVII.)

2254.   (vi.) SOPHIA[17], b. at Hebron, Dec. 15, 1782.

2255.   (vii.) EUNICE[17], b. at Hebron, July 24, 1788; m. Jedediah Elderkin, and settled in Western New York.

2256.   (viii.) DIMICE[17], b. at Hebron; m. and settled in Western New York.

2257.   (ix.) SALLY[17], b. at Hebron, Nov. 18, 1792; m. Nelson Elderkin and remained in Franklin, N. Y.

2258.   (x.) DIMICE[17], b. at Hebron, Aug. 27, 1796; m. Elijah Crocker and settled at Le Roy, N. Y. He d. there Oct. 9, 1877, æ. 90. His wife d. in 1888, æ. 92.

2259.   (xi.) MOSES[17], b. at Marlboro, Jan. 10, 1798 (of whom hereafter, 2379).

2260.   (2249.) RUTH KNEELAND[17] (*Joseph*[16], *Isaac*[15], *Benjamin*[14], *Edward*[13], *Edward*[12], *John*[11]—*Alexander*[1]). Eldest child of Joseph and Ruth (Pratt) Kneeland, b. at Hebron, Conn., May 21, 1773. She married her cousin, James Loveland. They reresided in Franklin, N. Y. She died there at the age of 56 and he at 44. They had four children, as follows:

Children of Ruth Kneeland[17] and James Loveland.

2261.   (i.) ELIPHAS LOVELAND[18], m. Desire Bartlett, and settled in Franklin County, N. Y.; from there he went to Livingston County, and later to Lenawee County, Mich., where he died July 28, 1838. Children:

2262.   (i.) *Ruth Loveland*[19], b. April 7, 1819. She married twice. Both husbands and the two children by the first husband are dead. She is 78 years old (1897) and her address is Ruth Loveland Warner, Delhi, N. Y.

2263.   (ii.) *Joseph Loveland*[19], d. at Lenawee County, Mich., æ. 2 years and 5 months.

Joseph Kneeland[18].

2264 and 2265. (iii. and iv.) Daughters, died in childhood, with their father, in 1838.

2266.   (v.) *Mrs. O. E. Bennett*[19]. She resided in Canonsville, N. Y., and had four sons. They are all dead.

2267.   (vi.) *Mrs. Wellington Northrup*[19]. She had two children. The elder,

2267A.   Charles Northrup[20], now lives at Franklin, N.Y.

2268 and 2269. (vii. and viii.) Two daughters. One died in infancy and the other lived to maturity in Franklin, N. Y.

2270. (ii.) RUTH LOVELAND[18]. She married her cousin, Deacon Beriah Bowers, of Franklin, N. Y. His mother was a Kneeland and he had a brother, Azel Bowers, living at the same place.

2271. (iii.) JOSIAH LOVELAND[18]. He went to Michigan with his brother Eliphas.

2272. (iv.) Child, buried in infancy.

2273. (2251.) JOSEPH KNEELAND[17] (*Joseph*[16], *Isaac*[15], *Benjamin*[14], *Edward*[13], *Edward*[12], *John*[11]—*Alexander*[1]). Eldest son of Joseph Kneeland[16], b. at Hebron (afterwards Marlboro), Conn., March 3, 1775-6; m. first, Elizabeth Eels, May 7, 1800. She was b. June 10, 1777, and d. Nov. 29, 1808. He m. second, Dolly Crocker, Aug. 17, 1809; she d. Aug. 29, 1855.

He lived all his life at Marlboro and died at the age of 76, within a few rods of his birthplace. He was loved and respected by all who knew him and was a very successful farmer, and generally "made the price" of all farm produce in his town. A man of great will power and an honor to the race.

Children of Joseph Kneeland.

2274. (i.) Child, unnamed, b. Sept. 10, 1801 ; lived 20 days.

2275. (ii.) JOSEPH[18], b. at Marlboro, Conn., Feb. 16, 1804 ; d. May 13, 1805.

Elizabeth Kneeland[19].

2276.   (iii.) ERASTUS[18], b. at Marlboro, Conn., Aug. 19, 1805
         (of whom hereafter, 2283).

2277.   (iv.) BETSEY E.[18], b. at Marlboro, Dec. 19, 1810; d. at
         Marlboro, Sept. 26, 1881 ; unmarried.

2278.   (v.) AUGUSTUS[18], b. Oct. 30, 1812, at Marlboro (of
         whom hereafter, 2321).

2279.   (vi.) DOLLY[18], b. at Marlboro, Nov. 12, 1814 (of whom
         hereafter, 2327).

2280.   (vii.) WILLIAM[18], b. May 8, 1817, at Marlboro (of
         whom hereafter, 2356).

2281.   (viii.) JANE[18], b. at Marlboro, May 18, 1818; d. Oct.
         21, 1818.

2282.   (ix.) JOSEPH[18], b. at Marlboro, June 25, 1826; d. there
         Sept. 18, 1880. He was the last of the direct line
         of Joseph Kneelands; was a wealthy farmer residing
         about two miles from the village of Marlboro, on
         the old homestead ; was married to Mary J. Foote,
         Jan. 11, 1863 ; they had no children.

2283.   (2276.) ERASTUS KNEELAND[18] (*Joseph[17], Jo-
         seph[16], Isaac[15], Benjamin[14], Edward[13], Edward[12],
         John[11]—Alexander[1]*). Second son of Joseph Knee-
         land[17], a prosperous farmer of Marlboro, Conn.; b.
         Aug. 19, 1805, at Marlboro, Conn.   He m. Percey
         Lord, Jan. 7, 1827 ; she was b. Aug. 30, 1804, and
         d. June 23, 1878.   Erastus resided at East Hamp-
         ton, Conn., where he died Feb. 9, 1870.   He had
         eight children and thirty-one grandchildren and
         great-grandchildren.

Children of Erastus and Percey (Lord) Kneeland.

2284.   (i.) JOSEPH[19], b. at Marlboro, Conn., July 31, 1830;
         d. Feb. 24, 1834.

2285.   (ii.) ELIZABETH[19], b. at Genesee, N. Y., Oct. 27, 1834;
         m. Edward N. Hinckley, Jan 1, 1863.   He was b.
         Sept. 30, 1835.   They reside at Lebanon, Conn.   It
         is to Mrs. Hinckley that I am indebted for precise
         information as to all the descendants of Joseph

Kneeland[17]. She has bombarded dilatory corres-
pondents and searched down stray bits of evidence
and rumaged clerks' offices with all the ardor and
zeal of a born and trained genealogist. I suppose
all the credit she will get, outside of this brief squib,
will be the "wonder why aunt Lizzie is so persistent about all these dates?" I hope to meet her
some day in heaven, where genealogy can be con-
structed with the precision of that absolute certainty
we mortals hope for but never realize. They had
three children, as follows:

2286.   (i.) *Mary Elizabeth Hinckley*[20], b. in Lebanon,
May 16, 1867; m. George F. Greene, March 2,
1888; d. Dec. 3, 1890. The family reside at
Lebanon, Conn. They had one child:

2286A.   Wm. H. Greene[21], b. Dec. 3, 1890.

2287.   (ii.) *William Edwin Hinckley*[20], b. at Lebanon,
Dec. 3, 1869.

2288.   (iii.) *Charles Lord Hinckley*[20], b. at Lebanon, Sept.
19, 1873.

2289. (iii.) CAROLINE KNEELAND[19], b. at Genesee, May 27,
1836; m. Elijah Watrous, of North Westchester,
Conn. He was b. March 12, 1817; d. Nov. 10,
1891. She still resides at North Westchester, Conn.
Children:

2290.   (i.) *Daniel Elijah Watrous*[20], b. Sept. 12, 1867; d.
Aug. 1, 1877.

2291.   (ii.) *Flora Celestia Watrous*[20], b. Jan. 2, 1870; d.
Jan. 8, 1870.

2292.   (iii.) *Lizzie Bell Watrous*[20], b. March 11, 1874;
m. Henry McDonald, of Colchester, Aug. 4,
1890. They reside at North Westchester,
Conn. Children:

2293.   (i.) Elizabeth May McDonald[21], b. Oct. 2, 1891.
2294.   (ii.) Carrie Pearl McDonald[21], b. May 16, 1893.
2295.   (iii.) Henry McDonald[21], b. Jan. 10, 1895.

2296. (iv.) DANIEL KNEELAND[19], b. at Genesee, March 17,
1838; m. Mary Cole, in 1864. She was b. Nov. 17,
1848. They now live at Sterling, Neb. Children:

Howard Buel Lord[21].

2297.   (i.) *George Daniel*[20], b. at Genesee, N. Y., Oct. 31,
          1866; m. Emma Van Ness, Oct. 25, 1892.
          They reside at Beatrice, Neb., and have two
          children.

2298 and 2299.   (ii. and iii.) Twins, b. Feb. 5, 1868; lived 48
          hours.

2300.   (iv.) *Grant*[20], b. Aug. 15, 1871; m. and have one
          child.

2301.   (v.) Infant son, b. and d. in 1840.

2302.   (vi.) WILLIAM[19], b. Nov. 9, 1841, in Ohio; m. Jane
          Catharine Bentze, July 4, 1866. Resides at Ster-
          ling, Neb. Children:

2303.   (i.) *Hattie Lucy*[20], b. May 21, 1867. She was the
          first child that was born in the town of Ster-
          ling, Neb. Married E. Ross Hitchcock, March
          30, 1884. One child:

2304.   William F. Hitchcock[21], b. May 5, 1885.

2305.   (ii.) *John*[20], b. in 1869; d. Sept. 18, 1881.

2306.   (vii.) ELLEN ELSIE KNEELAND[19], b. June 23, 1844;
          m. Erastus Watrous, Oct. 17, 1867. They reside
          at North Westchester, Conn. and had the follow-
          ing children:

2307.   (i.) *Alice Abigail Watrous*[20], b. Nov. 30, 1868; m.
          first, Byron O. Lord, Nov. 5, 1889; m. second,
          James Galvin, Sept. 3, 1894. One child:

2308.   Wm. C. Galvin[21], b. July 29, 1895.
          They reside at North Westchester, Conn.

2309.   (ii.) *Harriet I. Watrous*[20], b. June 29, 1873; d.
          Nov. 7, 1889.

2310.   (iii.) *Ellen F. Watrous*[20], b. June 3, 1875; m.
          Charles E. Chapin, Oct. 29, 1895. They
          resided at Comstock Bridge, Conn.

2311.   (iv.) *Albert E. Watrous*[20], b. June 10, 1882.

2312.   (viii.) LYDIA KNEELAND[19], b. Sept. 15, 1846; m.
          Roger Blish Lord, Nov. 10, 1864. Children:

2313.   (i.) *Emma E. Lord*[20], b. Sept. 8, 1865.

2314.   (ii.) *Frederick W. Lord*[20], b. Dec. 12, 1870; m.
          first, Hattie Buel, Feb. 18, 1891. Child:

2315.   Howard Buel Lord[21], b. Nov. 24, 1891.

Charles Augustus Kneeland[19].

Married, second, Laura D. Finley, Oct. 1, 1895.

2318. (iii.) *Annie I. Lord*[20], b. Nov. 5, 1872; d Oct. 5, 1889.

2319. (iv.) *Eugene B. Lord*[20], b. May 3, 1875.

2320. (v.) *Norman R. Lord*[20], b. Nov. 5, 1882.

2321. (2278.) AUGUSTUS KNEELAND[18] (*Joseph*[17], *Joseph*[16], *Isaac*[15], *Benjamin*[14], *Edward*[13], *Edward*[12], *John*[11]—*Alexander*[1]). Youngest son of Joseph Kneeland[17], b. at Hebron, Conn., Oct. 30, 1812; farmer; resided at Vernon Centre, Conn. Married, first, Hannah E. Ford, Dec. 10, 1838; she died Dec. 18, 1849. Married, second, Cornelia Hunt, Oct. 8, 1850.

My record, written in December, 1895, stated that Augustus "resides" at Vernon Centre. I have now to change it by substituting "resided." He died Jan. 30, 1896, aged 84 years. One more member of the family added to the "silent majority." He was considered to be the richest man in Vernon Centre. This is quite a novelty in a Kneeland.

Children of Augustus Kneeland, by Hannah E. Ford.

2322. (i.) EMILY FORD[19], b. Jan. 30, 1840; d. Sept. 7, 1854.

2323. (ii.) DWIGHT[19], b. June 25, 1842; enlisted in the war and died in the hospital March 1, 1865.

By Cornelia Hunt.

2324. (iii.) ELSIE EMILY[19], b. Dec. 5, 1855; m. Levi Merrill Pond, April 23, 1876. He was b. Oct. 18, 1848, and d. Sept. 14, 1894. They had no children. She resides at Vernon, Conn.

2325. (iv.) ARTHUR CROCKER[19], b. May 19, 1857. He went from home and was never heard from again.

2326. (v.) CHARLES AUGUSTUS[19], b. July 18, 1858; m. Rosella Elizabeth Price, Nov. 15, 1891. She was b. Feb. 8, 1860, at Ellington, Conn. They reside at Vernon Centre, Conn.

Dolly Myrtle Harvey[20].

2327. (2279.) DOLLY KNEELAND[18] (*Joseph[17], Joseph[16], Isaac[15], Benjamin[14], Edward[13], Edward[12], John[11] —Alexander[1]*). Sixth child of Joseph Kneeland[17], b. at Hebron, Conn., Nov. 12, 1814; m. Alfred Harvey, April 26, 1836. They resided at Scranton, Pa., and she still resides there. Mr. Harvey was born March 10, 1810, and died June 19, 1867.

Children of Dolly Kneeland[18] and Alfred Harvey.

2328. (i.) A daughter, unnamed, b. Jan. 30, 1837; lived eleven days.

2329. (ii.) JOSEPH KNEELAND HARVEY[19], b. Jan. 26, 1839; m. Emily H. Phillips, Oct. 7, 1863. Children:

2330.   (i.) *Alice Lenore Harvey[20]*, b. Sept. 12, 1864.

2331.   (ii.) A son, b. Sept. 20, 1865; d. unnamed.

2332.   (iii.) *Eugenia Harvey[20]*, b. Aug. 1, 1866.

2333.   (iv.) *Evangeline Harvey[20]*, b. Jan. 17, 1868.

2334.   (v.) *Joseph Kneeland Harvey[20]*, b. July 28, 1875; m. Rachel Robbins, Sept. 4, 1893.

2335. (iii.) JANE HARVEY[19], b. Feb. 23, 1841; lived 11 weeks.

2336. (iv.) ALFRED HARVEY[19], b. Aug. 9, 1842; d. Aug. 10, 1848.

2337. (v.) ALICE HARVEY[19], b. Jan. 26, 1845; m. Eugene Atwood, Dec. 31, 1865; d. July 5, 1873. Children:

2338.   (i.) *Alice Eugenie Atwood[20]*, b. Feb. 3, 1869; d. Jan. 10, 1872.

2339.   (ii.) *Agnes G. Atwood[20]*, b. April 26, 1870.

2340.   (iii.) *Alice Atwood[20]*, b. July 1, 1873; d. July 13, 1873.

2341. (vi.) A daughter, no name, b. and d. June 18, 1847.

2342. (vii.) ALFRED HARVEY[19], b. Oct. 20, 1848; m. Etta Babcock, Sept. 18, 1873. Children:

2343.   (i.) *Jaynes Egbert Harvey[20]*, b. Jan. 29, 1876; d. June 17, 1876.

2344.   (ii.) *Jennie May Harvey[20]*, b. May 9, 1877; d. May 17, 1883.

2345.   (iii.) *Dolly Myrtle Harvey[20]*, b. Oct. 4, 1882.

2346 and 2347.   (iv. and v.) Twin daughters, b. and d. Jan.
6, 1884.

2348.   (vi.) *Edith Mabel Harvey*[20], b. Dec. 11, 1885; d.
July 12, 1886.

2349.   (vii.) *Lura Norlaine Harvey*[20], b. May 30, 1888.

2350.   (viii.) ALBERT HARVEY[19], and

2351.   (ix.) AGNES HARVEY[19], twins, b. Aug. 3, 1850.   Agnes
died Feb. 2, 1884.   Albert married Virginia Anderson, Sept. 13, 1879.   Children:

2352.   (i.) *Alice May Harvey*[20], b. April 5, 1882

2353.   (ii.) *Albert James Harvey*[20], b. Sept. 20, 1891.

2354.   (x.) A daughter, unnamed, b. and d. March 17, 1853.

2355.   (xi.) ARTHUR HARVEY[19], b. July 3, 1854; d. May
1, 1882.

2356.   (2280.) WILLIAM KNEELAND[18] (*Joseph*[17], *Jo-
seph*[16], *Isaac*[15], *Benjamin*[14], *Edward*[13], *Edward*[12],
John[11]—*Alexander*[1]).   Born at Hebron, Conn.,
May 8, 1817.   He is a farmer, residing at Lebanon,
Conn.   Married, first, Lucy A. Park, Jan. 2, 1842;
she d. May 24, 1846.   Married, second, Betsey
McCall, Jan. 13, 1847; she d. Jan. 2, 1873.   Married,
third, Harriet N. McCall, May 12, 1874.

Children of William Kneeland by Lucy A. Park.

2357.   (i.) WILLIAM HENRY[19], b. at Hebron, June 5, 1844;
m. Maria A. Goodwin, Nov. 25, 1875.   They reside
at Columbia, Conn.   Children:

2358.   (i.) *Lucy Mary*[20], b. at Lebanon, June 1, 1880.

2359.   (ii.) *Julia Hattie*[20], and

2360.   (iii.) *Josephine Nettie*[20], twins, b. at Columbia,
Conn., April 28, 1884.

2361.   (ii.) EDWIN PARK[19], b. at Andover, Conn., Sept. 16,
1845; m. Mary Lovinia Park, of East Hampton,
Conn., Oct. 4, 1880.   They reside at Exeter, Lebanon, Conn.   Children:

2362.   (i.) *Mabel Louisa*[20], b. at Lebanon, March 7, 1885.

2363.   (ii.) *Lovinia Park*[20], b. at Lebanon, June 4, 1894.

Moses Kneeland[17].

By Betsey McCall.

2364. (iii.) JOHN GAGER[19], b. at Andover, Conn., Oct. 16, 1847; m. first, Harriet Adeline Tucker, Nov. 28, 1872; she was b. Aug. 7, 1850, and d. May 12, 1882. Married, second, Nellie Frances Tucker, Oct. 8, 1882; she was b. Sept. 9, 1864, and is still living (1897). John G. died April 6, 1889. The family reside at Lebanon, Conn. Children :

2365.   (i.) *Betsy[20]*, b. July 26, 1874.
2366.   (ii.) *Herbert Le Roy[20]*, b. Sept. 6, 1883.
2367.   (iii.) *Mattie Eliza[20]*, b. March 26, 1886.
2368.   (iv.) *John Gager[20]*, b. May 3, 1887.
2369.   (v.) *Bennie Tucker[20]*, b. Oct. 6, 1888; d. Aug. 11, 1889.

2370. (iv.) ANN ELIZA[19], b. May 26, 1849; d. Aug. 7, 1850.
2371. (v.) ALBERT GREEN[19], b. at Andover, April 11, 1852; m. Hattie J. Manning, Nov. 25, 1875. They reside at Lebanon, Conn. Children :

2372.   (i.) *William Albert[20]*, b. Feb. 17, 1877.
2373.   (ii.) ·*Warren Manning[20]*, b. Aug. 23, 1879.

2374. (vi.) HARRIET ELIZA[19], b. at Andover, July 12, 1854; m. William B. Loomis, March 12, 1873. They reside at Meadville, Mo. Children :

2375.   (i.) *Mary Belle[20]*, b. Nov. 13, 1875.
2376.   (ii.) *Albert William[20]*, b. May 23, 1879.
2377.   (iii.) *Arthur Anson[20]*, b. Dec. 6, 1882.
2378.   (iv.) *Carrie Evelyn[20]*, b. May 12, 1886.

2379. (2259.) MOSES KNEELAND[17] (*Joseph[16], Isaac[15], Benjamin[14], Edward[13], Edward[12], John[11]—Alexander[1]*). Youngest son of Joseph Kneeland[16], b. at Marlboro, Conn., Jan. 10, 1798; settled in Dearborn County, Indiana, where his two children were born. Afterwards, he went to Mississippi, and died there.

He was an honest, hard-working farmer, but filled with the roving characteristics inherited by the family from their Viking ancestry. This is the third Kneeland to marry a

"Mary Alden." There is nothing to show in this case that she descended from the Mayflower family, except the name. She accompanied her husband to the South, but whether there were any more children born unto them, or when or where they died, we have neither record nor tradition.

Children of Moses and Mary (Alden) Kneeland.

2380. (i.) JAMES HARDY[18], b. in Dearborn County, Ind., Dec. 15, 1825 (of whom hereafter, 2382).

2381. (ii.) MARY F.[18], b. in Dearborn County, Ind., Dec. 10, 1827; d. Feb. 24, 1852.

2382. (2380.) JAMES H. KNEELAND[18](*Moses[17], Joseph[16], Isaac[15], Benjamin[14], Edward[13], Edward[12], John[11] —Alexander[1]*). Born Dec. 15, 1825; m. Catharine L. Farrel, March 31, 1850.

The day after the marriage they started for Louisa County, Iowa, where he settled and remained until about 1855, when they went to Nebraska and took up a homestead, where they remained several years, but the newcomers in that region became so lawless that he sold out about 1859 and returned to Louisa County, Iowa, where they lived until after the war, when he finally settled near Chariton, Lucas County, and died there March 3, 1884. He was an intelligent farmer, one of the kind that has helped to build up our former West, but present Middle States, with the best of citizens. He had eight children, all but one of whom is now living (1897).

Children of James H. and Catharine L. (Farrel) Kneeland.

2383. (i.) MARY L.[19], b. in Iowa, Jan. 28, 1851; m. H. H. Robison, Feb. 2, 1869. Children:

2383A. (i.) *Lillie[20]*, b. Jan. 1, 1871.

2384. (ii.) *Henrietta[20]*, b. Dec. 15, 1874.

2385. (iii.) *Parry[20]*, b. July 8, 1876.

2386. (iv.) *Arthur[20]*, b. April 3, 1878.

2387. (v.) *Clarence[20]*, b. Oct. 25, 1879.

2388. (vi.) *Willis[20]*, b. May 3, 1881; d. Nov. 3, 1883.

2389. (vii.) *Stella[20]*, b. June 16, 1885.

2390. (viii.) *Charles[20]*, b. Oct. 13, 1886.

Marcus L. Kneeland[19].

2391.   (ix.) *Margaret[20]*, b. Dec. 10, 1890.

2392.   (ii.) SARAH E.[19], b. in Iowa, July 11, 1852; m. first, Geo. W. Smith, Nov. 30, 1874. They had one son:

2393.   (i.) *George W. Smith[20]*, who settled in Nebraska. Sarah E. Smith married, second, A. R. Erb, Feb. 13, 1882, and d. Feb. 1, 1894. By the second husband she had:

2394.   (ii.) *Frederick E. Erb[20]*, b. Dec. 4, 1882.

2395.   (iii.) *Florence E. Erb[20]*, b. Aug. 31, 1884.

2396.   (iv.) *Matilda L. Erb[20]*, b. Jan. 9, 1886.

2397.   (v.) *Charles E. Erb[20]*, b. March 22, 1887.

2398.   (vi.) *Aaron A. Erb[20]*, b. Aug. 20, 1888.

2399.   (vii.) *Bertie R. Erb[20]*, b. April 7, 1890.

2400.   (viii.) Infant daughter, b. and d. April 11, 1892.

2401.   (iii.) HENRIETTA M.[19], b. in Iowa, Dec. 23, 1854; m. R. C. Taylor, April 25, 1876. Children:

2401A.   (i.) *Charles E.[20]*, b. in 1877.

2402.   (ii.) *Nellie May[20]*, b. in 1879.

2403.   (iii.) *Emma Bell[20]*, b. in 1880.

2404.   (iv.) *Mabel Lulu[20]*, b. in 1884.

2405.   (v.) *Edna Pearl[20]*, b. in 1889.

2406.   (vi.) *Beulah Lamb[20]*, b. in 1893.

2407.   (iv.) GEORGE W.[19], b. in Nebraska, Nov. 29, 1856; m. Elijah J. Halton, Nov. 29, 1882. Children:

2408.   (i.) *Bertha O.[20]*, b. Oct. 3, 1883.

2409.   (ii.) *J. Earl[20]*, b. May 6, 1885.

2410.   (iii.) *Mary B.[20]*, b. Nov. 15, 1886.

2411.   (iv.) *James A.[20]*, b. Aug. 27, 1888.

2412.   (v.) *L. C.[20]*, b. July 22, 1890.

2413.   (vi.) *N. V.[20]*, b. Nov. 25, 1894.

2414.   (v.) JOHN S.[19], b. in Nebraska, Aug. 14, 1858; m. Anna M. Bingham, July 5, 1883. Children:

2415.   (i.) *Ethel Maude[20]*, b. May 14, 1884.

2416.   (ii.) *Jessie Gertrude[20]*, b. Jan. 4, 1887.

2417.   (iii.) *James Emerson[20]*, b. March 1, 1889.

2418.   (iv.) *Lila Margaret[20]*, b. Oct. 12, 1891.

2419.   (v.) *George Lee Glenn[20]*, b. Aug. 27, 1895.

2419A.   (vi.) MARCUS L.[19], b. in Iowa, March 15, 1860; m. Ellen Nelson, Aug. 30, 1892.

Alice Grace Kneeland[20].

2419B. (vii.) JAMES MANFORD[19], b. in Iowa, March 17, 1862 ; m. Nota V. Vogan, Oct. 2, 1887. I am indebted to him for the genealogy of the family from Moses down.

2420. (viii.) DAVID[19], b. in Iowa, Dec. 8, 1863 ; m. and has one daughter:

2420A. *Allie Grace*[20], b. April 10, 1895.

CHAPTER XXXVII.

THE MICHIGAN FAMILY.

(NOS. 2421 TO 2502.)

This branch of the Kneeland family starts from a most charming melo-drama, the scene of which is laid in the forests of New York State. The dramatis personæ forming the after-play are located throughout the union. I do not know why I localize this family by the name of "The Michigan Family," except that one of its prominent members resides in that State—one whom I have never seen save, possibly, among the troops "that passed by," in the old army days, but who has become much endeared to me by his kindly, systematic efforts in securing records of this branch. In my mind it has always been the "C. L. Kneeland family," from the name of that sterling representative of the race, Chas. L. Kneeland, of Lansing, Mich. With this brief prologue, we ring up the curtain for the first act.

2421. (2253.) DANIEL KNEELAND[17] (*Joseph*[16], *Isaac*[15], *Benjamin*[14], *Edward*[13], *Edward*[12], *John*[11], *William*[10], *James*[9], *Alexander*[8], *William*[7], *William*[6], *John*[5], *John*[4], *John*[3], *James*[2], *Alexander*[1]). Born at Hebron, near Marlboro, Conn., March 2, 1781.

In the spring of 1803, in company with his brother Benjamin, he went from Marlboro to Franklin, Delaware County, N. Y., then a complete wilderness. There is quite a romance connected with the outcome of this trip. It has come with slightly changing details from several different sources, but the following I find to be a correct statement thereof. The two brothers selected together a tract of 200 acres of land in Franklin, N. Y., cleared up a bit of it and commenced the erection of a log cabin for Benjamin's future wife, for be it known that prior to the journey he had become engaged to one of Marlboro's most beautiful damsels, as brave and strong as she was bonnie, and had agreed to become the mistress of the cabin, wild beasts and Indians to the contrary notwithstanding. About mid-summer, when the nest was nearly ready for its mate, Benjamin sent his brother back for her, while he prepared the cabin for the marriage festival. Late in the autumn, after a long and tedious journey, much of the way marked only by blazed trees, they arrived at the forest home. There was no "light in the window," no welcome for them. Benjamin was dead. What did they do? Retrace their steps through the forest snow-paths in the coming winter? Not a bit of it. They were cast in a more sensible mold. They just got married on the spot, and about two hundred descendants are glad of it. That is how we come to inscribe on these records the marriage of Daniel Kneeland to Grace Williams on the 23d of October, 1803. They remained on this homestead during their joint lives, and it is still in the family. Daniel cleared up with his own hands the 200 acres, made of it one of the best farms in the county, became wealthy and a power among the people, respected and loved by all. They and all their descendants were Congregationalists, save and except an occasional break through the fence to the neighboring fields of Presbyterianism. Daniel died May 28, 1842, and Grace followed him Oct. 24, 1845. I suppose both brothers waited for and welcomed her at the end of the last journey.

Children of Daniel and Grace (Williams) Kneeland.

2422. (i.) SOPHIA[18], b. Sept. 29, 1804, at Franklin, N. Y., m. Arastarkus Mann, of Otego, Otsego County, N. Y., a prominent farmer. She died April 3, 1889, aged, 85. They had the following children, all born at Otego:

25

Grace Melissa Kneeland[18].

2423. (i.) *Laura Mann*[19], b. Dec. 27, 1827; m. Giles Green, Feb. 6, 1865. They settled in Linden, Ill., and have a thousand acre farm there which is considered one of the finest in the State. Mr. Green was born at Willett, Courtland County, N. Y. •

2424. (ii.) *Lavancha Mann*[19], b. Nov. 25, 1829; d. April 1, 1867.

2425. (iii.) *Julia Rovella Mann*[19], b. Aug. 5, 1834; m. Belliott Orton, of Linden, Ill. They now reside at Boling, Kansas.

2426. (ii.) DANIEL[18], b. at Franklin, N. Y., Dec. 22, 1805 (of whom hereafter, 2439).

2427. (iii.) BENJAMIN[18], b. at Franklin, N. Y., Nov. 13, 1807; m. Minerva N. Hine, June 27, 1843. She was b. July 29, 1823. They lived on the old Kneeland homestead, at Franklin, and had one daughter:

2428. *Grace Abigail*[19], b. March 22, 1844; m. George Stillson, a hardware merchant, at Franklin, N. Y. Children:

2429. (i.) Libbie Minerva Stillson[20], b. June 18, 1866.
2430. (ii.) John Benjamin Stillson[20], b. May 29, 1872.

2431. (iv.) WILLIAMS[18], b. at Franklin, April 29, 1809 (of whom hereafter, 2453).

2432. (v.) ANNA H.[18], b. at Franklin, Feb. 5, 1811; m. Mr. Armstrong; went to Canada. No further information.

2433. (vi.) CAROLINE[18], b. at Franklin, Jan. 3, 1815; m. Sept. 21, 1842, Dr. Stephen G. Holbrook, of Kelloggsville, Ohio, and died there July 15, 1875. He d. Sept. 22, 1875. They had two children:

2435. (i.) *Flora Holbrook*[19], b. Aug. 14, 1846; m. June 30, 1867, Sanford L. Tobes.

2436. (ii.) *Stephen Abernathy Holbrook*[19], b. Sept. 7, 1851.

2437. (vii.) ISAAC[18], b. at Franklin, Aug. 26, 1821 (of whom hereafter, 2479).

2438. (viii.) GRACE MELISSA[18], b. Dec. 7, 1826; d. Feb. 21, 1855; unmarried.

Dr. Daniel Kneeland

No. 2439

2439. (2426.) DR. DANIEL KNEELAND[18] (*David*[17], *Joseph*[16], *Isaac*[15], *Benjamin*[14], *Edward*[13], *Edward*[12], *John*[11]—*Alexander*[1]). Eldest son of Daniel and Grace (Williams) Kneeland, of Marlboro, Conn., b. at Franklin, N. Y., Dec. 22, 1805.

He graduated at Cleveland (Ohio) Medical College and practiced medicine at Penn Line, Crawford County, Pa., until 1855, when he settled in Conneaut, Ohio, and had an extensive practice there until his death, on the 22d of February, 1861. He was highly respected in his profession and bore the love and esteem of numerous patrons, who were both friends and patients. He married, first, Susan Vaughn, Dec. 19, 1833; she died at Penn Line, Pa., April 1, 1848. Dr, Kneeland married, second, Olive A. Brown, June 20, 1850. They had children as follows:

Children of Daniel Kneeland, by Susan Vaughn.

2440. (i.) ANGELIA H. KNEELAND[19], b. at Penn Line, Pa., Jan. 27, 1838; she m. John Manning, of Cleveland, Ohio, and died there July 23, 1894. They had one son:

2440A.   *Seymour Kneeland Manning*[20], b. Jan., 1865.

2441. (ii.) GRACE E. KNEELAND[19], b. at Penn Line, Sept. 13, 1839; m. F. N. Hayne, of Conneaut, Ohio, Nov. 3 1864. Their children were:

2442.   (i.) *Arthur Kneeland Hayne*[20], b. at Conneaut, Nov. 21, 1865; d. April 7, 1867.

2443.   (ii.) *Walter N. Hayne*[20], b. at Conneaut, March 12, 1867.

2444.   (iii.) *Alice May Hayne*[20], b. at Conneaut, Oct. 25, 1869.

2445. (iii.) ADDIE M. KNEELAND[19], b. at Penn Line, Dec. 17, 1843.

By Olive A. Brown.

2446. (iv.) CLARENCE A. KNEELAND[19], b. at Penn Line, Dec. 7, 1851; m. at Conneaut, Ohio, Clara E. Kilburn, Oct. 20, 1875. Their children are:

Williams Kneeland[18].

2447.   (i.) *Leona C. Kneeland*[20], b. at Laidsay, Ohio, Oct. 3, 1876.

2448.   (ii.) *Harold M. Kneeland*[20], b. at Laidsay, Ohio, June 3, 1878.

2449.   (iii.) *Grace E. Kneeland*[20], b. at Conneaut, Ohio, April 23, 1881; d. Oct. 23, 1885.

2450.   (iv.) *Charles H. Kneeland*[20], b. at Conneaut, June 30, 1885.

2451.   (v.) AGNES MAY KNEELAND[19], b. at Conneaut, Ohio, Jan. 23, 1854. She still lives at Conneaut, and I am indebted to her for this history of Dr. Daniel Kneeland and his descendants.

2452.   (vi.) ARTHUR DANIEL KNEELAND[19], b. at Conneaut, March 25, 1861; d. Oct. 16, 1862.

2453.   (2431.) WILLIAMS KNEELAND[18] (*Daniel*[17], *Joseph*[16], *Isaac*[15], *Benjamin*[14], *Edward*[13], *Edward*[12], *John*[11]—*Alexander*[1]). Son of Daniel Kneeland, b. at Franklin, N. Y., April, 29, 1809; d. Dec. 3, 1868.

As a boy he was considered remarkably bright and quick but full of fun and harmless mischief, the adoration of his schoolmates and the terror of the teacher. His father, who was of the old Puritanic tendencies, staid and solemn in demeanor, was shocked at this specimen of coming America and concluded to tame him down by apprenticing him for five years to the trade of tanner, currier and shoemaker, these avocations being then united. He quieted down and became an industrious, honest and, but for extreme generosity, a prosperous man. He was a Democrat, which is not generally considered a Kneeland type or failing, and took an active part in politics but never accepted office. He was a great reader and had a wonderful memory, quoting verbatim any public document after reading it twice over. He was a good speaker and a deep thinker. He married Phoebe, daughter of Benjamin Kellogg, of Croton, N. Y. After his death she married a second time, May 15, 1872, to Sluman Follett, of Waverly, N. Y. He died May 3, 1886, and she now lives (age 87) with her son, J. H. Kneeland, at Waverly, N. Y.

No. 2461

Joseph Hart Kneeland[19].

Children of Williams and Phoebe (Kellogg) Kneeland.

2454.   (i.) EMILY[19], b. at Franklin, N. Y., July 13, 1835.
2455.   (ii.) JOSEPH HART[19], b. at Franklin, Delaware County,
           N. Y., April 3, 1838 (of whom hereafter, 2461).
2456.   (iii.) CHARLES L.[19], b. at Franklin, N. Y., June 5, 1841
           (of whom hereafter, 2466).
2457.   (iv.) ELLEN S.[19], b. Jan. 3, 1843; d. Nov. 13, 1864.
2458.   (v.) JULIA J.[19], b. Feb. 22, 1845; d. Aug. 14, 1848.
2459.   (vi.) REMUS A.[19], and
2460.   (vii.) ROMULUS A.[19], twins, b. Aug. 11, 1848 (of whom
           hereafter, 2474 and 2475).

2461.   (2455.) JOSEPH HART KNEELAND[19](*Williams*[18],
           Daniel[17], *Joseph*[16], *Isaac*[15], *Benjamin*[14], *Edward*[13],
           Edward[12], *John*[11]—*Alexander*[1]).   Born at Frank-
           lin, Delaware County, N. Y., April 3, 1838.

His mother is descended in the seventh degree from
Samuel Kellogg, one of the early Puritan fathers, who settled
at Hadley, Mass., in 1664.   She resides at the present time
with her son Joseph, and has already reached the advanced
age of nearly eighty-seven years.   Mr. Kneeland was educated
in the common schools and at the Delaware Literary Institute,
at Franklin, N. Y., in which institution he was an honored
member of the Independent Society.   At an early age he was
ambitious to acquire an education and to fit himself for the
profession of teaching, but the sudden death of his father
placed him at the head of a dependent family.   It was not
without sincere regret, but with courage undaunted, that he
gave up his studies and abandoned ambitious dreams of the
future by adopting his father's trade—that of a boot and shoe
maker.   To this business a tannery was afterwards added, and
with the assistance of his younger brothers a large family was
supported, and a debt of several hundred dollars, left by his
father at his death, was paid.   Later, with his brothers, he
assisted in conducting an extensive business in the sale of
musical instruments, in central New York, and while thus
occupied he began tuning, in which difficult profession he is
engaged at the present time with great credit to himself,

having acquired an excellent and extensive reputation. Mr.
Kneeland was married Feb. 10, 1864, to Josephine M. Shaw,
of Boston, Mass., who died July 25, 1889, aged 54 years. She
was the daughter of Mary Penniman and Josiah Shaw, of that
city. During the last eight years Mr. Kneeland has made his
home at Waverly, N. Y., where he resides at the present time
and is looked upon as a respected and influential citizen.

Children of Joseph H. and Josephine (Shaw) Kneeland.

2462.   (i.) HATTIE PETWIN[20], b. April 13, 1865; d. Sept.
            29, 1865.
2463.   (ii.) MARY STELLA[20], b. Aug. 27, 1866.
2464.   (iii.) JULIA JOSEPHINE[20], b. Nov. 27, 1872.
2465.   (iv.) ALICE MARIA[20], b. Jan. 6, 1876.

2466.   (2456.) CHARLES L. KNEELAND[19] (*Williams*[18],
            Daniel[17], *Joseph*[16], *Isaac*[15], *Benjamin*[14], *Edward*[13],
            Edward[12], *John*[11]—*Alexander*[1]). Son of Wil-
            liams and Phoebe (Kellogg) Kneeland, b. June 5,
            1841.
He, as well as his brothers, Joseph H., Remus and Romulus, was noted in his earlier years for his musical qualities.
In August, 1860, he raised a company of volunteers and was
commissioned Lieutenant, but soon afterward resigned to
accept the position of chief musician of the 144th N. Y. Vols.,
his company being the nucleus of that regiment. He served
three years, and a year or two later, Sept. 30, 1865, he married
Sarah H. L. Hollister, of Perrysburgh, Ohio, and settled down
for a while at his father's old business of tanner and currier, at
Franklin, N. Y. In 1868 he commenced the business of selling
musical instruments, building up a large trade and continuing
his mercantile pursuits for fourteen years. He then commenced
inventing and manufacturing a line of specialties in dairy
implements. His factory was at Unadilla, N. Y., until a few
years since, when he located at Lansing, Mich. A strong corporation was organized and is now doing business under the
name of " The Kneeland Crystal Creamery Co.," of which he
is President and Manager. Credit for the genealogy of this

CHARLES L. KNEELAND
No. 2466

EDWIN J. KNEELAND
No. 2468

FREDERICK KNEELAND
No. 2469

ANNA M. KNEELAND
No. 2473

HAROLD KNEELAND
No. 2467A

branch of the family, from Daniel Kneeland down, is herewith extended to him. For his kindly aid in this respect I give him the toast of Rip Van Winkle, "Here 's to your health and your wife's health and all your little family. May they live long and prosper."

Children of Charles L. and Sarah (Hollister) Kneeland.

2467.   (i.) FRANK WILLIAMS[20], b. Aug. 3, 1869; m. Carrie Avery, of Unadilla, N. Y., Sept. 10, 1889. They reside in Lansing, Mich., where he is engaged in the sale of pianos. They have one child:

2467A.   *Harold Kneeland*[21], b. May 22, 1890.

2468.   (ii.) EDWIN J.[20], b. Feb. 3, 1868; lives at Lansing, Mich.; is a jeweler and optician; unmarried at this writing. I expect to give the names of his wife, children and grandchildren in a later edition.

2469.   (iii.) FRED.[20], and

2470.   (iv.) CHARLES[20], twins, b. Feb. 27, 1871. Charles died March 10, 1871. Fred. resides with his father at Lansing, Mich., and is by profession a musician.

2471.   (v.) NELLIE[20], b. March 18, 1872; d. Sept. 30, 1877.

2472.   (vi.) LOTTIE[20], and

2473.   (vii.) ANNA M.[20], twins, b. July 29, 1879. Lottie died Sept. 30, 1880. Anna M. resides with her father at Lansing, Mich.

2473A.   (viii.) CLARA[20], b. Jan. 26, 1886; d. Aug. 11, 1886.

2474 (2459.) and 2475 (2460.) REMUS A. KNEELAND[19] and ROMULUS A. KNEELAND[19] (*Williams*[18], *Daniel*[17], *Joseph*[16], *Isaac*[15], *Benjamin*[14], *Edward*[13], *Edward*[12], *John*[11]—*Alexander*[1]). Twins; youngest sons of Williams Kneeland[18], b. at Franklin, N. Y., Aug. 11, 1848; settled at Benton Harbor, Mich., where they are now in business.

Remus A. was married at Benton Harbor, Sept. 17, 1873, to Nannie Van Dusen, who was born at Newark, N. Y., April 8, 1848, and was the daughter of James P. Van Dusen and Eliza H. Pomeroy. No children.

Frances Ceola Waldron[21].

Romulus A. married at Unadilla, N. Y., Aug. 24. 1870, to Mary Aurelia Randall, b. Oct. 11, 1853, at Lebanon, Conn., daughter of William Nelson Randall and Mary Barrett Backus.

Children of Romulus A. and Mary A. (Randall) Kneeland.

2476.   (i.) ANNIE NOWLEN[20], b. Oct. 29, 1874.
2477.   (ii.) HAZEL BELLE[20], b. July 28, 1889.
2478.   (iii.) MARGARET[20], b. Aug. 18, 1894.

2479.   (2437.) DR. ISAAC KNEELAND[18] (Daniel[17], Joseph[16], Isaac[15], Benjamin[14], Edward[13], Edward[12], John[11]—Alexander[1]). Youngest son of Daniel and Grace (Williams) Kneeland, b. at Franklin, N. Y., Aug. 26, 1821.

Studied medicine under Prof. Delamater. After graduation he commenced his practice at Berea, Ohio, and remained there until the autumn of 1857. His health then failing, he removed to Chariton, Iowa, where for twenty years he had a large and lucrative practice. He was a great reader and is credited with having been one of the best botanists in Western Iowa. Later, he moved to Burr Oak, Kansas, where he remained until his death, in March, 1886. He first married Eliza S. Proctor, a descendant of John Alden and Miles Standish. After her death, he married her sister, Susannah Church Proctor. She died in 1863, and he afterwards married Eleanor M. Crawford. He was buried at his old home in Chariton, by the Masonic fraternity, of which he had been a prominent member.

Children of Dr. Isaac Kneeland, by Eliza S. Proctor.

2480.   (i.) MYRA ELIZA[19], b. about Aug. 8, 1852; m. Joseph Bowlby, and settled in Oregon. Children:
2481.   (i.) Clara O. Bowlby[20], b. Nov. 2, 1871; she m. Alfred G. Waldron, of New Bridge, Ore. Children:
2482.   (i.) Datteen Oneta Waldron[21].
2483.   (ii.) Frances Ceola Waldron[21].

Frank W. Kneeland

No. 2467

Helen Kneeland[20].

2484.   (ii.) *Zora Elizabeth Bowlby[20]*, b. Jan. 15, 1873; m.
            Charles E. Slade. They had one child:
2484A.   Paul Francis Slade[21].
2485.   (iii.) *Arthur Cammel Bowlby[20]*, b. Feb. 21, 1875;
            drowned at Oswego, N. Y., in childhood.
2486.   (iv.) *Armand Insco Bowlby[20]*, b. Sept. 17, 1878;
            drowned in Snake River, Ore., when a child.

By Susannah C. Proctor.

2487.   (ii.) HERBERT[19], b. Jan. 24, 1855; m. Fannie M. Ross,
            Dec. 30, 1889. They now reside at Fort Gibson,
            Indian Territory, where he holds a government
            position. Their children are as follows:
2488.   (i.) *Harry Ross[20]*, b. Dec. 26, 1891.
2489.   (ii.) *Lonie Glenmore[20]*, b. Jan. 25, 1894.
2490.   (iii.) Son, not yet named, b. May 19, 1896.
2491.   (iii.) SAMUEL PROCTOR[19], b. Jan. 9, 1857; m. Julia M.
            Corning, April 18, 1889. No issue. He has resided
            at Des Moines, Iowa, for over twelve years, and
            most successfully manages the R. G. Dun & Co.
            mercantile agency there. He is a man of marked
            ability and good business habits, a most worthy
            member of the clan-Kneeland.
2492.   (iv.) WILLIAMS[19], b. Feb. 5, 1859; m. Carrie Lillian
            Allen, at Chariton, Iowa, April 30, 1885. They
            reside at Malvern, Iowa, where he has been en-
            gaged in the clothing and men's furnishing goods
            for several years with marked success. Their child-
            ren are:
2493.   (i.) *Ruth[20]*, b. Feb. 22, 1887.
2494.   (ii.) *Harry Lawrence[20]*, b. Nov. 30, 1888.
2495.   (iii.) *Paul[20]*, b. Sept. 7, 1890.
2496.   (iv.) *Helen[20]*, b. Aug. 28, 1892.
2497 and 2498. (v. and vi.) Twin daughters, b. Dec. 18, 1862;
            one d. same day, unnamed; the other, Susannah[19],
            d. about eighteen months afterwards.

THE MICHIGAN FAMILY.

Anna Sophia Kneeland[19].

By Eleanor M. Crawford.

2499. (vii.) MARY E.[19], b. Sept. 1, 1864; m. Harvey Scott Logan, June 13, 1895. They reside at Mankato, Kansas. Have one child:

2499A.   *Carleton Kneeland Logan[20]*, b. April 25, 1896.

2500. (viii.) LUCIUS DANIEL[19], b. June 14, 1866. Lives at Formosa, Kansas.

2501. (ix.) HARRIET[19], b. Jan. 1, 1868; d. June 23, 1869.

2502. (x.) ANNA SOPHIA[19], b. April 23, 1871; m. Cal. D. Hulbert, of Burr Oak, Kansas, April 23, 1889.

DR. ISAAC KNEELAND

No. 2479

CHAPTER XXXVIII.

THE OHIO FAMILY.

(NOS. 2503 TO 2692.)

It will be remembered that Isaac Kneeland[15] had two wives. By the first, Sarah Beach, he had one child only—Isaac Kneeland[16]. By the second wife, Content Rowley, he had many children, the descendants of whom have been fully considered. As nearly all the descendants of Isaac[16] located in Ohio, I have designated them as "The Ohio Family," and given them a place in a separate chapter. The third in name, Isaac Kneeland[17], settled about 1815 in the beautiful Western Reserve and laid in that attractive Ohio country the solid foundations for one of the most distinguished and successful tribes in the whole clan-Kneeland. To use a phrase somewhat familiar, though peculiar to this book, "of whom hereafter."

2503. (740.) ISAAC KNEELAND[16] (*Isaac*[15], *Benjamin*[14], *Edward*[13], *Edward*[12], *John*[11], *William*[10], *James*[9], *Alexander*[8], *William*[7], *William*[6], *John*[5], *John*[4], *John*[3], *James*[2], *Alexander*[1]). Only son of Isaac and Sarah (Beach) Kneeland, b. at Hebron, Conn., Oct. 13, 1741.

He enlisted with his brother Benjamin in Capt. Dunham's company, of Chatham, Conn. Isaac was the clerk of the company. They were "minute men" and fought in both Lexington and Bunker Hill. Isaac reënlisted near the close of the war and was present at the surrender of Cornwallis, and was, so to speak, the *Alpha* and *Omega* of the Revolution. He m. Hannah Adams, of the celebrated Adams family, and had the following children, all of whom are set forth in the Hebron and Chatham records:

Isaac Mills Kneeland[18].

Children of Isaac and Hannah (Adams) Kneeland.

2504. (i.) HANNAH[17], b. at Hebron, April 26, 1765.

2505. (ii.) ISAAC[17], b. at Hebron, April 26, 1765 (of whom hereafter, 2511).

2506. (iii.) DUDLEE[17], b. at Hebron, Jan. 28, 1767 (of whom hereafter, 2661).

2507. (iv.) SARAH BEACH[17], b. March 3, 1773, at Chatham.

2508. (v.) DEBORAH[17], b. Jan. 1, 1775; bapt. July 30, 1780.

2509. (vi.) LUCY[17], bapt. at Chatham, May 9, 1779.

2510. (vii.) RUSSELL[17], bapt. at Chatham, Nov. 28, 1785.

2511. (2505.) ISAAC KNEELAND[17] (*Isaac*[16], *Isaac*[15], *Benjamin*[14], *Edward*[13], *Edward*[12], *John*[11]—*Alexander*[1]). Eldest son of Isaac and Hannah (Adams) Kneeland, b. at Hebron—afterwards Marlboro—Conn., April 26, 1765. He m. first, Keziah Mills; she d. about 1806. He m. second, Philomela Robinson; she was b. March 12, 1776, and d. May 26, 1860.

He first located at Sandersfield, Mass. From there he went to the old homestead in Connecticut, and three years after, in 1815, they removed to the Western Reserve and located permanently at Shalersville, Ohio. He was a thrifty farmer, and assisted in establishing the beginning of things in that land noted for its beautiful farms and model Presidents. They had a good round dozen children, as follows:

Children of Isaac Kneeland, by Keziah Mills.

2512. (i.) CLARA[18], b. Nov. 7, 1790; d. Jan. 23, 1864 (of whom hereafter, 2524).

2513. (ii.) GEO. WYLLYS[18], b. Sept. 10, 1794; d. June 6, 1835 (of whom hereafter, 2574).

2514. (iii.) KEZIAH KATHERINE[18], b. Aug. 6, 1801; d. Feb. 11, 1865 (of whom hereafter, 2603).

2515. (iv.) HYRIA MARY[18], b. Aug. 10, 1803; d. June 9, 1877 (of whom hereafter, 2610).

2516. (v.) ISAAC MILLS[18], b. July 21, 1805; d. May 10, 1885 (of whom hereafter, 2637).

Eugene Laurens Whiting[20].

By Philomela Robinson.

2517. (vi.) PHILOMELA VOLUCIA[18], b. Feb. 6, 1808; d. Oct. 13, 1837.

2518. (vii.) RUSSEL SHERMAN[18], b. March 10, 1810; d. Oct. 14, 1882 (of whom hereafter, 2644).

2519. (viii.) FRED'K COOK[18], b. March 4, 1812; d. April 2, 1872 (of whom hereafter, 2657).

2520. (ix.) WILLIAM HOSMER[18], b. Aug. 17, 1814; d. Dec. 19, 1841.

2521. (x.) MILES ROBINSON[18], b. Oct. 22, 1817; d. April 18, 1818.

2522. (xi.) LUCIUS ROBINSON[18], b. Nov. 16, 1819; d. Feb. 19, 1820.

2523. (xii.) CHARLES LAURENS[18], b. Dec. 3, 1822; d. Dec. 4, 1844.

2524. (2512.) CLARA KNEELAND[18] (*Isaac*[17], *Isaac*[16], *Isaac*[15], *Benjamin*[14], *Edward*[13], *Edward*[12], *John*[11] —*Alexander*[1]). Eldest child of Isaac and Keziah (Mills) Kneeland, b. at Colebrook, Conn., Nov. 7, 1790; m. Sparrow Snow, of Sandersfield, Mass., Sept. 11, 1811.

He was b. at Sandersfield, Dec. 20, 1786, and d. at Austinburg, Ohio, Jan. 26, 1869, aged 83. She d. Jan. 23, 1864, aged 74. They had nine children, three born at Sandersfield, where they resided until about 1817, and the others at Austinburg, Ohio, where they subsequently resided.

Children of Clara Kneeland[18] and Sparrow Snow.

2525. (i.) EMILY LUCRETIA SNOW[19], b. at Sandersfield, Sept. 9, 1812; m. Nov. 12, 1841, at Austinburg, Ohio, Benjamin Whiting. She d. Nov. 11, 1891. He d. Aug. 25, 1876. They had two children:

2526. (i.) *Theodore Snow Whiting*[20], b. Aug. 12, 1842; d. July 20, 1847.

2527. (ii.) *Eugene Laurens Whiting*[20], b. Oct. 26, 1844; m. Alice Edna Pierce, Oct. 20, 1868. They reside at Austinburg, Ohio. Children:

Nellie Snow Ransom[21].

2528.   (i.) Ernest Eugene Whiting[21], b. Feb. 5, 1872; d. June 29, 1875.

2529.   (ii.) Roy Eugene Whiting[21], b. April 7, 1876.

2530.   (iii.) Eva Alice Whiting[21], b. Oct. 15, 1877.

2531.   (iv.) Lena Gertrude Whiting[21], b. Feb. 20, 1883.

2532.   (ii.) BETSY KEZIA SNOW[19], b. at Sandersfield, Mass., July 25, 1814; m. March 8, 1838, at Austinburg, Ohio, to John Calvin Shepard, of Great Barrington, Mass. They still reside at Austinburg. They had three children, as follows:

2533.   (i.) *Helen Frances Shepard*[20], b. Dec. 15, 1838; m. G. B. Miller, of Camden, N. Y. They reside in Rochester, N. Y.

2534.   (ii.) *Clara Gertrude Shepard*[20], b. Sept. 2, 1842. Address, Hosmer Hall, St. Louis, Mo.

2535.   (iii.) *Emily Anne Shepard*[20], b. Mar. 4, 1844; m. Rev. Cassius E. Wright, D.D. Residence, Austin, Minn.

2536.   (iii.) SAMUEL WYLLYS SNOW[19], b. at Sandersfield, July 27, 1816; m. Feb. 9, 1842, to Anne J. Strong. They resided in Sterling, Kansas. She died there April 17, 1895, and he April 6, 1895. Children:

2537.   (i.) *Edmund Strong Snow*[20], b. Jan. 25, 1845; m. Margaret Collins, Feb. 7, 1876. Residence, Lakin, Kansas.

2538.   (ii.) *Sparrow Alexander Snow, M.D.*[20], b. Jan. 15, 1847; m. Hulda Bird, May 26, 1880. Child:

2539.   Myra M. Snow[21]. Residence, North Branch, Michigan.

2540.   (iii.) *Eleanor Elizabeth Snow*[20], b. Sept. 11, 1848; m. Hamilton Irish, Nov. 7, 1872. Residence, Sterling, Kansas.

2541.   (iv.) *Mary Foster Snow*[20], b. and d. May 2, 1856.

2542.   (v.) *Martha Price Snow*[20], b. Aug. 5, 1862; m. J. Clinton Ransom, June 14, 1881. Residence, 2244 Guilford ave., Baltimore, Md. Children:

2543.   (i.) Nellie Snow Ransom[21], b. June 12, 1882; d. in 1890.

Kezia
Betsey (Kneeland) Shepard

No. 2532

2544. (ii.) Edmond Snow Ransom[21], b. Feb. 9, 1885.

2545. (iii.) Henry Conklin Ransom[21], b. July 27, 1886.

2546. (iv.) Clarence Albert Ransom[21], b. Jan. 25, 1891.

2547. (v.) Philip Moxom Ransom[21], b. Feb. 23, 1892.

2548. (vi.) Samuel John Ransom[21], b. April 13, 1893.

2549. (iv.) RHODA HELEN SNOW[19], b. at Austinburg, Ohio, June 20, 1818; m. Sept. 10, 1856, to Horace Dunbar, who was b. at Camden, N. Y., April 6, 1806. They resided at Ashtabula, Ohio. She died there Sept. 9, 1886, aged 68, and he, March 18, 1891, aged 85. One child:

2550. *Albert Ernest Dunbar*[20], b. Aug. 11, 1860; m. Clara Conklin, Aug. 11, 1885. They reside on West Prospect st., Ashtabula, Ohio. Children:

2551. (i.) Helen Conklin Dunbar[21], b. April 25, 1888.

2552. (ii.) Ruth Juliette Dunbar[21], b. Oct. 29, 1890.

2553. (iii.) Robert Alden Dunbar[21], b. Jan. 6, 1893.

2554. (v.) EDWARD SPARROW SNOW[19], b. at Austinburg, July 5, 1820; m. Oct. 22, 1851, Elizabeth Austin. They resided at Dearbone, Mich., where he died July 19, 1892. She still resides there. Children:

2555. (i.) *Herbert Montgomery Snow*[20], b. July 26, 1858; m. Mary Louise Martyn, Sept. 12, 1883. Residence, Dearbone, Mich. Children:

2556. (i.) Clara Louise Snow[21], b. July, 1884.

2557. (ii.) Harry Alfred Snow[21], b. May 7, 1889.

2558. (iii.) Gertrude Elizabeth Snow[21], b. April 28, 1892.

2559. (ii.) *Edward A. Snow*[20], b. March 7, 1863; d. Sept. 8, 1884.

2560. (vi.) CLARA ELIZA SNOW[19], b. at Austinburg, Feb. 6, 1822; m. June 28, 1854, George Green, who was b. at Remsen, N. Y., Aug. 3, 1818. He d. May 26, 1878, and she resides at No. 6 East street, Ashtabula, Ohio. Children:

2561. (i.) *Cornelia D. Green*[20], b. April 4, 1857.

2562. (ii.) *George Fowler Green*[20], b. April 5, 1861; m. Frances Theodora Beach, April 16, 1890. Address, Ashtabula, Ohio.

George Wyllys Kneeland[18].

2563. (vii.) LAURENS MILLS SNOW[19], b. at Austinburg, June 22, 1824; m. first, Elizabeth Henderson; she d. Sept. 23, 1863. Married, second, Nov. 22, 1864, Mina Woodworth. They reside at Austinburg, Ohio. They had one child:

2564. *Fred Laurens Snow*[20], b. Nov. 2, 1866; d. June 12, 1874.

2565. (viii.) ALBERT HENRY SNOW[19], b. at Austinburg, May 28, 1827; m. first, Juliette E. Watrous; she d. Jan. 2, 1867. Married, second, June 8, 1869, Cornelia L. Austin; she d. —— 25, 1894. He d. May 27, 1890, at Austinburg, Ohio. He had the following children. By Juliette E. Watrous:

2566. (i.) *Charles Albert Snow*[20], b. July 26, 1853; resides at Garrettsville, Ohio; m. Bertha J. Brown, by whom he had the following children :

2567. (i.) Charles Lee Snow[21], b. Nov. 23, 1876; d. Sept. 12, 1889.

2568. (ii.) Kneeland Sparrow Snow[21], b. March 10, 1879; d. Sept. 12, 1889.

2569. (iii.) Helen Griffith Snow[21], b. Dec. 6, 1881.

2570. (iv.) Albert Galen Snow[21], b. Feb. 14, 1892. By Cornelia L. Austin:

2571. (ii.) *Walter Austin Snow*[20], b. Sept. 13, 1872. Residence (1896), State University, Columbus, Ohio.

2572. (iii.) *Melissa Whitney Snow*[20], b. April 3, 1878. Residence, Dearbone, Mich.

2573. (ix.) THEODORE SNOW[19], b. at Austinburg, Ohio, March 15, 1830; d. in 1833.

2574. (2513.) GEORGE WYLLYS KNEELAND[18](*Isaac*[17], *Isaac*[16], *Isaac*[15], *Benjamin*[14], *Edward*[13], *Edward*[12], *John*[11]—*Alexander*[1]). Eldest son of Isaac and Keziah (Mills) Kneeland, b. at Colebrook, Mass., Sept. 10, 1794; m. Sally Carlton, of Mantua, Ohio, Nov. 25, 1816, and settled in Freedom, Ohio; d. at Freedom, June 6, 1835. She d. March 24, 1878, aged 84. They had four children:

Children of George Wyllys and Sally (Carlton) Kneeland.

2575. (i.) GILES WELLINGTON[19], b. in Shalersville, Ohio, Oct. 15, 1817; m. Amy A. Barbor, of Freedom, Ohio, Dec. 6, 1838; d. in Freedom, Ohio, Sept. 14, 1894. Children:

2576. (i.) *George Wyllys*[20], b. June 15, 1840; d. July 15, 1840.

2577. (ii.) *Sarah Keziah*[20], b. Nov. 6, 1841; m. Julian C. Harmon, of Ravenna, Ohio, Oct. 6, 1862; d. Aug. 26, 1886. Children:

2578. (i.) Orrin Giles Harmon[21], b. March 13, 1864.

2579. (ii.) Sabrina Augusta Harmon[21], b. Nov. 10, 1865.

2580. (iii.) Olive Franklin Harmon[21], b. April 23, 1871.

2581. (iii.) *Elbert Russell*[20], b. Nov. 28, 1843; m. Alice Brown, of Connecticut, and lives in Grand Traverse, Mich. Children:

2582. (i.) Frederick Atwood[21], b. in Freedom, April 11, 1869.

2583. (ii.) Mary Ann[21], b. July 29, 1871; d. Feb. 22, 1892.

2584. (iii.) Gertrude Blanche[21], b. Aug. 29, 1874.

2585. (iv.) *Charles J.*[20], b. Feb. 10, 1846 (of whom hereafter, 2602).

2586. (v.) *Myron Alphonso*[20], b. March 16, 1849; unmarried; lives in Freedom, Ohio.

2587. (vi.) *Elva Luella*[20], b. March 10, 1860; m. Arthur P. Rickard, May 31, 1889. No children.

2588. (ii.) SAMUEL ERASTUS MILLS[19], b. in Shalersville, Ohio, July 7, 1820; m. Feb. 25, 1841, Caroline C. Foote; d. at Freedom, Ohio, Nov. 6, 1882. He was for many years a Justice of the Peace. In 1861 he was appointed a member of the Military Committee for Ohio, and in 1864 was elected representative for Portage County to the Ohio Legislature. Children:

Dr. Charles J. Kneelana[19].

2589.   (i.) *George W.*[20], b. at Freedom, July 3, 1843 ; m. Caroline Robinson, Sept. 26, 1866; resides at Warren, Ohio. He is in partnership with his brother, under the name of Kneeland Bros., booksellers and stationers.

2593.   (ii.) *Edward S.*[20], b. at Freedom, June 22, 1846; m. Minnie A. Harmon, Oct. 21, 1868 ; resides at Warren, Ohio. Is in partnership with his brother. Children :

2594.   (i.) Willis H.[21], b. Dec. 8, 1872, at Warren, Ohio.

2595.   (ii.) Frederick Clyde[21], b. Jan. 23, 1878 ; d. April 13, 1879.

2596.   (iii.) George P.[21], b. at Warren, Ohio, April 29, 1879.

2597.   (iv.) Caroline E.[21], b. at Warren, Ohio, Dec. 12, 1882.

2598.   (iii.) *Velna D.*[20], b. at Freedom, Ohio, March 19, 1852; m. Dec. 2, 1874, A. D. Torrey. They reside at Garrettsville, and had one child :

2599.   Maude E. Torrey[21], b. July 4, 1885; d. in Garrettsville, Feb. 24, 1893.

2600.   (iii.) ISAAC ARAH[19], and

2601.   (iv.) KEZIAH SARAH[19], twins, b. in Freedom, Ohio, Aug. 6, 1829. Keziah Sarah d. July 5, 1841. Isaac Arah d. unmarried, Feb. 7, 1858.

2602.   (2585.) DR. CHARLES J. KNEELAND[19] (*George W.*[18], *Isaac*[17], *Isaac*[16], *Isaac*[15], *Benjamin*[14], *Edward*[13], *Edward*[12], *John*[11]—*Alexander*[1]). Youngest son of George Wyllys and Sally (Carlton) Kneeland, b. at Freedom, Ohio, Feb. 10, 1846.

His autobiographical sketch, written for my private information, is so exquisitely Kneeland that I take the liberty of inserting extracts therefrom instead of putting it in the third person. "I think I am a typical Kneeland. Am fifty years of age ; six feet high ; weight, 230 to 240 pounds ; never

Dr Charles J Kneeland

No. 2602

Keziah Katharine Kneeland[18].

in bed one whole day in my life; blue eyes (all Kneelands of true blood are blue eyed), brown hair and ruddy complexion; strictly temperate; a Congregationalist, and a good Republican. I am proud and independent in spirit, but full of work and grit. I think if occasion should demand, I could wield the Scotchman's broadsword or the Irishman's shovel." There is a description that harmonizes well with the characteristics of the clan. It even has a touch of the Scotchman's "conceit of himself" that is an unconscious attribute of us all.

Dr. Kneeland received his academic and collegiate education at Hiram College, Hiram, Ohio (Garfield's College), and graduated in medicine at Philadelphia. He went to what is now Traverse City, when Northern Michigan was an unbroken wilderness, and knows from personal experience the pioneer life of a physician. For twenty-five years he has stuck closely to his profession and has harvested the wealth and position that comes only to the sticker. Since 1873 he has been continuously a director of the Traverse City schools, and has always taken an interest in public matters though never accepting office. Dr. Kneeland married Estella I. Udall, July 12, 1870. She was of Vermont parentage. They have one son:

2602A. HAROLD SCOTT KNEELAND[20], b. at Traverse City, Mich. He is evidently a chip of the old block— blue eyed, tall and strong. He graduated at the Traverse City High School this season (1897). He will probably follow his father's profession, though he ought to be a lawyer, so as to preserve more evenly the due proportions of the liberal professions.

2603. (2514.) KEZIAH KATHARINE KNEELAND[18] (*Isaac*[17], *Isaac*[16], *Isaac*[15], *Benjamin*[14], *Edward*[13], *Edward*[12], *John*[11]—*Alexander*[1]). Second daughter of Isaac and Keziah (Mills) Kneeland, b. at Sandersfield, Mass., Aug. 6, 1801; went to Shalersville, Ohio, with her parents in 1815; m. to Simon Landfear, of Freedom, Ohio, Sept. 9, 1835. They resided there until her death, Feb. 10, 1865.

Lucius Russell Landfear[19].

Children of **Keziah K. Kneeland**[18] and **Simon Landfear.**

2604.   (i.) ELIZA LANDFEAR[19], b. at Freedom, June 24, 1836;
            m. George Earls, of Garrettsville, in 1868. They
            reside near Joplin, Mo., and had three children:

2605.   (i.) *Jennie Earls*[20].
2606.   (ii.) *George Earls*[20].
2607.   (iii.) *William Earls*[20]

2608.   (ii.) EMILY LANDFEAR[19], b. at Freedom, March 9,
            1838 ; m. first, May 25, 1861, Orville A. Taylor, of
            Garrettsville; he d. Oct. 4, 1871. Married, second,
            May 25, 1881, Egbert S. Hutchinson. They reside
            at Garrettsville, Ohio. I am indebted to Mrs.
            Hutchinson for a very complete genealogy relating
            to this branch of the family. She has worked
            most zealously and must have learned the diffi-
            culties to be " met up with " in unravelling the
            tangled snarl of the line of life extending over
            even a few generations. For all this she has both
            sympathy and thanks. By her first marriage
            she had one child:

2608A.   *Clarence Landfear Taylor*[20], b. July 25, 1869; m.
            Pearl E. Leeper, June 5, 1895. They reside
            at Alliance, Ohio.

2609.   (iii.) LUCIUS RUSSELL LANDFEAR[19], b. at Freedom,
            Ohio, Sept. 5, 1840. Removed with his parents to
            Hudson, Ohio, in 1852, where he was graduated
            from Western Reserve College (now Adelbert), in
            1861, and two years later received the degree of
            A.M. He graduated at the Miami Medical College
            of Cincinnati, receiving the degree of M.D. Hav-
            ing made the study of mental diseases a specialty,
            he was engaged as assistant physician of the Hos-
            pital for the Insane, at Dayton, Ohio, immediately
            after he graduated. Three years later he was
            appointed medical superintendent, which position
            he held until his death two years later. He re-
            ceived a blow on the head from a patient which
            caused his death July 25, 1869.

2610. (2515.) HYRIA MARY KNEELAND[18] (*Isaac*[17], *Isaac*[16], *Isaac*[15], *Benjamin*[14], *Edward*[13], *Edward*[12], *John*[11]—*Alexander*[1]). Third daughter of Isaac and Keziah (Mills) Kneeland, b. at Sandersfield, Mass., Aug. 10, 1803; m. James Crane, of Shalersville, Ohio.

Children of Hyria M. Kneeland[18] and James Crane.

2611. (i.) HENRIETTA R. CRANE[19], b. Oct. 14, 1826; m. George B. Hopkins, of Freedom, Ohio, Feb. 24, 1852; d. March 19, 1892, without issue.

2612. (ii.) PHILOMELA K. CRANE[19], b. May 5, 1829; m. Virgil Goddard, of Edinburg, Ohio, Oct. 12, 1859; d. at Alliance, Ohio, June 7, 1895. Children:

2613. (i.) *Dennis J. Goddard*[20], b. Sept. 5, 1860; m. Sadie Hamilton, of Buffalo, N. Y., and resides there. Children:

2614. (i.) Mary Goddard[21].
2615. (ii.) Ettie Goddard[21].
2616. (iii.) Sadie Goddard[21].
2617. (iv.) Joseph Goddard[21].

2618. (ii.) *Charles W. Goddard*[20], d. in 1882, without issue.

2619. (iii.) *Clifford V. Goddard*[20], m. Annie Gwin. They reside in Alliance, Ohio. Children:

2620. (i.) Roy C. Goddard[21].
2621. (ii.) Fred. O. Goddard[21].

2622. (iii.) FLORENCE EUGENIA CRANE[19], b. Aug. 25, 1832; m. Lester Olmstead, of Edinburg, Ohio, Oct. 3, 1854. They reside there. Child:

2623. *Ida Olmstead*[20], m. Watson Hollister. They reside at Edinburg, Ohio. Children:

2624. (i.) Eugenia W. Hollister[21], m. Samuel A. Stewart. They reside at Edinburg, and have one child (the 22d generation):

2625. *Ivan W. Stewart*[22], b. July 16, 1896.
2626. (ii.) Ernest L. Hollister[21].
2627. (iii.) Mabel E. Hollister[21].
2628. (iv.) Roy W. Hollister[21].

Julius Warren Watson[21].

2629.   (iv.) EMILY VOLUCIA CRANE[19], b. June 29, 1835; m.
        Jan. 26, 1861, J. Wesley McComb, of Edinburg,
        Ohio; d. in Shalersville. They had one child:

2630.   *Ray McComb[20]*, m. in 1891, Minnie Gledhill, of
                 Ravena, Ohio. They reside in Edinburg.

2631.   (v.) GEORGE WYLLYS KNEELAND CRANE[19], b. Sept.
        21, 1837; m. first, Loana Tuttle, of Painesville,
        Ohio, July 2, 1862. After her death he married,
        second, Orrel McClintock, Sept. 2, 1895. They
        reside in Shalersville, Ohio. Children:

2632.   (i.) *Flora M. Crane[20]*, b. May 27, 1870; m. A.
                 Lincoln Davidson, of Chardon, Ohio, June 21,
                 1893. They reside at Chardon. Child:

2633.   Howland C. Davidson[21], b. June 22, 1894; d.
                      Nov. 8, 1895.

2634.   (ii.) *Mary H. Crane[20]*, b. Nov. 11, 1873; d. Sept.
                 2, 1886.

2635.   (vi.) MARY HYRIA CRANE[19], b. Jan. 2, 1841; m. James
        S. Tull, of Ravena, Ohio, Jan. 31, 1863; d. in
        Whitehall, Wis. Child:

2636.   *Olive H. Tull[20]*, b. June, 1869. Resides in Chicago.

2637.   (2516.) ISAAC MILLS KNEELAND[18] (*Isaac[17]*,
        Isaac[16], *Isaac[15]*, *Benjamin[14]*, *Edward[13]*, *Edward[12]*,
        John[11]—Alexander[1]). Second son of Isaac and
        Keziah (Mills) Kneeland, b. July 21, 1805, at
        Sandersfield, Mass.; m. Electa Thompson, Jan. 6,
        1831; d. May 10, 1885, at Bethel, Branch County,
        Michigan.

Children of Isaac Mills and Electa (Thompson) Kneeland.

2638.   (i.) SHERMAN WYLLYS[19], b. Feb. 27, 1833; m. Frances
        H. Smith, of Shalersville, Ohio, Dec. 8, 1858; d.
        June 11, 1888, at Coldwater, Mich. Child:

2639   *Clara E.[20]*, b. Nov. 1, 1864; m. Joseph Watson,
                 Sept. 1, 1887. Resides at Coldwater, Mich.
                 Child:

2640.   Julius Warren Watson[21], b. in 1888.

RUSSEL KNEELAND

No. 2644

Emma Volucia Kneeland[19].

2641. (ii.) CORNELIA[19], and
2642. (iii.) CORDELIA[19], twins, b. Feb. 3, 1836. Cordelia died July 8, 1846. Cornelia married Christopher G. Babcock, of Bronson, Mich., Dec. 15, 1864. Residence, East Gilead, Branch County, Mich. No children.

2643. (iv.) ISAAC[19], b. May 2, 1842; d. Sept. 10th, 1842. This was the last of the Isaac Kneelands, being fifth in the direct line.

2644. (2518.) RUSSEL SHERMAN KNEELAND[18](*Isaac[17], Isaac[16], Isaac[15], Benjamin[14], Edward[13], Edward[12], John[11]—Alexander[1]*). Son of Isaac and Philomela (Robinson) Kneeland, b. in Sandersfield, Mass., March 10, 1810.

At the age of three years his parents moved to Connecticut, where he spent two years, and then they removed to Shalersville, Ohio. In 1835, he went to Illinois, from there to St. Louis, Mo., where he engaged as steamboat clerk on the upper Mississippi and Illinois rivers, and was afterwards in a flouring mill in St. Louis. He was married, Sept. 25, 1838, at Waukesha, Wis., to Electa Rossman, daughter of James and Irene Rossman. In April, 1847, he went to Hartford, Wis., and went into the mercantile business. About 1854 he was elected one of the directors of the old La Crosse and Milwaukee Railroad. His first wife died in November, 1848, and he was married to Olive Keith Harrington, daughter of Aaron Harrington, of Windsor, Vt. His business the latter part of his life was that of a conveyancer, collector, and he settled a large number of estates. He also held a number of public offices. He died suddenly of neuralgia of the heart while on a visit to his son Charles R., at Lamberton, Minn., Oct. 14, 1882. His widow resides at Minneapolis, Minn.

Children of Russel Sherman Kneeland, by Electa Rossman.

2645. (i.) EMMA VOLUCIA[19], b. at St. Louis, Mo., April 5, 1842; d. Aug. 28, 1843.

Lucius Harrington Lackor[20].

2646. (ii.) CLARA IRENE[19], b. at St. Louis, Mo., May 22, 1844; m. Arthur D. Parker, youngest son of Capt. Nathan Parker, of Stukeley, P. Q., at Hartford, Wis., Oct. 22, 1867. (Arthur was my old schoolmate in Stukeley, his sister Sophia being my first teacher.—S. F. K.) They reside at Carrington, N. D. Children:

2647.   (i.) *Charles Arthur Parker[20]*, b. April 13, 1870, at Fond du Lac, Wis.

2648.   (ii.) *Edna Elizabeth Parker[20]*, b. June 2, 1873, at Fond du Lac, Wis.

2649.   (iii.) *Andrew Abijah Parker[20]*, b. March 17, 1876, at Fond du Lac. Wis.

2650.   (iv.) *Russel Willard Parker[20]*, b. Jan. 1, 1883, at Fort Howard, Wis.

2651. (iii.) CHARLES ROSSMAN[19], b. at Shalersville, Ohio, Sept. 17, 1846; m. Kedie, daughter of Whitman Sayles, of Rubicon, Wis., at Waterville, Wis., July 19, 1866. He now resides at Lamberton, Minn.

By Olive Keith Harrington.

2652. (iv.) WYLLYS HOSMER[19], b. at Hartford, Wis., Dec. 10, 1850; d. May 26, 1851.

2653. (v.) EVA ELECTA[19], b. at Hartford, Wis., April 23, 1852.

2654. (vi.) RUSSEL SHERMAN[19], b. at Hartford, Wis., July 20, 1854; m. Mrs. Jennie Lynn Sackett, April 16, 1881. He resides at Orange, Texas. Children:

2654A.   (i.) *Eva Lynn[20]*, b. Jan. 26, 1882.

2654B.   (ii.) *Russel Clare[20]*, b. Nov. 29, 1883; d. at St. Peter, Minn., Nov. 25, 1886.

2654C.   (iii.) *Floyd Alfred[20]*, b. April 10, 1885.

2655. (vii.) EDNA OLIVIA[19], b. at Hartford, Wis., Oct. 28, 1857; m. Frederick William Lackor, son of Horace L. Lackor, of Minneapolis, at that city, Jan. 1, 1890. They still reside there, and have one child:

2655A.   *Lucius Harrington Lackor[20]*, b. July 7, 1893, at Minneapolis, Minn.

LUCIUS H. LACKOR
No. 2655A

EDNA (KNEELAND) LACKOR   EVA E. KNEELAND
No. 2655   No. 2653

MRS. EVETA R. KNEELAND

Dudlee Kneeland[17].

2656. (viii.) FRED. HALL[19], b. at Hartford, Wis., March 4, 1861; m. Alice Louise Nutter, of St. Peter, Minn., Nov. 25, 1886. Children:

2656A. (i.) *Fred. Lucius[20]*, b. Aug. 23, 1887, at Duluth Minn.

2656B. (ii.) *Harry Russell[20]*, b. April 17, 1892; d. at Brainard, Minn., Jan. 31, 1888.

2657. (2519.) FREDERICK COOK KNEELAND[18](*Isaac[17], Isaac[16], Isaac[15], Benjamin[14], Edward[13], Edward[12], John[11]—Alexander[1]*). Son of Isaac and Philomela (Robinson) Kneeland, b. March 4, 1812; d. April 2, 1872.

He was married, first, Oct. 11, 1838, at Hudson, Ohio, to Margaret A. Morton, of Blandford, Mass. They had two daughters. She died April 29, 1844, and in October of that year he married, second, Janutte M. Lyman, widow of Dr. James Lyman, of Andover, Ohio. In October, 1846, he moved to Waukesha, Wis., and in October, 1853, to Hartford of that State, where he remained until his death, April 2, 1872. His wife died Feb. 25, 1872.

Children of Frederick C. Kneeland, by Margaret A. Morton.

2658. (i.) ELLEN[19], b. July 23, 1839; m. Edward Mattison, and lives at Hartford, Wis.

2659. (ii.) AMELIA[19], b. Dec. 31, 1840; unmarried. Lived, 1896, at Milwaukee, Wis.

By Janutte M. Lyman.

2660. (iii.) MARY ELIZABETH[19], b. at Waukesha, Wis., Nov. 2, 1849. She now (1897) resides in Boston, Mass.

2661. (2506.) DUDLEE KNEELAND[17] (*Isaac[16], Isaac[15], Benjamin[14], Edward[13], Edward[12], John[11]—Alexander[1]*). Second son of Isaac and Hannah (Adams) Kneeland, b. at Hebron, Conn., Jan. 28, 1767. He married Mercy Knowles, Jan. 10, 1797. They had the following children, all born in Connecticut:

Horatio Hamilton Kneeland[19].

Children of Dudlee and Mercy (Knowles) Kneeland.

2662.   (i.) HORATIO[18], b. about 1798.

2663.   (ii.) DUDLEE[18], b. about 1800. He was a celebrated musician and violin manufacturer, too generous to reap anything in life but happiness.

2664.   (iii.) NATHANIEL KNOWLES[18], b. in 1802 (of whom hereafter, 2668).

2665.   (iv.) ISAAC[18], b. in 1805.

2666.   (v.) GILES ERASMUS[18], b. about 1808.

2667.   (vi.) MARCY[18], b. about 1814

2668.   (2664.) NATHANIEL KNOWLES KNEELAND[18], (*Dudlee[17], Isaac[16], Isaac[15], Benjamin[14], Edward[13], Edward[12], John[11]—Alexander[1]*). Second son of Dudlee and Mercy (Knowles) Kneeland, b. near Hartford, Conn., July 15, 1802.

He went to Massachusetts when quite young. From there he went to Sackett's Harbor, N. Y., thence to Watertown, N. Y., where he was married in 1831, to Lurancy Lyon, of that place, and several of his children were born there. From thence he went, in the spring of 1838, to Appleton, Ohio, and finally settled permanently at Newark, Ohio. He was in the boot and shoe business, which was adopted by his sons after him. He died Oct. 17, 1858, at the age of 56 years, three months and two days.

Children of Nathaniel K. and Lurancy (Lyon) Kneeland.

2669.   (i.) HORATIO HAMILTON[19], b. Sept. 14, 1835; m. Isabella M. Lane, at Newark, Ohio, Jan. 31, 1859; enlisted in Company D, 113th Ohio Regiment, which served in the 2d Brig., 2d Div., 14th Army Corps, during the campaign of the West, including the "march to the sea," under Gen. Sherman. He escaped without further harm than total deafness incurred in that celebrated tramp. Today, both he and his good wife are hearty and well. Although the mother of twelve children, she is, at the age of 53, stalwart and strong, without a gray

William L. Kneeland[20].

hair, and in perfect health. They live in Columbus, where he has been for many years engaged as a pension attorney. Children:

2670.   (i.) *Mary Alfaretta[20]*, b. Dec. 25, 1859, at Appleton, Ohio; m. Sept. 11, 1878, at Mt. Vernon, Ohio, to Clarence L. Davidson.

2671.   (ii.) *George Nathaniel[20]*, b. May 28, 1861, at Newark, Ohio; m. June 9, 1889, to Alfaretta Burnside, a relative of the late Gen. Burnside. They reside in Columbus, Ohio. Children:

2671A.   (i.) Maud Fay[21], b. Jan. 10, 1890.

2671B.   (ii.) Hugh[21], b. April 19, 1892; d. Oct. 21, 1893.

2671C.   (iii.) Mable Iona[21], b. Nov. 23, 1893.

2672.   (iii) *Joshua Hamilton[20]*, b. Jan. 8, 1863; m. Alice DeWitt, Jan. 1, 1886, at Mansfield, Ohio. They reside at Vedersburg, Ind.

2673.   (iv.) *Ida Bell[20]*, b. May 28, 1865, at Newark, Ohio, m. Charles Grimm. Resided at Columbus, Ohio. She is dead. They had one child:

2674.   Charles Grimm[21].

2675.   (v.) *Charles Frederick[20]*, b. May 22, 1867; married twice; resides at Vedersburg, Ind. First wife was Margaret Mahler, m. June 19, 1889; she d. July 17, 1894. They had three children:

2676.   (i.) Charles Hamilton[21], b. April 29, 1890; d. Nov. 26, 1893.

2677.   (ii.) Ethel E.[21], b. July 20, 1891.

2678.   (iii) Gertie Bell[21], b. April 4, 1893; d. May 17, 1894.

His second wife was Sarah Cochran, m. Dec. 15, 1895, at Vedersburg, Ind. They have one child:

2679.   (iv.) Robert[21], b. Sept. 7, 1896.

2680.   (vi.) *Murtie May[20]*, b. July 4, 1869, at Louisville, Ohio; m. William Otto Haen, Dec. 13, 1888. They reside at Columbus. No issue.

2681.   (vii.) *William L.[20]*, b. July 2, 1871, in Newark, Ohio; m. Nov. 3, 1892, to Rosie Steinfeld, at Mansfield, Ohio, where he now resides. They have a boy and a girl.

Elminia Kneeland[19].

2684.   (viii.) *Jesse Grant*[20], b. Aug. 17, 1874, in Mt.
Vernon, Ohio; m. April 5, 1894, to Clara
Strunk. They reside at Mansfield, Ohio, and
have no chidren.

2685.   (ix.) *Rolla Alfred*[20], b. Sept. 1, 1876, at Mt.
Vernon, Ohio. Resides at Columbus, Ohio.

2686.   (x.) *Arthur Ray*[20], b. Feb. 8, 1878, at Mt. Vernon,
Ohio.

2687.   (xi.) *Nellie Genevieve*[20], b. Sept. 2, 1879, at Mt.
Vernon, Ohio.

2688.   (xii.) *Bessie Daisy*[20], b. Sept. 1, 1882, at Columbus, Ohio.

2689.   (ii.) ELMINIA T.[19], b. in 1837; d. in 1839.

2690.   (iii.) LURANCY MARIA[19], b. in 1840; d. at Pittsburg,
Pa., in 1894.

2691.   (iv.) ALBERT N.[19], b. Aug. 19, 1846. He is living in
St. Joseph, Mo. He enlisted in the war at the age
of 16, and served three years.

2692.   (v.) ELMINIA[19]. She is now living in Columbus, Ohio.

CHAPTER XXXIX.

THE VERMONT FAMILY.

(NOS. 2693 TO 2798.)

2693. (725.) JOSEPH KNEELAND[16](*Joseph*[15], *Edward*[14], *Edward*[13], *Edward*[12], *John*[11], *William*[10], *James*[9], *Alexander*[8], *William*[7], *William*[6], *John*[5], *John*[4], *John*[3], *James*[2], *Alexander*[1]). Youngest son of Joseph[15] and Mirriam Kneeland and uncle of the celebrated divine, Rev. Abner Kneeland, was born in Harvard, Mass., Nov. 22, 1752 (see records of Harvard, Mass.); married Ruth Hartwell, had a large family and died at Hartford, Vt., in 1828, aged 76.

He lived many years at Fitzwilliam, N. H., and afterwards at Uxbridge, Mass. About the beginning of the present century his sons commenced business at Hartford, Vt. Edward's family moved there in 1811 and Joseph followed shortly after. Ruth Hartwell was the daughter of Samuel Hartwell and Anna Tarbell, and great-granddaughter of Rebecca Nurse, of Salem, who was hung for witchcraft, July 17, 1717 (see History of the Hartwell Family, p. 5). Joseph Kneeland settled in Fitzwilliam in 1774. The next year—April 23, 1775 —he enlisted in Capt. Whitcomb's company, from Fitzwilliam, Col. James Reid's regiment, and fought in the baptismal battle of the Revolution—Bunker Hill (see History of Fitzwilliam, pp. 143 and 249; also Rev. Records of N. H., No. 1, 111, and Vol. 1, p. 93, of the published Revolution Records). This makes all his descendants Sons or Daughters of the American Revolution.

Children of Joseph and Ruth (Hartwell) Kneeland.

2694. (i.) RUTH[17], b. at Fitzwilliam; m. Mr. Hazen. No further record.

Edward Kneeland[17].

2695.   (ii.) JOSEPH HARTWELL[17], b. at Fitzwilliam, N. H.
        The History of Hartford, Vt., mentions as among
        the earliest settlers, Edward Kneeland, who was
        located there in 1795, Joseph H. Kneeland who
        leased a factory in 1807, and states that the Olcott
        Falls paper mills was owned by Joseph H., Edward
        and David Kneeland. These were the sons of
        Joseph Kneeland[16]. A further history of their
        residence in Hartford appears in the article relating
        to the "Kneeland Twins" (No. 2713). The first
        Hartford, Vt., real estate transaction in which they
        are interested was the purchase of property by
        Joseph H. Kneeland, recorded on the 24th of De-
        cember, 1804. From that time forward the names
        of both Joseph H. and David Kneeland appear
        frequently in the records. The following old family
        record was sent me by Samuel E. Pingree, Town
        Clerk of Hartford, Conn.:

                "Joseph H. Kneeland Famely Record.

2696.   (i.) "*Almadorus*[18], their son, b. Aug. 29th, 1805.
2697.   (ii.) "*Emmalina*[18], their daughter, b. Sept. 14th,
             1806.
2698.   (iii.) "*Malvina*[18], their daughter, b. March 22d,
             1808.
2699.   (iv.) "*Diana Cornelia*[18], their daughter, b. June
             26th, 1813."
        From which we must assume that Joseph Hartwell
        Kneeland was well up in the classics. He and his
        brother David "went West"—that is, to Pennsyl-
        vania, which was "West" in those early days—and
        that is the last we have heard from either of them.
        I suppose that these sonorous names got quickly
        reduced to "Al.," and "Em.," and Mal.," and
        "Di.," so that the owners thereof never really got
        the benefit of their wonderful heritage.
2700.   (iii.) EDWARD[17], b. at Fitzwilliam, N. H., March 17,
        1782 (of whom hereafter, 2705).

Angeline Lucinda Kneeland[18].

2701. (iv.) DAVID[17], b. at Uxbridge, Mass., Jan. 10, 1784. As to history, see Joseph H. (No. 2695) and Angeline (No. 2713). He was married and had children, but some later chronicler must give their names and history.

2702. (v.) PRUDENCE[17], b. at Uxbridge, Mass.; m. A. Perley. No further record.

2703. (vi.) MIRRIAM[17].

2704. (vii.) LYDIA[17], married a Mr. Hall.

2705. (2700.) EDWARD KNEELAND[17] (*Joseph[16]*, *Joseph[15]*, *Edward[14]*, *Edward[13]*, *Edward[12]*, *John[11]* —*Alexander[1]*). Second son of Joseph and Ruth (Hartwell) Kneeland, b. at Fitzwilliam, N. H., afterwards settled at Hartford, Vt., with his father and brothers, Joseph H. and David (see History of Hartford, Vt.)

Quite an interesting sketch of some of the incidents in his life is contained in the history of two of his daughters, the Kneeland twins (No. 2713), also Joseph H. Kneeland (No. 2695). He married Charity Betsey Johnson, of New Haven, Conn., Jan. 15, 1806. They resided at Hampden, Conn., until about 1811, when he moved to Hartford, Vt., where he had for many years been interested in mills and factories. He died at Hartford, Vt., Dec. 4, 1862. His widow died at the residence of his daughter, Alpa, wife of Col. Nutt, of White River Junction, April 9, 1866. Among the marriage presents by the bride's parents were two negro slaves, John and Hannah. They formed a part of the personal property that the couple took to Vermont with them. Imagine this, in the nineteenth century. That they were well cared for, manumitted and afterwards married and lived in peace and happiness to the end of their days, is to be assumed, of course.

Children of Edward and Charity (Johnson) Kneeland.

2708. (i.) ADALINE MINERVA[18], and

2709. (ii.) ANGELINE LUCINDA[18], twins, b. Nov. 20, 1809 (of whom hereafter, 2713).

Angeline[18] *and Adaline Kneeland*[18].

2710.   (iii.) JANE ELIZABETH[18], b. April 6, 1811; m. Steven
         Carlton.

2711.   (iv.) ALPA LOUISA[18], b. May 25. 1819 (of whom here-
         after, 2793).

2712.   (v.) EDWARD ALPHONSO[18], b. Oct. 5, 1820.

2713.   (2708.) ANGELINE[18] AND ADALINE KNEE-
         LAND[18](*Edward*[17],*Joseph*[16],*Joseph*[15],*Edward*[14],
         Edward[13], *Edward*[12], *John*[11] — *Alexander*[1]).
         Twins, b. in Hampden, Conn., Nov. 20, 1809,
         daughters of Edward and Charity (Johnson) Knee-
         land. The following interesting sketch from the
         Manchester, N. H., *Union*, gives a glimpse of the
         homelife of these ladies.

"THE OLDEST IN NEW ENGLAND.

**"Interesting History of the Kneeland Twins.—Noteworthy Incidents in
the Lives of two Worthy Women.—Weight of Scores
of Years hangs lightly o'er Their Heads.**

   "It was one of those fine afternoons that come in spring
among the hills that the writer wended his way up the village
street in search of the Simpson homestead. The story of Mrs.
Angeline Kneeland Simpson and her twin sister, Mrs. Adaline
Kneeland Colby, is particularly interesting just now, since it
has appeared that they are the oldest living twins in New
England. The Fife sisters, of Petersborough, whose portraits
were printed in *The Union* a short time ago, were born August
11, 1811, making them nearly 83 years of age at the present
time. The Kneeland sisters were born November 20, 1809,
and are consequently nearly two years older that the Fife
sisters.

   "Adaline M. and Angeline L. Kneeland are daughters of
the late Edward Kneeland, a descendant of Abner Kneeland,
the distinguished orator and Universalist minister of Boston.
It was for this well-known clergyman that Kneeland street was
named. The sisters, Adeline and Angeline, were born in
Hampden, Conn., on Nov. 20, 1809. When the little girls
were two years old the family removed to Vermont, the
journey being made in a large covered wagon drawn by two

Angeline L. Simpson

No. 2713

Angeline[18] and Adaline Kneeland[18].

horses, the journey occupying several days. When the trip was about half completed an accident befell the party. The horses becoming frightened, the vehicle was partially over-turned down an embankment. Fortunately no one was seri-ously injured and the family arrived at Hartford, Vt., without further noteworthy incident. Mr. Kneeland was a prominent citizen in the village, where, besides being engaged in public affairs, he had an interest in a cotton factory. At this mill was carded and spun the yarn used by farmers' wives to make cloth on hand looms for home use. The cotton was distributed among the neighbors to be picked by hand. The method of picking was to spread the cotton out upon a sort of frame where it was beaten with two long sticks until the burrs and seed were loosened, after which they were picked out by the fingers. With the introduction of machinery the factory became one of importance. Mr. Kneeland being a man of great worth and enterprise, he naturally was called to offices of trust, and he was frequently called upon to decide important law points that arose in the town.

"While the sisters grew up in the healthful atmosphere of the quiet Vermont village, they received the best education the schools afforded. The school they attended derived a special advantage in being taught by advanced students from Hanover. The bright, handsome girls were naturally the belles of the village and moved in the best society, while their gentle manners and cultured bearing won the respect of the neighborhood. Miss Angeline L. Kneeland was married, Feb. 13, 1829, to Dr. Daniel L. Simpson, of Rumney. Soon after marriage they settled in Londonderry, where the doctor carried on a farm in addition to his medical practice. These were bright, happy days of rural life by the banks of the Merrimack; and now the sweet paths of memory run along the scented clover fields by the river side. Dr. Simpson had an extensive practice at Londonderry and often rode to Litchfield, Hudson and Manchester.

"In 1833 the Simpson family removed to Windham. After a short residence in Windham and Nashua, they went to Rumney and settled in the part of the town for many years known as Morse Village, now West Rumney. It was in the

27

Angeline[18] *and Adaline Kneeland*[18].

good old stage coach times, when the great, lumbering, yellow vehicle had headquarters at Morse's tavern. Here the genial Robert Morse, well known up and down the valley, kept the public house and was proprietor of the stage line. About this time Dr. Simpson was appointed postmaster, which office he held up to the time of his death, July 15, 1879. In all his public work Dr. Simpson had the intelligent sympathy and valuable help of his wife.

"Mrs. Angeline Simpson is the mother of thirteen children, twelve of whom are living. One son, Lieut. Henry C. Simpson, died in the army and was buried in Carr Hill Cemetery, at Louisville, Ky. Two other sons were in the service. The children are widely scattered; one in Nebraska, one in Minnesota, four in Massachusetts, while the others are in New Hampshire. Her days are cheered by the memory of a kind husband and the watchful care of dutiful children. Her descendants number forty-one grandchildren and fourteen great-grandchildren. Mrs. Simpson has always taken an active part in the church and in all affairs of public improvement. She is still an active, handsome woman, whose glossy hair and bright eyes betray no sign of her 80 years and more. A vein of sunny wit runs through her conversation, and when the writer spoke of her youthful appearance, her eyes sparkled as she said: 'You remind me of a book agent who called here a little while ago. After supper—I let him stay to supper—he moved his chair up by the window where I was sitting, and after looking thoughtful a minute, said, 'Mrs Simpson, you remind me of the very woman my first wife said she wanted me to have, if I ever married again.'' 'Mercy, how old do you think I am, sir?' 'Why, I suppose about 60,' said the book man. 'Well, sir, I am 85.' 'Thunder, I never thought it.'

"The twin sister, Mrs. Adaline M. Colby, resides in Fairlee, Vt. In 1836 she married John Colby, a well-known lawyer of that place. Her intelligence and education enabled her to greatly assist her husband in his duties, and many town records are done in her beautiful handwriting. Her husband held several offices of trust, and was at one time judge of the court. Of her four children, three are living. Like her sister, she still possesses much of the beauty of younger years.

Dwight Ezra Douglass[21].

These amiable sisters have always taken a cheerful view of life and its affairs; their sunny dispositions have shed its perplexities like summer rain; and as the summer of their days drifted into autumn, and autumn into winter, they still saw the warm light of the evening sun shining upon their paths."

Angeline married Dr. Simpson, Feb. 13, 1829. Of the thirteen children, one died in the army, and *the remaining* twelve are still living (1897)—a wonderful record, considering that they range from 65 years down.

But this is not all. Their oldest son died in the army and his wife followed him to the grave a few months later, leaving two orphaned children, who were adopted and brought up by the grandparents, making, really, fifteen children to care for. In addition to the care of this little household, the troubles of an army of patients seem to have been rolled upon the shoulders of the doctor's wife. She was constantly watching by the bedside of the sick, cheering the last moments of the dying. She prepared their souls for eternity, and after death, their bodies for the grave. In the absence of her husband she took up his labors, administering remedies and even performing surgical operations. She is now enjoying the "Indian summer" of life, with the remembrance of golden days in the past and the benedictions of a wide circle of friends.

Children of Angeline L. Kneeland[18] and Dr. D. L. Simpson.

2714.   (i.) HENRY CLAY SIMPSON[19], b. Jan. 29, 1830 (of whom hereafter, 2768).

2715.   (ii.) EDWARD ALPHONSO SIMPSON[19], b. April 1, 1831 (of whom hereafter, 2779).

2716.   (iii.) MINERVA JANE SIMPSON[19], b. Dec. 28, 1832; m. James Marshall Douglass, Dec. 27, 1852. Children:

2719.   (i.) *Frederick H. Douglass[20]*, b. March 3, 1854; m. Celia May Humphrey, Oct. 3, 1882. Children:

2720.   (i.) Carl E. Douglass[21], b. Dec. 11, 1883; d. Aug. 13, 1884.

2721.   (ii.) Beulah Alice Douglass[21], b. Jan. 14, 1885.

2722.   (iii.) Dwight Ezra Douglass[21], b. July 30, 1887.

Evelyn L. Simpson[19].

2723.   (iv.) Keith Frederick Douglass[21], b. Nov. 7, 1889.
2724.   (v.) Ruth Olive Douglass[21], b. Dec. 4, 1893.
2725.   (vi.) Mark Lyle Douglass[21], b. Jan. 25, 1896.
James M. Douglass served in the U. S. army during the war, and participated in Sherman's famous "march to the sea." They reside at Anoka, Minn.
2726.   (ii.) *William Henry Douglass[20]*, b. Sept. 1, 1856; d. March 25, 1857.
2727.   (iii.) *James Edward Douglass[20]*, b. June 21, 1858; m. Maud Battarff, June 21, 1892. No children.
2728.   (iv.) *Henry C. Douglass[20]*, b. March 29, 1860; d. May 2, 1861.
2729.   (v.) *Alice M. Douglass[20]*, b. March 11, 1862; d. Jan. 8, 1874.
2730.   (vi.) *Benjamin S. Douglass[20]*, b. Nov. 24, 1871; d. April 26, 1874.
2731.   (vii.) *Kenneth V. Douglass[20]*, b. Oct. 26, 1877.
2732. (iv.) HELEN MARIA SIMPSON[19], b. May 17, 1834; m. Alpheus G. Hobbs, April 7, 1864. They reside at Pelham, N. H. Children:
2733.   (i.) *Sherman Hobbs[20]*, b. Jan. 29, 1865; unmarried.
2734.   (ii.) *Helen Abiah Hobbs[20]*, b. Jan. 6, 1871; unmarried.
2735. (v.) CHARLES DANIEL SIMPSON[19], b. Jan. 31, 1836; m. Rose G. Pitman, Sept. 19, 1859. They had one son:
2736.   *Louie W. Simpson[20]*, b. Sept. 30, 1860, and who married Mabel Johnson, of Ord, Neb., Jan. 1, 1890. They live at Elyria, Neb., and have two children:
2737.   (i.) Luella Pearl Simpson[21], b. Dec. 19, 1890.
2738.   (ii.) Hazel Kirk Simpson[21], b. Oct. 30, 1892.
2739. (vi.) MARY LANG SIMPSON[19], b. March 24, 1838; m. Joshua R. Fessenden, of Windham, N. H., Dec. 7, 1864. They had one son:
2740.   *William Lang Fessenden[20]*, b. Nov. 10, 1865; d. Feb. 21, 1867.
2741. (vii.) EVELYN LOUISA SIMPSON[19], b. Feb. 11, 1840; m. Henry Clark, of Windham, N. H., Jan. 2, 1869.

Harriet Frances Simpson[19].

They reside at Windham, and have the following children:

2742.   (i.) *George Henry Clark[20]*, b. Sept. 2, 1869.
2743.   (ii.) *Joanna Bodge Clark[20]*, b. March 24, 1871.
2744.   (iii.) *Rosa Jane Clark[20]*, b. June 11, 1875.
2745.   (iv.) *Angeline E. Clark[20]*, b. March 6, 1877.
2746.   (viii.) OLIVER EVERETT SIMPSON[19], b. July 24, 1842; m. Georgiana Merrill, Jan. 9, 1877; resides at West Rumney, N. H.   He was the third son of the family to join the Union army at the time "that tried men's souls."   On the 22d of August, 1862, at the age of 22, he enlisted in Company E, 12th N. H. Vols.; was mustered in Sept. 5, and joined the army of the Potomac Sept. 27, 1862.   The change from the pure air of New Hampshire to the miasma of the swamps of Virginia proved too great.   He was stricken with typhoid fever, and the stalwart youth of 160 pounds was reduced to a skeleton of 87 pounds.   He lost a portion of his left foot, was discharged and has ever since suffered from the effects of that contest with the swamps and "gray backs" of "old Virginny."   It took more real heroism, though realizing less fame, to face the fever-laden meadows of that God-forsaken country than to breast up against the leaden hail of the rebel armies.   Children of Oliver E. Simpson:

2747.   (i.) *Susan Caroline Simpson[20]*, b. Dec. 19, 1888.
2748.   (ii.) *Sarah Alberta Simpson[20]*, b. Oct. 22, 1890.
2749.   (iii.) *Frank Edwin Simpson[20]*, and
2750.   (iv.) *Henry Alphonso Simpson[20]*, twins, b. Oct. 22, 1893.
2751.   (ix.) HARRIET FRANCES SIMPSON[19], b. June 23, 1844; m. Dr. Dixie Crosby Smalley, of Lebanon, N. H., March 19, 1866.   Dr. Smalley was the youngest son of Dr. Adonixon Smalley, of Lebanon, Conn., and a relative of Judge Smalley, of Vermont.   He practiced medicine in Corinth, Vt., Lyme, N. H., and Lebanon, N. H.   He died in 1873, leaving his most capable wife in sole charge of a son of two

Frank Edwin Simpson[19].

years and five months, and another of five months.
They both graduated at Dartmouth in June, 1894,
and their grandmother, 85 years old, journeyed to
Hanover to witness the commencement exercises.
The oldest son, Bertrand, was the class poet and is
now in Boston, on the *Evening Record* and the
Morning Advertiser. The younger, Fred., is studying medicine. I desire to thank their mother in
this semi-public manner for her earnest labors in
my behalf, she having secured the records in full of
the descendants of Mrs. Dr. Simpson. She resides
with her mother at West Rumney, N. H. Children of Harriet F. Simpson and Dr. Smalley :

2752.   (i.) *Nellie Rosamond Smalley*[20], b. Oct. 2, 1867 ;
            d. April 25, 1868.

2753.   (ii.) *Ina Mystic Smalley*[20], b. May 21, 1869 ; d.
            Jan. 18, 1870.

2754.   (iii.) *Bertrand A. Smalley*[20], b. Oct. 29, 1870.

2755.   (iv.) *Fred. Lyman Smalley*[20], b. Nov. 1, 1872.

2756. (x.) SUSAN CAROLINE SIMPSON[19], b. June 17, 1846 ;
            m. Vernon E. Atwood, of West Rumney, N. H.
            Child :

2757.   *Rexford U. Atwood*[20], b. and d. Nov. 14, 1890.

2758. (xi.) ALICE OLENA SIMPSON[19], b. April 9, 1848 ; m.
            Aaron M. Hamblett, Feb. 2, 1869. They reside at
            Brockton, Mass. Children :

2759.   (i.) *Lillian Mabel Hamblett*[20], b. April 20, 1870 ;
            m. Edward Tinkham, July 8, 1895.

2760.   (ii.) *Ina Beatrice Hamblett*[20], b. March 27, 1873.

2761.   (iii.) *Harry Arthur Hamblett*[20], b. July 9, 1875.

2762. (xii.) ELIZABETH SIMPSON[19], b. April 18, 1850 ; m.
            William Flynn, of South Boston, where they now
            reside. Children :

2763.   (i.) *Harry W. Flynn*[20], b. Aug. 19, 1882.

2764.   (ii.) *Lillian E. Flynn*[20], b. March 21, 1884.

2765.   (iii.) *Frank E. Flynn*[20], b. May 4, 1889.

2766.   (iv.) *Ralph E. Flynn*[20], b. July 29, 1892.

2767. (xiii.) FRANK EDWIN SIMPSON[19], b. July 5, 1853 ;
            m. Lucy Holbrook, Sept. 11, 1878. No children.

LIEUT. HENRY C. SIMPSON

No. 2768

Ernest Henry Simpson[20].

2768. (2714.) HENRY CLAY SIMPSON[19] (*Angeline Knee-land*[18], *Edward*[17], *Joseph*[16], *Joseph*[15], *Edward*[14], *Edward*[13], *Edward*[12], *John*[11]—*Alexander*[1]). Eldest son of Angeline L. Kneeland and Dr. Daniel L. Simpson, b. Jan. 29, 1830; m. Elizabeth Corson, Nov., 1850; d. at Lebanon Junction, Ky., Dec. 1, 1861.

I have received from his family the following sketch of his life: "Being a youth of more than ordinary ability, he was early apprenticed to learn the printer's trade, in the office of Mr. Towle, who edited the *Granite State Whig*, at Lebanon, N. H. He completed his course Jan. 29, 1850, at the age of twenty years, but continued in the same place until his marriage, in the fall of the same year, when he secured a position in New York City. Later, he edited a paper at Potsdam, N. Y. About 1856 he removed his family to Minnesota and edited a paper at Watopa—the *Watopa Journal*. At the breaking out of the Rebellion, he responded personally to Lincoln's proclamation calling for 75,000 volunteers for three months, and served his time. Returning home he sold out his business (printing) and reënlisted in Comp. C, 2d Reg., Minn. Vol., and was chosen First Lieutenant when ordered to the seat of war, early in October, 1861, the captain being on a furlough on account of sickness."

Children of Lieut. Henry C. Simpson and Elizabeth Corson.

2769. (i.) HELEN MINERVA SIMPSON[20], b. in New York City, Dec. 12, 1851; m. Loren E. Bailey, June 2, 1873. They reside at Salem Depot, N. H. Children·

2770.   (i.) *Edith Clare Bailey*[21], b. Sept. 9, 1874; d. Sept. 6, 1875.

2771.   (ii.) *Ethelyn Mary Bailey*[21], b. May 11, 1876.

2772.   (iii.) *Henry Loren Bailey*[21], b. Feb. 19, 1879.

2773.   (iv.) *Helena Josie Bailey*[21], b. April 27, 1881.

2774.   (v.) *Shirlie Ernestine Bailey*[21], b. Feb. 11, 1883.

2775.   (vi.) *Daniel Simpson Bailey*[21], b. Nov. 4, 1891.

2776 and 2777. (ii. and iii.) ERNEST HENRY SIMPSON[20], and twin sister, b. June 29, 1869. The sister died six months after. Ernest Henry married Eva K. Joyce, April 15, 1889. One child:

2778.   *Helen Mattie Simpson²¹*, b. in Williams, Arizona,
Jan. 25, 1896, and resides there with her parents.

Ernest and his twin sister were born in the
township of Watopa, Minn., in a small log cabin
on the White river, in close vicinity of a large
lodge of Sioux Indians. At the outbreak of the
Civil War, 1861, they removed to West Rumney,
N. H., to live with the grandparents until the close
of the war, the family going as far as Cairo, Ill.,
with the father and husband, with the 2d Minn.
Vols. on their way to the front. There they parted
forever, the father to meet his doom under the
clear, blue southern skies of Kentucky, the mother
to soon die in a few weeks in the wintry climate
of New England, in the quiet little town of West
Rumney, N. H. At the age of 17 Ernest was sent
to learn the printer's trade in the office of the
Manchester, N. H., *Daily Mirror.* He worked at
the business in Boston, Mass., and Augusta, Me.,
until the spring of 1881, when he started for the
great West, stopping at Chicago, Ill., Omaha, Neb.,
and Denver, finally locating at Leadville, Col., then
the greatest mining camp in America. Here he
engaged in mining and other pursuits until the fall
of 1881, when he removed south to the Arizona
frontier, locating on the great cattle ranges of that
territory, where he followed the life of a vaguerio
until 1888. He then accepted a situation as manager of a general merchandise store and Indian
trading post, which position he retained until 1894,
when he accepted the management of the Grand
Cañon Hotel, the leading hotel of North Arizona,
where he at present resides. His life on the
frontier has been full of adventure and narrow
escapes, he having passed through the bloody
Apache Indian wars of 1882 and 1886 unharmed,
being favored with the acquaintance and compan-
ionship of the gallant Gen. Crook and the late
Capt. Banks, 3d U. S. Cavalry. He rendered them

Edward Alphonso Simpson[19].

great service in the struggles that finally broke the
power of the Apaches. He was married April 15,
1889, in National City, Cal., to Eva K., daughter of
P. A. Joyce, division road-master of the Atlantic
and Pacific Railway, and a veteran of the Civil
War (10th Iowa Vols.) They are blessed with
one child, a daughter, Helen M., who was born
in Williams, Arizona, Jan. 25, 1896. He is a charter
member of Gen. Fremont Camp, No. 48, S. of V.,
U. S. A., Los Angeles, Cal.

2779. (2715.) EDWARD ALPHONSO SIMPSON[19] (*An-
geline*[18], *Edward*[17], *Joseph*[16], *Joseph*[15], *Edward*[14],
Edward[13], *Edward*[12], *John*[11]—*Alexander*[1]). Sec-
ond son of Daniel L. and Angeline (Kneeland)
Simpson, was born April 1, 1831; m. Augusta Fox,
Jan. 1, 1855.

He bore a most honorable part in the War of the Rebellion, 1861-5, enlisting in Company B, 30th Regt., Mass. Vols.,
Oct. 12, 1861, at Camp Chase, Lowell, Mass. Leaving camp
on the second day of January, 1862, embarked on board the
steamship Constitution, at Boston, bound for the rendezvous
of Gen. Butler's expedition at Ship Island, Mississippi Sound,
to prepare for the capture of New Orleans and the control of
the lower Mississippi river. Was present at the " battle of the
forts." His regiment was the second to land at New Orleans
after its surrender, the 1st of May, 1862. He was engaged in
the battle of Baton Rouge, Aug. 5, 1862; was at the siege of
Port Hudson, 27th May to the 8th July, under fire every day;
at the battle of Kox's Plantation, near Donaldsonville, La.,
July 13, 1863. He was also on the Bayou Teche campaign, in
the autumn and winter of 1863-4. Was engaged in the battle
of Carrion Crow Bayou, Sept., 1863. He reënlisted Jan 1,
1864. After a brief furlough at home, returned to New
Orleans and up the Mississippi river to Morgansie Bend ; there
met the army of Gen. Banks returning from its disastrous
Red River campaign. Soon after, the 19th Corps, to which
his regiment belonged, was ordered north to join the army of
Gen. Meade in front of Petersburg. Arriving in Hampton

D. Clinton Colby[19].

Roads at the time of Gen. Early's raid around Washington, the 19th Corps was sent immediately to that point to protect the Capitol. Thereafter he was engaged in that vicinity and in the Shenandoah Valley, in Virginia; was in the engagement at Snicker's Gap and Berryville; at the battle of Halltown Heights; at the battle of Winchester, Sept. 19; the battle of Fisher's Hill, Sept. 23; the engagement at New Market, Sept. 24, also at the battle of Cedar Creek, Oct. 19, 1864, where he received a wound in the ankle which necessitated the amputation of the left leg and closed his military career. Subsequently he suffered two more amputations, one at the middle of the thigh and the other near the hip-joint. After one year of suffering in the hospital, he was discharged to spend the remainder of his life on crutches. A few years later he was chosen postmaster at Middlesex Village, Lowell, Mass., where he resided and continued to hold that office until it was discontinued in 1896.

Children of Edward Alphonso and Augusta (Fox) Simpson.

2780. (i.) ISABELLE MINERVA SIMPSON[20], b. Nov. 12, 1855; m. De Clinton Nichols, of Southboro, Mass., June 20, 1877. The family reside there. Children:

2781. (i.) *Grace Isabella Nichols*[21], b. June 9, 1879.

2782. (ii.) *Charlotte Augusta Nichols*[21], b. Jan. 28, 1884; drowned Sept. 8, 1887.

2783. (iii.) *Edward Clinton Nichols*[21], b. June 21, 1889.

2784. (ii.) ANNIE AUGUSTA SIMPSON[20], b. July 20, 1858; m. Willis H. Bean, of Lowell, Mass., June 9, 1880. Children:

2785. (i.) *Alice Gertrude Bean*[21], b. July 21, 1884.

2786. (ii.) *Winthrop Simpson Bean*[21], b. May 28, 1892.

2787. (iii.) EVA GERTRUDE SIMPSON[20], b. March 2, 1868; unmarried.

Children of Adaline L. Kneeland[18] and Judge Colby.

2788. (i.) JANE E. COLBY[19], b. April, 1838; m. Mr. Bragin; d. in 1894.

2789. (ii.) D. CLINTON COLBY[19], b. Dec., 1839; m. and had one child:

Fannie Louise King[20].

2790.   *Roland Browning Colby[20].*

2791.   (iii.) HENRY COLBY[19], b. in August, 1841; d. in Nov., 1845.

2792.   (iv.) ELLEN L. COLBY[19], b. in 1843.

2793.   (2711.) ALPA LOUISE KNEELAND[18] (*Edward*[17], *Joseph*[16], *Joseph*[15], *Edward*[14], *Edward*[13], *Edward*[12], *John*[11]—*Alexander*[1]). Born at Hartford, Vt., May 25, 1819; m. Col. Alonzo Nutt, in 1844, and has ever since resided at White River Junction.

She is thus introduced to me by Samuel E. Pingree, the clerk of Hartford, Vt., in partial answer to my enquiry for facts relating to the Hartford family of Kneelands: " Mrs. Col. Alonzo Nutt, of White River Junction, Vt., *née* Alpa L. Kneeland, daughter of Edward Kneeland, is one of our brightest women, and can give you much lore about her family in Hartford, during this century." Subsequent communications from her have abundantly verified this statement. She is as bright, as witty and as jolly as—a Kneeland. If you wish a statement as to her death you will, I trust, have to wait many years and apply to some other chronicler.

Children of Alpa Louise Kneeland[18] and Col. Alonzo Nutt.

2794.   (i.) ALICE L. NUTT[19], b. in 1845; m. to C. Vreeland, in 1868. They reside in Jersey City, N. J., and have one daughter:

2795.   *Jennie Louise Vreeland[20]*, b. Nov. 2, 1872. She is unmarried and lives with her parents in Jersey City.

2796.   (ii.) AMANDA H. NUTT[19], b. in 1848; d. in 1868.

2797.   (iii.) SARAH B. NUTT[19], b. in 1849; m. W. J. King, in 1875. They have one daughter:

2798.   *Fannie Louise King[20]*, b. Dec. 21, 1874.

CHAPTER XL.

THE MAINE FAMILY.

(NOS. 2799 TO 3218.)

2799. (736.) AARON KNEELAND[16] (*Philip*[15], *Philip*[14], *Edward*[13], *Edward*[12], *John*[11], *William*[10], *James*[9], *Alexander*[8], *William*[7], *William*[6], *John*[5], *John*[4], *John*[3], *James*[2], *Alexander*[1]). Third son of Philip and Mary (Potter) Kneeland, b. at Topsfield, Mass., Nov. 10, 1749; m. Hannah Ramsdell, of Topsfield, May 10, 1773, and had ten children, all born there.

He was one of the "minute men" on the Lexington alarm list from Topsfield, and fought at Bunker Hill. That battle satisfied his military ambition, and he settled down and commenced raising potatoes and children—both crops proving sound, healthy and numerous. About 1808 he went to Harrison, Cumberland County, Me., and his descendants now populate that and the surrounding county. They possess all the New England virtues and peculiarities, hardy, honest, religious, shrewd and thrifty. The average of life in his family was 78 years.

Children of Aaron and Hannah (Ramsdell) Kneeland.

2800. (i.) DANIEL[17], b. at Topsfield, Oct. 23, 1774; m. Betsy Rolf, of Topsfield, May 3, 1797; resided at Topsfield, Mass.; d. May 23, 1861, aged 87. They had three children, as follows:

2801.   (i.) *Eunice*[18], b. May 11, 1799; m. Joseph Andrews, of Harrison, Me., Nov. 13, 1821. Had one child:

2802.   Lizzie[19].

David P. Kneeland[17].

2803 and 2804.   (ii. and iii.) *Nathaniel*[18] and *Lois*[18], twins, b. May 12, 1803. Lois d. Sept. 25, 1804. Nathaniel m. Eunice Chaplin, Sept. 19, 1829.

2805.   (ii.) AARON[17], b. June 27, 1776; m. Lucy Hobbs, of Topsfield, Mass., March 6, 1799, and resided there; d. Dec. 6, 1854, aged 78. Their children were:

2806.   (i.) *Humphrey*[18], b. Nov. 15, 1800; m. Mary Chipman, of Ipswich, Dec. 25, 1822. Had a son:

2807.   Alfred[19], who died Jan. 13, 1828, aged four months.

2808.   (ii.) *Cyrus*[18], b. Sept. 25, 1804; m. Sally G. Boardman, of Topsfield, Sept. 30, 1832.

2809.   (iii.) *Aaron Porter*[18], b. Nov. 21, 1815.

2810.   (iii.) MARY[17], b. March 24, 1778; m. Geo. Hobbs, of Topsfield, Mass. (brother of Aaron's wife), Dec. 17, 1818; d. July 1, 1860, aged 82.

2811.   (iv.) JOHN[17], b. Nov. 28, 1780; m. Rhoda Hobbs, of Topsfield (another sister of Geo. Hobbs); settled in Topsfield, and died there June 23, 1855, aged 75 (of whom hereafter, 2818).

2812.   (v.) MOSES[17], b. Nov. 16, 1782; m. Priscilla Peabody, Aug. 23, 1808; d. March 17, 1838, aged 56 (of whom hereafter, 2836).

2813.   (vi.) EZRA[17], b. Oct. 6, 1784 (of whom hereafter, 2897).

2814.   (vii.) NEHEMIAH[17], b. May 5, 1789; m. Polly Goodhue, founder of Topsfield, Me.; d. June 28, 1867, aged 79 (of whom hereafter, 2950).

2815.   (viii.) ASA[17], b. Jan. 20, 1791; m. Sally Kneeland, a second cousin; he lived several years in Harrison, Me., and afterwards moved East and died Jan. 10, 1882, aged 91. No further information.

2816.   (ix.) SIMEON[17], b. Feb. 25, 1793; m. Hannah, daughter of Elijah Richardson, of Waterford; d. Jan. 1, 1873, aged 80 (of whom hereafter, 3098).

2817.   (x.) DAVID P.[17], b. May 24, 1798 (of whom hereafter, 3152).

2818. (2811.) JOHN KNEELAND[17] (*Aaron*[16], *Philip*[15], *Philip*[14], *Edward*[13], *Edward*[12], *John*[11]—*Alexander*[1]). Third son of Aaron Kneeland, b. at Topsfield, Mass., Nov. 28, 1780; d. there June 23, 1855, aged 75.

He was a prominent, public spirited citizen and held in high esteem by his neighbors. He served in the Topsfield company during the War of 1812, as his father did in the War of the Revolution and his grandson, John N. Kneeland, in the War of the Rebellion. He married Rhoda Hobbs, whose sister Lucy married his brother Aaron, and whose brother, George Hobbs, married his sister Mary. Considerable Hobnobbing between these families!

Children of John and Rhoda (Hobbs) Kneeland.

2819.   (i.) LEVI[18], b. at Topsfield, Mass., Feb. 17, 1802; m. Margaret Conant, Aug. 18, 1822.

2820.   (ii.) JOHN[18], b. at Rowley, Mass., June 30, 1804 (of whom hereafter, 2829).

2821.   (iii.) NOAH[18], b. Oct. 17, 1806, at Topsfield, Mass.

2822.   (iv.) RHODA[18], b. at Ipswich, Sept. 19, 1808.

2823.   (v.) AARON[18]. b. Sept. 8, 1811, at Ipswich, Mass.; now living at Georgetown, Mass.

2824.   (vi.) DAVID[18], b. at Ipswich, May 5, 1814.

2825.   (vii.) LYDIA[18], b. at Ipswich, Aug. 30, 1816.

2826.   (viii.) ALMIRA[18], b. Jan. 13, 1819, at Ipswich, Mass.

2827.   (ix.) MARY E.[18], b. at Rowley, Mass., Aug. 2, 1823; m. her cousin, Daniel Kneeland, and had ten children (see No. 3099).

2828.   (x.) HARRIET[18], b. at Rowley, Mass., June 11, 1826.

2829.   (2820). JOHN KNEELAND[18] (*John*[17], *Aaron*[16], *Philip*[15], *Philip*[14], *Edward*[13], *Edward*[12], *John*[11] —*Alexander*[1]). Born at Rowley, Mass., June 30, 1804, and resided there until his death, in 1863. He married Lydia Peabody, of Topsfield, Mass. (a relative of the London banker), April 10, 1829. They had two children.

Children of John and Lydia (Peabody) Kneeland.

2830.   (i.) JOHN N.[19], b. at Ipswich, June 4, 1840; now living at Rochester, N. Y. (of whom hereafter, 2832).

2831.   (ii.) MARY E.[19], b. at Rowley, Mass., Oct. 31, 1845.

2832·   (2830.) JOHN N. KNEELAND[19] (*John*[18], *John*[17], *Aaron*[16], *Philip*[15], *Philip*[14], *Edward*[13], *Edward*[12], *John*[11]—*Alexander*[1]). Eldest son of John Kneeland, b. at Ipswich, June 4, 1840; now resides at Rochester, N. Y.

He has the unique record of being the representative of all our wars: the Colonial, by Edward[13], who was in King Philip's War; the Revolution, by Aaron[16], who was one of the "minute men;" the War of 1812, by his grandfather, John[17]; and the Rebellion, in his own person.

Children of John N. and Jane (Wilson) Kneeland.

2833.   (i.) MARY L. A.[20], b. Jan. 20, 1872, at Palma, N. Y.

2834.   (ii.) THOMAS WILSON[20], b. at Rochester, N. Y., Sept. 15, 1873.

2835.   (iii.) ALFRED R.[20], b. at Greece, N. Y., June 25, 1877.

2836.   (2812.) MOSES KNEELAND[17] (*Aaron*[16], *Philip*[1,5], *Philip*[14], *Edward*[13], *Edward*[12], *John*[11]—*Alexander*[1]). Fourth son of Aaron Kneeland and Hannah Ramsdell, b. Nov. 16, 1782; m. Priscilla Peabody, a relative of the London banker; settled at Harrison, Me., where he died March 17, 1838.

Children of Moses and Priscilla (Peabody) Kneeland.

2837.   (i.) SARAH[18], b. in 1814; m. Aug. 20, 1839, to William Leslie; d. Sept. 2, 1875. They had six children:

2838.   (i.) *Lucy C. Leslie*[19], b. Feb. 14, 1843; m. Alfred Rowe, of Harrison. Children:

2839.   (i.) Hermon Rowe[20], b. Nov. 22, 1866.

2840.   (ii.) Harry C. Rowe[20], b. Dec. 13, 1867.

2841.   (iii.) Chas. B. Rowe[20], b. June 20, 1870.

2842.   (iv.) Alfred H. Rowe[20], b. Aug. 12, 1872.

2843.   (v.) Lizzie B. Rowe[20], b. June 29, 1874.

David Thomas Leslie[19].

2844.   (ii.) *Melvin Leslie*[19], b. Jan. 17, 1845; m. and had
two children. He d. Feb. 14, 1873. Children:

2845.   (i.) Arthur C. Leslie[20], b. May 4, 1871.

2846.   (ii.) Melvin W. Leslie[20], b. Nov., 1872.

2847.   (iii.) *Charles Leslie*[19], b. April 17, 1847; m. May
4, 1875. Children:

2848.   (i.) William B. Leslie[20], b. March 2, 1876.

2849.   (ii.) Allie B. Leslie[20], b. Sept. 3, 1880.

2850.   (iv.) *Harriet N. Leslie*[19], b. Jan. 20, 1849; d. Oct.
29, 1861.

2851.   (v.) *William P. Leslie*[19], b. Dec. 24, 1851; d. Sept.
11, 1853.

2852.   (vi.) *William P. Leslie*[19], b. Jan. 5, 1855; d. Jan.
13, 1882.

2853.   (ii.) PEABODY[18], b. in Feb., 1816 (of whom hereafter,
2890).

2854.   (iii.) JOSIAH[18], b. in 1817; m. in 1838; d. in 1846.
Children:

2855.   (i.) *Lucy*[19], b. in 1839; m. Mr. Westcott, in 1865,
and had seven children.

2864.   (ii.) *Melvin*[19], b. in 1843; m. in 1862. Had four
children.

2870.   (iv.) LUCY[18], b. in 1819; d. in 1838; unmarried.

2871.   (v.) JOSEPH[18], b. in Dec., 1821; m. Harriet Kneeland,
of Rowley, Mass. They had two children:

2872.   (i.) *Orestus*[19], b. in 1852; d. in 1875, without issue.

2873.   (ii.) *Annie*[19], b. in 1860; m. in 1875. No further
record.

2874.   (vi.) CYNTHIA[18], b. July 4, 1826; m. James B. Leslie,
in April, 1849; d. in 1880. They had five children:

2876.   (i.) *James W. Leslie*[19], b. Jan. 30, 1851; m. Clara
E. Joy, May, 1876. Children:

2877.   (i.) Mary Louise Leslie[20], b. March 7, 1877.

2878.   (ii.) Raymond E. Leslie[20], b. May 15, 1878.

2879.   (iii.) Carrie Mabel Leslie[20], b. Oct. 18, 1880.

2880.   (iv.) Emery Clayton Leslie[20], b. Feb. 23, 1883.

2881.   (v.) Edmund W. Leslie[20], b. Aug. 22, 1885.

2882.   (ii.) *David Thomas Leslie*[19], b. Nov. 2, 1853; d. in
1856.

2883. (iii.) *Louise C. Leslie*[19], b. July 27, 1855; m. Rives C. Mitchell, Sept. 10, 1879. One child:
2884. Rives Herbert Mitchell[20], b. June 5, 1887.
2885. (iv.) *Charles Arthur Leslie*[19], b. Oct. 23, 1857; m. Minnie H. Sancton, Jan. 8, 1884. Children:
2886. (i.) Eva Maud Leslie[20], b. Sept. 20, 1884.
2887. (ii.) Ethel Louise Leslie[20], b. Aug. 14, 1890.
2888. (v.) *Samuel Chase Leslie*[19], b. Feb. 13, 1859; m. Julia A. Marriner, in Nov., 1883. They had one child:
2889. Freeman Leslie[20], b. in Nov., 1884.

2890. (2853.) PEABODY KNEELAND[18](*Moses*[17], *Aaron*[16], *Philip*[15], *Philip*[14], *Edward*[13], *Edward*[12], *John*[11]— *Alexander*[1]). Son of Moses and Priscilla (Peabody) Kneeland; farmer; resided at Harrison, Me. He m. Abigail Cummings, of Topsfield, Mass. Mrs. Kneeland died in 1895. Had four children:

Children of Peabody and Abigail (Cummings) Kneeland.

2891. (i.) CHARLES[19], b. Aug. 28, 1843, at Chelsea, Mass.; m. Harriet Clark, of Boston.
2892. (ii.) SAMUEL A.[19], b. May 25, 1846, at Bridgton, Me. He is a farmer, residing at Harrison, Me., and writes me that he is "not married, I hope—an old bach. yet." Thanks for many a lift on this pedigree.
2893. (iii.) AUGUSTUS[19], b. May 16, 1849, in Bridgton, Me.; m. Alma C. Harman, of Harrison, Me.; d. May 2, 1891. Had two children:
2894. (i.) *Lee*[20], b. in 1877.
2895. (ii.) *Ira*[20], b. in 1883.
2896. (iv.) THOMAS[19], b. June 19, 1851; m. Josie W. Underwood. He is a successful and prosperous lawyer, practicing at Minneapolis, Minn. Has no children.

2897. (2813.) EZRA KNEELAND[17] (*Aaron*[16], *Philip*[15], *Philip*[14], *Edward*[13], *Edward*[12], *John*[11]—*Alexander*[1]). Fifth son of Aaron Kneeland, born at Topsfield, Mass., Oct. 6, 1784; he m. Polly Harden,

28

Nehemiah Kneeland[18].

and settled in Harrison, Me. After residing there for many years he went to Albany, Me., where he died May 30, 1868, aged 83.

Children of Ezra and Polly (Harden) Kneeland.

2898. (i.) LOUISE[18], b. in 1804; m. Thos. Funnel. Children :
2899.   (i.) *Edward Funnel*[19], b. in 1835.
2900.   (ii.) *Matilda Funnel*[19], b. in 1843.
2901. (ii.) EBEN H.[18], b. in 1807; m. Hannah Tibbetts. Children :
2902.   (i.) *Mary E.*[19], b. in 1835 ; d. in 1839.
2903.   (ii.) *Hannah*[19], b. in 1837; d. in 1852.
2904.   (iii.) *William H.*[19] (of whom hereafter, 3190).
2905.   (iv.) *Ira A.*[19], b. in 1841 ; m. Hattie E. Garmon. Children :
2906.   (i.) Cory[20], m. Lizzie Libbie.
2908.   (ii.) Albert[20], b. in 1872; unmarried.
2909.   (v.) *Eben*[19], b. in 1842; m. Sophia Wheeler. They had one child :
2910.   Ernest[20], b. in 1874; unmarried.
2911.   (vi.) *Emaline*[19], b. in 1843; m. Charles Jackson. Children :
2912.   (i.) Eva Jackson[20].
2913.   (ii.) Warren Jackson[20].
2914.   (iii.) Edward Jackson[20].
2915.   (iv.) Emma Jackson[20].
2916.   (v.) Hattie Jackson[20].
2917.   (vi.) Minnie Jackson[20].
2918.   (vii.) *Thomas*[19], b. in 1845 ; unmarried.
2919.   (viii.) *Lizzie*[19], b. in 1852; unmarried.
2920. (iii.) MARY[18], b. in 1809; m. Geo. Funnel. Children :
2921.   (i.) *Charles Funnel*[19].
2922.   (ii.) *Mary Funnel*[19].
2923.   (iii.) *George Funnel*[19].
2924.   (iv.) *Lizzie Funnel*[19].
2925.   (v.) *Clarence Funnel*[19].
2926.   (vi.) *Nelson Funnel*[19].
2927. (iv.) NEHEMIAH[18], b. in 1811; m. Hannah Tucker.
2928.   (i.) *Clara*[19].

Ephraim Kneeland[18].

2929. (ii.) *Edward[19]*.
2930. (iii.) *Warren[19]*.
2931. (v.) EZRA[18], b. in 1816; m. Nancy Hazelton. Children:
2932.   (i.) *Alonzo[19]*, b. in 1844; m. Lizzie Knight. No
             children.
2933.   (ii.) *Melissa[19]*, b. in 1846; m. Daniel Wood.
             They had six children.
2940.   (iii.) *Nellie[19]*, b. in 1848; m. Samuel Walker.
             Has children.
2945.   (iv.) *Elizabeth[19]*, b. in 1850; m. Henry Hazelton.
             Has one child.
2947.   (v.) *Ida[19]*, b. in 1852; m. Charles True. Has one
             child.
2948.   (vi.) *Alice[19]*, m. Wallace Sanborn. No issue.
2949. (vi.) CYRUS[18], b. June 13, 1820; m. Eliza Hazelton (of
             whom hereafter, 3200).

2950. (2814.) NEHEMIAH KNEELAND[17] (*Aaron[16]*,
             Philip[15], *Philip[14]*, *Edward[13]*, *Edward[12]*, *John[11]*
             —*Alexander[1]*). Sixth son of Aaron Kneeland, of
             Topsfield, Mass., b. at Topsfield, Mass., May 5,
             1789; m. Mary Goodhue, of Salem, Mass.
       He went to Harrison, Me., about the year 1818. After-
wards—about 1827—he moved to Lincoln, Maine, and in
March, 1832, in company with a few neighbors, he loaded his
family and household goods on a sled driven by four oxen
and went forty miles into the wilderness. They commenced
a clearing in the umbroken forests of Maine and founded a
new town, which they named in honor of their old home,
Topsfield. There he died June 28, 1867, and there some of
his descendants still live.

Children of Nehemiah and Mary (Goodhue) Kneeland.

2951. (i.) ELIZA[18], b. in Topsfield, Mass., Feb. 10, 1812; m.
             Joseph Loring, of Perry, Me. They had five child-
             ren, four boys and one girl, of whom three are
             still living.
2957. (ii.) EPHRAIM[18], b. in Topsfield, Mass., Jan. 7, 1814;
             m. Henrietta Johnson, of Effingham, N. H.; d. at

John J. Kneeland[19].

Topsfield, Me., Nov. 17, 1893. I copy the following obituary notice from a local paper: " Ephraim
Kneeland, who recently died at his home in Topsfield, at the advanced age of 79 years, was the last
son of a large family of Nehemiah Kneeland, who
came from Topsfield, Mass., in 1832 and was the
first settler in Topsfield, at that time an unbroken
wilderness. By the death of Mr. Kneeland another
old land-mark has been removed. He was well
known and highly esteemed by many acquaintances,
an active Christian, and leaves a number of children and grandchildren to mourn his loss." Their
children were as follows:

2958.   (i.) *Charles F.*[19], b. Dec. 8, 1842; m. Sarah Fogg,
of Princeton, Me. They had one son:
2959.   Nehemiah W.[20], b. July 25, 1895. They reside
at Princeton, Me.
2960.   (ii.) *Sarah Atha*[19], b. Jan. 9, 1844; m. Eugene
Hough, of Topsfield, Me. They resided at
Machias, Me., and have the following children:
2961.   (i.) Ellen A. Hough[20], b. Jan. 22, 1866.
2962.   (ii.) Henrietta J. Hough[20], b. July 5, 1869.
2963.   (iii.) Bertha L. Hough[20], b. Sept. 17, 1871.
2964.   (iv.) Charles W. Hough[20], b. July 11, 1875.
2965.   (v.) Morris E. Hough[20], b. March 28, 1877.
2966.   (vi.) Justin E. Hough[20], b. Oct. 20, 1879.
2967.   (vii.) Anna M. Hough[20], b. Oct. 29, 1881.
2968.   (viii.) Ray Hough[20], b. Oct. 15, 1887.
2969.   (iii.) *Anette*[19], b. Oct. 24, 1845; d. May, 1853.
2970.   (iv.) *Edwin*[19], b. Oct. 10, 1847. He served in the
Union army during the war, returned home
safe and sound and was killed in the woods by
a limb three years afterwards.
2971.   (v.) *John J.*[19], b. March 3, 1850, at Topsfield, Me.;
m. Emily J. Loring. They reside at Topsfield,
Me., and I am indebted to him for much information relating to the descendants of Nehemiah Kneeland. They had five children, as
follows:

Cynthia A. Kneeland[19].

2972.	(i.) Lottie C.[20], b. May 26, 1883.
2973.	(ii.) Justin C.[20], b. June 8, 1886.
2974.	(iii.) Maud A.[20], b. June 5, 1888.
2975.	(iv.) Lina M.[20], b. June 30, 1891.
2976.	(v.) Helen G.[20], b. March 23, 1893.

2977.　　(vi.) *Amanda J.*[19], b. March 18, 1852; m. first, Lewis D. Bean, and second, Charles E. Cary, both of Topsfield. She resides at that place, and had five children:

2978.	(i.) Burley E. Bean[20], b. Dec. 16, 1874.
2979.	(ii.) Ethel M. Bean[20], b. Nov. 30, 1881.
2980.	(iii.) Blanche Bean[20], b. Feb. 22, 1886.
2981.	(iv.) Lavina A. Bean[20], b. Dec. 2, 1889.
2982.	(v.) Ruth A. Cary[20], b. May 28, 1895.

2983.　　(vii.) *Howard E.*[19], b. Sept. 18, 1856; m. Ida Hodgman, of Milltown, Me. They reside at Topsfield, Me.

2984.　(iii.) MANASSEH[18], b. in Waterford, Mass., June 9, 1815; m. Emily L. Coffin, of Belfast, Me. They settled at Lincoln, Me., and remained there until 1860, when he moved to Silver Ridge, Me., where most of his descendants still reside. He died at Monarda, Me., April 7, 1883. His widow still resides (1897) at Silver Ridge, her present name being Emily L. Dow. Their children were:

2985.　　(i.) *Albin M.*[19], b. Feb., 1849; unmarried.

2986.　　(ii.) *Willis*[19], b. Feb. 12, 1854; unmarried, and resides at Carmer, Me.

2987.　　(iii.) *Lucinda*[19], b. Aug. 7, 1856; m. Abram Perry. They reside at Staceyville, and have children:

2988.	(i.) Raymond Perry[20], b. May 10, 1878.
2989.	(ii.) Ellie Perry[20], b. March 8, 1884.

2990.　　(iv.) *Cyrus H.*[19], b. Oct. 26, 1858; m. first, Cora Royal, who d. June 5, 1881; m. second, Lucy Kimball, May 30, 1890; she d. May 27, 1893. He is a merchant and postmaster at Silver Ridge.

2991.　　(v.) *Cynthia A.*[19], b. March 24, 1861; m. Henry Neal. They reside at Silver Lake, and have the following children:

Emily Kneeland[20].

2992.	(i.) William Neal[20], b. June 8, 1878.
2993.	(ii.) Maud Neal[20], b. Nov. 16, 1891.
2994.	(iii.) Emma Neal[20], b. Dec. 11, 1891.
2995.	(vi.) *Lillian A.*[19], b. May 12, 1863; m. Sylvanus F. Kneeland. They reside at Silver Ridge, and have three children:
2995A.	(i.) Eva E.[20], b. Aug. 29, 1891.
2996.	(ii.) Alice M.[20], b. March 31, 1894.
2997.	(iii.) Donald R.[20], b. March 1, 1896.
2998.	(vii.) *George N.*[19], b. March 16, 1866; married. They reside at Sherman, Me., and have the following children:
2999.	(i.) Lena M.[20], b. May 16, 1888.
3000.	(ii.) Bessie J.[20], b. June 28, 1889.
3001.	(iii.) Verna L.[20], b. May 5, 1895.
3002.	(iv.) OBED[18], b. at Topsfield, Mass., in 1816; m. Eliza Hannonell, of Topsfield, Me.; d. at Topsfield, Me., in 1861. He had five children, as follows:
3003.	(i.) *Delon S.*[19], b. March 28, 1848, at Lincoln, Me.; m. Hannah E. Hurd. No issue. Resides at Lynn, Mass.
3004.	(ii.) *Delphina*[19], b. March 26, 1850; m. Mr. Fayle, and had five children. They reside in Lee, Me. Children:
3005.	(i.) Sydney P. Fayle[20], b. May 13, 1871.
3006.	(ii.) Margaret E. Fayle[20], b. July 31, 1872; d. Aug. 14, 1872.
3007.	(iii.) Alfred W. Fayle[20], b. May 11, 1874.
3008.	(iv.) Constance L. Fayle[20], b. May 22, 1882.
3009.	(v.) Wilmot B. Fayle[20], b. July 28, 1884.
3010.	(iii.) *Sylvester H.*[19], b. at Lincoln, Me.; m. Rubie E. Carson, of Carroll, Me. He resides at Winn, Me. Children:
3011.	(i.) Rubie[20], b. Sept. 3, 1879.
3012.	(ii.) Sylvester H.[20], b. Aug. 20, 1881.
3013.	(iii.) Belgora[20], b. Feb. 14, 1884.
3014.	(iv.) Eliza Eldora[20], b. June 9, 1887.
3015.	(v.) Emily[20], b. May 20, 1891.

Lester C. Fitch[20].

3016.   (iv.) *Isabella H.*[19], b. Jan. 6, 1855, at Lincoln, Me.;
          m. George H. Bailey. They reside at Jackson,
          N. H. Their children are :
3017.   (i.) Myrtle C. Bailey[20], b. April 7, 1874.
3018.   (ii.) Calista G. Bailey[20], b. Sept. 14, 1877.
3019.   (iii.) Emma O. Bailey[20], b. Dec. 5, 1879.
3020.   (iv.) George F. Bailey[20], b. Nov. 29, 1886.
3021.   (v.) Harry P. Bailey[20], b. March 24, 1889.
3022.   (v.) *Ada M.*[19], b. June 15, 1859, at Topsfield ; m.
          Simon Scribner. They reside at Kossuth, Me.,
          have ten children, as follows :
3023.   (i.) Kate B. Scribner[20], b. March 13, 1877.
3024.   (ii.) Chloe M. Scribner[20], b. Nov. 4, 1878.
3025.   (iii.) Blanche E. Scribner[20], b. April 14, 1880 ;
                 m. Oct. 25, 1896, to Asa F. Richardson.
3026.   (iv.) Lucia A. Scribner[20], b. June 29, 1882.
3027.   (v.) Lura E. Scribner[20], b. April 12, 1884.
3028.   (vi.) Lee B. Scribner[20], and
3029.   (vii.) Lila B. Scribner[20], twins, b. Aug. 31, 1886.
3030.   (viii.) Violet M. Scribner[20], b. March 14, 1888.
3031.   (ix.) Nina P. Scribner[20], b. April 16, 1890.
3032.   (x.) Raymond Scribner[20], b. May 12, 1893.
3033. (v.) ISAAC[18], b. at Harrison, Me., Nov. 3, 1819 ; m.
          Sarah Sherman, at St. Davis, N. B.; d. at Prince-
          ton, Me., May 2, 1891. Children :
3034.   (i.) *Oren*[19], b. Dec. 3, 1847 ; m. Jennie Hawkins.
                 They reside at Princeton, and have the follow-
                 ing children :
3035.   (i.) Annie E.[20], b. Oct. 23, 1891.
3036.   (ii.) Earl E.[20], b. Oct. 8, 1893.
3040.   (ii.) *Maria*[19], b. Oct. 3, 1849 ; m. Briggs Fitch, of
                 Topsfield. They had the following children :
3041.   (i.) Orina Fitch[20], b. July 21, 1870.
3042.   (ii.) Mertie B. Fitch[20], b. July 13, 1873.
3043.   (iii.) Everett C. Fitch[20], b. Dec. 20, 1877.
3044.   (iv.) Gussie L. Fitch[20], b. Aug. 23, 1880.
3045.   (v.) Bertha M. Fitch[20], b. May 4, 1883.
3046.   (vi.) Lily L. Fitch[20], b. Jan. 2, 1887.
3047.   (vii.) Lester C. Fitch[20], b. Jan. 22, 1889.

3048 and 3049.   (viii. and ix.) Two children, d. in infancy.
3050.   (iii.) *Albert*[19], b. Feb. 15, 1855; m. Amelia Stone, of Princeton, Me.   Their children are:
3051.   (i.) Ernest[20], b. June 29, 1876.
3052.   (ii.) George[20], b. Sept. 22, 1878.
3053.   (iii.) Harvey[20], b. May 15, 1880.
3054.   (iv.) Charles[20], b. July 23, 1882.
3055.   (v.) Blanche[20], b. Sept. 11, 1884.
3056.   (vi.) Harry[20], b. Aug. 3, 1887.
3057.   (vii.) Ralph[20], b. Aug. 6, 1888.
3058.   (viii.) Percy[20], b. Nov. 15, 1890.
3059.   (ix.) Guy[20], b. Jan. 4, 1895.
3060.   (x.) There was one other child, who died young.
3061.   (iv.) *Alden*[19], b. Sept. 3, 1858; m. Stella Simmons, of Princeton.   Children:
3062.   (i.) Kate E.[20], b. March 29, 1884.
3063.   (ii.) Alice L.[20], b. Jan. 5, 1891.
3064.   (v.) *Hannah*[19], b. Nov. 4, 1861; m. Hazen Bailey, of Princeton.   Children:
3065.   (i.) Helen Bailey[20], b. Dec. 20, 1879.
3066.   (ii.) Frederick Bailey[20], b. Aug. 7, 1883.
3067.   (iii.) Roy Bailey[20], b. March 21, 1896.
3068.   (vi.) *Moses*[19], b. Sept. 7, 1865: m. Della Henderson, of Burlington, Me.   They reside at Princeton, Me.
3071.   (vi.) HUMPHREY[18], b. in Harrison, Me., Jan. 13, 1826; m. Lydia Thornton, of Calais, Me.; d. in Foxcroft, Me., in 1887.   Their children were:
3072.   (i.) *Eliza*[19], b. Sept. 24, 1849, at Topsfield, Me.; m. Albion K. Kneeland, of Lincoln, Me.   They reside at Lee, Me., and had nine children, all born there, viz.:
3073.   (i.) Nellie[20], b. Sept. 25, 1870.
3074.   (ii.) Harry[20], b. Dec. 22, 1872.
3075.   (iii.) Inez[20], b. July 19, 1875.
3076.   (iv.) Percy[20], b. April 9, 1878.
3077.   (v.) Della[20], b. Jan. 29, 1881.
3078.   (vi.) Clara[20], b. Jan. 20, 1884.
3079.   (vii.) Eda[20], b. April 12, 1887.

3080.   (viii.) Ardie[20], b. Feb. 11, 1890.

3081.   (ix.) Earl[20], b. Oct. 18, 1894.

3082.   (ii.) *Mary E.*[19], b. Aug. 1, 1851; m. David Ketchel. They resided at Sebec, Me., and had nine children.

3092.   (iii.) *Walker*[19], b. Jan. 12, 1855; unmarried; resides at Dover, Me.

3093.   (iv.) *Samuel*[19], b. May 16, 1865. He is married and resides at Dover, Me.

3097.   (vii.) LUCINDA[18], b. in Lincoln, Me., in 1828; m. Evan Powell, of Nova Scotia; d. in Topsfield, Me., in 1846. No issue.

3098.   (2816.) SIMEON KNEELAND[17] (*Aaron*[16], *Philip*[15], *Philip*[14], *Edward*[13], *Edward*[12], *John*[11]—*Alexander*[1]). Eighth son of Aaron Kneeland, of Topsfield, Mass., and Harrison, Me., b. Feb. 25, 1793, at Topsfield; m. Hannah, daughter of Elijah Richardson, of Waterford, Me., and settled in Harrison. He d. Jan. 1, 1873, aged 80. His widow died Sept. 23, 1876. They had eleven children, as follows:

Children of Simeon and Hannah (Richardson) Kneeland.

3099.   (i.) DANIEL[18], b. July 27, 1820; m. Mary E. Kneeland, daughter of his uncle, John Kneeland (see No. 2827). They settled in Harrison and had the following children:

3100.   (i.) *Mary*[19], b. March 8, 1842; m. in 1858, to Mr. Spinney. No issue.

3101.   (ii.) *Osgood*[19], b. April 11, 1844; m. Dec. 12, 1863, to Lizzie Manson. Children:

3102.   (i.) Edgar[20], b. in 1864; d. in 1867.

3103.   (ii.) Warren[20], b. Feb. 17, 1866; unmarried.

3104.   (iii.) Edna[20], b. in 1868; married. Children:

3105.   (i.) *Gladys*[21].

3106.   (ii.) *Fred*[21].

3107.   (iii.) *Hasland*[21].

3108.   (iv.) Mabel[20], b. March 14, 1871; unmarried

Lillian Kneeland[19].

3109.   (iii.) *Esther*[19], b. Nov. 20, 1845; m. Feb. 17, 1864, to Freeman Manson, of Waterfield. No issue.

3110.   (iv.) *Oliver*[19], b. Nov. 17, 1849; m. in 1860. They have two children.

3111.   (v.) *Hattie E.*[19], m. Mr. Winworth. Children:

3112.   (i.) Edward Winworth[20], b. June 10, 1870.

3113.   (ii.) Weston Winworth[20], b. Sept. 8, 1871.

3114.   (iii.) Willis Winworth[20], b. Nov. 6, 1872.

3115.   (iv.) Clarence Winworth[20], b. April 3, 1876.

3116.   (v.) Myrtle Winworth[20], b. July 23, 1878.

3117.   (vi.) Almeda Winworth[20], b. July 27, 1882.

3118.   (vii.) Maud Winworth[20], b. Dec. 6, 1885; d. Aug. 30, 1886.

3119.   (vi.) *Emily*[19], b. April 13, 1857; m. Moses Gillman. Children:

3119A   (i). Otis Gillman[20].

3120.   (ii.) Dalmas Gillman[20].

3121.   (iii.) Etta Gillman[20].

3122.   (vii.) *Amanda*[19], b. July 18, 1859; m. Sarah Hazelton. No issue.

3123.   (viii.) *Charles H.*[19], b. Jan. 16, 1863; m. 1886, to Etta Kimbal. No issue.

3124.   (ix.) *William P.*[19], b. in 1865; d. in childhood.

3125.   (x.) *Manson*[19], b. Feb. 3, 1867; d. Feb. 1, 1892.

3126. (ii.) CHARLOTTE[18], b. Oct. 21, 1821; m. first, Charles Augier; second, Geo. H. Hamblin, of Waterford, where she subsequently resided. She had one daughter by first marriage:

3127.   *Lizzie Augier*[19], b. in 1855; unmarried.

3129. (iii.) ESTHER R.[18], b. Jan. 29, 1823; m. Otis Bean, and resided at Worcester, Mass. No children.

3130. (iv.) OLIVER P.[18], b. Sept., 1824; d. the same year.

3131. (v.) OLIVER P.[18], b. Aug. 11, 1825; m. Frances Baker, of Shoreham, Me., and had children:

3132.   (i.) *Zenas*[19].

3133.   (ii.) *Ella*[19].

By his second wife, Caroline Richardson, he had:

3134.   (iii.) *Sidney O.*[19]

3135.   (iv.) *Cora*[19].

3136.   (v.) *Lillian*[19].

3137. (vi.) ELIZABETH E.[18], b. Sept. 23, 1829; m. J. Wales Brown, of Worcester, Mass.

3138. (vii.) THOMAS F.[18], b. Feb. 1, 1831; m. Jane S. Hamblin, daughter of Joshua, of Lowell, and had children:

3139. (i.) *Herbert O.*[19], b. April 20, 1860; m. Nov. 15, 1884, to Colby Needham, of Harrison. No children.

3140. (ii.) *Albert S.*[19], b. March 15, 1866; m. April 20, 1890, to Jennie Libby, of North Bridgton, Me.

3141. (iii.) *Delano B.*[19], b. June 7, 1876; d. Nov. 13, 1877.

3142. (viii.) HASKELL P.[18], b. Oct. 14, 1832; m. Marietta Leary, of Harrison, Me., and settled in Bridgton, Me. Children:

3144. (i.) *Myrtie N.*[19], b. June 24, 1867; m. Oct. 21, 1893.

3145. (ii.) *Nettie M.*[19], b. April 28, 1874; d. Aug. 28, 1874.

3146. (ix.) GEORGE H.[18], b. July 16, 1835; m. Jane Brown; resided in Harrison. Children:

3147. (i.) *George E.*[19], b. July 27, 1864.

3148. (ii.) *Rev. F. B.*[19] He was a preacher; m. July 7, 1892, to Mary Bean, of Otisfield, Me.

3149. (x.) GREENFIELD B.[18], b. July 30, 1838; m. Mary Whitney, of Worcester. Had sons:

3150. (i.) *Harry*[19].

3151. (ii.) *Frederick G.*[19]

3152. (2817.) DAVID P. KNEELAND[17](*Aaron*[16], *Philip*[15], *Philip*[14], *Edward*[13], *Edward*[12], *John*[11]—*Alexander*[1]). Youngest son of Aaron Kneeland, b. May 24, 1798; m. Mercy Watson, daughter of James Watson, of Harrison, Me., Jan. 21, 1817; settled in Harrison and had following children:

Children of David P. and Mercy (Watson) Kneeland.

3153. (i.) ALMON[18], b. June 23, 1817; m. Dorcas Sands. He lived in the village of Harrison, and kept the "Elm House." Children:

3154. (i.) *Amelia M.*[19], b. June 10, 1842; m. Sherburn Ricker, Aug. 24, 1871. No issue.

Mercy Kneeland[18].

3155.   (ii.) *David P.*[19], b. Aug. 21, 1846; m. Dec. 30, 1866, Caroline Walker.   He now keeps the " Elm House."   Children :

3156.   (i.) Jennie[20], b. March 10, 1867; m. in 1884, and had one child.

3158.   (ii.) Grace[20], b. July 23, 1870; m. in 1889, and had one child.

3160.   (iii.) James F.[20], b. Dec. 10, 1872; unmarried.

3161.   (iv.) H. V.[20], b. June 29, 1877; unmarried.

3162.   (iii.) *Orlando*[19], b. Feb. 8, 1849; m. July 27, 1889, to Mary Hunters.   No issue.

3163.   (iv.) *Evans*[19], b. Jan. 9, 1851; d. July 14, 1880, without issue.

3164.   (ii.) EUNICE[18], b. Nov., 1818; m. in 1842, to Asa P. Whitney, of Bridgton.   Children :

3165.   (i.) *Edward P. Whitney*[19], b. Nov. 29, 1843; d. Jan. 25, 1874.

3166.   (ii.) *Charles Whitney*[19], b. March 20, 1846; m. Mr. Johnson, and had two children.

3169.   (iii.) SETH[18], b. Jan. 24, 1820; m. Mary Jane Whitney, March 28, 1853, and settled in Harrison, Me. Children :

3170.   (i.) *Silas*[19], b. March 7, 1854; m. May 5, 1881, to Lizzie Hervey.   No children.

3171.   (ii.) *Walter*[19], b. June 14, 1856; m. Carrie Gregory, July 20, 1881.   No children.

3172.   (iii.) *Mary A.*[19], b. Aug. 18, 1858; m. Feb. 4, 1891, to F. Philbrook.   Children :

3173.   (i.) Carroll Philbrook[20], b. April 28, 1892.

3174.   (ii.) Jessie Philbrook[20], b. April 20, 1895.

3175.   (iv.) *Ernest*[19], b. Dec., 1861; m. April 5, 1891, to Clara Welch.   Child :

3176.   Edith[20], b. March 15, 1892.

3177.   (v.) *Arthur B.*[19], b. May 20, 1867; unmarried.

3178.   (vi.) *Zula A.*[19], b. Sept. 20, 1869; m. Oct. 9, 1894, to E. Haskell.   No issue.

3179.   (iv.) MERCY[18], b. in 1822; m. Nov. 22, 1852, to Mr. Emerson.   They had two children :

3180.   (i.) *Horace B. Emerson[19]*, b. in 1854; m. July 22, 1875.
3181.   (ii.) *Arthur W. Emerson[19]*, b. May 21, 1854; m. Feb. 21, 1881. No further records.
3182.   (v.) CHRISTINA[18], b. in 1825; unmarried; d. July, 1871.
3183.   (vi.) SABRINA[18], b. in 1827; m. to Mr. Johnson. Children:
3184.   (i.) *Charles Johnson[19]*.
3185.   (ii.) *Nellie Johnson[19]*.
3186.   (iii.) *Walter Johnson[19]*.
3187.   (vii.) SARAH[18], b. in 1837; m. Mr. Emerson, Nov. 23, 1861. Children:
3188.   (i.) *Edward L. Emerson[19]*, b. Aug. 30, 1863.
3189.   (ii.) *Lillian S. Emerson[19]*, b. July 25, 1868.

3190.   (2904.) WILLIAM H. KNEELAND[19] (*Eben[18], Ezra[17], Aaron[16], Philip[15], Philip[14], Edward[13], Edward[12], John[11]—Alexander[1]*). Eldest son of Eben and Hannah (Tibbetts) Kneeland, b. Aug. 30, 1839, at North Waterford, Me.

After exhausting a limited local means of education he went to Brookline, Mass., and remained there until the war broke out. In 1862 he enlisted at South Royalton, Vt., in the 9th Vermont Vols., serving there until he was taken prisoner at Harper's Ferry. After his release he served in the 7th Vermont, which was in the celebrated Vermont Brigade that won the highest honors of the war. Although of the same name and in the same brigade, we fought together for two years without knowing of each other's existence. Among other battles he took part in the celebrated Shenandoah Valley campaign, under Sheridan, and also in the Florida, Alabama and Texas contests. After the close of the war, April 8, 1867, he married at Charlestown, Mass., Mary Proctor, of Dundee, Scotland, and finally settled, Oct. 6, 1879, at Lowell, Mass., and was thereafter for twelve years in the employ of that city as assistant superintendent of the street lighting department. He then retired to private life at Chelmsford, Mass. He was a life-long and enthusiastic Republican, and is a prominent member of the Grand Army of the Republic. They had seven children, all of whom are living.

Children of William H. and Mary (Proctor) Kneeland.

3191. (i.) WARREN JAMES[20], b. Dec. 10, 1867, at Charlestown, Mass. He is a "hustler from Hustlerville," as may be imagined from his position of superintendent of the advertising department of C. I. Hood & Co.—"Hood's Sarsaparilla." This keeps him "on the road" for fourteen months in the year; the other two months he "lays off" among the mountains of Maine. If this statement seems incredible, you must remember that some people are capable of placing fourteen months of work into ten months of time. Warren James is one of that kind. It is singular that he is single, but a fact nevertheless.

3192. (ii.) MINNIE BLANCHE[20], b. at Westford, Mass.; m. G. Davis. They had two children:

3193.   (i.) A daughter. Died in infancy.

3194.   (ii.) *Frederick Davis*[21].

3195. (iii.) WILLIAM HENRY[20], b. Aug. 30, 1872, at Westford, Mass. He is unmarried and in the fruit business.

3196. (iv.) HARRIET ROSE[20], b. at Harrison, Me., Oct. 14, 1875; m. Thomas Hartwell, a druggist at Holyoke, Mass.

3197. (v.) WALTER ALLEN[20], b. at Poland, Me., Oct. 10, 1878; single; in the drug business.

3198. (vi.) SARAH E.[20], b. at Lowell, Mass., Sept. 2, 1880.

3199. (vii.) ARTHUR HERBERT[20], b. at Lowell, Mass., June 3, 1883.

3200. (2949.) CYRUS KNEELAND[18] (*Ezra*[17], *Aaron*[16], *Philip*[15], *Philip*[14], *Edward*[13], *Edward*[12], *John*[11] —*Alexander*[1]). Son of Ezra and Polly (Harden) Keeeland, b. in the town of Lincoln, Me., June 13, 1820; m. Eliza Hazelton.

When he was eighteen he began life for himself on wild land, in the town of Albany, and for many years lived in a log house. More than fifty years he had been engaged in lumber-

CYRUS KNEELAND

No. 3200

ing, in that time building one water mill and one steam mill, in which he manufactured oak staves and spool strips. In politics he was a staunch and true-blue Republican. In 1888 he was elected representative to the State Legislature. He was a member of Crescent Lodge, No. 17, I.O.O.F. Died June 12, 1894.

Children of Cyrus and Eliza (Hazelton) Kneeland.

3201.   (i.) EDWARD R.[19], b. in 1841; m. Mrs. Alice A. Bolton; They reside at Norway, Me. Have no issue.

3202.   (ii.) LOIS[19], b. May 2, 1843; m. Alonzo B. Littlefield; reside at Waterford, Me. Their children are:

3203.   (i.) *Flora Littlefield[20].*

3204.   (ii.) *Claton Littlefield[20].*

3205.   (iii.) *Addie Littlefield[20].*

3206.   (iv.) *Roland Littlefield[20].*

3207.   (v.) *Lillian Littlefield[20].*

3208.   (vi.) *Frederick Littlefield[20].*

3209.   (iii.) LOUISA B.[19], b. in 1848; m. David Jordan, in 1868; they reside at Norway, Me. Their children are:

3210.   (i.) *Mattie M. Jordan[20].*

3211.   (ii.) *Myrtie A. Jordan[20].*

3212.   (iii.) *Annie E. Jordan[20].*

3213.   (iv.) *Gertrude L. Jordan[20],*

3214.   (v.) *Carl D. Jordan[20].*

3215.   (vi.) *Lou E. Jordan[20].*

3216.   (vii.) *Roy F. Jordan[20].*

3216A. (iv.) WELLINGTON E.[19], b. in 1858; m. Ella Proal, of New Hampshire. They now reside in the city of New York.

3217.   (v.) ELLSWORTH F.[19], b. in 1860; m. Lizzie Waterhouse, and reside at Waterford, Me. They have one child:

3218.   *Raymond Waterhouse Kneeland[20]*, b. in 1895.

CHAPTER XLI

DESCENDANTS OF HENRY KNEELAND, OF NEW YORK.

(NOS. 3219 TO 3300.)

3219. (719.) HENRY KNEELAND[17] (*Ebenezer*[16], *Ebenezer*[15], *Benjamin*[14], *Edward*[13], *Edward*[12], *John*[11], *William*[10], *James*[9], *Alexander*[8], *William*[7], *William*[6], *John*[5], *John*[4], *John*[3], *James*[2], *Alexander*[1]). Eldest son of Ebenezer and Elizabeth (Sedgwick) Kneeland; eighth in descent from Dr. Samuel Fuller and Edward Fuller, of the Mayflower, and seventh in descent from Major-Gen. Robert Sedgwick, commander-in-chief of the colony; b. at Hartford, Conn., May 9, 1779; located in New York City, prior to 1793; m. Ann Taylor, daughter of Capt. Willett and Mary (Bogert) Taylor; d. at Hyde Park, N. Y., July 6, 1837, aged 58.

This is the summary of the life of one of the best known and most successful of the "old merchants of New York" and the head of a distinguished metropolitan family. Henry Kneeland was a born merchant. His father, who had a fulling and dyeing establishment at Hartford, Conn., died in 1786, at the early age of 33, when Henry was only nine years of age, leaving a small estate, of which Henry received a double portion, being the eldest son. He afterwards inherited some money through his mother, from the Sedgwick family, but substantially his entire fortune was made by his own exertions. In 1795, when he was only 16 years of age, we find him recorded in the New York directory as in business at No. 7, Burling Slip. The address is the same in the directory of 1797, but the name then disappears until 1805, and there-

Henry Kneeland[17].

after continues in the directory until shortly before his death. We have no date as to his arrival in New York, but we know that his uncle, Lieut. Seth R. Kneeland (see Chap. XXXIV.), was settled there as early as 1793, and it was probably through the latter's influence that Henry came here about two years later. It is remarkable that these two New York families, so closely related, so drifted apart that none of the present generation knew of any connection between them. It was through Mrs. Mitchill the youngest daughter of Seth R., that I first learned that Henry was her first cousin. She knew that he was her father's nephew, but did not know the name of his father, and I am indebted to Miss Adele Kneeland, the granddaughter of Henry, for the connecting link between the two families. The completion of data as to this family was so delayed that I have been forced to make this chapter the Omega instead of the Alpha of the history of the Kneelands in America.

The commercial career of Henry Kneeland is best stated by giving a history of the firm with which his family was connected for more than half a century. When he was 18 he became supercargo of a vessel running from New York to Savannah, and soon after became engaged in business in the latter city, remaining there until 1805, which accounts for the absence of his name in the New York directory during that period. From that time forward he was part and parcel of the commercial house of Bogert & Kneeland.

HISTORY OF THE FIRM OF BOGERT & KNEELAND.

On or about April 28, 1783, at the close of the Revolutionary War, Peter Bogert, of New York, formed a copartnership with his brother-in-law, Petrus Byvanck, under the name of Byvanck & Bogert, as merchants who were engaged at that early period in the European trade, and which connection was dissolved about March 2, 1793. During the years 1788, '89 and '91, he appears to have been concerned with his brother-in-law, George Barnwall, in commercial business, under the firm of George Barnwall & Co. Prior to 1796 he formed a business connection with Joseph Hopkins, under the firm of Bogert & Hopkins, which was dissolved by the death of Mr.

Jan Louwe Bogert[1].

Hopkins, of yellow fever, near Flushing, L. I., about Oct. 3, 1798. Subsequently he formed a copartnership for the transaction of a commercial business, with Col. Samuel Mansfield, under the firm of Bogert & Mansfield, which continued up to April, 1803. During several years prior to 1806 he was a partner with Samuel Mansfield, and Henry Kneeland in the house of Henry Kneeland & Co., doing business in Savannah, Ga. He, with Benjamin Story and Henry Kneeland, composed the firm of Kneeland & Story, Savannah, Ga., from October, 1806, to October, 1810. In 1803, October 19, the New York business commenced under the firm of Bogert & Kneeland, which connection ceased May 1, 1818, Mr. Bogert retiring from business pursuits to his farm at White Stone, L. I. Henry Kneeland continued to transact business under the name of Bogert & Kneeland until May 1, 1824, when Henry K. Bogert, son of Peter, became a partner. On May 1, 1829, Charles Kneeland, son of Henry Kneeland, was taken into the house and these three composed the firm of Bogert & Kneeland until the death, on July 6, 1837, of Henry Kneeland. The firm was afterwards continued by the surviving partners, Henry K. Bogert and Charles Kneeland, until May 2, 1851, when Edward C. Bogert, son of Henry K. Bogert, was admitted as partner, and as thus composed it continued until the withdrawal, on May 1, 1858, of Edward C. Bogert. Thereafter the firm of Bogert & Kneeland was composed of and continued by Henry K. Bogert and Charles Kneeland. Under the date of May 2, 1870, the copartnership was dissolved but not published until May 14, 1870, in the *Journal of Commerce* and *Morning Times* of this city, showing Henry K. Bogert's membership of the firm to have been 46 years, and Charles Kneeland's, 41 years.

Sketch of the Bogert family, ancestors of Ann (Taylor) Kneeland.

JAN LOUWE BOGERT[1], born in Schoonduwoerd, Holland, settled at Bedford, L. I., about 1663, where he had a large tract of land. After nine years he went to Haarlaem (1672) and purchased the Montagne farm of 200 acres. He was chosen Magistrate in 1675 and reëlected in 1676. He married Cornelia Everts and lived in Harlem for thirty-five years; then he sold his lands and moved to New York, remaining there until his death (see Riker's Harlem, p. 491). He had ten children, including:

NICHOLAS BOGERT[2], b. in 1668, who married in 1695, Bellitie, daughter of Hendrick C. Van Schaick, by whom he had two children, the eldest being:

JOHN BOGERT[3], b. in 1697. He married, March 10, 1716, Hannah, daughter of Jan Peeck by his wife Elizabeth, daughter of Dr. Gysbert and Rachel (Montagne) Van Imbroch (as to whom, see hereafter). John died in New York, in 1775. They had eight children, the eldest being:

JOHN BOGERT, JR.[4], born in 1718; m. March 16, 1737, Abigail, daughter of Alderman Jacobus Quick. John, Jr., was a distinguished and prosperous New York merchant and an alderman from 1756 to 1766. He then refused the offer of the mayoralty of the city and retired from public and commercial life to his country seat in Harlem, where he purchased his grandfather's (Dr. Johannes Montagne) bouewerie of 200 acres lying between Ninety-third street and the Harlem river. When the Revolution opened and the Provincial Convention held its session in the Harlem church, the records were kept at Bogert's house, he being a good Whig. He died in 1772, leaving eight children, the youngest being:

MARY BOGERT[5], born in 1742; m. in 1760, Capt. Willett Taylor (see Riker's Harlem, p. 494). They had several children, including:

ANN TAYLOR[6], born at Jamaica, L. I., who married Henry Kneeland and became the ancestor of the New York City branch of the Kneeland family.

Sketch of Gov. La Montagne, ancestor of Ann (Taylor) Kneeland, wife of Henry Kneeland, of New York.

DR. JOHANNES LA MONTAGNE, a distinguished officer of the Colonial Government, was born at Saintoyne, France, in 1592, just three years before the edict of Nantes restored order to the realm and peace to the Huguenots. When the troubles arose again he escaped to Holland. His was the first of the families of refugees. He studied medicine at the University of Leyden, and was an intimate associate of the

Dr. Johannes La Montagne.

Mayflower pilgrims and of their celebrated pastor, John Robinson. He arrived at New Netherland (New York) in 1637. In 1638 he was appointed the sole member of the council under Kieft and placed in command of an expedition against the English at Fort Good Hope (now Hartford, Conn.), to maintain the Dutch rights there against the encroachments of their fellow-pilgrims, the English. In 1643 he saved the life of Gov. Kieft when attacked by Maryn Adriaensen, and the same year was sent to Staten Island with three companies to put down the Indians, from which he returned laden with the spoils of several hundred bushels of corn. In 1644 he headed an expedition against the Indians of Long Island, when 120 savages were killed. In 1645 he accompanied Kieft to Fort Orange to secure the friendship of the Mohawks, on which occasion he analyzed the war paint of the natives and discovered gold therein, much to the joy of the renowned Director. In 1647 he was retained in the council by Gov. Stuyvesant and the next year was dispatched by him to the South river to secure the possessions at that place, which was done. In 1656, on the retirement of De Decker, he was appointed Vice Director (Deputy Governor) at Fort Orange. In 1664 he surrendered Fort Orange to the English and swore allegiance to the new government. His bouwerie in New York was east of Eighth avenue and extended from Ninety-third street north of the Harlem river, containing 200 acres (see O'Callahan's History of New Netherland; Documents relating to the Colonial History of New York, and Early Records of Albany County, N. Y., by Pearsall, p. 9).

La Montagne was a great friend of Gov. Stuyvesant, who referred to him as "our very learned Montagne." Their correspondence is preserved in the Colonial History of New York. Miss Lamb, in her history of New York City (Vol. I., p. 83), speaking of Gov. Kieft, says: "The West India Company had accorded him the privilege of selecting the members of his council. He warily chose *one* man. The favored individual was Dr. Johannes La Montagne, a learned and highly-bred French Huguenot who had escaped from the rage of religious persecution the year before (1637), and found his Canaan in the Dutch settlement on Manhattan Island.

John T. Kneeland[18].

His parents belonged to the *Ancienne Noblesse* of France. He was a widower with four interesting children, upon whom he bestowed great care and affection. The three daughters grew up to be the most attractive women of their day in the Province and his son became a man of fortune and position. Two of his daughters married physicians—Dr. Hans Kiersled and Dr. Van Imbroeck." Mrs. Van Imbroeck was captured by the Indians at the Esopus Massacre of June 7, 1663. She escaped and personally led as a guide an armed force in pursuit of the Indians. She conducted them to the Indian Castle where she last saw the warriors (Lamb's History of N. Y., Vol. I., p. 200). Her father, Dr. Van Imbroeck, was a resident of Esopus, L. I., and represented it at the Landtag or Diet called April 10, 1664, by Gov. Stuyvesant, for the purpose of taking into consideration the precarious condition of the Province (id.) Genealogical descent:

DR. JOHANNES LA MONTAGNE[1], born at Saintoyne, France, in 1592; married Angeritie Gillis Ten Waert, widow of Arent Corsen, and had eight children, including:

RACHEL LA MONTAGNE[2], born in 1634; she married Dr. Gysbert Van Imbroch, whose descendants write their name "Van Amburgh." He was one of the Schepens at the time of his death, in 1665. They had three children, including:

ELIZABETH VAN IMBROCH[3], born in 1659. She moved to New York and married Jan (John) Peeck (see Appendix B, Riker's Harlem). They had several children, including:

HANNAH PEECK[4], born in 1695; married John Bogert (id., p. 493), whose descendants to Ann (Taylor) Kneeland we have already given.

Children of Henry and Ann (Taylor) Kneeland.

3220. (i.) HENRY[18], b. in New York, in Oct., 1806 (of whom hereafter, 3231).

3221. (ii.) CHARLES[18], b. at New York, March 3, 1808 (of whom hereafter, 3258).

3222. (iii.) GEORGE[18] (of whom hereafter, 3270).

3223. (iv.) JOHN T.[18] He d. at Hyde Park, Aug. 8, 1838. Unmarried.

Francis Kneeland Grain[20].

3224. (v.) ELIZABETH S.[18], m. Ogden Haggerty, Esq., and
d. in 1888. He d. Aug. 30, 1875. They had four
children, two of whom died young. The others are:

3225. (i.) *Anna K. Haggerty*[19]. She m. Robert G. Shaw.
They have no children.

3226. (ii.) *Clemence Haggerty*[19]. She m. James Mason
Crafts. Their children are:

3227. (i.) Anna K. Crafts[20].

3228. (ii.) Marian M. Crafts[20].

3229. (iii.) Elizabeth S. Crafts[20].

3230. (iv.) Clemence Crafts[20].

3231. (3220.) HENRY KNEELAND[18] (*Henry*[17], *Ebenezer*[16], *Ebenezer*[15], *Benjamin*[14], *Edward*[13], *Edward*[12], *John*[11]—*Alexander*[1]). Eldest son of Henry
and Ann (Taylor) Kneeland, b. in New York City,
in October, 1806.

He was a well equipped and thoroughly educated gentleman. Married Margaret Barr, of Baltimore, Md., a refined
and most beautiful lady, who is still living with one of her
daughters, at Utica. They resided most of the time at his
country residence, at Hyde Park, near Poughkeepsie, N. Y.
He was content to allow his younger brother, Charles,
to run the mercantile business in New York, while he attended
to his investments and enjoyed the quiet comfort of country
life with an accomplished family of daughters, who inherited
their mother's beauty and their father's charm of manner.

Children of Henry and Margaret (Barr) Kneeland.

3232. (i.) ALICE[19], b. Oct. 18, 1833; m. first, Francis H. Grain.
He was born in England, of a distinguished family,
his father having been for many years the commandant of Gibraltar. He (the son) was a resident
of New York and a partner in the banking house
of Duncan Sherman & Co. They had one child;

3233. *Francis Kneeland Grain*[20].
After Mr. Grain's death, she m. second, Hon.
J. B. Curtis, a prominent lawyer of Stamford, Conn.
Mr. Curtis has held the offices of State Senator
and Judge of Probate in Connecticut. They now
live in Stamford.

Kate Kneeland[19].

3234. (ii.) MARY[19], b. March 13, 1835, at Hyde Park, N. Y. a suburb of Poughkeepsie. She m. E. T. Parkinson, Esq., of Boston, in February, 1860, and d. Sept. 8, 1873. Their children were:

3235. (i.) *Arthur Parkinson[20]*, b. Dec. 6, 1860.

3236. (ii.) *Jane Hodgkinson Parkinson[20]*, b. Dec. 23, 1864.

3237. (iii.) *Alice Grain Parkinson[20]*, b. March 8, 1866; m. Oct., 1887, to William Livingston Watson, son of Dr. Watson, of Utica, one of the Regents of the University of the State of New York. They had one child:

3238. Alice Watson[21], b. July, 1890.

3239. (iv.) *Charles Outram Parkinson[20]*, b. March 9, 1871.

3240. (v.) *Edward Kneeland Parkinson[20]*, b. July 21, 1872.

There were several other children, who died in infancy.

3241. (iii.) ELIZABETH[19], b. in 1837; d. in 1839.

3242. (iv.) FANNIE[19], b. Feb. 21, 1839: d. July, 1893. She m. Baron William Von Restorff, an officer in one of the royal regiments of the Prussian army. They had three children:

3243. (i.) *Frederich Von Restorff[20]*, b. in 1869.

3244. (ii.) *Karl Von Restorff[20]*, b. in 1871.

3245. (iii.) *Courtlandt Von Restorff[20]*, b. in 1873.

3246. (v.) ELIZABETH[19]. She m. first, Smith A. Schuyler, a descendant of the famous New York families of Schuylers and Van Rensselaers. They had two children:

3247. (i.) *Cortlandt Van Rensselaer Schuyler[20]*, b. in March, 1864.

3248. (ii.) *Frank H. Schuyler[20]*, b. Nov. 25, 1865; m. Nov., 1894, to Harriet J. Fosdick. They had one child:

3249. Philip Kingsland Schuyler[21], b. Dec., 1895.

3250. (vi.) KATE[19]. She m. first, Smith W. Anderson, of New York. He also was a descendant of the Schuylers and Van Rensselaers, of New York and Albany, by whom she had one child:

Dr. Thomas Rodman[1].

3251.   *Harriet Schuyler Anderson*[20], b. in 1862; m. Jan.,
1885, to Rev. R. H. Nelson, of New York,
an Episcopal clergyman, now (1897) rector of
St. Peter's, Philadelphia. Their children are:

3252.   (i.) Katharine Kneeland Nelson[21], b. Nov.,
1885.

3253.   (ii.) McDonald Nelson[21], b. in 1890.

3254.   (iii.) John Low Nelson[21], b. in 1895.

3255. (vii.) ANNA H.[19], b. March 9, 1842. She is unmarried
and resides with her mother, nominally at Utica,
though most of their time is spent in Europe.

3256. (viii.) HENRY[19], b. in 1845; m. Frances Keeling.

3257. (ix.) CLARA[19], b. in 1852; d. in infancy.

3258. (3221.) CHARLES KNEELAND[18] (*Henry*[17], *Ebenezer*[16], *Ebenezer*[15], *Benjamin*[14], *Edward*[13], *Edward*[12], *John*[11]—*Alexander*[1]). Second son of
Henry and Ann (Taylor) Kneeland, b. in New
York, March 3, 1808.

He early acquired a liberal education and then entered
the employ of Bogert & Kneeland, the old cotton house
of which his father was a member. On May 1, 1829, having arrived at full age, he joined the firm and remained a
partner thereof until its final dissolution, May 14, 1870, a
period of forty-one years. Though a liberal provider and
generous by nature, he nevertheless succeeded in acquiring an
extensive property, which is now administered for the heirs by
Henry L. Bogert, of New York. Charles Kneeland married
Joanna Hone, daughter of Philip J. and Anna (Hazard)
Hone, of New York. The ancestry of Mrs. Kneeland I give
herewith.

**Sketch of Joanna (Hone) Kneeland's descent from Dr. Rodman, Gov.
Clarke and Col. Willett.**

DR. THOMAS RODMAN[1], b. Dec. 26, 1640, at Barbadoes;
was the eldest son of John Rodman, a wealthy planter of that
place. He came to Newport, R. I., in 1675, and was an
eminent physician and surgeon there. He married, Nov. 26,
1691, Hannah Clarke, the daughter of Walter Clarke, Governor
of Rhode Island. They had six children, including:

Capt. Jeremiah Clarke[1].

SAMUEL RODMAN, ESQ.[2], b. July 23, 1703; d. Feb. 27, 1749. He was a prominent resident and Justice of the Peace at Newport. He married, May 16, 1723, Mary Willett, of Flushing, L. I., the daughter of Col. Thomas Willett, of that place. They had nine children, the eldest being:

THOMAS RODMAN[3], b. at Newport, Feb. 29, 1724; m. Mary Borden, daughter of Abraham and Elizabeth (Wanton) Borden, of Newport. He was in the merchant marine service and was lost at sea in one of his vessels, Nov. 16, 1766. They had eight children, including:

ANNA RODMAN[4], b. at Newport, June 24, 1761; d. June 14, 1845. She married Thomas Hazard, of New York City, and afterwards resided in the latter place, and had six children, including:

ANNA HAZARD[5], b. in New York, in 1785; m. Oct. 2, 1809, to Philip J. Hone, Esq., of New York. He was a son of John Hone, Sr., one of New York's wealthiest merchants, whose brother, Philip Hone, was elected Mayor of New York in 1828. A picture of Mayor Hone and of his residence on Broadway, opposite City Hall Park,, is contained in Vol II., of Mrs. Lamb's History of New York City. They had one child:

JOANNA HONE[6], b. June 26, 1811, who married Charles Kneeland of New York, as hereinbefore stated. It will be noted that the present descendants of Charles Kneeland had an ancestry of 150 years in Newport and 125 years in New York City. Much of the information contained herein is gained from the History of the Rodman Family.

The Clarke Family.

CAPT. JEREMIAH CLARKE[1], son of Carew Clarke, Esq., "Gentleman," of Ruffum, Suffolk County, England (I have his history four generations further back); married Frances Dungan, of the same place, and came to Newport, R. I., in 1638. He was one of the founders of that celebrated resort. The original compact for the government of the colony constituted one judge and eight elders as supreme authority. In this compact, which was signed by Jeremiah Clarke, he was named as elder. He was created Freeman in 1641, Lieutenant in 1642, Captain in 1644, Treasurer of the Province from 1644 to 1648, and President Regent and Acting Governor in 1648. He died in November, 1651. He had several children, including:

GOV. WALTER CLARKE[2], b. in 1640; d. May 22, 1714. He was Deputy Governor of the Rhode Island plantations for 42 years and Governor for five years (1676, '77, '86, '96 and 1698), filling the above official positions continuously for 47 years, probably the longest record of like service in the history of the country. He was married three times. By his second wife, Hannah Scott, he had:

HANNAH CLARKE[3], who married Dr. Rodman, and was, the ancestor of the Charles Kneeland family, as hereinbefore set forth.

Children of Charles and Joanna (Hone) Kneeland.

3259. (i.) CHARLES, JR.[19], b. March 3, 1830; m. May 11, 1854, to Louise Taintor, daughter of Hon. John A. Taintor, of Hartford, Conn. Mr. Taintor represented this country as U. S. Minister to France, and was one of the most distinguished of Connecticut's sons. Charles Kneeland was associated with his father in the firm of Bogert & Kneeland, and was an educated and refined gentleman. He died May 18, 1866, at the early age of 36, and is buried in the Kneeland plot at the Lenox (Mass.) Cemetery. His father survived him many years. They had the following children:

3260. (i.) *Adele[20]*, b. April 23, 1856. She is unmarried, and resides at 6 East Thirty-eighth street, New York, and Lenox, Mass.

3261. (ii.) *George[20]*, b. May 19, 1859; unmarried; d. July 3, 1883.

3262. (iii.) *Alice Taintor[20]*, b. Nov. 23, 1861; m. Oct. 1, 1885, to Henry Whitney Munroe. Their children are:

3263. (i.) George Kneeland Munroe[21], b. May 28, 1888.

3264. (ii.) Louise Munroe[21], b. Dec. 27, 1890.

GEORGE KNEELAND. 459

Prof. John McVickar, A.M., S.T.D.

3265.   (iii.) John Munroe[21], b. April 19, 1892.

3266.   (iv.) —— Munroe[21], b. April 13, 1897.

3267. (ii.) GEORGE[19], b. Aug. 4, 1832; d. June 13, 1859;
        unmarried; buried at Lenox, Mass.

3268. (iii.) HENRY[19], b. April 10, 1834; d. June 13, 1859;
        unmarried; buried at Lenox, Mass.

3269. (iv.) ANNA[19], b. Sept. 12, 1836; d. Aug. 2, 1858;
        unmarried; buried at Lenox, Mass.

NOTE.—At the time of the execution of the will of
Charles, Sr. (December, 1881), all his children were dead, and
his sole descendants were his grandchildren, Adele, George
and Alice T. Kneeland. George died two years later, without
issue, leaving Adele Kneeland and Alice T. (Kneeland) Munroe the only descendants and heirs-at-law of Charles Kneeland, Sr.

3270. (3222.) GEORGE KNEELAND[18] (*Henry*[17], *Ebenezer*[16], *Ebenezer*[15], *Benjamin*[14], *Edward*[13], *Edward*[12], *John*[11]—*Alexander*[1]). Third son of Henry
        and Ann (Taylor) Kneeland; ninth in descent from
        Dr. Samuel and Edward Fuller of the Mayflower,
        and eighth in descent from Major-Gen. Robert
        Sedgwick.

He resided principally in New York City, but had his
country residence at Hyde Park. He married Fanny, daughter of Rev. Dr. John McVickar, and great-granddaughter of
Washington's physician, Samuel Bard (as to whom, hereafter).
The line of ancestry through the McVickars and Bards is so
full of interest and honor that I give a full sketch thereof.
The female descendants of George Kneeland are entitled to
admission to the Society of Colonial Dames, with at least four
bars for qualifying ancestors. He resided at Hyde Park, near
Poughkeepsie, and died there in 1850.

**Sketch of Rev. John McVickar, father, and the Bard family, ancestors, of
Frances (McVickar) Kneeland, wife of George Kneeland.**

PROF. JOHN McVICKAR, A.M, S.T.D., was born in New
York City, August 10, 1787. He was the son of a wealthy
New York merchant, who gave personal attention to his son's

Col. Peter Bard¹.

education. The son was carefully reared and after graduation at Columbia, in 1804, spent several years in England with his father, devoting most of his time to study at Cambridge. Upon his return he studied for the ministry, and in 1811 was ordained in the Protestant Episcopal ministry, and became rector of St. James' Church, Hyde Park, N. Y., where he remained until 1817, when he accepted the chair of Moral Philosophy, Rhetoric and Belleslettres in Columbia, which position he held for nearly fifty years. To his chair was subsequently added Evidences of Christianity. He was Superintendent of the Society for Promoting Religion and Learning, in New York, and labored earnestly to secure a training school for the diocese, which resulted in the establishment of St. Stephen's College, at Annandale. He was also chaplain to the U. S. troops at Governor's Island for nearly twenty years. In 1864 declining health made it desirable for him to retire from active college work, when he was honored with the title of Professor Emeritus. He had already received from his alma mater the degree of A.M., in 1818, and S.T.D., in 1825. Dr. McVickar's wife was the granddaughter of Samuel Bard (of whom hereafter).

In 1822 Dr. McVickar wrote and published "A Domestic Narrative of the Life of Samuel Bard;" in 1825, the "Outlines of Political Economy," and later, a comprehensive memoir of Bishop Hobart. In addition thereto he was the author of numerous essays, addresses, reviews and occasional publications. He held important positions in the church and in the diocese. As a college professor, Dr. McVickar pursued the higher interests of the subjects entrusted to him with original tact and ability. His course of instruction was eminently clear and practical, while he quietly led the pupil in the discipline of taste and philosophy. He died in New York, Oct. 29, 1868.

The Bard family, ancestors of Fanny (McVickar) Kneeland.

COL. PETER BARD¹ was an exile from France in consequence of the revocation of the Edict of Naples, and came to this country in 1703 as a merchant. He married the daughter of Dr. Mannion, and was for many years a member of the

Charles Handfield Wyatt[20].

Council and a Judge of the Supreme Court, at Burlington, N. J. In 1722 he was the Colonel commanding a regiment of foot. He had one son:

DR. JOHN BARD[2], born at Burlington, N. J., Feb. 1, 1716. He studied medicine in Philadelphia and was an intimate friend of Dr. Franklin. He came to New York in 1743, leaving a lucrative practice in Philadelphia. His further history is given hereafter, in connection with his son:

DR. SAMUEL BARD[3]. Mrs. Lamb, in her History of New York (Vol. II., p. 305), thus speaks of Drs. John and Samuel Bard: "The eldest and most successful physician of the time (1786) was Dr. John Bard. He was 73, a Huguenot by descent, and noted for his skill and learning, and for his extreme urbanity of manner. In 1788 he became the first President of the New York Medical Society. His son, Samuel Bard, who studied medicine at Edinburgh and married his cousin, Mary Bard, organized the first medical school connected with Kings (Columbia) College, and took the chair of Physic in 1769, subsequently becoming dean of the faculty. He succeeded to his father's practice and when Washington was inaugurated President, became his family physician."

"The New York Hospital was created by an Act of Assembly passed in 1773, but the scheme originated three years before in the minds of three physicians—Drs. Middleton, Jones and John Bard. They started a subscription list and secured $18,000 before the passage of the bill." (Lamb's History of New York, Vol. I., p. 761.)

The granddaughter of Dr. Samuel Bard married Rev. John McVickar, the father of Fanny (McVickar) Kneeland, as hereinbefore mentioned.

Children of George and Fanny (McVickar) Kneeland.

3271. (i.) ELIZABETH[19], usually designated "Liza," b. Friday, July 31, 1840; m. Wednesday, Oct. 8, 1862, to Charles Handfield Wyatt, of Baltimore, youngest child of Rev. William Edward Wyatt, D.D. They had four children:

3272.   (i.) *Lisa Kneeland Wyatt*[20], b. March 24, 1864.

3273.   (ii.) *Charles Handfield Wyatt*[20], b. Oct. 11, 1866.

Euphemia Mc Vickar Haight[20].

3274.   (iii.) *John McVickar Wyatt[20]*, b. July 9, 1867; d. Jan. 1, 1891.

3275.   (iv.) *Frances Wyatt[20]*, b. Jan. 1, 1869.

3276. (ii.) EUPHEMIA[19], b. at Poughkeepsie, N. Y., Feb. 13, 1842; m. at Trinity Chapel, New York, Sept. 19, 1865, to Charles Coolidge Haight, architect, of New York, only son of the Rev. Benj. J. Haight, assistant rector of Trinity Church, New York, born in that city, March 17, 1841; graduated from Columbia College in the class of 1861; studied at the law school of Columbia; enlisted and served with the Seventh Regiment, in Baltimore, in 1862; served with the 31st N. Y. Volunteers as First Lieutenant and Adjutant from October, 1862, and as Captain of the 39th N. Y. Volunteers from December, 1863, to November, 1864; was severely wounded while in command of his regiment in the Battle of the Wilderness, and in consequence obliged to retire from active service. He was elected and served as Vice-Commodore of the New York Yacht Club in 1886, and reëlected the following year. He is a trustee of the New York Society Library; of the Society for the Promotion of Religion and Learning; and of the Corporation for the Relief of Widows and Children of Deceased Clergymen. Among the prominent buildings designed by him are those erected by Columbia College on its Madison avenue property; the Manhattan Eye and Ear Hospital; the New York Cancer Hospital; the buildings of the General Theological Seminary, New York; the American Theatre, New York; Vanderbilt Hall and Phelps Hall, at Yale University; the Keney Memorial Tower, at Hartford, Conn., and others. They reside in New York, and have issue:

3277.   (i.) *Euphemia McVickar Haight[20]*, b. at Irvington-on-the-Hudson, Aug. 20, 1866; d. in New York, April 23, 1893.

Frederick Nevell Kneeland[20].

3278.   (ii.) *Sarah Bard Haight*[20], b. at Orange, N. J.,
          Feb. 8, 1869.
3279.   (iii.) *Charles Sidney Haight*[20], b. at New York,
          May 11, 1877.
3280.   (iv.) *John McVickar Haight*[20], b. at New York,
          Oct. 11, 1882.
3281. (iii.) MARY[19], b. at New York, March 16, 1845; m.
          Albert McNulty, of West Orange, N. J., Oct. 1,
          1867.   Their present postoffice address is South
          Orange, N. J.   They had nine children, as follows:
3282.   (i.) *George Kneeland McNulty*[20], b. Dec. 5, 1871.
3283.   (ii.) *Frank Pendleton McNulty*[20], b. March 17, 1873.
3284.   (iii.) *Henry Augustus McNulty*[20], b. Feb. 22, 1874.
3285.   (iv.) *Mary Bard McNulty*[20], b. Sept. 5, 1876; d.
          March 14, 1888.
3286.   (v.) *Allan Bertram McNulty*[20], b. July 18, 1878;
          d. March 29, 1888.
3287.   (vi.) *Dorothea Noël McNulty*[20], b. Dec. 25, 1880.
3288.   (vii.) *John Archibald McNulty*[20], b. April 14, 1883.
3289.   (viii.) *Eleanor Susan McNulty*[20], b. July 17, 1885.
3290.   (ix.) *Donald Stuart McNulty*[20], b. Dec. 6, 1891.
3299. (iv.) JOHN HENRY[19], b. at Columbia College, College
          Place, New York, May 11, 1847; d. Nov. 13, 1888;
          m. Sept. 28, 1871, Arabella C. Fishbourne, daugh-
          ter of Edward Gustace Fishbourne, youngest son of
          William Fishbourne, of Holly Mount, Queen's
          County, Ireland, and Elizabeth Nevell, daughter
          of William Nevell, of Ballymoney, County Wicklow.
          The original name was de Fissebourne, but was
          changed to Fishbourne.   The family settled in
          Ireland in the time of Cromwell.   They were des-
          cendants of Hugh Puset (or Pudsey), first Bishop
          of Durham.   Children:
3299A.   (i.) *Charles Gustace Kneeland*[20], b. March 25, 1875.
3300.   (ii.) *Frederick Nevell Kneeland*[20], b. Oct. 4, 1877.

INDICES.

INDEX I.

GIVEN NAMES OF KNEELANDS.

[Reference is to Numbers.]

Asa..........735, 772, 911, 916
        974, 1439, 1676, 2815
  " L...............1150, 1153
Athrea M.................1311
Augusta...................226
Augustus. 2278, 2321, 2893
Austin L.................2064

Bartholomew.......38, 60, 85, 224
Bela...... 2001
Belgora 3013
Belle G..................1671
Benjamin 63, 117, 217, 225, 647, 652
        671, 672, 689, 690, 743
        1433, 1441, 1490, 1860
        2000, 2027, 2252, 2427
  ·· B.............252, 271
  ·· C. R.............581
  " F..1346, 2007, 2009, 2166
  ·· L.............1486
  ·· M.............927
  " T.............1710
Bennie T................2369
Bertha A................1167
  " L................1219
  " M................1170
  " O................2408
Bessie D................2688
  " J................3000
  " K................1928
  " M................303
Betsey 2155
  " E................2277
Betsy........354, 791, 1456, 2365
Blanch L................1504
Blanche 3055
  " G..............545

Carey C................1779
Caroline......517, 1858, 2289, 2433
  " C.........229, 1879
  " E.........260, 2597
Carrie M................1502
Cassius L...............1668
Catharine. 1686
  " V.............1881
Charles..........540, 567, 1680
        1685, 2390, 2470, 2891
        3054, 3221, 3258, 3259
  ·· A.........1228, 2326
  ·· B.............556
  ·· E.........1225, 1344
  ·· F.........2675, 2958
  ·· G.........1155, 3299a
  ·· H.....257, 272
        1178, 2450, 2676, 3123
  ·· J........1497, 2585, 2602
  ·· L........2456, 2466, 2523

Charles R................2651
  " S................2207
  " W.........249, 262, 265
Charlotte.........1482, 3126
Childis B. D.............1662
Christina.... 3182
Christopher..........368, 1243
Clara........1625, 2473a, 2512
        2524, 2928, 3078, 3257
  " E.............2639
  " I.............2646
  " J......537
  " L......1157
  " S......1307
Clarence................2387
  " A......2446
  " H......332
  " R......1236
Clarinda................1610
Clarissa...... ....454, 2065, 2160
  " A......1314
Clayton................2136
Clementine A 512
Clytie Z................330
Content.................741
Cora....................3135
  " C......1208
  " M......1232, 1602
Cordelia.... 2642
Cornelia.........1689, 2130, 2641
  " S......1870
Cory....................2906
Cynthia.. .. 844, 1449, 1638, 2874
  " A......2991
  " I......976
Cyrus........2808, 2949, 3200
  " F. 1801
  " H......2990

Daisy I................583
Daniel.......360, 2253, 2296, 2421
        2426, 2439, 2800, 3099
David........659, 723, 733
        745, 1854, 1855, 1863
        1891, 2420, 2701, 2824
  " F......1634
  " M......1927
  " P..1878, 1880, 2817, 3152, 3155
  " R......1930
Debby.. 356
Deborah. ...686, 716a, 2143, 2508
Delano B................3141
Della........2022, 3077
Delon S 3003
Delphina................3004
Dewitt C................1619
Diana C................2699
Dimice.............2256, 2258
Dolly..........1789, 2279, 2327

Everett L...................1163
Ezra............2813, 2897, 2931

F. B.......................3148
F. Wayland...........1772, 1774
Fannie.....................3242
  "   J.....................1529
Fanny W...................1164
Fletcher..................231
Flora B....................1674
  "   I.....................1313
Florence A.................2195
  "   M...................1234
Floyd......................282
  "   A..................2654c
Frances............1766, 1973
  "   A..................2225
  "   O..................1953
  "   S..................1929
Francis....................1591
  "   F..................1154
Frank......................1945
  "   E.....524, 548, 1601, 1641b
  "   G..................1819
  "   H..................277
  "   J............1641, 1648
  "   L..................1181
  "   W.......2080, 2081, 2467
Franklin E..........1833, 1834
Fred......................2469
  "   H..................2656
  "   L..................2656a
Frederick A................2582
  "   B..................1603
  "   C.....2519, 2595, 2657
  "   G..................3151
  "   L..................838
  "   N.......2208, 2212, 3300
  "   R..................267
Furman L.........2129, 2138

Gardner.............923, 1188
  "   A..................1232a
George............2187, 3052
    3222, 3261, 3267, 3270
  "   A..................1173
  "   D..................2297
  "   E............1332, 3147
  "   F..................280
  "   H..................3146
  "   J..................268
  "   L..................2419
  "   M..................1204
  "   N............2671, 2998
  "   P..................2596
  "   S..................261
  "   W....261a, 1140, 1309, 2407
    2513, 2574, 2576, 2589

Gertie B...................2678
Gertrude...................2060
  "   B..................2584
Gilbert B..................975
  "   H..................1811
Giles E....................2666
  "   W..................2575
Grace...........357, 1769, 3158
  "   A..................2428
  "   B..................2228a
  "   E.......1179a, 2441, 2449
  "   M........1884, 1921, 2438
Grant.....................2300
Greenfield B...............3149
Guy.......................3059

H. V.......................3161
Hannah 41, 54, 118, 148, 169, 589, 706
    2154, 2504, 2903, 3064
  "   G............914, 1058
  "   M...........795, 929
  "   S..................1114
Harmon J...................1661
Harney....................2153
Harold....................2467a
  "   E..................278
  "   M.............531, 2448
  "   S..................2602a
Harriet........94, 1623, 2501, 2828
  "   A..................263
  "   E.............1823, 2374
  "   H..................511
  "   J..................2209
  "   R..................3196
  "   U..................827
  "   W...........1240, 1279
Harris B...................1200
Harry..........3056, 3074, 3150
  "   B..................1227
  "   C..................281
  "   L..................2494
  "   R..........2488, 2656b
Harvey L....2163, 2189, 2197, 3053
  "   T..................2196
Haskell P..................3142
Hattie.............833, 2170
  "   B..................1498
  "   E..................3111
  "   L.............505, 2303
  "   M..................534
  "   P..................2462
Hazel B....................2477
Hector....................1683
Helen...........1684, 2139, 2496
  "   G..................2976
Henrietta...........1694, 2384
  "   H..................1925
  "   M..................2401

Jonathan 1429, 1432, 1436, 1633, 1640
Joseph 51, 96, 97, 115, 141, 142, 668
    683, 720, 725, 744, 2144
    2145, 2149, 2161, 2188
    2248, 2251, 2273, 2275
    2282, 2284, 2693, 2871
  " A.................... ..2063
  " B............. 1832
  " C.............2162, 2183
  " H... ..... 2455, 2461, 2695
Josephine....................2182
    " M................1249a
    " N...............2360
Joshua.......... 590
  " H 2672
Josiah.............554, 1121, 2854
Joy P....................1670
Judith A.................. 1515
  " M....................1127
Julia 1865
  " A...................1882
  " E...................1209
  " H 2359
  " J................2458, 2464
  " M........1190, 1326, 1837a
Juliana 237
Justin C....... 2973

Kate.......... 3250
  " E. 3062
Katharine.................568
    " L.................335
    " M . ... .550
Katie L....................302
  " W...................2021
Keziah K............2514, 2603
  " S.............. 2601

L. C.... 2412
Laura A.................251, 1006
Lauriette 2171, 2172
Lawrence........2098, 2126, 2131
Leander.....................1174
  " S....................831
Lee 2894
Lena.......................832
  " M. 2999
Leona C..................2447
Leonard................922, 1147
    " J...................1203
Leota 261d
Lerwick L...................835
Leslie C.......... 1202
Levi..............788, 841, 2819
  " B.................812, 830
  " H. 1286
  " S................... .1312
Lewis B.................. .1624

Lila M......................2418
Lillian.....................3136
  " A...................2995
  " C...................1605
  " F..................2210
  " J...................1201
Lillie...................2383a
  " J..................1663
Lina M.......................2975
Linda 2016
Lindley M..................532
Lizzie.............1790, 2919
  " S............ 538
Lloyd B...... ... .261b
  " R....................1776
Lois....................2804, 3202
Lonie G....................2489
Lorenzo D............2061, 2084
  " P.... 2003
Lorinda................. .1593
Lottie......................2472
  " C...................2972
  " M............ 506
Louis G.............. ...1161
Louisa B...................3209
  " M....................796
Louise...................2898
Lovina...............1479, 1487
Lovinia P.................2363
Lucinda...............1244, 1791
    2146, 2156, 2987, 3097
Lucius. 319
  " D.................. :2500
  " R................. 2522
Lucy.......752, 774, 780, 846, 1287
    1348, 2509, 2855, 2870
  " A..............794, 1182
  " M...................2358
  " S............. 1673
  " W...................1148
Lurancy M..................2690
Luther A...................503
Lydia...127, 132, 375, 653, 664, 724
    2157, 2312, 2704, 2825
  " A...........1231, 2165, 2216
  " L............ ....977, 993
  " M 1211
Lyle A.................. 1609

Mabel.................. 3108
  " L.................. 2362
Mable I.... ... .2671c
Malvina....................2698
Manasseh 2984
Mandana P...................984
Manson................. ..3125
Marcus L..................2419a
Marcy.................... 2667

INDEX II.

CPSIA information can be obtained
at www.ICGtesting.com
Printed in the USA
BVHW040850170219
540195BV00003B/5/P

9 781332 194896